Categorizing Sound

The publisher gratefully acknowledges the Otto Kinkeldey Endowment of the American Musicological Society, funded in part by the National Endowment for the Humanities and the Andrew W. Mellon Foundation.

Categorizing Sound

*Genre and Twentieth-Century
Popular Music*

David Brackett

UNIVERSITY OF CALIFORNIA PRESS

University of California Press, one of the most distinguished university presses in the United States, enriches lives around the world by advancing scholarship in the humanities, social sciences, and natural sciences. Its activities are supported by the UC Press Foundation and by philanthropic contributions from individuals and institutions. For more information, visit www.ucpress.edu.

University of California Press
Oakland, California

A portion of an earlier version of chapter 7 appeared in "The Politics and Musical Practice of 'Crossover' in American Popular Music, 1963–65," *Musical Quarterly* 78, no. 4 (Winter 1994): 774–97. A portion of an earlier version of chapter 8 was published as "(In Search of) Musical Meaning: Genres, Categories, and Crossover," in *Popular Music Studies: International Perspectives,* ed. David Hesmondhalgh and Keith Negus (London: Arnold Publishers, 2002), 65–83. An early version of chapter 1 appeared as "Popular Music Genres: Aesthetics, Commerce, and Identity," in *The Sage Handbook of Popular Music Studies,* ed. Steve Waksman and Andy Bennett (Los Angeles and London: Sage Publications, 2015), 189–206.

Library of Congress Cataloging-in-Publication Data

Names: Brackett, David, author.
   Title: Categorizing sound : genre and twentieth-century popular music / David Brackett.
   Description: Oakland, California : University of California Press, [2016] | Includes bibliographical references and index.
   Identifiers: LCCN 2015046200 (print) | LCCN 2015049245 (ebook) | ISBN 9780520248717 (cloth : alk. paper) | ISBN 9780520291614 (pbk. : alk. paper) | ISBN 9780520965317 (ebook)
   Subjects: LCSH: Popular music genres—Social aspects—United States. | Popular music—United States—History and criticism.
   Classification: LCC ML3918.P67 B72 2016 (print) | LCC ML3918.P67 (ebook) | DDC 781.64—dc23
   LC record available at http://lccn.loc.gov/2015046200

Manufactured in the United States of America

25   24   23   22   21   20   19   18   17   16
10   9   8   7   6   5   4   3   2   1

For Lisa

CONTENTS

LIST OF FIGURES

LIST OF TABLES

LIST OF MUSICAL EXAMPLES

ACKNOWLEDGMENTS

Those scanning the publication information about previous versions of a few of these chapters may notice the date "1994." That's no typo. The idea for that article goes back even further, at least as far as an afternoon when I sat in the office of a former mentor of mine, Don Randel, and discussed an article he had recently published on Rubén Blades that focused on the *salsero*'s penchant for "crossing over." What, I wondered, did Don think of the idea that such crossings-over actually strengthened the genres in question rather than weakening them, as commonly believed? And didn't such genres depend on one another for their mutual self-definition? I dimly recall Don replying that my ideas might have some merit. Like another Don tilting at windmills, thus began my joust with the chimera of genre. Unlike Cervantes's Don Quixote, who abandoned his confrontation with the windmills for other battles, genres did turn out to be giants for me, and my struggle continued for a long time.

One could not indulge in such lengthy projects without a job that provides the time to explore one's occasionally intractable ideas. I therefore follow my acknowledgment of Don Randel by thanking the institutions that supported me. In a line of work that comes with many privileges, perhaps the greatest perk of all is the sabbatical. Two sabbaticals seven years apart helped jump-start and then complete this project after many years of scattered paper presentations and articles. McGill University, in addition to employing me and granting me those sabbaticals, has furnished a wonderfully supportive environment for intellectual exchange at many levels, beginning with my colleagues in the Musicology/Music History area: Tom Beghin, Julie Cumming, Steven Huebner, Roe-Min Kok, and Lloyd Whitesell. The benefits of this environment radiate outward from the musicology area to the Department of Music

Research, to the Schulich School of Music, to the wider university community, with colleagues at each level, too numerous to name, who have stimulated my thinking about music in one way or another. A special thank you goes to Dean Don McLean, who hired me and was a source of support in numerous ways. I began thinking about genre and crossover while at the State University of New York at Binghamton, and I want to thank that institution and my former colleagues in the Department of Music for many years of support and camaraderie. Finally, two granting agencies in two countries, the National Endowment for the Humanities (NEH) and the Social Sciences and Humanities Research Council of Canada (SSHRC), provided funds that enabled me travel to conferences to present this work, and to hire research assistants, without whom a project of this scope would have been impossible.

Due to the long gestation of this book, the number of individuals I would like to thank is almost, but not quite, proportional to the time taken to write it. Because so many people contributed in so many different ways, I am bound to omit many of them, and I apologize in advance to anyone that I've left out. First, several generations of grad students at McGill who acted as research assistants and sounding boards were indispensable: Mel Backstrom, Vanessa Blais-Tremblay, Laura Dymock, Meghan Dzyak, Michael Ethen, Dana Gorzelany-Mostak, Claire McLeish, Mimi Haddon, Erin Helyard, Sean Lorre, Farley Miller, Julie Mireault, Laura Risk, Eric Smialek, Matthew Testa, and Cedar Wingate. Special thanks to Sean Lorre for copying some of the musical examples in chapters 2 and 3, and to Laura Risk for her transcription of Eck Robertson and Henry Gilliland's recording of "Arkansas Traveler." In addition to these graduate students were all the students in the numerous seminars I was fortunate enough to teach at McGill, who debated with me many of the ideas presented in these pages.

Friends and colleagues at McGill and the greater Montreal area form a vibrant intellectual and artistic community that provides part of the larger context for the writing of this book. I would like to thank, among many others, Giovanni Burgos, Katie Fallon, Tom and Christine Lamarre, Brian and Katharine Manker, Carrie Renschler, Udayen Sen, Jonathan Sterne, and Will Straw. Outside of Montreal, support of a similar nature came from Kofi Agawu, David Ake, Susan Cook, Richard Crawford, Eric Drott, Ellie Hisama, Tammy Kernodle, Jeff Magee, Gayle Sherwood Magee, Winslow Martin, Steve Meyer, Noel Murray, Guthrie Ramsey, Corinne Schippert, Van and Caroline Stiefel, Eileen Strempel, Judy Tsou, Anton Vishio, Steve Waksman, and Richard Will—thanks for tossing ideas around, reading part of the manuscript, or simply being good company. A special shout out to Bernie Gendron for years of intellectual companionship and for reading the entire manuscript. Thanks to Susan Fast, Samuel Floyd Jr., David Hesmondhalgh, Eric Lewis, Richard Middleton, Keith Negus, Steve Waksman, and Eric Weisbard for inviting me to write for conferences or edited volumes—experiences that allowed me to develop some of the ideas presented here.

I am indebted to Georgina Born for many years of dialogue on both the topic of this book and music scholarship in general, as well as for being the driving force behind a conference staged at McGill in September 2014, "Music and Genre: New Directions," which devoted an entire weekend to a conversation with many of the leading music genre scholars in the world. Thanks to all the scholars who participated in that event as well as to Dean Sean Ferguson of the Schulich School of Music for his support of the conference; and to Mimi Haddon, whose work on the conference was truly beyond the call of duty.

I was extremely lucky to work at an institution with an unusually fine library and an exceptional staff of librarians whose knowledge of research methods and music never ceases to amaze me. Led by the indefatigable Cynthia Leive, the staff also included or includes John Black, David Curtis, Cathy Martin, Brian McMillan, Melanie Preuss, Andrew Senior, and Gale Youster. Special thanks go to Photoshop wizard Joel Natanblut for helping with the illustrations.

I am grateful to Jason Hanley for his hospitality while in Cleveland, both for his role in providing opportunities to present my work at the Rock and Roll Hall of Fame and for introducing me to the archives there. Head archivist Andy Leach and his staff made sifting through their collection as enjoyable as it possibly could be. While at the National Museum of American History in Washington, DC, Wendy Shay and her staff aided immensely in sorting through boxes of old sheet music and other artifacts.

Throughout much of my academic career, the International Association for the Study of Popular Music (IASPM) has been my scholarly home away from home, where I was first encouraged to pursue the work that eventually became this book. In addition to those already mentioned above, Anahid Kassabian and the late David Sanjek were an integral part of that experience. I also benefited enormously from presenting my work at the Center for Black Music Research, the Society for American Music, the American Musicological Society, the Society for Music Theory, the Experience Music Project, and the "Jazz Beyond Borders" conference hosted by the Amsterdam Conservatory. Invitations from Cornell University, UCLA, the University of Pennsylvania, the University of Toronto, the University of Texas at Austin, the University of British Columbia, and the University of Alberta provided ideal forums for the presentation and exchange of ideas. The conferences, colloquia, and meetings of the major collaborative research initiative "Improvisation, Community, and Social Practice" (funded by SSHRC) also encouraged me to explore directions that I otherwise might not have. Special thanks to Eric Lewis for facilitating my involvement in that project.

I can still remember the day in the summer of 1999 when I received a call from Mary Francis, the music editor at the University of California Press, who was interested in reprinting my first book, *Interpreting Popular Music,* in paperback. My gratitude to Mary extends back to bringing that work to a larger audience, and for possessing the perfect mixture of patience, encouragement, firmness, intellectual understanding, and a sense of the practical that many authors (including this one) lack. Mary also deserves credit for finding such excellent external readers for the manuscript, whose comments helped me refine my arguments and tighten up the manuscript.

I would be remiss if I did not state rather emphatically that this work rests on the shoulders of all the musicians and recordists who made the sounds, and all the writers, critics, and journalists who wrote the words that created the texts that are the subject of the analysis of this book.

With sadness I note that one of my greatest intellectual heroes, my uncle Bernd Lambert, passed away as this manuscript neared completion. Embodying the ideal of scholarly and personal generosity, I was not alone in benefiting from his humor, kindness, and encyclopedic knowledge about almost everything. I'm selfish enough to want to think that this book would have ended up on his long list of "armchair books." I'm sorry that he will never read it; if not for him, my life may have well followed a different path.

I thank the rest of my family—my parents Stan and Marion for their continued support of me in various ways, great and small, and my brothers Joe and Buzz for passionate conversations about music, and for being a source of inspiration. In Philadelphia, the Bargs, led by Pop-Pop Bernie, always provide the home base that sustains and nurtures. My cousins Margy and Jim Bauman have been a real lifeboat during difficult times in too many ways to count.

To my children—Fred, who has a special fondness for the *Time-Life Rhythm & Blues: 1964* collection, and Sophie, for whom "Papa's Got a Brand New Bag" is endowed with special meaning—thank you for enduring many long car rides while listening to compilations of songs organized by year, for your love of music that grows stronger with time and becomes part of a collective experience of sound, and for asking me endless questions about what type of music we are listening to. When it comes to talking about genre, you are truly precocious.

To be able to share one's life with another is a rare gift. To be able to experience intellectual camaraderie and the sharing of one's half-baked theories with one's partner is a matter of indescribable luck. Last but not least, the greatest acknowledgment of all goes to Lisa Barg, the dedicatee of this book, without whom this work—and life in general—would be unimaginable.

Introduction

They Never Even Knew

A *New Yorker* cartoon depicts an elderly couple crossing a line from a territory marked "pop" to one marked "easy listening" with a territory labeled "rock" receding into the background, the couple having evidently already crossed from "rock" into "pop" at some indeterminate time in the past. The caption reads, "They Never Even Knew" (figure 1).

This cartoon, even in a single frame, compresses many ideas about the relationship between genre and identification. Boundaries separate the categories of "rock," "pop," and "easy listening," yet consumers regularly traverse these boundaries. Categories of music are often associated with categories of people, but these associations often change over time. In one possible reading of the cartoon, the associations change because the tastes of a particular group shift as the members of the group age: the couple is crossing over to easy listening because pop music now seems just a little too wild. The caption—"they never even knew"—suggests another, more likely interpretation: associations change because the way that the music is categorized has changed. In other words, the couple has continued to like the same type of music, but the music that was once "pop" (and before that "rock") is now classified as "easy listening." In either interpretation, the couple remains oblivious to the reclassification of their taste: they never even knew.

Categories, or genres, of popular music exist in an odd kind of limbo in public and scholarly discourse. On the one hand, musicians and consumers often resist requests to categorize themselves, insisting that their tastes are unclassifiable. It is common to hear discussions that have invoked the idea of genre end with the declaration that musical genres do not really exist, that they are mere fabrications of the music industry. Yet despite these disavowals, in addition to the cartoon just

FIGURE 1. "They Never Even Knew," by Bruce Eric Kaplan, *The New Yorker*, November 2, 2009. Reprinted by permission of Condé Nast Publications.

discussed, the use of genre labels to describe taste continues to return in a wide variety of contexts. For example, on an episode of the television series *Glee*, the character Mercedes (who is African American) explains to the character Puck (who is white) that a romance is simply not in the cards: "It's never going to work. You're Top 40 and I'm rhythm and blues."[1] Even songs confirm the quotidian value of genre: Lonnie Mack proclaimed in 1988 that he was "too rock for country, too country for rock 'n' roll" in a recording with the same title.[2] And no listing of "musicians wanted" ads (i.e., musicians looking for other musicians to play with) could function without an extensive listing of genre labels in order to indicate the musicians' interests to one another.[3]

These anecdotes illustrate that the issue of genre is complex, possibly contentious, and difficult to escape. The *New Yorker* cartoon, the exchange from *Glee*, Lonnie Mack's song, musicians wanted ads, and many other texts suggest that the question of genre in popular music is often inextricably tied to how people identify with different types of music. Such genre designations indicate or imply the assumed audience for a particular type of music, and frequently raise questions about who produces and consumes the music. At the same time, much of the resistance encountered in discussions of genre implies an awareness of the instability of genres over time (e.g., music with similar stylistic traits is reclassified— and, even if "they never even knew," occasionally participants in popular music dimly sense this impersonal process), of the porousness of boundaries (despite the clear lines drawn in the *New Yorker* cartoon), and of the way in which no two people define a genre in the same way. Similarly, something seems to be amiss in how categories of people are associated with categories of music in that these relationships are constantly changing and never seem to accurately describe all those who participate in a particular type of music. This lack of a tight, unwavering fit occurs at least partly because categories of people are subject to the same type of transience that affects categories of music. The ability of popular music genres to evoke a demographic group also seems odd in that some categories, such as country music and rhythm and blues, evoke a category of people much more clearly than do others (Top 40 or mainstream popular music, for example).

Despite many contradictions, however, genre labels for popular music continue to be used in numerous contexts, and they continue to evoke connotations of particular types of people (albeit some more than others). Contradiction and inconsistency need not signal the undesirability of a critical enterprise. In my case, they sparked the beginning of an odyssey, which has consisted of the search for answers to a series of questions, beginning with the most basic: What is a popular music genre? This chapter will also consider in turn what I term the "relational" quality of genre; the role of scale or level; the process of iterability or citationality in the emergence, stabilization, and transformation of genres; the issue of authorship; and the nature of the relationship between categories of music and categories of people.

WHAT IS A POPULAR MUSIC GENRE?

The term "genre," in its most basic sense, refers to "type" or "kind" (in French the word is synonymous with one of the most basic ways of classifying human beings, namely gender). This definition may seem straightforward until we inquire about the basis of the similarity of texts that are grouped together. Doubts arise because inspection of an individual text in terms of style, form, or content inevitably raises questions as to genre identity: the more that we examine a given grouping of texts, the more dissimilar individual texts begin to appear. The obverse of this situation lies in the impossibility of imagining a genre-less text—that is, a text so dissimilar to other texts that it could not under any circumstances be grouped with another.[4] Similarly, the more closely one describes a genre in terms of its stylistic components, the fewer examples actually seem to fit.[5] And although the range of sonic possibilities for any given genre is quite large at a particular moment, it is not infinite. Simply because a musical text may not (to paraphrase Jacques Derrida) belong to a genre with any stability does not mean that it does not participate in one, a distinction that emphasizes the temporal, experiential, functional, and fleeting quality of genres while nonetheless retaining the importance of the genre concept for communicating about texts. Put another way, genres are not static groupings of empirically verifiable musical characteristics, but rather associations of texts whose criteria of similarity may vary according to the uses to which the genre labels are put. "Similar" elements include more than musical-style features, and groupings often hinge on elements of nation, class, race, gender, sexuality, and so on.

Indeed, while musical style traits may alert us to general tendencies that differentiate artists and recordings at a given moment, without other types of information about producers, consumers, critical discourse, and the music industry (to name but a few other factors), these traits will not suffice, as it will be possible to find musical examples with these traits that were categorized some other way, or, as in the *New Yorker* cartoon, to find clusters of musical texts that were categorized differently at some point in the past. In other words, the "effects" of genre cannot be traced to the "cause" of musical style in a direct, one-to-one relationship.

Another question (or difficulty) emerges in the relationship between popular music genres such as rock, pop, and easy listening, and the notion of genre as it has existed previously in musicological study or in the scholarship in other media, such as literature or cinema. In studies of Western art (classical) music, the large category of music with which the discipline of musicology has been primarily concerned, genre has tended to refer to formal and stylistic conventions, focusing on textual distinctions between the symphony, concerto, opera, character piece, et cetera. Other types of groupings do occur in the study of art music, such as those by historical period (Baroque, classical, Romantic) or nationality or geography, or, in post-Romantic music, by compositional approach (serialism, neoclassicism, minimalism), but these are not generally conflated with the idea of genre.[6]

Classical studies of genre in literature began with Aristotle's formulation of a tripartite scheme for analyzing poetry in terms of syntactical schemes: epic, lyric, drama. Subsequent discussions of genre until the mid-nineteenth century regarded Aristotle's model as sacrosanct; in the words of the film scholar Rick Altman, "By accentuating poetry's internal characteristics rather than the kinds of experience fostered by poetry, Aristotle set genre theory on to a virtually unbroken course of textual analysis."[7] Altman's dire prognosis may be contradicted by recent activity on the subject (including his own), especially in the fields of literature and film studies, but it must be said that musicological studies have tended to follow the traditional literary emphasis on style traits. Emphasis in these situations tends to rely more on retroactive grouping based on what is already known or assumed to be the contents of a genre rather than on the emergence of a category during a particular historical period and the conflictual contemporaneous understandings that often compete while a genre is becoming established. The study of epic, lyric, and drama lends itself to a focus on syntactic processes and semantic content due to their historical distance, and the resulting difficulty in recovering whatever social connotations these genres may have possessed at one time.

In cinema, to take a different medium in which scholars have extensively debated the issue, genres have often been retroactively fitted to formal characteristics and conventions of plot, setting, and character. Cinematic genres would seem to lend themselves to formalist groupings, as genres such as the musical, action-adventure, and biopic do not raise connotations of identity in the same manner as does, say, foreign music, a category of popular music prominent in the early twentieth century. This is not to say that these genres do not suggest different audiences; however, due to the production and distribution costs associated with films, most film genres of necessity overtly court audiences that transcend demographic divisions, and promotional materials often seek to blur generic boundaries for that reason. Cases in which types of film are explicitly matched with types of people are rare, as in the case of the early-twentieth-century form Yiddish cinema, or in the 1970s with Blaxploitation. The latter notwithstanding, few cinematic parallels exist to the various categories of popular music that have existed since the 1920s and that have evoked communities of participants, often with great specificity. This is the case even though action-adventure movies filled with high-tech explosions, animated features filled with adorable fuzzy animals, and "women's films" all clearly connote a demographic slice of the pie. Beginning in the late 1970s, film studies underwent its own questioning of formalist and presentist approaches to genre.[8] Unlike cinema studies, however, popular music studies has not displayed the same attention to issues of genre, and, despite scattered attempts to address the issue, has not generated anything approaching a sustained, theoretically informed debate around a series of shared issues.

What Does It Mean to Write a History of Genre?

Recently, a turn away from retroactive grouping and toward a more historicist approach has appeared in the work of music and film scholars.[9] The opposition between presentist and historicist approaches contrasts the retroactive grouping of texts into a genre based on a presumed stylistic consistency and critical consensus with the study of the conflictual meanings of categories via a reconstruction of a historical horizon of meaning. Mikhail Bakhtin stressed the interdependence of the two concepts, and made the following description of the effect they have on interpretation: one approach, the historicist, "encloses" the work "within the epoch," while the other, the presentist, reads the work on the basis of one's scholarly disposition, in the process "modernizing" it. Neither of these approaches, according to Bakhtin, is particularly valuable by itself.[10]

This book, in addition to explicitly contrasting historicist and presentist concepts, also employs an approach toward categorization that could be described, following Michel Foucault, as genealogical, in that such a method attends to a period's historical accidents and forgotten trivialities and to the role of these in struggles in cultural production. Rather than focusing on *what* constitutes the contents of a musical category, the emphasis here falls on *how* a particular idea of a category emerges and stabilizes momentarily (if at all) in the course of being accepted across a range of discourses and institutions. The point is to question the "self-evident" aspects of a genre that bind together different instantiations of it over time, and thus to emphasize the conditions that support the singularity of the function, use, and meaning of particular genres. At the same time, long-range historical narratives, with their tendency toward a unitary view of genre, are reread here in terms of the struggles over categorical labels that dominate accounts of a category's emergence. The purpose of using the concept, genealogy, is not to contrast simply a presentist view of history—a role that might be filled by canonical narratives in which a cause-and-effect teleology leads from a point of origin to the present in order to confirm contemporary beliefs about a subject—with a historicist approach that reconstitutes the historical horizon in which events and texts emerge. Rather, such a genealogical approach seeks both to analyze the conditions that make it possible for an event to occur and, at the same time, to not occlude the current events to which an interest in the past is responding, what Foucault termed a "history of the present."[11]

Franco Fabbri and Genre as a System of Difference

If the study of genre has not attained as high a profile in popular music studies as in the study of cinema or literature, this is not due to a lack of trying on the part of several scholars of popular music. Perhaps the first, and certainly one of the most celebrated, salvos was fired by Franco Fabbri in two articles published in 1982.[12] The more extensive of these, "A Theory of Musical Genres: Two Applications," maps out a rigorous approach to the study of genre. Most accounts of the study of genre in popular music studies begin here and focus on elaborating one of Fabbri's opening statements: A musical genre is "a set of musical events (real or possible) whose course is governed by a definite set of socially accepted rules" (52). Fabbri divides these rules into five categories: 1) "formal and technical rules"; 2) "semiotic rules"; 3) "behavior rules"; 4) "social and ideological rules"; and 5) "economic and juridical rules."

From the foregoing summary, it is clear that Fabbri regards as indivisible what are usually divided into the musical and social aspects of genre—that is, he argues implicitly that it is impossible to understand a given genre without consideration of both (what are conventionally divided into) social and musical elements (even as he divides the musical and the social into separate categories for heuristic purposes). Rules, however, give the appearance of something fixed. They invoke the law, a set of strictures that may be interpreted but which appear to be outside of history. In a word, the idea of multiple sets of rules conjures up something cold and forbidding.

A piece of scholarship is a product of a specific time and place. Fabbri initially wrote "A Theory of Musical Genres" for presentation at the first conference of the

International Association for the Study of Popular Music in 1981. The almost sci-
entistic quality of some of the passages in the article may be ascribed to the powerful sway over the humanities and social sciences held by structuralism in the late
1970s and early 1980s.

Another, and perhaps more convincing, line of defense for Fabbri's article
against criticism of its being overly deterministic is suggested by a close reading of
the article itself, which reveals that these rules are not quite as austere and static as
they might appear at first sight. The article may, at times, give the impression that
identifying a given genre and the texts that participate in it is synonymous with
toting up how a given text does or does not correspond to a genre's rules. However,
a careful examination of Fabbri's discussion of a test case—the system of *canzone*
in Italy today—and the transformation of a particular subgenre of *canzone*—the
canzone d'autore—makes it clear that genres exist in a system of difference operating during a specific period of time, and that the rules are derived inductively after
the analyst has already observed the arrangement of genres within the system. This
inductive method may beg the question as to how one is able to identify a given
genre in the first place, or how one is able to delimit the system, but what is possibly a tautological problem does not negate the observation that these rules are
thus descriptive rather than prescriptive, inductive rather deductive, a heuristic
tool rather than a series of rigid containers. This relational quality of genres within
a system enables Fabbri to avoid an essentialist approach to the description of
genres, and his account of generic transformation clarifies that genres are not
static entities with stable boundaries.[13]

It is curious, upon reflection, how little attention the relational aspect of genres
in Fabbri's work has received, even though citation, and at least a brief description,
of the article is a rite of passage for most popular scholars who would enter the fray
of genre study. Fabbri himself does not emphasize this relational quality, even
though the following statement appears prominently at the opening of his essay:
"The only solution I have found to this problem [of excessive broadness of defini-
tion] is to decide each time whether a certain set of musical events is being considered *in relation* to other opposing sets in which case I will call it a genre—or *in
relation* to its sub-sets—in which case I will call it a system" (52–53, my emphasis).
Later in the essay, Fabbri evokes the idea of relationality via a discussion of musical
systems: "A new genre is not born in an empty space but in a musical system that
is already structured" (60). By invoking (via implication) Ferdinand de Saussure's
notion of meaning as created through a system of difference without positive
value, Fabbri strongly suggests that musical genres become meaningful only in
relation to one another, as part of a "musical system," and cannot be identified
according to a list of positive terms. His rules thereby become a mechanism for
describing difference as it is found to exist within a system during a particular
period of time.

The idea of deriving the meaning of a genre from its place within a system can be traced back to the Russian formalist school of literary criticism of the 1920s, which moved away—most prominently in the work of Yuri Tynyanov—from the idea of genres developing autonomously and organically, and instead stressed the mutual interdependence of genres on one another for their definition and meaning. In Tynyanov's formulation, "evolution," rather than referring to an autonomous and organic unfolding, describes an ever-changing constellation of genres in which a shifting hierarchy results in a "dominant" genre, which reveals itself in its influence upon other subordinate genres.[14] Eventually, the influential reign of the dominant is spent, as its characteristic stylistic devices become overused and clichéd, and the generic hierarchy gradually reassembles with a different dominant.

Various accounts of genre invoke the notion of a system of difference, although this approach has thus far been more common in literary and cinema studies than in music.[15] This approach has the virtue of avoiding the problems of a trait-based approach noted earlier, as definition becomes a purely "negative" affair, resembling other structuralist-influenced approaches to cultural production, such as Pierre Bourdieu's notion of a "field."[16]

Levels of Genre

In one of the quotes reproduced earlier, Fabbri's distinction between sets and subsets suggests an additional challenge for the study of genre in popular music: the importance of recognizing different *levels* of genre.[17] He initially leaves the issue somewhat ambiguous—what exactly is the difference between "sets" and "subsets," and to what do these terms refer?—but the subsequent discussion of the system of *canzone* and the different types of *canzone* offers a plausible example of what might be meant by this distinction (63–74). Thus the different types of *canzone* inhabit one level, and the *canzone*, in contrast to other types of Italian (and possibly international) popular song, another. These levels could be continued with increasing degrees of abstraction. In the schema summarized in figure 2, popular music *in toto* in contrast to Western art music, jazz, et cetera occupies one level; Western music in opposition to various forms of non-Western music forms yet another level, and so on.

In theory, this branching process could continue indefinitely in either direction with subsets of different types of *canzone d'autore* indicating greater specificity, continuing down to the idiolect of individual performers, and, in the other direction, with Earth music as distinct from music from other planets, solar systems, and galaxies.[18] Plentiful examples of this branching tendency will be explored throughout this book, but no example illustrates this more clearly than the subject of chapter 2, foreign music (itself a subset of popular music), which in the early decades of the twentieth century boasted more than thirty subgenres, including Jewish, Italian, Irish, German, Swedish, Croatian, Hawaiian, and many others.

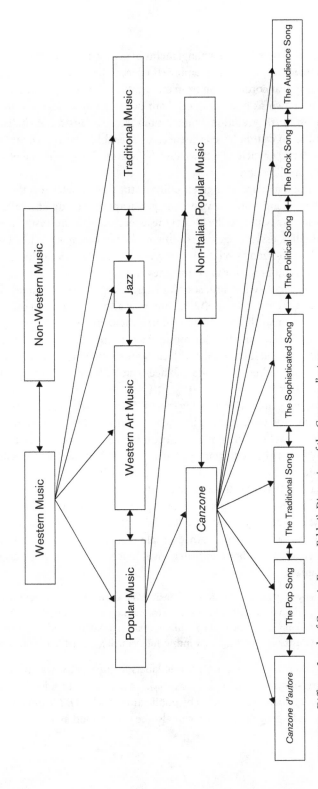

FIGURE 2. Different Levels of Genre in Franco Fabbri's Discussion of the *Canzone d'autore*.

Although this table presents the arrangements of genres according to different levels as a strict hierarchy, it does not capture the bleed-through that occurs between categories that appear cordoned off from one another. For example, simply because the *canzone* is shown as branching off from popular music does not mean that jazz, Western art music, traditional music, non-Western music, non-Italian popular music, and so on cannot have influenced it. The table reflects an analysis of the discussion in Fabbri's article as well as how the relationships are frequently understood in everyday discourse.

The notion that a genre, at a given point in time, articulates together notions of musical style, identifications, visual images, ways of moving and talking, and myriad other factors is akin to the idea of the assemblage. In contrast to the notion of organic totalities, assemblages, according to the philosopher Manuel DeLanda, are "wholes characterized by *relations of exteriority.* . . . The exteriority of relations implies a certain autonomy for the terms they relate."[19] Thus, in the study of genre, the components (be they musical, social, material, expressive, et cetera) that may characterize a genre at a given point in time may also participate in other genres at the same time, or in the past or the future. The components are not part of a seamless, organic whole, and their meaning in a particular genre formation derives from their relations and interactions with each other over time. As with the theory of levels presented earlier, larger assemblages can be formed by the grouping of smaller assemblages.[20]

Conceiving of genre as operating on different levels simultaneously has other implications as well. Although much of Simon Frith's discussion of genre centers on the impact of different contexts on the use of genre labels, his discussion also highlights the importance of distinctions between different levels of genre. Sometimes the necessity of this distinction becomes clear when genre labels do not provide an effective interface between production and consumption. While on the one hand "The point of music labels is, in part, to make coherent the way in which different music media divide the market," on the other, "this doesn't always work smoothly."[21] An example of failure to coordinate different media is the relationship between categorical labels used by radio stations and record companies:

> The peculiarity of generic definitions in music radio terms is that programmers are using the sounds to put together an audience (or market or demographic) for delivery to advertisers. Sometimes the radio definition of this market-by-taste coincides with the record industry's (as with country music, for example); often it does not. (79)

Examples of other media that use generic labels in different ways given by Frith include the music press and nightclubs (84). To this I might add the names of popularity charts, such as those used by publications such as *Billboard* and *Variety*. These variations in generic function can also be understood as variations in level

TABLE 1 Different Levels of Genre, ca. 2001

Marketing Category	Rhythm and Blues (Black Popular Music)	Pop (Mainstream)	Country
Chart Name	hot R&B/hip-hop	Hot 100	country
Radio Format	R&B, urban contemporary, hip-hop, quiet storm, soul	Top 40, mainstream Top 40, adult Top 40, adult contemporary, modern rock, mainstream rock, AOR	country
Critic-Fan Genres	hip-hop, R&B, funk, disco, rap, new jack swing, neo-soul, quiet storm	modern rock, mainstream rock, teen pop, adult contemporary	new traditionalists, hat acts, alt-country

or scale: the use of different generic labels may vary in terms of their duration and the scope of the audience, real or implied, toward which they are directed. Table 1 displays the different labels in use in the early 2000s in different media for the main categories of U.S. popular music.[22] Both the consistency of the labeling of country music in this chart and the greater variation within rhythm and blues and pop (the mainstream), which illustrates the failure to coordinate the different levels of production, bear out Frith's observation in the foregoing quote.

Although I use the terms "category" and "genre" somewhat interchangeably throughout this book, the usage in table 1 does correspond to an aspect of everyday discourse. That is, "genre" is often used with greater specificity than "category," a tendency reflected in table 1, where the most general level is "marketing *category*" while the most specific is "critic-fan *genres*." This greater specificity is partly why I use "genre" in my book: I'm sure I would draw blank looks were I to tell people that I was working on a book on popular music "categories." On the other hand, the greater specificity of "genre" can create its own difficulties, as people tend to have more rigid conceptions of the term than they do of "category."

Genre as Citation/Iteration

Differences in the usage of labels according to level and media exist on a meta level, as discussed in the previous section. This type of inconsistency addresses variations in how individual texts are grouped together according to changing contexts and the functions of genre labels, but does not account for the relationship between individual texts and the genres into which they are grouped. Consideration of the relationship between individual text and genre leads to questions about the role of stylistic prototypes and whether each individual text refers to a generalized model. I have already questioned the idea that genres can be understood as a bundle of style traits that are repeated, but does this rule out the notion that individual works can refer to stylistic conventions that are associated with a particular genre?

To begin to answer this question, we can turn to the idea of citation (or iteration), which, when understood in a broad sense, can be fruitful for construing the continued efficacy of the concept of genre despite the fact that no single text seems to fit all the "rules" of a given genre, and even as texts that seem to fit many of the rules of a genre are understood as participating in a different genre. The pertinence of the concept of citation derives from how a text and its associated paratexts (which include stylistic traits, visual associations, and a wide range of discursive connections as well as sonic-stylistic features), in the course of participating in a genre, cannot help but invoke the conventions of a genre in which they participate. This relationship of a text to the conventions of a genre that it invokes leads us to consider how a text becomes associated with a genre label in the first place, and how a text achieves legibility, that is, how it becomes capable of being understood as participating in a genre at a given place and time. In addition to this, the notion of citation or iteration emphasizes the collective, impersonal nature of how genres are formed, as well as the impossibility of finding the moment when a genre could be said to have definitively begun.

Here a reference to J.L. Austin's distinction between "performative" and "constative" utterances may be useful. Constative utterances in Austin's parlance consist of statements of fact, whereas performatives consist of statements that perform an action (Austin gives the example of "I do take this woman to be my lawful wedded wife" as performed at a wedding ceremony).[23] Jacques Derrida's critique of this essay problematizes certain aspects of Austin's formulation of the performative, demonstrating how Austin relies on a distinction between "serious" and "non-serious" speech acts, a distinction that reintroduces the notion of authorial intention that Austin had earlier proscribed.[24] A grievous case of how serious versus non-serious distinctions trouble notions of the performative, from Austin's perspective, is the quotation or citation of a performative speech act such as occurs in a theatrical performance. Yet Derrida argues that the very possibility of quoting a performative speech act is the condition of a performative's possibility, for only when the conventions of such a performative can be enacted on a stage is it possible to recognize such a speech act in real life. In other words, if a performative speech act could not be recognized as such on stage, it could not be effective in a nontheatrical setting. Derrida thus claims that such citationality or iterability is a necessary condition for all communication.

Extending this discussion to the notion of musical genre, one could argue that unless it is possible to cite a genre out of context (as in, for example, parody or pastiche), such a genre cannot otherwise be legible in situations in which texts are not perceived as quotations. I am not arguing that all enactments of a musical genre are quotations in the sense of a literal or parodic quotation, but that the difference between such quotations and other iterations of genre relies on what Derrida terms a "differential typology of forms of iteration" (326) rather than on an absolute separation between quotations and non-quotations. The effects of quotation and non-quotation do not exclude one another but rather rely on each other and "presuppose [each other] in dyssemtrical fashion, as the general space of their possibility" (327). Put differently, once the citation (or non-literal quotation) of socio-musical conventions acquires relative stability and is associated repeatedly with a genre label, it can be quoted (literally) out of context with the quotation then being recognized as a generic reference. Many of the chapters that follow are concerned precisely with the citation by musical texts of previous conventions governing meaning and sound, the gradual coalescence of a cluster of socio-textual elements, and the increasing stability with which these elements are then associated with a genre label.

The idea of citationality may help resolve some of the seemingly unresolvable contradictions of how genres function, in particular their instability over time and the different ways in which individuals interpret genre labels. For it is a condition of the legibility of a text that a listener can place it in the context of a genre, that is, in the context of how sounds, lyrics, images, performer personae, musical rhetoric, and a generic label (among other things) can be related. In order for this to occur, texts must cite or refer to generic conventions that predate them. A musical text that is not a literal quotation can only be understood as participating in a genre if that genre is capable of being quoted outside of, or beyond, the initial context in which it was created, and if that genre is legible to addressees beyond the initial audience for the genre.

This is to say that musical genres operate on the principle of general citationality or iterability. They refer to generic conventions that are constantly being modified by each new text that participates in the genre. A pervasive framework of citationality, and the constant (however slight) modification of a genre created by each individual instantiation of it, means that texts refer to a model that they are bringing into existence.[25] The attempt to establish a prototypical example of a genre that functions as a point of origin thus appears as an act of constant deferral. When a text or a group of texts is retrospectively figured as the origin of a genre, it is thus figured on the basis of its citation as the origin in the present.[26] The continued legibility of a genre is only possible, however, as long as its conventions are cited. Another way of putting it would be to say that no genre identity exists behind expressions of genre; genre is performatively constituted by the very expressions that are said to be its results. The conventions of a genre may continue to be cited even as its generic context changes, thus leading to a relabeling of the "same" genre, a process without a locus of agency: they never even knew.

Do Genres Have an Author?

An Artist shoots in the dark, not knowing whether he hits or what he hits.
GUSTAV MAHLER[27]

Such an emphasis on iterability as a condition of the possibility of genre focuses on the activation and constant modification of conventions, and thus moves the understanding of genre away from an emphasis on exemplary works or on the meaning of the text springing from the intention of an individual author (not that exemplary works and prototypes do not continue to play an important role in folk taxonomies). Removing the idea of authorial intention from an understanding of genre also has important implications for how we understand authorship and creativity. For related to the idea of a generalized iterability of genre is the idea of genres as the result of collective creativity rather than the product of an autonomous auteur. Authorship and creativity thus come to seem less an act of individual inspiration leading to a rupture of tradition, of channeling inspiration from a heavenly source, than of entering into an ongoing dialogue with other participants in a given artistic field. An awareness, conscious or not, of the potentials and constraints of the genre or genres in which they have chosen to work informs the decisions of artists as they adjust their aims to the audiences they are addressing.

Bakhtin's notion of addressivity (as formulated in his discussion of "speech genres") echoes some of the ideas of Derrida discussed earlier—in that the conventions invoked by a text also imply an addressee—but enters more directly into debates about authorial creativity. As Bakhtin explains, "The style of the utterance depend[s] on those to whom the utterance is addressed, [and] how the speaker (or writer) senses and imagines his addressees." Furthermore, "Each speech genre in each area of speech communication has its own typical conception of the addressee, and this defines it as a genre."[28] At the same time, the "audience member" of today may become the "artist" of tomorrow; the "artist" of tomorrow may become the music critic or music industry executive of the day after tomorrow. In other words, the dialogue about how to interpret sounds with generic labels includes participants in the popular music field regardless of their current role in it.[29]

The discussion of an artist's adjustments to an imagined audience may appear to re-import the notion of artistic intention through a back door. The idea of artistic intention is rewritten here to signify the decision (often not wholly conscious) of an artist to exploit a genre's semantic potential. The value of this idea might then be found in how the creation of music (and, to some extent, lyrics and visual images associated with music) enables listeners to experience the world in a new way through rhetorical processes that convey particular modes of feeling and emotion. Genres here, too, may be understood as modes of feeling, and as ways of experiencing embodied emotion. Musical texts may thus convey meanings or "truths" of which the author is unaware, but that only become apparent in the course of later hearings/readings.

Bakhtin applied his notions of heteroglossia and dialogism developed in other essays to the idea of particular forms of rhetorical address in his essay on speech genres, especially in the idea of assimilation:

> The unique speech experience of each individual is shaped and developed in continuous and constant interaction with others' individual utterances. . . . Each utterance is filled with echoes and reverberations of other utterances to which it is related by the communality of the sphere of speech communication. Every utterance must be regarded primarily as a *response* to preceding utterances of the given sphere.[30]

Bakhtin adds to Derrida's notion of iterability the idea of the social resonance embedded in each utterance. To those who may object that a speech genre is not the same as a musical genre, in that individual songs or pieces are not uttered in direct response by an individual to another individual, I would argue that the parallels between the foregoing statements of Bakhtin and the process of creating musical works are strong enough to outweigh such objections. Musical texts, in the process of citing the conventions of genre, are "shaped and developed in continuous and constant interaction with" the musical texts of others working in similar genres. Each musical text "is filled with echoes and reverberations of other" musical texts "to which it is related by the communality of the" musical genre. Every musical text "must be regarded primarily as a *response* to preceding" musical texts of the given genre.

Bakhtin's notions of creativity and genre evoke a grand dialogue among the participants in a particular genre or genres, as ideas circulate among producers, consumers, and mediators of all types, resulting in the constant sharing of ideas and the modification and cross-pollination of genres. According to this point of view, genre affords us a different perspective on creativity, emphasizing its social nature, and the interconnections between artists (producers) and audiences (consumers).[31] From this perspective, Gustav Mahler's words in the epigraph can be understood as undercutting one of the most enduring images of the High Romantic composer: on one level, throwing into doubt notions about artistic intentionality, Mahler's statement also underscores how even artists who exemplify the notion of individualistic genius participate collectively in what Howard Becker dubbed an "Art World."[32]

The Reception of Genre

Understanding a genre as part of an ever-shifting system still raises many difficult questions. Such a system-based approach, while avoiding an emphasis on style traits, and thus a genre's diachronic unity, nonetheless could seem to verge on a quasi-mechanistic approach that unfolds in its own hermetically sealed world in which musical genres interact with each other, but little else. The factor most clearly lacking in such an approach is the audience, and an initial step might be to emphasize (once again) that genres cannot be understood solely in textual terms, whether this be through a diachronic unfolding of a single genre, through a synchronic analysis of a genre system at a given moment in time, or through the citation of stylistic traits. Several popular music scholars, such as Simon Frith, Keith Negus, and Jason Toynbee, following the lead of the film scholar Steven Neale, have emphasized the role of listeners' expectations and the relation of these expectations to "conventions that circulate between industry, text and subject."[33] Neale's theory of genre in turn draws on the literary theories of Hans Robert Jauss, especially Jauss's notion of a "horizon of expectations." Jauss's theory stresses both the importance of synchronic analysis—that genres are defined in relation to one another—as well as how individual texts are related to a genre in a processual manner. Each new text inherits the conventions and expectations of a genre, but then transforms the genre's conventions, but not so much as to alienate fans of the genre.[34] Once again, we seem to have returned to a relational approach in which "conventions," which emphasize the text, have been flipped around to include "expectations." Voilà, the listener appears!

I have already argued that the meaning-producing relationship extends beyond what occurs between a text and a listener, and depends on a feedback loop in which ideas and assumptions about genre circulate among music producers (musicians and music-industry workers), audience members, and critics. I have also underscored the transitory possibilities of the roles inhabited by participants in the popular music field. Nonetheless, it is undeniable that participants, based on how they understand their current role, use genre terms differently. The music industry operates on a belief in a temporary reification of these roles, making assumptions about who will consume music; musicians use the terms to communicate with each other about what kind of music they play, which includes their attitude about playing it; consumers use the terms in order to recognize the music they wish to consume as well as to communicate with one another; and critics use or invent terms in order to mediate between producers and consumers. Genre labels are vital for communicating about music to all these groups, and such labels both participate in the creation of new genre-audience alliances and reinforce existing ones.

MUSIC/IDENTIFICATION

In the preceding paragraphs I've indicated the need to go beyond abstractions such as "addressees" and the expectations of "listeners." This may be easier said than done, however, as no ideas about popular music genres have occasioned more discussion and debate than the question of how they evoke, respond to, correspond to, or connote specific audiences or communities. In other words, who are these people being addressed? Why do popular music genres conjure up images of particular groups of people despite all the contradictions and logical inconsistencies involved? The interest in this matter transcends academia, and, fortunately for us, mass culture provides many examples of public fascination with the relationship between categories of music and categories of people. David Chappelle, in a skit that aired on his televised comedy show in 2004, began one such example with the following preamble:

> All my life I've heard that white people can't dance. I don't believe it. I don't think it's so much that white people can't dance. It's just that they like certain musical instruments. That instrument, my friends, is electric guitar. It speaks directly to the soul of the white person. They find it irresistible.[35]

The skit continues with Chappelle and John Mayer, playing his guitarist sidekick, visiting a corporate board meeting attended only by white people. Mayer commences to play some pentatonic improvised lines reminiscent of the jam band genre. The people in the room quickly leave their seats and start the sort of interpretive dancing associated with audiences at jam band concerts; one woman becomes so uninhibited that she removes her blouse and bra. As soon as the music stops, the people stop dancing. Next, the dynamic duo visits a "chic Manhattan restaurant" filled with (in Chappelle's words) "a lot of [George W.] Bush voters"—in other words, a conservative crowd. Mayer plays a heavy metal riff replete with distorted power chords and the restaurant's clientele begin to behave very aggressively, dancing enthusiastically, overturning tables, and fighting one another. Again, once the music stops, the people return to their tables and continue their lunches.

But then, "every experiment needs a control." At a "Harlem barbershop" filled with African Americans and Latinos, Mayer's blues-rock improvisations are met impatiently with requests to "shut the fuck up." Chappelle then announces, "Let's see how the blacks respond to drums." He pulls back a tarp to reveal drummer Questlove, who then proceeds to lay down a funk-based groove. The African Americans in the barbershop immediately begin dancing, and one even freestyles a rap to go with it. Finally, Chappelle observes that "some of the Latin people were nodding their heads, but they weren't really feeling it the way I thought they would." The solution? To add an electric piano playing a *montuno* or *guajeo* figure, which Questlove complements with a salsa drum pattern. The punchline to the skit comes in the final scene, in which Chappelle and Mayer, now back out on the street, are confronted by two policemen who threaten to fine them for filming without a permit. Mayer starts playing a country song, and both policemen, one white, one black, begin to sing along. Chappelle asks the black cop, "Hey, my man. How you know that song?" The cop replies, "I'm from the suburbs, man. I can't help it." Intertitles follow that read: "People of Earth. No Matter What Your Instrument. Keep Dancing."

The skit brilliantly begins by parodying stereotypes, which rely on the idea of homology (i.e., that categories of people are directly related to categories of music). Chappelle pairs not only instruments with people, as he claims to be doing, but *instruments* with *genres* with *people* with *kinesthetic responses* with *affect*: white people can't resist *dancing* in a *spacy* or *aggressive* manner to the *electric guitar,* especially when that guitar plays *jam band* music or *heavy metal*. Black people can't resist dancing to the drums, especially when they are playing a funk or hip-hop groove. And Latinos respond automatically to electric pianos and percussion, especially when playing salsa. Yet the punch line carries us beyond biological essentialism (the idea that one's identity is defined by biology): if one grows up in the suburbs, then location (and the cultural context found in that location) trumps racial identity. The laughter accompanying all segments of the skit only confirms the "truth" of both models: the essentializing homology, and the imaginary identification in which genre and identity don't seem to fit.

Chappelle underscores how a major difference between the labels used for popular music genres (R&B, country, pop, easy listening, rock) and those for classic literature (epic, lyric, drama) is that popular music genres call attention to the identity of the people associated with a particular type of music. Take, for example, race music, an important category of popular music in the United States from the mid-1920s until the late 1940s: a code label for African American music. Various instantiations of race music could be associated with other examples of race music through textual references (or iterations) to previous texts associated with race music, and the category of race music could be established through its difference from other categories of popular music circulating at the same time. Race music, however, could not plausibly be understood as race music unless it had something to do with African Americans. Contradictions arise when we ponder how race music may not have found favor with all people who identified as African American, and that some non–African Americans were race music's biggest fans.

This lack of a tight, one-to-one fit between popular music genres and demographic groups constitutes one of the greatest challenges in theorizing genre-audience relations, a challenge taken up by numerous popular scholars.[36] The fascination with the relationship between demographics and popular music categories long predated popular music studies, however, and figured prominently in the emergence of both the notion of popular-music-as-mass-mediated music and the culture industry itself.

Genre-Demographics-Population

The history of popular music categories, and their relationship to different demographic categories, is long and complex, and formed an inextricable part of the U.S. commercial recording industry in the late nineteenth and early twentieth centuries. The desire to categorize did not originate with the distribution of music on sound recordings, but rather continued a process of organizing music in terms of categories of difference associated with demographic divisions. Commercial music prior to sound recording, however, was limited to those types of music performed in professional venues (classical music concerts, vaudeville, minstrelsy) or distributed as printed music (classical music, parlor music, religious music). Technological transformations in the realm of sound recording and transmission extended and modified the conception of relations between different types of music and processes of group identification, and made a variety of musics widely available that were previously unable to circulate beyond a circumscribed locale.

Dating back to the mid-nineteenth century, popular music in the United States has been divided into categories that refer to specific (or implied) group identifications. The form of popular music that dominated the nineteenth century, minstrelsy, is emblematic in this respect, as it arose as a genre that focused on the performance of (what was believed to be) black identity by white working-class men. The development of sound recording facilitated new ways of linking a type of music to a type of people, as dispersed groups of people could find themselves connected to others through their consumption of a particular type of music. Unlike minstrelsy, however, in which the mode of musical identification was primarily imaginary or performative, the modes pursued by the music industry in the early years of sound recording were often based on the idea of a one-to-one correspondence between the social connotations of the genre and the identity of the audience (and often the performers as well).

The notion of discrete markets correlated to particular formations of musical sounds paralleled the growing importance of the concept of population in the nineteenth century, with its emphasis on the measurement and tracking of individuals, and the compilation of statistics about birth, death, disease, and so on. The classifications of groups of human beings stored in government and medical files found echoes in the new forms of cultural production, characterized by mechanical reproduction, which arose in the late nineteenth century.[37] When compared to the dominant modes of classifying individuals, which emphasized the importance of groups at the expense of individuals, commercial sound recording appeared as a paradox, confirming group identifications staked out by demography even as it individualized.[38] And although sound recordings were able to confirm already extant, homological identifications—a characteristic that was particularly clear in the music industry categories of various foreign recordings that flourished in the years 1890 to 1930—they also continued processes of imaginary identification begun earlier in the nineteenth century with musical practices such as minstrelsy, the coon song, songs invoking the stereotypical white yokel, and songs caricaturing various groups of new immigrants. If sound recording extended the possibilities for individuated listening and isolated identifications, then one of the most significant effects of sound recording was to change the perception of how these newly individualized listeners might belong in a group.

From Homology to the Exotic

By the time that the record industry practice of relating categories to identities was in high swing in the 1920s, none other than Theodor W. Adorno himself weighed in on the practice. In his essay "The Curves of the Needle," Adorno contended that "what the gramophone listener actually wants to hear is himself, and the artist merely offers him a substitute for the sounding image of his own person, which he would like to safeguard as a possession."[39] What Adorno refers to here as the artist I would argue can be extended to entire categories of music. His testament to the one-to-one-correspondence or homology model (i.e., listeners hear themselves or a representation of what they imagine themselves to be) thus suggests one possible way in which artists or genres might relate to categories of people (even though Adorno would probably argue that the self thus heard is not predated by a "sounding image of his own person," or a stable, unified self anchored in a demographic classification). Minstrelsy, however, as already discussed, clearly cannot be explained by recourse to this homological model. Genres could thus exist in a homological relation to a group of people, or they could exist in a performative relation.

The mode of identification found in minstrelsy persisted into the twentieth century (as did the practice of minstrelsy itself) alongside the newfound emphasis on homology. Many modalities of identification were needed, both for commercial reasons and to describe the complex world of interactions between musicians, music industry personnel, and audiences in the early twentieth century. Georgina Born has developed a four-pronged model of music and identification relations ranging from those that are homologous to those that are primarily fantasized, such as those involved in exoticist relationships to musical identification. In between these two extremes, ways of conceptualizing music-identity relations often fall into two other categories based on the temporality of the identificatory relation: a nostalgic or retroactive relation, in which an identification is mapped onto the past, as in what occurs with many nationalist uses of folk music, and imaginary identifications that prefigure an emergent, and potentially homologous, social grouping.[40] These emergent identifications can be formed by a new articulation of music and identity, such as what has occurred with numerous forms of music initially associated with African Americans that later found success with white audiences.[41] Such imaginary relations emphasize the contingency of musical and identificatory categories, drawing attention to the permeability of their borders. The notion of "articulation" is also crucial here, as it suggests that the range of genre-identity relations does not arise as a natural or biological connection (even in the most seemingly straightforward cases of homology) but rather must be sutured together through the repetition of social practices in which a generic label brings together categories of people.[42]

Notions of articulation and assemblage help account for the complex relations between music and social identifications, in which different categories of people may feel an affinity for a category of music, or, conversely, the same category of people may identify with multiple categories of music. A flexible relationship

TABLE 2 Record Catalog (before 1939) and Popularity Chart (after 1939) Nomenclature, 1920–97

Categories	1920–39	1939–49	1949–69	1969–82	1982–90	1990–97
Mainstream	Vocal with Accompaniment / Instrumental Dance	Popular	Popular / Hot 100	Hot 100	Hot 100	Hot 100
African American	Colored Records (1921–22) / Race Music (1923–42)	Harlem Hit Parade (1942–44) / American Folk (1945) / Race (1946–49)	Rhythm and Blues	Soul	Black	Rhythm and Blues
White, Southern, Rural	Old-Time Tunes, Old-Familiar Tunes, Southern Records (1924–33), Hillbilly (1933–39)	Hillbilly (1939–42) / American Folk (1945–49)	Country and Western/ Country (1962)	Country	Country	Country
Foreign Music	Foreign Music	Foreign Music (1939–44)				

between popular music categories and identities characterizes the studies of genre in the history portrayed in this book. The main categories that were to play the largest role in structuring the U.S. popular music industry from the 1920s onward were based on an oscillation between the poles of imaginary and homological identification. These categories have assumed a variety of names but can be summarized as a category of music associated with African Americans (known variously as race, rhythm and blues, and soul), one associated with rural, white Americans (old-time, hillbilly, and country), and one that is nominally unmarked in terms of identity, but which implies a white, middle- or upper-class, urban subject (no official name, but often referred to as mainstream popular music). Another important category based largely on homology, foreign music, played a central role beginning at the dawn of the recording era in the 1890s, but its significance waned before becoming moribund during the 1940s (see table 2).

Table 2 reveals that the period from 1920 to 1950 was one of great turbulence in the U.S. music industry, where uncertainty reigned as to how to label the different categories. This book correspondingly spends the majority of its chapters on this period, although later chapters also examine briefer moments of uncertainty after 1950.

Musical Communities: Imagined, Constellated, or Phantasmatic?

It could be argued that even the earliest forms of mechanical reproduction, such as printing, created the possibility of imagined communities: individuals dispersed in space related to one another through the consumption of the same object. Benedict Anderson's influential study of nationalism, *Imagined Communities,* makes precisely the point that the emergence of printing in local vernaculars, combined with the development of print journalism, served to unite individuals unknown to one another into nations.[43]

The film scholar Rick Altman has proposed an extension of Anderson's concept, what he dubs "constellated communities," to take into account those media associated with the early twentieth century, such as cinema and sound recording, which, Altman argues, created new forms of identification, and new relationships with different categories of cultural production.[44] One could visualize Altman's "constellated communities" as fissuring the nation conjured up by Anderson's "imagined communities," breaking the latter into interwoven formations allied through identification with categories or genres of mass cultural production. Unlike the newspapers of the early nineteenth century, which form the paradigm for Anderson's study, the categories and genres of the new media were directed across the full range of demographic divisions in the society, and could either bring these groups together by appealing across divisions (as in, for example, mainstream popular music, or many film genres) or appeal to a sense of particularity (e.g., various types of foreign music, race music, old-time music, or Yiddish cinema). Furthermore, sound recording and cinema could make people aware that they belonged to a group they never knew existed, or that they might be categorized with people whom they had previously believed were very different from themselves and whose primary awareness of one another was through the mass media itself.[45] To paraphrase Altman, textual resemblances in the realm of syntax and semantics are insufficient to establish a genre; rather, audience members must have the sense that others are interpreting texts similarly to themselves, one of the cornerstones of what he terms "lateral communication": the way in which textual or generic meaning is shaped by audience members' communication with each other as much as by "frontal communication" between audiences and texts.[46]

As suggested earlier, such processes of identification could work in a variety of ways. In some cases, a recording category referred to a preexisting demographic category; this was the case to some extent with both race music and old-time music. Yet even in these cases, industry categories might collapse significant distinctions. For example, African Americans born in Detroit in the 1920s into a family where the father worked for the Ford Motor Company might be aware that they belonged to the "negro" or "colored" demographic group with African Americans born into a sharecropping family in Mississippi, but they would also be acutely aware of their differences.[47] Marketing firms working in the music industry, however, would have targeted both families in their race record catalogs. Thus, the race record audience was formed, in part, by the knowledge that other fans of race music were interpreting the music similarly, a practice facilitated by marketing and adapted to extant practices of touring live performers.

A similar collapsing of internal distinctions could be observed in the formation of the old-time category, which would have included white workers in Southern cities as well as that almost mythological representative of the folk, the mountain man, and then, rather quickly, (mostly) rural, (mostly) white people in the rest of North America. In order to create difference with the unmarked mainstream, consisting of (what were assumed to be) white, middle- or upper-class Northern urban dwellers, the old-time category's relationship to a demographic group could not be accounted for by beliefs in visual difference characteristic of the racialist thinking of the time, but had to include class and geography in ways that resonated with a conception of racial difference peculiar to the period in which this category was formed.[48] For its part, foreign music functioned to create a sense of unity among specific categories of immigrants dispersed across North America.

As the previous paragraph suggests, popular music in the era of mechanical reproduction was particularly well suited to the production of homologous music-identity relationships—that is, identifications in which a category of music corresponds to a preexisting demographic category of some kind. In this mode of identification, a race record finds an African American audience; an old-time record finds a rural, white, Southern audience; a mainstream record finds a white, bourgeois, Northern, urban audience; and a foreign record finds a foreigner. Such formulations based on the idea of homology support the impression that audiences, musical genres, and the relations between them are stable and clearly demarcated from one another. However, such direct correspondences would not suffice in the twentieth century for the complex relations of consumers and producers required for maximum circulation of recordings, and neither did they correspond to the experiences of musicians and audiences. This failure of the homological model to provide for either maximum commercial efficiency or the range of possible musician-audience relationships to genre recalls the need for a model such as Born's typology of music-identity relations. A question still remains, however, around the notion of imaginary relations to genre, and whether it is possible to have a truly non-imaginary relation.

A psychoanalytic theory of musical identification might argue that all identifications are imaginary to some extent, in that they occur through a relationship either to one's own image or through identification with, and recognition by, others.[49] Such an observation touches on how identification with cultural others (or with our own image) may fulfill psychic needs, yet even if we accept the theoretical model of psychoanalysis, Born's model has the advantage of indicating how some types of identification with forms of mass culture are *relatively* homologous, in that they rest on an identification with an extant social or demographic category. These contrast with those that may or may not prefigure a grouping, but which do not refer to a preexisting identification in which audience members hear the "sounding image of his/her own person." Such a distinction is crucial to understanding the functioning of musical categories in popular music even if the extant categories are themselves in a constant state of flux, and are modified once they are pressed into service. Put differently, if people at a young age assume an identification that is socially recognized, then due to its unstable character, this identification is also produced through iterations that then refer to a model that, in a certain sense, does not yet exist. This way of understanding identification has sometimes been referred to as performative. "Performative" in this case, however, does not refer to a voluntaristic act of identificatory affiliation, but rather to how successive iterations of an identification constantly modify the conventions (and thus the constraints) of the category (or categories) with which people identify, uncannily paralleling the iterative processes of musical categories discussed earlier.[50] Attempts to understand musical and identificatory categories seem to share the same central conundrum: how to evoke simultaneously a shared system alongside numerous individual instantiations and interpretations that threaten to undo the legibility of the system.

This way of understanding identification can also be thought of as phantasmatic, in that the subject incessantly restages (as in fantasy) the assumption of an identity, which is dispersed in fantasy into different identificatory positions, and which inevitably engages in revising prior identifications in light of subsequent events. If iteration refers to the public expression and perception of an identification, then referring to identification as phantasmatic evokes the interior process of continual recitation and modification.[51]

An iterative or phantasmatic theory of identification does not minimize the role played by the distinctions already proposed between homologous and imaginary relations to music. Rather, this theory can help shed light on how some popular music categories refer specifically to demographic divisions while others represent affiliations that might emerge against the background of one's own demographic classification, such as, to take two examples from the 1920s, the white fan of hot jazz, or that other sign of rebellious white youth in the 1920s, the flapper. Sound recording and cinema participated both in consolidating homologous identifications and in expanding the range of imaginary affiliations via new forms of audience building. Altman stresses that the role of homologous identity-genre relations is minimal in the formation and circulation of film genres. However, as Born argues, the situation in popular music would seem to be more complex. To be sure, plentiful cases do exist in music in which individuals learn to recognize that they are part of a generic, constellated community through the efforts of merchandisers, producers, advertisers, et cetera, only conscious of each other through the media (one of Altman's central contentions), but this cannot erase the central organizing principle of homology in the music business. Indeed, I have been arguing that it is the combined deployment of a wide range of possible imaginary identifications with those that emerge against the background of these apparently more stable formations that so strongly marks the new musical categories that appeared at the turn of the twentieth century.[52] This combination of the imaginary and the homologous represents the practical result of the phantasmatic identificatory positions described in the previous paragraph.

Born's model implies a temporality of musical identification on the level of both the individual and the social, in which the concept of homology corresponds to those identifications that are most deeply felt and experienced as "natural," as "who we really are," that is, those identifications that formed before we were conscious that they were forming. The various imaginary identifications parallel those aspects of our selves that we are conscious of learning how to "perform," with the acknowledgment here that these two distinctions often bleed into one another. On the social-historical level, the temporality of music-identificatory relationships could be exemplified by blues-rock. As shown in Chappelle's skit, blues-rock is currently (and has been since the 1960s) identified primarily with white people. Yet the blues on which blues-rock is based has strong historical associations with African Americans. What appeared initially to be an exoticist relation for white people could have been interpreted by the mid-1960s as an emergent relation, and then, by the 1970s, as a homologous relation.

Returning to the early decades of the twentieth century, one finds all of these modes of identification at work as exemplified by foreign music, which had existed as a recording category since the 1890s, and by the race and old-time categories, both of which emerged in the 1920s and were to have particular significance for the future of genre-identity relations. The assumed unity and homological quality of the foreign, race, and old-time categories could be projected into the past, as was done by folklorists, to argue that some types of people had always listened primarily to a certain type of music; the music associated with the foreign, race, and old-time categories could be adopted by mainstream audiences, to the point where it became part of the mainstream; or identification could be treated as a performance, as with the remaining vestiges of minstrelsy and popular music with Asian themes.

Race music, old-time music, and the mainstream have formed the poles between which a great deal of popular music in the United States has circulated since the 1920s. The resulting musical categories are enshrined in institutional practices—from radio formats, production categories, and journalistic and fan discourse all the way to the graphic interface of iTunes—that have a profound effect on the circulation of music. One implication of the foregoing argument about identifications and genres is that categories of music and people are neither true nor false, but rather ideological, in that they speak to a shared, tacit understanding about which differences are meaningful as well as how these differences are meaningful. Adorno, in the essay cited earlier, even underscored the relation between this aspect of genre and identificatory homologies: "Most of the time records are virtual photographs of their owners, flattering photographs—ideologies."[53] At the same time, and contra Adorno, an aspect of ideology is that it never speaks to everybody in the same way at the same time. Genre, because it acts as a kind of cultural shorthand, is one of the arenas in which the patterns and contradictions of ideology become visible.[54] Consistency of musical style-genre-audience associations can underscore the deeply entrenched nature of these connections, while rapid changes in the relationship between any of these three terms can underscore their contingency.

Crossover: The Fulcrum of Genre/Identification

If neither genres nor identifications are ever finally fixed or stable—if musical genres are differentiated in terms of music style, and demographic groups are differentiated in terms of musical taste—then the perpetual reclassification of musical texts comes to seem inevitable. Thus, the appeal of musical texts may extend across generic boundaries, individual tastes may change or expand, or some people may never even know when the music they prefer is reclassified without their consent. Because popular music genres are so often read in terms of the people with whom they are associated, such reclassifications offer particularly revealing moments for studying the processes of articulation that bind together categories of music and people. The concept of crossover thus has broad implications pertaining to social mobility, the formation of new audiences and social alliances, and shifts in the beliefs of producers and consumers of popular music. Instances of generic crossover often highlight those moments when identification with a category of music shifts from a homologous to an imaginary form.

The interest in crossover derives from the way in which the process appears, on the one hand, to reinforce category-identity relations, while at the same time (and paradoxically) exposing inconsistencies in the way these relations are understood. In other words, the crossover process relies on preexisting categories, which provide sites to move away from and toward, and may therefore seem to reinforce these categories, yet the process of recordings moving from one category to another also undermines assumptions about connections between categories and audiences, and points to the complexity and instability of individual genres and identities. Crossover highlights the tension between the differentiated practices that people experience in their daily lives, and the imagined unities of categories of people and music that enable the use of genre and identificatory labels in communication—what I elsewhere described as the tension between lived and imagined conceptions of genre.[55] While the notion of crossover as a boundary-exceeding or boundary-reinforcing process appears prominently in chapters 3 through 7, the history of the concept is explored in chapter 8 as a prelude to an analysis of its function in the early 1980s.

CHARTING POPULARITY

For my analysis of the categories of music used in discourse about the music industry in the United States during the twentieth century, I rely heavily on the publications produced by and for the music industry such as *Talking Machine World, Billboard, Variety,* and *Cash Box.* I frequently refer to and analyze the popularity charts found in these publications from the late 1930s onward. To open a copy of *Billboard* published after 1940 (or *Cash Box* after 1955, or *Record World* after 1964) is to enter a space dominated by charts, numbers, hierarchies, predictions, and speculations. Accompanying these numerically organized lists are articles that describe the charts in terms of the trends, the surprises, and the legal battles of companies. These articles thereby create a narrative that accompanies the information paradigmatically arranged in the charts. The charts themselves contain a syntagmatic dimension, as they display a song's position relative to its position in previous weeks. The articles attempt to explain both paradigmatic and syntagmatic dimensions of the charts, to elaborate what the numbers imply. And, in addition to this, ads for products related to the recording industry occupy almost half of the total space of the magazine. The charts and articles also function as free advertising for the same products, and this all makes a certain kind of sense, since the putative audience for *Billboard* consists of record shop retailers, radio personnel, jukebox operators, and others who are trying to maximize their profits in dealing with recorded products in one form or another.[56] In this respect, industry publications such as *Billboard* function similarly to commercial radio and music television, in which advertisements alternate with the playing of recordings and videos to stimulate sales of recordings.[57]

The emphasis on numeracy in the charts, on paradigmatic hierarchies and syntagmatic narratives, finds echoes in other aspects of mass culture, most prominently in the business and sports pages. Like sports, the emphasis on statisticity may explain the interest of the charts for consumers; unlike sports, the pop charts tell a story with information that is more clearly directed toward retailers.[58] Numbers have had the ability to confer legitimacy on media events since at least the 1830s, when numerically based accounts of "disease, madness, and the state of the threatening underworld . . . created a morbid and fearful fascination for numbers upon which the bureaucracies fed."[59] This relationship between numbers and legitimacy only increased when, in response to the more than thirteen thousand questions in the 1890 U.S. census, mechanical means of manipulating data were developed.[60] It's a small leap from the mechanical operations of the census of 1890 to the pride with which *Billboard* announced in 1991 *its* mechanical means of tabulating record sales. Mechanical tabulation devices extend the way in which numeracy and the marshaling of quantitative facts can become a means of legitimating information by distancing the facts from the background practices that make them possible.

The numeracy of the charts as presented in *Billboard* may only partly explain the fascination they hold for consumers. After all, upon its inception in 1935, *Your Hit Parade* quickly became one of the most-listened-to radio shows in the United States.[61] In a sense the charts perform a kind of self-citation similar to that of the public opinion poll: opinion surveys allow citizens to assume that others believe what they can't believe themselves.[62] Beyond even this quality of self-citation, the charts possess an oft-cited circularity. The Hot 100 is supposedly based on a combination of radio play and record sales, although *Billboard* has never explicitly revealed the way in which these factors influence the charts. Yet for much of its history, radio play directly influenced record sales and was itself based on record sales or promotional pitches from record companies (as well as the taste of disc jockeys, particularly prior to 1970) and the ranking of recordings in popularity charts.[63] As Irv Lichtman, an editor for *Cash Box* from the 1950s onward, explains: "A lot of the chart was intuitive; it was projecting based not on actual statistics necessarily but perhaps a buzz, perhaps something more concrete."[64]

More significant, however, is how the charts function as a form of symbolic, expressive coding, and as an observable sign of otherwise-invisible material forces that create social boundaries of exclusion and inclusion. As the most visible sign of the intersection between marketing categories and the representation of the popularity of individual recordings, charts provide information about the asymmetrical distribution of resources that accrue to categories of sound according to implicit social divisions. Charts also participate in the production of imagined or constellated communities by synchronizing the popularity of recordings across widely dispersed regions.[65]

The charts present themselves as authoritative, as statistical facts, an appearance that occludes the very real human activity that compiles the charts in the first place. By not attempting to penetrate frequently beyond the chart's facade to the human creators behind them, I assign a kind of agency to the charts. This way of presenting the charts is not an accident: popularity charts serve as a paradigmatic example of what Bruno Latour calls a nonhuman agent—a mediator that does not merely transfer information from one site to another, but one that makes a difference by creating its own effects.[66] Popularity charts create effects in those who encounter them that cannot be anticipated by the humans who formulate them. Because readers respond to the charts rather than to the humans who compile them, the charts assume a sort of autonomy. The numeracy of the charts, so important in granting them their authority, also leads to a neglect of their crucial role.

Such is the fate of a mediator that communicates largely through numbers rather than words.

A Note on Sources

In chapters 2 through 4, the printed source on which I rely most heavily is *Talking Machine World*, while in chapters 5 through 8, I cite *Billboard* more often than any other source. My main reason for this is that these two publications are the richest source of information about popular music making and the music industry during the periods in question. Although I do rely heavily on these two publications, which are directed primarily to music industry workers, other publications are cited as a way of showing how the discourses analyzed in *Talking Machine World* and *Billboard* are not sui generis but indicative of discussions transpiring in other publications and in other forums. And while it is true that the different interests of these publications do inflect the debates in particular ways, the same terms circulate and are used in roughly the same ways in a wide range of media and publications.

It could appear as if the focus on *Talking Machine World* and *Billboard* privileges an analysis of genre that is driven by music industry sources to the relative neglect of how fans form their interpretations or how musicians are influenced by notions of genre. The argument here is that the role of genre for fans and musicians cannot be separated from how the producers of *Billboard* think about genres.[67] To be sure, what I call music industry categories probably figure more in the discourse of the *Billboard* writers than they do in the discourse of fans and musicians, and what I call critic-fan genres feature more in the discourse of fans and critics (and musicians), but these worlds are connected, and a change in one sphere of discourse will have its ramifications in the other. Fans and musicians are not completely impervious to what the creators of *Billboard* think, and the reverse is also true: *Billboard* considers what will make sense to fans and musicians. At certain points in the chapters that follow, when *Billboard*'s conception of its large categories diverges from what is happening with critic-fan-musician discourses, I search for statements to clarify this divergence. This happens most spectacularly in chapter 7, when *Billboard* discontinued its R&B charts, an event that exemplifies the tensions inherent in the practice of categorization. I not only sought out statements in *Billboard* itself that addressed the contradictory elements of this event, but also consulted other sources, such as a column in the African American newspaper the *Chicago Defender*, in which teenagers compiled their own column about what they and their peer group were listening to. Several chapters explore the relationship between the different levels of genre in a detailed way so as to show the reciprocal effect of music industry categories, radio formats, and critic-fan genres. Other examples of the interactions between critic-fan genres and marketing categories come to the fore in chapter 5, which explores the relationship of swing and novelty to the mainstream and race categories, and in chapters 3 and 6, in which the term "hillbilly," although active in critical discourse, never quite achieved stability as a marketing category label.

Related to the issue of printed sources is the focus in *Categorizing Sound* on sound recordings as both objects of discourse and as sources of sonic information, although videos of performances are consulted whenever possible, as are journalistic accounts of performances. Chapters 3, 5, and 6 discuss live performance in detail. From these examples, it is clear that the ways in which genre terms were being used and the functions they served in other media did not differ significantly from how they operated in discussions of recordings.

. . .

Categorizing Sound will largely focus on the large categories used by the U.S. music industry, how these categories map certain aspects of musical style onto categories of group identification, and how these categories interact with critic-fan genres. Although on the face of it such a study runs the risk of reification, both of music and of identifications, the discussion in this chapter on popular music genres and processes of group identifications has indicated how this study will emphasize the singularity of the event over notions of resemblance and the same.[68] Rather than order the events of the past so as to construct a teleological chain that arrives to confirm our present-day beliefs about categories of music and humans, this book focuses on the moment of emergence of the categorical labels themselves. This is especially true in chapters 3 and 4, which chart the formation of race music and old-time music, events that established the two principal minority categories of popular music in the 1920s. Chapter 2 discusses some of the popular music categories that preceded race music and old-time music, principally foreign music, which created a template for the use of homologous music-identity relations that would figure so prominently thereafter.

The other chapters are primarily concerned with periods of flux in the popular music genre system, when uncertainty gripped participants in the world of popular music as to which sounds should be assembled into what genres with which group of people and with what generic label. Thus, in the 1940s (the subject of chapters 5 and 6), while categories had already been established for music associated with African Americans and rural white people, the rise and fall of swing music in the mainstream affected the perception of both of these "specialized" musics in the first part of the decade, while the growth of novelty recordings toward the end of the decade led to a further repartitioning of the popular music field. *Billboard* had rechristened race music and old-time music (which by the early 1940s was being referred to as hillbilly or folk music) as rhythm and blues and country and western by the end of the 1940s, a decade during which both categories experienced enormous growth in their public circulation.

Although no major sea changes occurred in the names of the categories themselves between the late 1940s and the early 1960s, the constant minute modifications that characterize genre histories guaranteed that the meaning of the categories would not stabilize entirely. Such minute inflections can sometimes lead to what may seem to be an abrupt shift. Chapter 7 takes an anomalous event as its starting point: the disappearance of the rhythm and blues chart from *Billboard* during a fourteen-month period from November 1963 to January 1965. Given the intense interconnections between musical categories and group identifications, and the way in which musical categories function as social allegories, what can it have meant for an influential organization such as *Billboard* to decide that one of its three main categories should disappear and then reappear fourteen months later? This period of turbulence for the popular music category associated with African Americans also gave rise to a new label, soul, a label strongly bound up with then-current political movements around African American self-definition. Such shifts in labels are never innocent, but are rather tied to institutional acts of classification, with corresponding implications in terms of access to material resources and assumptions about audiences.

Chapter 8 focuses on the early 1980s, the period when the debate over crossover reached its peak—a debate closely tied to a transformation in popular music radio formats during the 1970s. Country music experienced a brief moment of mainstream prominence during this period, the category for African American music was renamed yet again (this time to "black music"), and the launching of MTV redefined notions of the mainstream and made issues about genre and racial identification visible in a novel and literal way.

If the approach to categories in this book could be broadly dubbed genealogical, then such an approach does not assume that categories are pre-given and universal, but rather encourages an analysis of the processes through which they are formed, of the play of power and the violent suppressions of difference in the name of the identical necessary to promulgate the notions of resemblance enshrined in categories—a violence attested to by the struggles over the various labels for popular music genres and notions about musical popularity itself. The components of an assemblage that are recognized as similar are then able to attain legibility, visibility, and audibility, and to become the conventions of categories as they are invented, consolidated, and accepted by the public. In the United States in the early and mid-twentieth century, musical categories grew out of and contributed to a preoccupation with race, class, and geographical regions and how these might be articulated to technological developments and the imperatives of economics. Thus, knowledge about people and music participated in the process of finding an efficient model for the music industry that would coordinate production and consumption.

One concern of this book that I have attempted to develop in this chapter is how genres create a way of communicating about music between artists, music industry middle-people, and audiences, none of whom are strictly separable. If the roles that they perform differ, all of these agents inhabit the same, or similar, or overlapping social worlds. If the labels that are used to group musical utterances together are not broadly legible, they will not gain currency. The process through which this occurs has no single agent or point of origin. A single individual or group of individuals (no matter how powerful) cannot will a genre label into existence ("they never even knew").[69] Genres are therefore neither top-down, in that they cannot be imposed by the music industry if the connections projected by the categorical labels are not legible to the public, nor bottom-up, created by consumers willy-nilly in a voluntaristic feat of individual will. The counterpoising of top-down and bottom-up is not meant to eviscerate the effects of power, but rather to indicate that the tendency from the 1920s onward toward ever-finer divisions of the audience meant that the effects of power transcended the role played by the agency of music industry executives as well as consumers. Capitalism channels desire into the production of categories of music and humans that continue to proliferate, forming a grid that becomes increasingly available as a source of information and that thus leads to greater possibilities of surveillance (be they conventional or cybernetic). Individualizing even as they group people together, genre labels arise through broad processes that create projections of our shared and not-entirely-conscious social preoccupations, somewhat in the sense of modern-day mythical fables in which a society works out its collective concerns.

NOTES

1. Initially broadcast on May 10, 2010.

2. Mack's song is used as an example in Thomas O. Beebee, *The Ideology of Genre: A Comparative Study of Generic Instability* (University Park: Pennsylvania State University Press, 1994), 249–50.

3. For an example, see http://www.bandmix.com/new-york/, accessed April 19, 2012. I will note that musicians often use individual artists, rather than entire genres, as reference points in these advertisements. In these cases, I would argue that the individual artist stands in for an entire genre while affording a greater degree of stylistic specificity.

4. Jacques Derrida, "The Law of Genre," in *On Narrative*, ed. W. J. T. Mitchell (Chicago and London: University of Chicago Press, 1981), 61.

5. On this point see also Keith Negus, *Music Genres and Corporate Cultures* (London and New York: Routledge, 1999), 29; and Jason Toynbee, *Making Popular Music: Musicians, Creativity and Institutions* (London: Arnold, 2000), 105.

6. For a sampling of some of the explicit invocations of genre in scholarship on Western art music, many of which range beyond a concern with formal and stylistic conventions, see Carl Dahlhaus, "New Music and the Problems of Musical Genre," in *Schoenberg and the New Music*, trans. Derrick Puffett and Alfred Clayton (Cambridge: Cambridge University Press, 1990), 32–44; Julie Cumming, *The Motet in the Age of Du Fay* (Cambridge: Cambridge

University Press, 1999), 7–40; Mark Everist, *French Motets in the Thirteenth Century: Music, Poetry, and Genre* (Cambridge: Cambridge University Press, 1994); Jeffrey Kallberg, "The Rhetoric of Genre: Chopin's Nocturne in G Minor," in *Chopin at the Boundaries: Sex, History, and Musical Genre* (Cambridge, MA: Harvard University Press, 1996), 3–29; Laurence Dreyfus, *Bach and the Patterns of Invention* (Cambridge, MA: Harvard University Press, 1996), 103–33; Eric Drott, "The End(s) of Genre," *Journal of Music Theory* 57, no. 1 (Spring 2013): 1–45; Matthew Gelbart, *The Invention of "Folk Music" and "Art Music": Emerging Categories from Ossian to Wagner* (Cambridge: Cambridge University Press, 2007).

7. Rick Altman, *Film/Genre* (London: British Film Institute, 1999), 2–3.

8. This reassessment includes Stephen Neale's oft-quoted assertion that "genres are not to be seen as forms of textual codifications, but as systems of orientations, expectations and conventions that circulate between industry, text and subject." Stephen Neale, *Genre* (London: British Film Institute, 1980), 19. See also Rick Altman's reformulation of the role of "syntax and semantics" in "A Semantic/Syntactic Approach to Film Genre," *Cinema Journal* 23, no. 1 (Spring 1984): 6–18 and *The American Film Musical* (Bloomington: Indiana University Press, 1987). For a collection that charts shifts in approaches to genre in film studies, see Barry Keith Grant, *Film Genre Reader III* (Austin: University of Texas Press, 2003).

9. In film studies, Rick Altman has stressed the importance of studying the "producer's game" (based on historical emergence) in order to counter the prevalence of the "critic's game" (retroactive grouping) (*Film/Genre*, 30–48). Steven Neale, in his most recent book on genre in film, arrives at a similar questioning of the retroactive approach in his emphasis on the "production of culture" perspective. Steven Neale, *Genre and Hollywood* (London and New York: Routledge, 2000), 207–30. In popular music scholarship, examples of this kind of work can be found in Karl Hagstrom Miller, *Segregating Sound: Inventing Folk and Pop Music in the Age of Jim Crow* (Durham, NC, and London: Duke University Press, 2010); Keir Keightley, "Tin Pan Allegory," *Modernism/Modernity* 19, no. 4 (November 2012): 717–36; Steve Waksman, *This Ain't the Summer of Love: Conflict and Crossover in Heavy Metal and Punk* (Berkeley: University of California Press, 2009); and Diane Pecknold, *The Selling Sound: The Rise of the Country Music Industry* (Durham, NC, and London: Duke University Press, 2007). Matthew Gelbart offers a historicist interrogation of the main categories of Western European music in *The Invention of "Folk Music" and "Art Music."* See also Karin Barber's discussion of the role of history in studies of genre, which she frames in terms of the opposition between etic/emic and macro/micro approaches, in *The Anthropology of Texts, Persons and Publics* (Cambridge: Cambridge University Press, 2007), 36–45.

10. Mikhail Bakhtin, "Response to a Question from the *Novyi Mir* Editorial Staff," in *Speech Genres and Other Late Essays*, ed. Caryl Emerson and Michael Holquist (Austin: University of Texas Press, 1986), 4. This passage of Bakhtin's is discussed in Gary Saul Morson and Caryl Emerson, *Mikhail Bakhtin: Creation of a Prosaics* (Stanford, CA: Stanford University Press, 1990), 286.

11. For the clearest explanation of his genealogical approach to history, see Michel Foucault, "Nietzsche, Genealogy, History," in *Language, Counter-Memory, Practice: Selected Essays and Interviews* (Ithaca, NY: Cornell University Press, 1977), 139–64. The term

"history of the present" comes from Michel Foucault, *Discipline and Punish: The Birth of the Prison* (New York: Vintage Books, 1979), 31.

12. Franco Fabbri, "A Theory of Musical Genres: Two Applications," in *Popular Music Perspectives,* ed. D. Horn and P. Tagg (Göteborg, Sweden, and London: IASPM, 1982), 52–81 (subsequent citations in this chapter to this work are noted by page numbers in parentheses); and Franco Fabbri, "What Kind of Music?," *Popular Music* 2 (1982): 131–43. Fabbri has continued to revise his theory of genre; for a recent discussion focused on temporality, see "How Genres Are Born, Change, Die: Conventions, Communities and Diachronic Processes," in *Critical Musicological Reflections: Essays in Honour of Derek B. Scott,* ed. Stan Hawkins (Farnham, England: Ashgate, 2012), 179–91. The following also include explicit theorizations or arguments about genre in popular music: Simon Frith, *Performing Rites: On the Value of Popular Music* (Cambridge, MA: Harvard University Press, 1996), 75–95; Robert Walser, *Running with the Devil: Power, Gender and Madness in Heavy Metal Music* (Hanover, NH, and London, 1993), 26–34; Keith Negus, *Music Genres and Corporate Cultures* (London and New York: Routledge, 1999); Jason Toynbee, *Making Popular Music: Musicians, Creativity and Institutions* (London: Arnold, 2000), 102–29; Fabian Holt, *Genre in Popular Music* (Chicago: University of Chicago Press, 2007); David Brackett, "Questions of Genre in Black Popular Music," *Black Music Research Journal* 25, nos. 1–2 (Spring–Fall 2005): 73–92; Adam Krims, *Rap Music and the Poetics of Identity* (Cambridge: Cambridge University Press, 2000), 46–92; David Hesmondhalgh, "Subcultures, Scenes or Tribes? None of the Above," *Journal of Youth Studies* 8, no. 1 (2005): 21–40; Steve Waksman, *This Ain't the Summer of Love.* For studies that focus on categories of popular music over longer durations, see Philip Ennis, *The Seventh Stream: The Emergence of Rocknroll in American Popular Music* (Hanover, NH, and London: Wesleyan University Press, 1992); Charles Hamm, *Yesterdays: Popular Song in America* (New York and London: W. W. Norton, 1979); and William Howland Kenney, *Recorded Music in American Life: The Phonograph and Popular Memory, 1890–1945* (New York and Oxford: Oxford University Press, 1999).

13. Previous theorists of genre have used a relational approach in order to circumvent stylistic essentialism. Such relational approaches to genre have received more attention in literary studies, and can be traced to the Russian formalists; see Yury Tynyanov, "On Literary Evolution," in *Reading in Russian Poetics: Formalist and Structuralist Views,* ed. L. Matejka and K. Pomorska (Cambridge, MA: MIT Press, 1971), 66–78; and P. N. Medvedev, *The Formal Method in Literary Scholarship: A Critical Introduction to Sociological Poetics,* trans. Albert J. Wehrle (Cambridge, MA: Harvard University Press, 1985). Walter Benjamin's meditation on *The Origin of German Tragic Drama* (London and New York: Verso, 1998) produces striking insights about the dependence of a genre on its generic neighbors. Later approaches that treat genre as a relational construct include Hans Robert Jauss, "Theory of Genres and Medieval Literature," in *Towards an Aesthetic of Reception* (Minneapolis: University of Minnesota Press, 1982), 76–109; Thomas O. Beebee, *The Ideology of Genre*; and John Frow, *Genre* (London and New York: Routledge, 2006).

14. See Yury Tynyanov, "On Literary Evolution."

15. For literature, see Hans Robert Jauss, "Theory of Genres and Medieval Literature"; for cinema studies, see Steven Neale, "Questions of Genre," *Screen* 31, no. 1 (Spring 1990): 45–66. Heather Dubrow's notion of a "counter-genre" (in Heather Dubrow, *Genre* [London:

Methuen, 1982]) relies on the notion of a realization of genre's meaning in relation to other genres, a notion that has been explored by Steve Waksman in his study of punk and heavy metal (*This Ain't the Summer of Love,* 9–10). Thomas O. Beebee has developed an approach to genre that focuses on a genre in relation to what he calls its neighboring genres (*The Ideology of Genre*). Keith Negus refers to the idea of relationality in reference to Neale (*Genres and Corporate Cultures,* 53).

16. See Pierre Bourdieu, "The Field of Cultural Production: or the Economic World Reversed," in *The Field of Cultural Production: Essays on Art and Literature* (New York: Columbia University Press, 1993), 29–73.

17. For one of the most thoroughgoing examinations of the impact of different levels on how individual texts are understood to participate in a genre or genres, see Eric Drott, "The End(s) of Genre."

18. Fabbri himself confronts this last possibility, with his mention of "'terrestrial music' (a union of all the types of musical production and consumption on this planet) or 'galactic.'" Franco Fabbri, "A Theory of Musical Genres," 53.

19. Manuel DeLanda, *A New Philosophy of Society: Assemblage Theory and Social Complexity* (London: Bloomsbury, 2006), 10–11. DeLanda's concept of the assemblage is in turn adapted from the work of Gilles Deleuze; see Gilles Deleuze and Félix Guattari, *A Thousand Plateaus: Capitalism and Schizophrenia* (Minneapolis: University of Minneapolis Press, 1987); and Gilles Deleuze, *Foucault* (Minneapolis: University of Minnesota Press, 1988). For an application of the notion of the assemblage to the analysis of musical production, see Georgina Born, "On Musical Mediation: Ontology, Technology and Creativity," *twentieth-century music* 2, no. 1 (2005): 7–36.

20. Manuel DeLanda, *A New Philosophy of Society,* 17–18.

21. Simon Frith, *Performing Rites,* 77. Subsequent citations in this chapter are noted by page numbers in parentheses. Jennifer C. Lena has recently expanded on Frith's discussion of the importance of function in genre analysis in *Banding Together: How Communities Create Genres in Popular Music* (Princeton, NJ, and Oxford: Princeton University Press, 2012).

22. Names given in the "radio format" and "genre" categories are an amalgamation of names that have been used from the early 1980s up to the early 2000s.

23. J.L. Austin, *How to Do Things with Words* (Cambridge, MA: Harvard University Press, 1962).

24. Jacque Derrida, "Signature, Event, Context," in *Margins of Philosophy,* trans. Alan Bass (Chicago: University of Chicago Press, 1982), 307–30. Subsequent citations in this chapter are noted by page numbers in parentheses.

25. Writing about genre in cinema, Stephen Neale did much to bring attention to the role of convention, and of repetition and difference, in the functioning of genre (*Genre,* 19, 48–55).

26. Judith Butler discusses the continuing viability of the law in similar terms in *Bodies That Matter: On the Discursive Limits of "Sex"* (New York: Routledge, 1993), 107–8. This aspect of the principle of citationality also accounts for the "retroactive" groupings that have dominated genre study as discussed earlier in the chapter.

27. Quoted in Alma Mahler, *Gustav Mahler: Memories and Letters* (London: Cardinal, 1990), 105.

28. Mikhail Bakhtin, "Problems of Speech Genres," in *Speech Genres and Other Late Essays* (Austin: University of Texas Press, 1986), 95.

29. This dialogical property of genre production illustrates one of the properties observed recently by Georgina Born: the ability to articulate together four interlocking planes of sociality. These include the following: those experienced by musicians in the act of performance, those experienced as imagined communities, those refracting wider social identity formations, and those "bound up in social and institutional forms." Georgina Born, "Music and the Materialization of Identities," *Journal of Material Culture* (2011): 376–88.

30. Mikhail Bakhtin, "Problems of Speech Genres," 89, 91. See also Mikhail Bakhtin, *The Dialogic Imagination: Four Essays*, ed. Michael Holquist, trans. Caryl Emerson and Michael Holquist (Austin: University of Texas Press, 1981). This kind of "distributed creativity" is also the focus of Howard Becker's *Art Worlds* (Berkeley: University of California Press, 1982), which studies the creative production of art as the result of a creative network. The notion of "distributed creativity" is explored and applied in Georgina Born, "On Musical Mediation." Born, in turn, draws on the work of the anthropologist Alfred Gell, *Art and Agency* (Oxford: Oxford University Press, 1998). Anahid Kassabian has developed the related notion of "distributed subjectivity," a mode of subjectivity connected to what she terms "ubiquitous listening" in *Ubiquitous Listening: Affect, Attention, and Distributed Subjectivity* (Berkeley and Los Angeles: University of California Press, 2013).

31. Jason Toynbee offers a more elaborated theory of artistic creativity than that presented here in *Making Popular Music*, 34–67. For another study of what might be called "distributed creativity," which in this case analyzes how a network is created through intra- and intertextual dialogues of sonic generic references, see Charles Kronengold, "Exchange Theories in Disco, New Wave, and Album-Oriented Rock," *Criticism* 50, no. 1 (Winter 2008): 43–82.

32. Howard Becker, *Art Worlds*.

33. Jason Toynbee, *Making Popular Music*, 103; Simon Frith, *Performing Rites*; Keith Negus, *Music Genres and Corporate Cultures*; Steven Neale, *Genre*, 19; and Steven Neale, "Questions of Genre."

34. Hans Robert Jauss, *Towards an Aesthetic of Reception*, 79; Steven Neale, "Questions of Genre," 56–57.

35. "White People Can't Dance Experiment," *The Dave Chappelle Show* season 2, episode 3, first broadcast February 4, 2004.

36. The idea that a popular music genre produces its audience rather than corresponding to it in a direct fashion has been the focus of much of the work on subcultures and scenes; a complete listing of this work would be enormous, but for important signposts, on subcultures see Stuart Hall and Tony Jefferson, eds., *Resistance Through Rituals: Youth Subcultures in Post-War Britain* (New York: Routledge, 1993); Paul Willis, *Profane Culture* (London: Routledge and Kegan Paul, 1978); Dick Hebdige, *Subculture: The Meaning of Style* (London and New York: Routledge, 1979); Ken Gelder, ed., *The Subcultures Reader*, 2nd ed. (London and New York: Routledge, 2005). On scenes, see Will Straw, "Systems of Articulation, Logics of Change: Communities and Scenes in Popular Music," *Cultural Studies* 5, no. 3 (1991): 368–88; Will Straw, "Scenes and Sensibilities," *Public* 22–23 (2002): 245–57; Barry Shank, *Dissonant Identities: The Rock 'n' Roll Scene in Austin, Texas* (Hanover, NH, and

London: Wesleyan University Press, 1994); and Andy Bennett and Richard A. Peterson, eds., *Music Scenes: Local, Translocal, and Virtual* (Nashville, TN: Vanderbilt University Press, 2009).

37. The discussion of population here is indebted to the work of Foucault; see Michel Foucault, *History of Sexuality: An Introduction, Volume 1* (New York: Pantheon, 1978), 133–59; and Michel Foucault, *Security, Territory, Population: Lectures at the Collège de France, 1977–78* (Houndmills, England: Palgrave MacMillan, 2007).

38. A phenomenon well described by William Howland Kenney's pithy phrase "alone together" (*Recorded Music in American Life*, 4). The simultaneous individualizing and grouping characteristic of listening to sound recordings had already been prepared by the "audile technique," which, according to Jonathan Sterne, had developed in the context of medical training, and that, in turn, relied on a prior "segmentation of acoustic space." Jonathan Sterne, *The Audible Past: Cultural Origins of Sound Reproduction* (Durham, NC, and London: Duke University Press, 2003), 174, 161. Matthew Gelbart argues that the division of Western European musics into "art" and "folk" dating from the early nineteenth century relies on a similar assumption about demographic partitioning. Matthew Gelbart, *The Invention of "Folk Music" and "Art Music."*

39. Theodor W. Adorno, "The Curves of the Needle," in *Essays on Music*, ed. Richard Leppert, trans. Thomas Y. Levin (Berkeley and Los Angeles: University of California Press, 2002), 274. This essay was originally published in 1927 and revised in 1965.

40. Georgina Born, "Music and the Representation/Articulation of Sociocultural Identities" and "Techniques of the Musical Imaginary," in *Western Music and Its Others: Difference, Representation, and Appropriation in Music*, ed. Georgina Born and David Hesmondhalgh (Berkeley: University of California Press), 31–47. For another mapping of possible articulations of music and identity, see Kay Kaufman Shelemay, "Musical Communities: Rethinking the Collective in Music," *Journal of the American Musicological Society* 64, no. 2 (Summer 2011): 349–90.

41. Charles Keil coined this phenomenon the "appropriation-revitalization process" way back in 1966. Charles Keil, *Urban Blues* (Chicago: University of Chicago Press, 1966), 43.

42. On the concept of articulation, see Stuart Hall, "On Postmodernism and Articulation: An Interview with Stuart Hall," *Journal of Communication Inquiry* (1986): 45–60. On the value of a theory of articulation for understanding connections between music and the social, see Richard Middleton, *Studying Popular Music* (Milton Keynes, England: Open University Press, 1990), 1–33. On the utility of "articulation" for the study of genre-identity relations in popular music, see Jason Toynbee, *Making Popular Music*; and David Hesmondhalgh, "Subcultures, Scenes or Tribes?"

43. Benedict Anderson, *Imagined Communities: Reflections on the Origin and Spread of Nationalism* (London and New York: Verso, 1991).

44. Rick Altman, *Film/Genre*. For a related notion of "interpretive community," albeit one that stresses social affiliation through different modes of responding to texts, see Stanley Fish, *Is There a Text in This Class? The Authority of Interpretive Communities* (Cambridge, MA: Harvard University Press, 1980), especially 147–74. Georgina Born highlights the importance of shared values in establishing a sense of community organized around genre in what she terms a "values community" in her essay "The Social and the Aesthetic:

For a Post-Bourdieuian Theory of Cultural Production," *Cultural Sociology* 4, no. 2 (2010): 171–208.

45. Rick Altman, *Film/Genre*, 184.

46. Ibid., 162.

47. For a discussion of how the emergence of the race music category participated in a growing sense of African American solidarity, see Eric Porter, *What Is This Thing Called Jazz?: African American Musicians as Artists, Critics, and Activists* (Berkeley and Los Angeles: University of California Press, 2002), 7.

48. The "mainstream" is a particularly vexed term. A provisional explanation might look like this: music perceived by the music industry (and thus by the rest of the society in which the music industry participates, as the agents in the industry do not exist in a cordoned-off realm) to be marketed toward the largest, most heterogeneous audience possible. Within this ideal, however, there frequently exists an unstated default audience which, during the period in question, consisted of white, bourgeois, northeastern urban dwellers in the United States. Despite the patent importance of the mainstream concept, and its ubiquitous deployment in writing about popular music, it has rarely been analyzed or theorized in any detail, although that appears to be changing in recent years. For exceptions see Sarah Thornton, *Club Cultures: Music, Media and Subcultural Capital* (Hanover, NH, and London: Wesleyan University Press, 1996), 87–115; Jason Toynbee, "Mainstreaming: Hegemony, Market and the Aesthetics of the Centre in Popular Music," in *Popular Music Studies: International Perspectives*, ed. David Hesmondhalgh and Keith Negus (London: Arnold Publishers, and New York: Oxford University Press, 2002), 149–63; Timothy J. Dowd, "Concentration and Diversity Revisited: Production Logics and the U.S. Mainstream Recording Market, 1940 to 1990," *Social Forces* 82 (2004): 1411–55; Alison Huber, "What's in a Mainstream? Critical Possibilities," *Altitude* 8 (2007): 1–12; Sarah Baker, Andy Bennett, and Jodie Taylor, eds., *Redefining Mainstream Popular Music* (New York and London: Routledge, 2013).

49. Georgina Born acknowledges this usage of "imaginary" and states that her intention is "to expand theoretically on the dictum that identification is always imaginary." Georgina Born, "Music and the Representation/Articulation of Sociocultural Identities," 36. For a useful overview and discussion of different approaches to identification, see Stuart Hall, "Introduction: Who Needs Identity?," in *Questions of Cultural Identity*, ed. Stuart Hall and Paul du Gay (London: Sage Publications, 1996), 1–17.

50. The theory I have been describing is strongly associated with the theories of Judith Butler, which she has elaborated over the course of the last two decades. The formulation expressed above is most indebted to her theories presented in *Gender Trouble: Feminism and the Subversion of Identity* (New York: Routledge, 1990) and *Bodies That Matter*. The notion of the iterative or citational aspects of identification has also been explored by theorists associated with postcolonialism. For two of the most influential examples, see Paul Gilroy, *The Black Atlantic: Modernity and Double Consciousness* (Cambridge, MA: Harvard University Press, 1993) and Homi K. Bhabha, *The Location of Culture* (London and New York: Routledge, 1994).

51. Judith Butler clarifies the relationship between phantasmatic and iterative identification in "Phantasmatic Identification and the Assumption of Sex," in *Bodies That Matter*, 93–119. For an account of the relation between fantasy and early acts of identification, see

Jean Laplanche and Jean-Bertrand Pontalis, "Fantasy and the Origins of Sexuality," in *Formations of Fantasy*, ed. Victor Burgin, James Donald, and Cora Kaplan (London: Methuen, 1986), 1–34. For an excellent discussion of phantasmatic identification and nationalism, see Marilyn Ivy, *Discourses of the Vanishing: Modernity, Phantasm, Japan* (Chicago and London: University of Chicago Press, 1995).

52. To be fair, Rick Altman stresses the role played by "lateral communication" among audience members, thereby emphasizing the importance of the circulation of meaning from side-to-side, as it were, as much as top-down. Elsewhere, in his parole-based theory of signification, he proposes a theory similar to that of the iterative theory discussed above. Rick Altman, *Film/Genre*, 173–78. The difference between the theory presented here and Altman's is the apparently minimal role played by homology in Altman's theory of generic identification, due to its rarity in cinematic practice.

53. Theodor W. Adorno, "The Curves of the Needle."

54. See Thomas O. Beebee, *The Ideology of Genre*, 18.

55. See David Brackett, "Black or White? Michael Jackson and the Idea of Crossover," *Popular Music and Society* 35, no. 2 (2012): 169–85. The scholarship on crossover in popular music rivals that on studies of genre noted earlier. The following provides a sample: Reebee Garofalo, "Crossing Over: 1939–1989," in *Split Image: African-Americans in the Mass Media*, ed. Jannette L. Dates and William Barlow (Washington, DC: Howard University Press, 1990), 57–121; Reebee Garofalo, "Black Popular Music: Crossing Over or Going Under?," in *Rock and Popular Music: Politics, Policies, Institutions*, ed. Tony Bennett, Simon Frith, Lawrence Grossberg, John Shepherd, and Graeme Turner (London and New York: Routledge, 1993), 231–48; Don M. Randel, "Crossing Over with Rubén Blades," *Journal of the American Musicological Society* 44 (Summer 1991): 301–23; Jon Fitzgerald, "Motown Crossover Hits 1963–1966 and the Creative Process," *Popular Music* 14, no. 1 (January 1995): 1–11; Steve Waksman, "Metal, Punk, and Motörhead: The Genesis of Crossover," in *This Ain't the Summer of Love*, 146–71; Albin Zak, "Crossing Over," in *I Don't Sound Like Nobody: Remaking Music in 1950s America* (Ann Arbor: University of Michigan Press, 2010), 110–42.

56. These are the groups specified in a January 9, 1961, *Billboard* editorial, "The 'New' Billboard" (3).

57. YouTube and other web 2.0 technologies possibly represent an extension or new stage in the interaction of recordings and other media, in which commercial recordings are now used primarily to sell other products rather than functioning as advertisements for themselves.

58. The connection between the emphasis on statistics in the business and sports sections of the newspaper is adapted from Bill Brown, "The Meaning of Baseball in 1992 (with Notes on the Post-American)," *Public Culture* 4, no. 1 (Fall 1991): 43–71, especially 57–61. Regarding the paradigmatic and syntagmatic aspects of the charts, Martin Parker has preceded me with a similar formulation in "Reading the Charts: Making Sense with the Hit Parade," *Popular Music* 10, no. 2 (1991): 212. Ernest Hakanen further discusses the evolution of popularity charts in "Counting Down to Number One: The Evolution of the Meaning of Popular Music Charts," *Popular Music* 17, no. 1 (January 1998): 95–112. Fredric Dannen discusses the manipulation of the charts in response to external pressures in his scathing account of the music industry in *Hit Men: Power Brokers and Fast Money Inside the Music*

Business (New York: Times Books, 1990), 173–74, 210–11. For a study of charts from the production of culture perspective, see Gabriel Rossman, *Climbing the Charts: What Radio Airplay Tells Us About the Diffusion of Innovation* (Princeton, NJ: Princeton University Press, 2012).

59. Ian Hacking, "Biopower and the Avalanche of Printed Numbers," *Humanities in Society* 5, nos. 3–4 (1982): 287. For a fuller account of this argument, see Ian Hacking, *The Taming of Chance* (Cambridge: Cambridge University Press, 1990).

60. Ian Hacking, "Biopower and the Avalanche of Printed Numbers," 290.

61. Charles Hamm, *Yesterdays*, 337.

62. This statement paraphrases the following by Michel de Certeau: "Replacing doctrines that have become unbelievable, citation allows the technocratic mechanisms to make themselves credible for each individual *in the name of the others.* To cite is thus to give reality to the simulacrum produced by a power, by making people believe that others believe in it, but without providing any believable object." Michel de Certeau, *The Practice of Everyday Life* (Berkeley: University of California Press, 1984), 188–89. See also Pierre Bourdieu, "Opinion Polls: A 'Science' Without a Scientist," in *In Other Words: Essays Towards a Reflexive Sociology,* trans. Matthew Adamson (Stanford, CA: Stanford University Press, 1990), 168–74. For Bourdieu's earlier reflections on the topic, see his notorious essay "Public Opinion Does Not Exist," in *Communication and Class Struggle,* ed. Armand Mattelart and Seth Siegelaub (New York: International General, 1979), 124–30.

63. See Fredric Dannen, *Hit Men,* for an argument about the power of promotional pitches in determining airplay.

64. John Broven, *Record Makers and Breakers: Voices of the Independent Rock 'n' Roll Pioneers* (Urbana and Chicago: University of Illinois Press, 2009), 201.

65. Ibid., 195.

66. Bruno Latour, *Reassembling the Social: An Introduction to Actor-Network-Theory* (New York: Oxford University Press, 2005), 39–40.

67. As Eric Weisbard puts it in his discussion of A&M records during the 1970s, just as "record men" (i.e., producers) had to anticipate the desires of consumers in order to complete the feedback loop, so too did consumers have to learn "to think like a record man." Eric Weisbard, *Top 40 Democracy: The Rival Mainstreams of American Music* (Chicago: University of Chicago Press, 2014), 116.

68. The opposition between "the singularity of the event over notions of resemblance and the same" is derived from the discussion in Michel Foucault's "Theatrum Philosophicum" in *Language, Counter-Memory, Practice,* 165–96. This essay, in turn, is a discussion of two books by Gilles Deleuze, *Difference and Repetition* and *The Logic of Sense.*

69. Foucault addresses the issue of how new discursive regimes gain traction in an interview conducted in 1977: "In order for there to be a movement from above to below there has to be a capillarity from below to above at the same time." Michel Foucault, "The Confession of the Flesh," in *Power Knowledge: Selected Interviews and Other Writings 1972–1977,* ed. Colin Gordon (New York: Pantheon, 1980), 201.

2

Foreign Music and the Emergence of Phonography

We entered a new world of musical and cultural values. One had to erase all memories of the music of European opera-houses and concert-halls: the very foundations of my musical training were undermined.

—FREDERICK W. GAISBERG, *THE MUSIC GOES ROUND*, 1942[1]

As all languages seem to have once been contained in an ancient universal tongue and all of the hundreds of languages and dialects to have emanated, by gradual degrees, from the Aryan, so all modern music seems to have proceeded from the Spanish and Italian schools.... They seem to have been almost identical in the beginning. The music of the great composers in Russia, Germany, [and] France stems from the Spanish and Italian groundwork.

—*THE COLUMBIA RECORD*, MAY 1905[2]

These quotes come from recording scouts employed by the Columbia and Victor recording companies in the first decade of the twentieth century, who were reflecting upon their early encounters with a type of music that these companies classified as "foreign." Their statements contain ideas that were constitutive of the popular music category of foreign music in the years to follow, a category that was to play an important role in the emergence of other categories of popular music in the 1920s.

Foreign music, which existed as a category in music company catalogs dating back to the 1890s, moved through various stages, encompassed a broad range of music, and progressed on domestic and international fronts. In the 1890s this category included recordings both of notated arrangements of European art and folk music by military bands in the United States, and of European vocal concert music in Europe. The 1890s also witnessed the beginning of recordings that depicted stereotypes of immigrants produced by what William Howland Kenney calls the "Coney Island Crowd"—a group of professional vaudeville singers based in New York. The range of foreign recordings expanded in the early 1900s when scouts such as Frederick Gaisberg (quoted in the epigraph) embarked on recording missions in Central and South America, and South and East Asia, recording music by westernized professional entertainers (rather than traditional musicians) with the aim of selling this music to local inhabitants overseas. Finally, during World War I, the domestic branch of foreign music that had formerly been associated with the Coney Island Crowd became dominated by foreign-born immigrants, who in effect began to perform their own identities on recordings. The idea of foreign music initially thus sought both to explore exotic musical territory and to match the music of faraway places with corresponding immigrant groups back home. The spirit of adventure found in the early travelogues of the scouts yielded over time to shrewd calculations about homegrown productions focused on locating and pleasing narrowly divided audiences of immigrants.[3]

Within this general transformation of foreign music during the early decades of the twentieth century, two ideas presented in the epigraphs resonated with notions then holding powerful sway over how cultural value and categories of music and people were routinely connected. The first was that a "new world of musical and cultural values" could possibly "undermine" the "foundations" of the "musical training" of the recording scouts and executives charged with finding new commercial pathways to tread. The scouts and the owners of the recording companies, and more generally the middle and upper classes in the United States at that time, took for granted the aesthetic and cultural superiority of Western European art music. In this "new world," the ties that bound musical practice and aesthetic value were frayed, and the scouts, in order to function professionally, were encouraged to suspend their embodied musical values in order to better evaluate the "musical and cultural values" of the foreign lands that they visited.

The second epigraph presents another idea that evokes the then-popular practice of tying cultural hierarchy to theories of evolution. The belief circulated widely that the geographical origin of a group of people could be located and mapped in relation to the degree of evolution believed to characterize that group. Just as "all languages and dialects . . . emanated . . . from the Aryan," so did all "the music of the great composers" come "from the Spanish and Italian groundwork." This theme was reworked in the music industry discourse of the time in many forms. At times, the further a type of music and people were, geographically and culturally, from Western Europe (the center of which was Germany for music, England for people) the less "evolved" they were. At other times, like "Spanish and Italian" music, music of distant lands was perceived as temporally and evolutionarily prior to the music of the West, and thus understood as providing the "groundwork."

That this particular cluster of associations between group identity and sound should be pursued and produced so avidly within the nascent recording industry also references—because of the structure of the industry at the time—the not-incidental proximity between social and business practices, and the technics of sound recording itself. Music production and promotion were intertwined with the development of sound reproduction technologies, which were developed and marketed by the same companies that were responsible for the production of recordings. Changes in recording technologies were, in turn, made in response to shifting conceptions at the time about music as an autonomous practice, divorced from social function or value; the type of listening that might be appropriate to autonomous musical sounds; and (related to the first two ideas) the social function and place of music. The dispersed sense of connection fostered by the imagined or constellated communities that were made possible by mechanical reproduction was accompanied, in contrary motion, by an intensified interest in individuated listening, as music consumption increasingly became an isolated affair focused on the internal experience of recordings and separated from the physical gestures necessary to produce musical sound.[4]

This chapter thus considers—before delving further into the production of the foreign music category—the new modes of listening associated with sound recordings. Rapid changes in technology that affected the circulation of music and its meaning were but one aspect of the social upheaval that shaped the categorization of music in the first decades of the twentieth century. Changes in immigration laws, demographic shifts, the redrawing of high-low cultural-aesthetic boundaries, and the reorganization of institutions involved with the circulation of music, among other factors, transformed the way in which categories of people and music were produced and connected.

Cultural and technological shifts contributed to creating the conditions of possibility for constellated communities and thus for the emergence of music industry categories in the eras of mechanical and electronic reproduction; this section thus extends the discussion of musical communities begun in chapter 1. Of the categories in operation between 1890 and 1920, foreign music is the most apposite in terms of the larger project of this book. In this chapter and the two that follow I will argue that foreign music provided a way of understanding how identifications and musical categories could be related that was subsequently adopted by the race and old-time categories. The focus in this chapter will be on how foreign music in the early decades of the twentieth century up through the mid-1920s set the stage for the emergence during the 1920s of a four-prong model (including foreign, race, old-time, and mainstream popular musics) of musical categories that would structure the U.S. music industry, a model that would soon transform into a three-prong model sans foreign music by the 1940s (the subject of chapters 5 and 6).

SOUND RECORDING AND NEW MODES OF THE MUSICAL IMAGINARY

The historical status of sound recording plays a central role in the genealogy of popular music categories presented here. Because I am writing during the period that might be considered the post-recording era, in which sound recordings as consumable objects are in the process of being dethroned from their premier position as the barometer of cultural meaning in the popular music industry, it may be helpful to recall that the period from 1890 to 1930 is often figured by historians of sound recording as the pre-recording era. In the early decades of the twentieth century, sound recordings were in the first stages of establishing themselves as a viable commodity, achieving only a nebulous status in relation to the "hardware" of talking machines and radios on the one hand, and to an alternative form of "software," sheet music, on the other.[5]

This nebulous status was echoed in journalism about the music industry. A question frequently asked by writers of the time concerned the viability of the sound recording as a commercial object of exchange. Because it was as yet untested, many articles expressed astonishment at the popularity and profitability of shellac discs. Part of this incredulity undoubtedly derived from the dual role of record peddlers as purveyors of both software and hardware—early record stores served as dealerships for phonographs and radios as well. An advertisement for the Pathé recording company from 1924 illustrates this manufacturing versatility, with phonographs, radio sets, and records promoted side by side.[6] Indeed, the recording companies produced sound reproduction and broadcasting equipment first, and recordings second. Vendors concentrated on hardware, hoping to make a profit on a single sale many times that of what could be made from a recording. Also contributing to the precarious state of the sound recording was its role as a newcomer with respect to sheet music. More space was devoted in nonspecialized entertainment industry publications to pondering the negative effect of recordings on sheet music sales than to appreciating the sales potential of the new medium.[7]

The relation of sound recordings to sheet music is particularly instructive in understanding the transition in emphasis in the music industry from one to the other. The difference in listening practices between the two media, often characterized as dispersed (sound recording) versus participatory and present (the performance of sheet music), played a prominent role in the formation of contemporary notions of popular music genres. The participatory world of sheet music required face-to-face contact, the means to buy a piano or an organ, and the time and resources to learn how to read music. Even if consumers of sheet music were aware that other folks like themselves were somewhere playing the same music, this awareness of an imagined musical community was reinforced by music participation within the family or immediate (non-imagined) community. The sense that people elsewhere buying and playing this music were somehow just like you found confirmation in the music played by people in your immediate vicinity who seemed to be just like you. In other words, even if imaginary communities were important in the sheet music–dominated phase of economically mediated musical exchange, a tangible community existed at the same time to reinforce the sense of what was imagined. A similar observation about the role of music in the construction of imagined communities can be made about the world of performance in the nineteenth century, where touring ensembles would have provided a bridge to exotic, faraway places, and diligent listeners could have perused reviews of distant performances in newspapers and journals.

If, on the other hand, the idea of dispersed listening is emphasized in discussions of a post-recording or broadcasting mode of musical participation in the early twentieth century, then it is important to point out that this mode did not consist only of serialized experiences by isolated consumers communicating laterally. Concerts still brought audiences together, people within relatively bounded communities continued to make music together, and professional musicians continued to perform and tour. However, an indicator of the anxiety provoked by the changing state of affairs manifests in articles and advertisements of the era, such as that found in an advertisement for Edison published in *Talking Machine World* in 1923. This sprawling advertisement (spanning two pages), titled "Re-Creation," evoked social gatherings and dances organized around recording equipment where the talking machine took on the role of a performer rather than a mere accompanist, claiming that the "phonograph is an instrument . . . with a fidelity that challenges the final, supreme test—direct comparison with the voice of the living artist."[8] Even as the new technology of mechanical reproduction disturbed long-held beliefs about the role of music in society, the use of phonograph and radio equipment was understood as an extension of social practices associated with the piano and other forms of communal performance. The phonograph and radio console (sometimes joined together) were elegant pieces of furniture to be placed in the parlor and chosen by the lady of the house, who would also be required to keep the children's needs in mind, a set of associations depicted in another sprawling *Talking Machine World* ad from 1925.[9] At the same time, as will be discussed in chapters 3 and 4, the substitutability of gramophone for human created a situation in which notions of liveness came to depend on an opposition with recorded sound for their very definition.

The Talking Machine and the Loss of Visuality

If talking machines were employed in an attempted act of mimicry, then the failure of this act left a significant residue. Recordings brought performances in a material form into domiciles in a fashion that had previously not been possible. Rather than abstract instructions for a performance, as found in sheet music,[10] sound recordings conveyed the particularity of a performance and the corporeal traces of the humans who produced it, but, crucially, without the visuality associated with musical performances. Lisa Gitelman has argued that the case of Plessy v. Ferguson in the United States in 1896 (which consecrated Jim Crow practices) separated the idea of race from physical appearance and that, hence, it was a small step for sound recording to separate the sound associated with a particular form of identi-fication from how the recording artist might be identified socially.[11] This disasso-ciation of sound from visual identification expanded the range of significations that could become associated with recordings, or categories of recordings, some of which could either retain prior associations of group identity, or rearticulate these prior associations altogether.

The resulting destabilization of musical identities played an important role in how the disembodied and dispersed material manifestations of particular bodies participated in the emergence of constellated communities. The bourgeois con-sternation that seems to have accompanied this newfound ambiguity almost from the beginning resulted, at least in part, from the associations of identity that already accompanied popular entertainments such as the minstrel show or the coon song. Both of these cases, however, differed significantly from one another. In the min-strel show, the performers were visible, even if identification was masked (or corked), but masked in a conventional way so as dispel any confusion; the audi-ence did not need to be reassured that white minstrel performers were white (or that black minstrel performers were black).[12] Recordings of coon songs, like the sonic emissions of white minstrels, were identificatory simulacra, but now cru-cially no longer tethered to a visibly sounding body (as coon songs would have been in theatrical or domestic performances), and thus they required additional documentation of some sort to allay fears of domestic contamination. The Edison Company attempted to provide such documentation when it published an article in its own trade journal in 1905 testifying that Arthur Collins, one of Edison's best-known performers of coon songs, was white.[13]

The coon song distilled aspects of the minstrel show into a compact, commod-ity form. The name of the genre itself, however, did not refer to a homologous connection between a type of music and the group identity of the assumed audi-ence, as would later categories and genres associated with sound recording.[14] Like the minstrel show, the coon-song-as-printed-composition presented a simu-lacrum of African Americans for white people that could also be performed by white people (and, similar to the minstrel show from the 1860s onward, African Americans participated in the creation and performance of coon songs). New York–based professional singers continued the legacy of the simulacrum propa-gated by the coon song by expanding their range to include other types of material, such as negro or Southern melodies, and fiddle tunes.

In all these types of music the loss of music's visuality created ambiguity, lead-ing white listeners to question the white racial identity of the performers. Sound recordings thus appeared as if already placed into musical categories that predated them, even if the new medium produced unnerving modifications of those catego-ries, an aspect of the iterative process described in chapter 1. That is, the emerging genre identification typology associated with sound recordings drew upon a typology that predated sound recordings. Recorded voices disturbed this prior set of associations because they were not initially a citation of a prior recorded sound and could not be placed within a typology of how recorded voices might be matched with identities. African American appearance could still be cited, as in the minstrel show, but the idea of how sounds could be cited without a visual corollary had not yet taken hold. This development could also be understood as a shift from one mode of imaginary identification to another, with sound recordings suggesting new genre identity connections. Paradoxically, sound recordings, even though they severed a tangible link to the performer, presaged the rise of homological identifications circulating throughout constellated communities.

That the sound recording proved (eventually) to be extraordinarily well suited to the commodity form is beyond dispute. Even though the way had been paved by sheet music and player pianos, the uniqueness of the performances captured by the disc was only enhanced by the surplus value of its unparalleled corporality—its status as a thing to be possessed and listened to—and the prestige generated via its association with what Jonathan Sterne has termed "audile technique."[15] Even as the sound recording may have introduced "schizophonia" (to use R. Murray Schaefer's term), it brought corporeal traces of the performers into environments that both reinforced and transcended preexisting group identifications with music, enabling listeners to come into contact with music that they would have been unlikely to encounter before.[16] That is, the source was split from the sound in the circulation of recordings even as a new way of creating an association between the presumed identity of the people at the source and the sound came into being.

CATEGORY AND GENRE, CA. 1920: A SPECIAL CASE

In the years during and immediately following the First World War, participants in the world of popular music labored to develop new categories and to adapt existing ones adequate both to the flood of novel musical utterances that burst onto the scene, and to a rapidly changing awareness of who was making and listening to these musics. As stated earlier, many factors played a role, including changes in sound reproduction and transmission technology, the way and the rate at which cultural texts circulated, immigrant and patent law, and shifting demographics within the United States, to name but a few.

The loosening of patent restrictions on what material form records could take increased the range of music that could circulate and the number of people who had access to the full spectrum of recorded music. Prior to 1919, only Columbia and Victor could produce records in which the needle moved side to side (lateral cut), which were playable on phonographs made by their companies, and this type of phonograph was by far the most commonly owned across a wide demographic spectrum. Lower-income families were unlikely to own a phonograph that could play the "hill and dale" records (or vertical cut, in which the needle moved up and down) produced by the smaller record companies. The synchronization of hardware, in which restrictions to lateral-cut recording were lifted, was a huge boon for the smaller companies, who could begin to compete with Columbia and Victor without requiring their customers to own a separate phonograph. Now guaranteed access to a larger public, these companies, such as OKeh, began to search for hitherto-unexplored sectors of the audience to exploit.

Changes in access to technology and sound recordings were complemented by migrations of rural white Southerners and African Americans to urban areas in the North, and by legal statutes affecting immigrants—changes that made themselves felt in the popular music field. On the level of musical categories referring to group identification, at the beginning of the 1920s one found a variety of foreign records as well as other broad categories such as dance music and vocal music. These latter categories did not indicate an audience with the clarity of foreign records, but their very opacity confirmed the superfluousness of marking dominant identifications, and also perpetuated vestiges of pre-1920 methods of categorization.[17] These larger categories were further divided into what could be called genres, which referred to song or dance types such as fox-trot, waltz, ballad, or coon song, or, alternatively, to vocal type and accompaniment format, such as tenor with orchestra accompaniment, or contralto-baritone duet with banjo and accordion. Many other descriptive terms were used at the level of genre on a more ad hoc basis, including "novelty," "Irish quadrille," and so on. The rationale for this distinction between category and genre becomes clear from examining two streams of information: the listings for upcoming record releases and advertisements in music industry publications, and catalogs issued by the recording companies.[18]

The sections of upcoming record releases in publications such as *Talking Machine World* and the *Phonograph and Talking Machine Monthly* listed recordings organized by record company and category, with entries detailing the song title, performer, and genre. An example of a particular instance of this categorizing process can be found in the following list from the August 16, 1916, issue of *Talking Machine World*:

COLUMBIA GRAPHOPHONE CO.

Blue-Label Double-Disc Records

Double-Disc Records

Symphony Double-Disc Records

VICTOR TALKING MACHINE CO.

Popular Songs for September

Dance Records
Miscellaneous Instrumental Records
Pipe Organ Records
Blue and Purple Label Records
Red Seal Records

THOS. A. EDISON, INC.
New Edison Diamond Disc Records

EDISON BLUE AMBEROL RECORDS
Concert List
Regular List
Songs and Ballads
Bands and Orchestras
Instrumental Hits
French Records
Swedish Records

PATHE [PATHÉ] FRERES PHONOGRAPH CO.
New Vocal Foreign Records
New French Songs
Vocal Specialties with Bird Effects
New Foreign Instrumental Records
New Hawaiian Records—Vocal and Instrumental

OPERAPHONE MANUFACTURING CORP.
[no categories]

EMERSON PHONOGRAPH CO.
7-Inch Emerson Double Discs
Popular Dance Records
Standard and Miscellaneous Selections

In addition to the striking lack of synchronization across companies, several items
in the above taxonomy claim our interest, for instance many terms that refer to the
physical properties of the medium itself (indicating size of record, how many sides
are used for the recording, the color of the label), and items ranging from high or
low cultural divisions ("Popular Songs," "Concert List") to instruments and ensembles ("Pipe Organ," "Bands and Orchestras") to time of the year ("Popular Songs
for September") to novelties ("Vocal Specialties with Bird Effects").[19] Foremost

among these items are the categories that allude to group identifications of some sort, such as "French Records" (or "New French Songs"), "New Vocal Foreign Records," "Swedish Records," and "New Hawaiian Records—Vocal and Instrumental." That Pathé Frères Phonograph Co. would have a category for "New French Songs" is not surprising, as the company was based in France. But that does not explain why Edison Blue Amberol would also have a similarly named category, or why Swedish and Hawaiian recordings would have been of any particular concern.

Genre, Otherness, and Hawaiian Music

Advertisements reveal a similar set of distinctions between category and genre as the "Upcoming Record Releases," and a similar sense of confusion. Like the "Upcoming Record Releases," advertisements displayed the shifting hierarchy of categories pegged to different audience niches. At the beginning of the 1920s, one finds recordings occasionally listed almost entirely according what I described earlier as genres, illustrated by a representative ad for OKeh Records taken from the April 7, 1920, issue of *Phonograph and Talking Machine Weekly*. Recordings are identified by performer, their catalog number, their size, their genre (either fox-trot, one-step, or waltz), and whether they are an instrumental or a vocal (and if a vocal, the type of voice and accompaniment is given). The ad makes no distinction according to category or type. A few distinctions, however, are apparent: one song has the title "Blues," referring to the blues craze that had been ongoing since W. C. Handy's "Memphis Blues" and other blues titles were published in 1912.[20] Other songs bear markers that were used to modify the ubiquitous "fox-trot," such as "Arabianna" by Vincent Lopez, described in a later ad for OKeh Records as an "Oriental Fox-Trot Sensation."[21] As these examples indicate, even in the most capacious, and thus nominally unmarked, mainstream categories, one finds an obsession with identification and otherness. Thus, the blues craze initially formed part of the middle- and upper-class obsession with minstrelsy, ragtime, and the coon song, and "Arabianna" and the "Oriental" in the "Oriental Fox-Trot Sensation" derived from a popular music cycle featuring Asian stereotypes.[22]

Even popularity charts, that form of list relying most strongly on numerically enhanced notions of objectivity, reproduced the same obsession with stereotypical difference.[23] A curious chart taken from the June 4, 1920, issue of *Variety*, titled "Week's Six Best Sellers" (even though, curiously, far more than six titles are listed), is divided into categories featuring the two dominant record companies of the day (Victor and Columbia) and by price ("30c music" and "10c music"), and includes titles such as "My Sahara Rose," "Ching-a-Ling's Jazz Bazaar," "Hiawatha's Melody of Love," "Abe Kabibble Monologues," and "Lazy Mississippi." These examples evoke a world in which popular music already relied on categories and genres that articulated notions of group identification to various confabulations of musical style traits, although important distinctions existed between these examples, some of which presumed homological connections (foreign music), and the others, which relied on a variety of imaginary or exoticist relations. And, to reiterate a point made earlier, these particular articulations did not arise magically on their own or at the behest of a few powerful individuals but rather traded on notions of otherness and musical style that already had circulated extensively among musicians and consumers—concepts that were, in a word, legible to the participants in the musical field at the time.

The history of the category of Hawaiian music is particularly instructive for how it formed its association between musical style and identification. Recordings with Hawaiian associations were a ubiquitous presence in lists of upcoming record releases and record catalogs well into the 1920s, sharing variants such as "New Hawaiian Novelties," "Hawaiian Guitars," "Hawaiian Music by Hawaiian Artists," "Louise and Ferera and Their Waikiki Orchestra Play Popular Successes," "Hawaiian Guitars and Instrumental Trios," and "Enchanting Music by the Hawaiians." Most of the companies listed in the "Upcoming Record Releases" section of *Talking Machine World* featured a Hawaiian category at one time or another, or Hawaii-associated recordings in their unmarked categories. As Charles Hiroshi Garrett has argued, Hawaiian music was a dominant force throughout the 1910s, resulting from a confluence of factors: the attention brought to Hawaii following its annexation by the United States in 1898; a successful musical, *Bird of Paradise,* which featured Hawaiian musicians and opened in 1912; many successful tours of Hawaiian musicians throughout the decade; a well-placed exhibit of Hawaiian cultural wares in the 1915 Panama Pacific International Exposition, held in San Francisco, which prominently featured Hawaiian music; following from these, an increased number of recordings of Hawaiian musicians playing both traditional Hawaiian songs and *hapa haole* compositions (new songs written by Hawaiians featuring some English lyrics and references to current U.S.-based popular music); and a large number of Hawaiian-style numbers written by Tin Pan Alley–based composers. These recordings reached a peak during the years 1915 to 1917, and were nurtured by utopian fantasies about Hawaii as a paradise, and by images of the colonial potency of the United States. Although many of the recordings of traditional music and *hapa haole* songs were popular in Hawaii itself, their popularity among the white bourgeoisie in the United States undoubtedly thrived on colonialist fantasies about Asian femininity not far removed from the impetus for such high-cultural narratives as *Madame Butterfly.* The continuation of the Hawaiian category in the United States in the 1920s relied increasingly on white performers playing Tin Pan Alley–generated compositions, producing an imaginary form of identification somewhat at odds with foreign music, the category of popular music to which Hawaiian music bore the closest resemblance.[24]

FIGURE 3. "Types of the Races of Man" (1886)[25]

FOREIGN MUSIC: FROM RACE TO ETHNICITY

More capacious and central to the U.S. music industry than Hawaiian music, foreign music provides a fascinating window through which to study the debates over the proper social and political position for Europeans who had immigrated in successive waves to the United States beginning in the 1840s. Allowed to immigrate by dint of the 1790 naturalization law declaring the gates of the nation open to all "free white persons," national understandings of race quickly shifted in order to distinguish the "native" Anglo-Saxons from the foreign-born Celts, Teutons, Hebrews, Slavs, and others, giving rise to charts such as those found in figure 3.[26] Bound up in contemporary scientific discussions about the biological basis of race, physical as well as moral attributes were ascribed with certainty to these different races. The debate was played out in the public sphere in terms that were both rhetorically and physically violent. The striking presence of the category of foreign music in the early years of the twentieth century attests to the persistence of this mode of racial thinking, as well as to the central importance of fine distinctions between different types of whiteness. Indeed, the preoccupation with otherness in general (as already seen in the discussion of music associated with Asians and Pacific Islanders) gave voice to the concern over the unstable nature of these identifications.

The years that form the focus of this chapter cover a crucial moment in the history of how white "new immigrants" were perceived and classified, including, as it does, the period leading up to and following the Johnson-Reed Act of 1924, which restricted immigration by the different white races to quotas based on how many members of each race already resided in the United States.[27] These races were increasingly assimilated during and after the 1920s into the category of Caucasian and gradually reconceptualized as ethnicities precisely at the same time as the recognition of African Americans as musical consumers summoned the category of race music into being.[28] In fact, one could argue that, in addition to the Johnson-Reed Act, it was the heightened presence of African Americans and Asian Americans in major urban areas that provided the impetus for the consolidation of the various white races. These white races, now simply Caucasians, were increasingly defined after 1930 in opposition to a form of difference based largely on culture rather than on biology, and conceptualized in a three-pronged model consisting of "Negroid," "Mongoloid," and "Caucasoid."[29] Members of these in-between non–Anglo Saxon white races, however, always had the possibility of being perceived as white, something that could not be said for African Americans and Asian Americans.[30] The shift in paradigms had a curious resonance with the rearrangement of popular music categories and the fate of various cyclical trends during the 1920s.

Jewish Music, a Case Study

As stated in the opening of this chapter, foreign music and its various subcategories underwent a significant transformation during World War I to music mostly recorded by immigrants in the United States who were representatives of a given foreign race. Changes in the location and identities of the performers also affected the type of material recorded, as the orchestral arrangements of traditional and religious music that dominated the category before the war gave way to newly composed music of a more populist nature.[31] The public rhetoric accompanying this category contrasts with the exoticist connotations of the Hawaiian category, and the occasional moral panic associated with evocations of Chinese immigrants in numerous popular songs of the period (or in coon songs, for that matter).[32] Although the record companies were not above parodying these hailings of variegated whiteness or employing negative stereotypes (especially in recordings made before the war by popular singers outside of the racial group in question), foreign music recordings were, by and large, presented as relatively neutral presentations of difference. As immigrants became increasingly involved in the recording process during the 1920s, many recordings presented a more sympathetic, insiders' view of the immigrant group in question in a shift that could be temptingly analyzed as a precursor or parallel to the reconception of racial whiteness that was soon to follow.

A close examination of one subcategory of foreign music, Jewish music (which was also termed "Hebrew" or "Yiddish" music by the industry at the time) cautions against a simple trajectory from negative stereotypes toward an insiders' perspective that resists such stereotypes, and, indeed, might profitably shift our attention to how such stereotypes are produced. At the turn of the last century, a Jewish comic type emerged, replete with a long nose, derby hat, bulging eyes, and disheveled appearance—in fact, a mask with such features was sold for domestic comedians who wished to perform in "Jew face."[33] While the early Hebrew or Yiddish recordings were performed and written by non-Jews (Kenney's Coney Island Crowd), by the early 1910s Jews dominated the production of such recordings, one of whom made the first comedy record to sell more than a million copies (Joe Hayman's "Cohen on the Telephone").[34] What are we to make of the fact that Jews participated so actively in what may now seem to be a demeaning form of humor? On the one hand, the phenomenon could be understood as the Jewish entertainer's response to the audience's demand to produce a public identity authorized by WASP taste, an interpretation that highlights similarities with the practice of African Americans performing in blackface.

On the other hand, however, a more nuanced picture emerges from a tangled web of historical transactions, as well as from the analysis of recordings that constituted the category of Jewish music during the period, 1900 to 1920 (a similar move could be carried out on African American minstrelsy as well). One could simply describe a transitional arc from the caricature of Jewish physiognomy in "When Mose with His Nose Leads the Band," recorded in 1906 by Arthur Collins and Byron Harlan (performers better known, not coincidentally, for their renditions of coon songs), in which neither the songwriters nor the performers were Jewish, to the self-deprecating mockery of Monroe Silver's "Pittsburgh, PA," a song written and recorded by Jews.[35] The Collins-Harlan number is sung straight, without a stereotypical Jewish accent or Yiddish-isms (save for an interjected "Oi, oi, oi, mazel tov," sung to a minor-key, klezmer-inflected strain), and describes a bandleader who doesn't need a baton due to his abundantly endowed schnoz. The diegetic band members are listed by name and instrument in a manner that leaves neither racial identity nor musical inclination (nor the Freudian symbolism) in doubt: for example, "Julius Meyer he can toot / with the fiddle or the flute."

But a comparison with "The Original Cohens," recorded a year earlier in 1905, throws such a tidy narrative into question. "The Original Cohens," like "Mose with His Nose," was written and recorded by gentiles, performed on this recording by two leading stars of the day, Ada Jones and Len Spencer, and it even begins with the same melodic-harmonic strain that accompanied Harlan and Collins's declamation of "Oi, oi, oi, mazel tov" (musical example 1). Jones and Spencer perform with broad Eastern European accents, substituting *v*'s for *w*'s and making malapropisms associated with Jewish immigrants. The sound of the routine does not differ substantially from the Jewish recordings made from the mid-1910s onward that were produced and recorded by Jews, even if the lyrics may have lacked some of the affectionate self-deprecation of the later recordings. If "The Original Cohens" makes a joke out of selling a man half a suit when it is marked "half off," Monroe Silver's "Pittsburgh, PA" (1920) is content to render absurd the proclivity of Jewish surnames to end in "burg" or "berg" by describing a party attended by "Greenberg, Romberg, Blomberg, Bromberg / Bamberg, Hamburg, Goldberg, too / . . . the 'bergs' all came from everywhere / every 'berg' in the world was there / and where do you think they held the affair? In Pittsburgh, P-A." Like the "Oi, oi, oi, mazel tov" phrase of "The Original Cohens" and "When Mose with His Nose," the second section of "Pittsburgh, PA" shifts into something approximating the *freygish* scale (or *shteyger* in Yiddish), a mode found in Eastern European folk songs.[36] This melodic trope, which I call the Yiddish minor when used in popular songs of the time, employs the harmonic minor with the prominent use of the raised fourth scale degree as a lower neighbor to (scale degree) five, creating an augmented second interval with scale degree three, and thereby conjuring up aural stereotypes of the Eastern European shtetl (see musical example 2). The punch line of the refrain shifts back to the relative (gentile?) major in which the song begins (musical example 3).

What emerges from this brief description is the difficulty of establishing and maintaining stable boundaries between racial groups believed to be absolutely separate. One can speculate that the gentiles responsible for producing "The Original

MUSICAL EXAMPLE 1. Intro to "The Original Cohens" (and a quote of "Oi, oi, oi, mazel tov" from "When Mose with His Nose Leads the Band")

MUSICAL EXAMPLE 2. "Yiddish minor" from "Pittsburgh, PA"

MUSICAL EXAMPLE 3. Refrain from "Pittsburgh, PA"

Cohens" had already been exposed to vaudeville routines coded Jewish by the time the recording was made, and, in fact, that the stereotypes on which this humor drew had circulated in both Europe and North America for many years before sound recordings were commercially available.[37] By the time Jews became more involved in the production of these recordings, the conventions of the Hebrew-Yiddish category were already established and well known, so that to make Jewish records meant to offer a particular blend of Yiddish accent, Eastern European–influenced skewered syntax, and Klezmer-inflected, minor-key melodies, all of which would have reminded Jewish (and some non-Jewish) listeners of a type of musical routine predating the early recordings. The continuity with WASP-produced recordings recalls the idea of a public identity authorized by WASP taste, but does not explain why even these early recordings were so popular with Jewish audiences, unless we accept that this widely circulated public identity was already impure, emerging as a relational construct defined by changing notions of Jewishness and gentile-ness during the period, with antecedents rooted in nineteenth-century European cultural exchange.[38]

The convolution of what might seem on the surface to be a relatively straight-forward form of homology returns us to some of the ambiguous aspects of musical identification discussed in chapter 1. The Hebrew-Yiddish musical category is homologous, in that it refers to a preexisting demographic group, which the music industry assumed was its main audience, even as it spoke to the exotic fantasies of consumers who did not identify with that preexisting demographic. This produc-tion of exotic homologies also returns us to a comparison made in chapter 1: the way in which the extensive lists of categorical difference in the recording industry produced a striking contrast to the role of identifications in cinema, that form of mechanical reproduction that emerged in almost perfect synchrony with sound recording. With production costs low compared to the film industry, and con-sumption focused domestically by the 1910s, the recording industry realized quickly that a divide-and-conquer strategy would be most effective. A profit could be made with relatively low sales, making it advantageous to segment the audience as finely as possible. However, this meant determining what sort of divisions were significant and how to link production with consumption. The early decades of the twentieth century are fascinating precisely because of the uncertainty over the sig-nificance of different potential segments of the listening public, and because of the clashes between economic imperatives and ideological assumptions about the characteristics of the people who might be targeted.

An Almost Bewildering Variety

While occasionally grouped within the catchall category of foreign records, as in the listing for Pathé above, recordings directed toward immigrants were often clas-sified with greater specificity. Far from being limited to Hebrew or Yiddish music, or to the French and Swedish categories listed in the previous example of upcom-ing record releases, foreign music could produce an almost bewildering variety. An ad for Lyraphone Co. of America from the July 15, 1917, of *Talking Machine World* (36) illustrates this multiplicity: in addition to categories that may well sur-prise the contemporary reader due to their finely tuned approach to difference ("Neapolitan" and "Italian"? "German" and "Schwabish"? "Jewish" and "Hebrew"?), the list ends with the telling conclusion of "etc., etc.," implying an infinite set of permutations. To some extent these overlapping classifications reflect an uncer-tainty over the guiding principle of categorization—should it be the location of ancestral origin, language, or race as it was understood at the time? This extrava-gant multiplicity remained remarkably stable throughout the 1910s and 1920s. For example, an ad for Columbia from 1924 touting "Columbia *New Process* RECORDS for all Nations" lists recordings in twenty-eight languages compared to Lyraphone's mere sixteen, but minus Lyraphone's gesture toward the infinite ("etc., etc.").[39]

This multilingual virtuosity not only existed in the listings of recordings, but found its way into the practices of sales staff as well, managing in the process to transcend regional boundaries. A brief article describing the expansion of a phonograph store in Oakland, California, for example, boasts that "records in twenty-six languages are now stocked by this firm and a staff of salesmen who are capable of speaking the more important ones is maintained."[40] Yet even this number of languages pales in comparison to Victor's claim from three years earlier, in which the company of His Master's Voice appeared to have already claimed victory in the battle for the most foreign languages: "Victor serves a clientele of persons speaking thirty-four different languages and dialects with music played on native instruments and sung or played by active artists."[41]

Given the interest in racial otherness, the outpouring of discourse on foreign music would seem to follow inevitably, but the form of this discourse betrays more than mere curiosity or anxiety. Many of the commentaries in music industry publications adopted the benign, paternal tone of a tolerant older relative, and often underscored how foreign records relied on a logic of homology. An article from 1918, titled rather strikingly "How Recognition of the Pride of Race Will Increase Record Sales," exemplifies this logic by stating the "obvious": "We all realize that it is the Italian to whom Italian records most appeal, or the Swede who takes most interest in Swedish records, and so on." The author, Frank E. Parsons, encourages dealers to study "racial sympathies" in order to get "results that count" and observes that when it comes to motivating record buyers, "nationality" is almost as important as pure "musical value."[42] Not only referencing how ideas about the value of absolute music had thoroughly penetrated the sphere of journalistic criticism, such comments also speak to the fundamental connection between sound reproduction technologies and the "construction of sound as a carrier of meaning in itself" dating back to the development of what Sterne calls "audile technique" in the nineteenth century.[43] Parsons recognizes in this passage that the power of consanguinity might almost equal the ineffable allure of music existing outside of time and place.

Five years after Parsons's article appeared, the basic philosophy of the music industry toward foreign music had not changed significantly, yet a comment by Jack Kapp, a record company executive who would boast a long and influential career aided by a keen ear for crossover material, noted how identification may not always function in a strictly homological fashion, but may vary according to the performer, and, one can only assume, the nature of the recorded performance. Kapp observed "the fact that the greatest purchasers of Jewish comical records such as the famous 'Cohen on the Telephone' records and 'Levinsky at the Wedding' are the Jews themselves, yet very few Irish buy the Casey records made by Michael Casey. They, however, are the largest purchasers of jigs and reels which not many others seem to enjoy." Indeed, this may be seen as a call for finer distinctions to be made in the study of the consumption habits of foreign races, and a bid to devise a course of action for sales staff when the sharing of biological traits is not enough. Other writers in *Talking Machine World* also occasionally disputed the tight fit of the homological model, warning against such a reductionist approach. One particularly pithy comment cautioned that "too many dealers work by a rule and believe that all people coming from Norway like accordion records; from Russia, balalaika; Poland, polka dances, and so on. While this is true to a certain extent, it does not apply in all cases or even in a majority of instances."[44]

Some eight months after Kapp, another columnist for *Talking Machine World* noted that such musical identifications were not limited to those of European extraction; indeed, the author momentarily implies equivalence between East Asians and Eastern Europeans (a white race rather low in the cultural hierarchy), as "Chinese laundrymen" were almost granted the humanity of Russian immigrants, notwithstanding the stereotypical association of race with occupation. The author, however, does seem impatient to switch from an Asian subject to a European one (even if it is Eastern European) once the heart (and soul) of the listener becomes the topic: "Although the playing of a group of Chinese records serves to excite Chinese laundrymen to a point where they are willing to spend real money for the records and a machine to play them on," when "an immigrant from the heart of Russia" buys a record "of some folk-song of his childhood . . . he is buying happiness and a cure for homesickness."[45] Immigrants from many continents and of different racial types might, in other words, be able to learn to appreciate the magical properties of the commodity fetish, which would keep them content enough to do other people's laundry or perform other menial occupations. Happiness, or at least a cure for homesickness, was available for purchase as long as one heard her- or himself—the "sounding image of his [*sic*] own person," to return to Adorno's pithy evocation of homology—in the grooves of their latest purchase.[46]

So important, in fact, was the category of foreign records that commentary on it even found its way into articles dedicated to what might appear to be somewhat distant topics. In a prescient piece devoted to praising the utility of sound recordings for the teaching of music history, the author James Humphris turns for a moment to the subject of folk music recordings. While he bemoans the paucity of recordings suitable for a historical study of music, he applauds the number and diversity of "folk-songs" and "folk-dances" that are available. This music, Humphris confesses, was produced to "supply the needs of foreigners in our midst," and while "most of these are quite worthless from an educational standpoint . . . many are gems." The true value of these recordings, which becomes clear as the article progresses, lies in the homily that "travel in space is similar to travel in time," a common theme in much of the scientific literature on race of the late nineteenth and early twentieth centuries, and one that also formed one of the bases for the theories associated with eugenics. A frequent corollary derived from these theories, similar to that found in the second epigraph to this chapter, suggested that "other cultures" represented an earlier stage of civilization, through which

Europeans had already passed.[47] Along these lines, Humphris remarks, "Not the least interesting are certain Greek, Turkish, Syrian, and other Levantine records. These are made by natives in the native and give vivid reality to the oft-repeated assertion of our musical histories that our music originated in the East." As odd as these recordings may sound, however, they sound downright familiar next to those from East Asia: "Chinese, Japanese, and other unusual records are also obtainable. Sometimes the effects are laughable, even painful, but the careful music student cannot fail to detect the relationship between these grotesque sounds and our own most cherished music. Here is the raw material from which Liszt evolved his elaborate ornamentations."[48] These comments provide startling confirmation that even as musical evidence supported the hierarchical differences among white races, it also maintained an even greater difference between these white races and Asians, prefiguring the eventual transformation of the white races into the monolithic category of Caucasians, similar to one another and utterly distinct from the Negroid and Mongoloid races.

The reaction to the popularity of foreign records, the sense in which these recordings seemed to speak to the already-formed stable identities of immigrants (and therefore to confirm by default the identities of the non-immigrant writers), provoked two differing approaches. On the one hand, these recordings were welcomed, providing evidence for the emotional largesse of Anglo-Saxons, who could tolerate space for difference because of the security of their position. On the other hand, however, these recordings could evoke feelings of anxiety: if the immigrants felt *too* welcome, perhaps their numbers would swell uncontrollably, eventually constituting a threat to "American culture." "Who knows," the authors of these articles seem to be asking, "perhaps those foreigners will hold onto their strange ways and never fit in?" The discourses of self-congratulation and anxiety were occasionally mixed with justifications of the civic and economic utility of the talking machine: "the 'talker' has become a community leader so to speak" by helping people learn folk songs—it's a "great cultural work." Not only did the talking machine provide a cure for homesickness, then, but it also proved adept at mixing business with pleasure, anticipating the use of programmed music such as Muzak: "Acquainting millions of people with the very best in all forms of instrumental and vocal music, . . . it is proving a potent factor as a stimulator of labor in the factories where it is becoming a great power for contentment and pleasure."[49]

Not satisfied with increasing contentment or its ability to stimulate labor, the talking machine was far from exhausted. Even as it confirmed immigrants in their Old World identities, the talking machine might also be able strengthen their ties to the New World in the same stroke. The emergence of a new rhetoric of assimilation, spurred by the greater access to "American musical ideals" through "American songs," could result ultimately in "the Americanization of the great mass of people of foreign birth who are now residing in this country."[50] As if that were not enough, the talking machine could make thousands of foreigners stand at attention and sing the national anthem, according to an anonymous writer from *Talking Machine World*, a certain tip-off that they were learning to appreciate the democratic spirit of America.[51] For Americans who feared being overrun by a bunch of lazy, recalcitrant immigrants who stubbornly clung to their strange customs, nothing could be more comforting, simultaneously confirming mainstream identification and the democratic spirit, tolerance and chauvinism, in a single gesture.[52]

Yet by the mid-1920s another discourse had emerged that stressed the statistical importance of immigrant populations, as well as positive characteristics such as their thriftiness and reliability as customers, reinforced by the foreigner's tendency not to go anywhere and to keep "right on buying those things which appeal to him." New possibilities for demographic research and advertising beckoned, and music industry procedures were yoked to the United States census. The desire to communicate with multiple imagined or constellated communities was fueled by the belief that immigrants formed a vast majority of the metropole's populace—as much as 73.5 percent in the case of New York City! Other cities could not quite compete with this percentage, but "the average percentage of foreigners" in "most of our large industrial cities . . . is nearly 30 per cent, perhaps more," according to H. L. Wasserman, a dealer who "has all this information tabulated upon cards and has won the confidence of his following."[53] Beyond confirming the uses of marketing research as a form of surveillance, the pages of journals such as *Talking Machine World* attest to the striking importance of foreign music to the music industry at this time, with the number of advertisements, short blurbs, and feature articles on the subject far outstripping those of other types of music that figure much more prominently in subsequent narratives about popular music in the United States (and which will form the focus of the next two chapters).

. . .

In short, from the early years of the twentieth century until the early 1920s, the most important overarching category of difference in the U.S. music industry was that of foreign records, a distinction shared to some extent with Hawaiian music (which was sometimes folded into it). The recording industry recognized (primarily) white immigrants as fertile turf for marketing. The significance of this market for the nascent commodification of sound recording cannot be overemphasized. At once consolidating techniques of individuated listening that continued the transformation of domestic space into a receptacle for standardized goods, assimilation, and the reinforcement of group identifications that transcended national borders, foreign records provided a forum for the working out of debates over the proper place for new immigrants and racial hierarchies.[54] Two other markets, however, that developed during the early 1920s catering to native-born migrants proved to be of greater long-term importance to the record industry. For it was not only the new immigrants who used sound recordings to spread and interweave their constellated communities and to allay feelings of homesickness; workers in the urban North recently arrived from the rural South, both black and white, were soon to be enshrined in their own music industry categories.

NOTES

1. Frederick W. Gaisberg, *The Music Goes Round* (New York: MacMillan, 1942), 54.

2. *The Columbia Record* 3, no. 5 (May 1905): 135, quoted in William Howland Kenney, *Recorded Music in American Life: The Phonograph and Popular Memory, 1890–1945* (New York: Oxford University Press, 1999), 70–71.

3. This history is derived largely from William Howland Kenney, *Recorded Music in American Life*, 65–87. For more background see also *Ethnic Recordings in America: A Neglected Heritage* (Washington, DC: American Folklife Center, 1982).

4. The emphasis on individual experience in the development of sound recording is one of the arguments made by Jonathan Sterne in *The Audible Past: Cultural Origins of Sound Reproduction* (Durham, NC, and London: Duke University Press, 2003).

5. The role of technology in the mechanical reproduction of art and its impact on the formation of modernity has been and continues to be addressed from numerous points of view. It was famously, and perhaps first, addressed in 1936 by Walter Benjamin, "The Work of Art in the Age of Mechanical Reproduction," in *Illuminations*, ed. Hannah Arendt, trans. Harry Zohn (New York: Schocken Books, 1969), 217–52. The following give some idea of the range of activity around the topic: William Howland Kenney, *Recorded Music in American Life*; Jonathan Sterne, *The Audible Past*; Lisa Gitelman, *Scripts, Grooves, and Writing Machines: Representing Technology in the Edison Era* (Stanford, CA: Stanford University Press, 1999); Friedrich Kittler, *Gramophone, Film, Typewriter* (Stanford, CA: Stanford University Press, 1999); Michael Chanan, *Repeated Takes: A Short History of Recording and Its Effects on Music* (London and New York: Verso, 1995); Mark Katz, *Capturing Sound: How Technology Has Changed Music* (Berkeley and Los Angeles: University of California Press, 2004); Michael Taussig, *Mimesis and Alterity: A Particular History of the Senses* (New York and London: Routledge, 1993); Jacques Attali, "Repeating," in *Noise: The Political Economy of Music*, trans. Brian Massumi (Minneapolis: University of Minnesota Press, 1985), 87–132; Alex Ross, "Infernal Machines: How Recordings Changed Music," in *Listen to This* (New York: Farrar, Straus and Giroux, 2010), 55–68.

6. *Phonograph and Talking Machine Weekly*, July 24, 1924, 17.

7. See for example "Popular Music," *Variety*, December 31, 1920, 75; and "Too Much Repetition in Music Game," *Billboard*, August 14, 1926. This topic was also a regular feature of the "Land O' Melody" column in *Billboard* during the mid-1920s.

8. *Talking Machine World* (hereafter *TMW*), August 15, 1923, 26–27. This advertisement also evokes a promotional practice popular at Edison during this time, the tone test, which will be discussed in greater detail in chapter 4 in conjunction with the career of Vernon Dalhart. The idea of verisimilitude with musical instruments could be taken to extremes: William Howland Kenney discusses the development by Columbia of the Columbia Symphony Grand, a phonograph in the shape of a grand piano, in *Recorded Music in American Life*, 51.

9. *TMW,* January 15, 1925, 36–37. The identification of women with the talking machine could take many forms. A broad sampling of advertisements taken in chronological order reveals the following: a woman in a bathing suit in a rural scene adorns an ad for Starr Phonograph, presumably creating an easy equation between the naturalness of the setting, the natural quality of Starr Phonographs, and woman as nature, with the caption "The difference is in the tone" (*TMW,* December 15, 1923, 110); an ad for Thorola speakers features a woman in a form-fitting classical Grecian-type garment above a caption reading "I am the voice" (*TMW,* February 15, 1925, 115); an ad for the Sonora Phonograph Company, with the heading "About the Girl I Am Going to Marry," promotes the gramophone as an ideal way to combine the excitement of nightlife and the tranquility of domesticity—all so a young woman might encourage the man of her dreams to propose to her (*TMW,* October 15, 1926, 78–79). Femininity and records could also blend into one another, as illustrated by an ad for the Empire Talking Machine Co. in which a cascade of records substitutes for the lower half of a woman's body (*TMW,* June 15, 1920, 55). For more on the early recognition of women as the primary consumers of talking machines, see the articles collected in Timothy D. Taylor, Mark Katz, and Tony Grajeda, eds., *Music, Sound, and Technology in America: A Documentary History of Early Phonograph, Cinema, and Radio* (Durham, NC: Duke University Press, 2012), 70–78.

10. Or the pianola, which represented an intermediate phase in terms of mechanical reproducibility but lacked the ability of the recorded voice to invoke the bodily presence of the performer.

11. Lisa Gitelman, *Scripts, Grooves, and Writing Machines,* 133–35. Gitelman is referring to the "one-drop" rule in which one became African American by virtue of having one great-great-grandparent of African descent. Hence, after Plessy v. Ferguson it was not necessary to have the visual characteristics associated with being African American to be defined as African American.

12. For much of the minstrel show's history, male members of white immigrant groups, who were themselves marginalized, used minstrelsy to confirm their Americanness and their whiteness, not to mention their virility. For more background on minstrelsy, see Robert Toll, *Blacking Up: The Minstrel Show in Nineteenth-Century America* (New York and Oxford: Oxford University Press, 1974); Eric Lott, *Love and Theft: Blackface Minstrelsy and the American Working Class* (New York and Oxford: Oxford University Press, 1993); Annemarie Bean, James V. Hatch, and Brooks McNamara, eds., *Inside the Minstrel Mask: Readings in Nineteenth-Century Blackface Minstrelsy* (Hanover, NH: Wesleyan University Press, 1996); Dale Cockrell, *Demons of Disorder: Early Blackface Minstrels and Their World* (Cambridge and New York: Cambridge University Press, 1997); W. T. Lhamon, *Raising Cain: Blackface Performance from Jim Crow to Hip Hop* (Cambridge, MA: Harvard University Press, 1998). For discussions of *The Jazz Singer* (1927) in these terms, see Michael Rogin, *Blackface, White Noise: Jewish Immigrants in the Hollywood Melting Pot* (Berkeley and Los Angeles: University of California Press, 1996), 73–120; Krin Gabbard, *Jammin' at the Margins: Jazz and the American Cinema* (Chicago and London: University of Chicago Press, 1996), 35–63; and Matthew Frye Jacobson, *Whiteness of a Different Color: European Immigrants and the Alchemy of Race* (Cambridge, MA: Harvard University Press, 1998), 119–22.

13. This anecdote is described more fully in Lisa Gitelman, *Scripts, Grooves, and Writing Machines,* 136.

14. The coon song has not attracted the same level of attention as has minstrelsy. Extant literature includes the following: Sam Dennison, *Scandalize My Name: Black Imagery in American Popular Music* (New York: Garland Publishing, 1982); James H. Dormon, "Shaping the Popular Image of Post-Reconstruction American Blacks: The 'Coon Song' Phenomenon of the Gilded Age," *American Quarterly* 40 (December 1988): 450–71; David R. Roediger, *The Wages of Whiteness: Race and the Making of the American Working Class* (London and New York: Verso, 1991), 95–131; and Lynn Abbott and Doug Seroff, *Ragged but Right: Black Traveling Shows, "Coon Songs," and the Dark Pathway to Blues and Jazz* (Jackson: University Press of Mississippi, 2007), 11–38. Thomas L. Riis discusses coon songs in the context of different song types found in early black musical theater productions in *Just Before Jazz: Black Musical Theater in New York, 1890–1915* (Washington, DC, and London: Smithsonian Institution Press, 1989).

15. Sterne gives the following explanation of audile technique: "The objectification and abstraction of hearing and sound, their construction as bounded and coherent objects . . . was a prior condition for the construction of sound-reproduction technologies. . . . [Audile technique is] a set of practices of listening that were articulated to science, reason, and instrumentality and that encouraged the coding and rationalization of what was heard." Jonathan Sterne, *The Audible Past*, 23. Recordings very quickly became part of a new mode of musical transmission, as musicians began to learn from recordings, in a kind of second-degree aurality. For examples of this phenomenon see David Hatch and Stephen Millward, *From Blues to Rock: An Analytical History of Pop Music* (Manchester, England: Manchester University Press, 1987), 53–54; and Karl Hagstrom Miller, *Segregating Sound: Inventing Folk and Pop Music in the Age of Jim Crow* (Durham, NC, and London: Duke University Press, 2010), 233–34.

16. R. Murray Schaefer, *The Tuning of the World* (New York: Alfred A. Knopf, 1977), 90–91. Schaefer is referring to the splitting of a sound from its source.

17. "Dance Music" and "Vocal Music" belong to the category of "popular music," which doesn't appear in catalogs but is referred to in other modes of discourse found in music industry publications.

18. This usage of "category" and "genre" as distinct terms will be unique to my discussion of the 1920s. As will become clear, the distinction between these terms is less tenable after this period, in which the use of terms reliant on style characteristics such as "fox-trot," "waltz," and so on became increasingly rare, and terms that refer to a cluster of socio-musical associations became more common, be they the large music industry categories of rhythm and blues, country and western, et cetera, or critic-fan-derived terms such as rock and roll, folk-rock, and the like. The distinct usage of category and genre does parallel the general tendency elsewhere in this book of using "category" to refer to relatively larger groupings, and "genre" to refer to groupings marked with greater specificity.

19. Novelty songs featuring birds appear to have been a popular subcategory, as witnessed by the attention lavished on a recording released several years later; see "Series of Records Made by Chorus of Sixteen Canaries Trained by a German: Melody-Singing Birds the Result of Years of Breeding and Training—Birds Were Never Permitted to Hear Other Feathered Songsters—A Unique Series of Records," *TMW*, March 15, 1926, 58. Evidently, judging from the rest of the article, the fact that a German trained the canaries guaranteed

the seriousness of the endeavor. The sense that the soul of European art music was embodied by Germans extended to the memoirs of African American popular musicians as well. W. C. Handy, for one, makes clear in his autobiography the particular importance of his encounters with various German musical mentors, an importance that would have hardly been unique at the time. W. C. Handy, *Father of the Blues: An Autobiography* (New York: Da Capo Books, 1969), 32.

20. The subject of the blues prior to 1920 will be addressed in the next chapter.

21. *Phonograph and Talking Machine Weekly,* March 5, 1924, 39.

22. For more on the use of Asian stereotypes in the popular music of this era, see Charles Hiroshi Garrett, *Struggling to Define a Nation: American Music and the Twentieth Century* (Berkeley and Los Angeles: University of California Press, 2008), 121–64; Judy Tsou, "Gendering Race: Stereotypes of Chinese Americans in Popular Sheet Music," *repercussions* 6, no. 2 (1997): 25–62; Larry Hamberlin, "Visions of Salome: The Femme Fatale in American Popular Songs Before 1920," *Journal of the American Musicological Society* 59, no. 3 (Fall 2006): 631–96; Krystyn R. Moon, *Yellowface: Creating the Chinese in American Popular Music and Performance, 1850s–1920s* (New Brunswick, NJ: Rutgers University Press, 2004); Robert G. Lee, *Orientals: Asian Americans in Popular Culture* (Philadelphia: Temple University Press, 1999).

23. Although it should be noted that popularity charts were still in nascent form in the 1920s and could not project the type of authority they were to acquire in the 1930s and 1940s.

24. Charles Hiroshi Garrett, *Struggling to Define a Nation,* 165–213. See also Pekka Gronow, Ethnic Recordings: An Introduction," in *Ethnic Recordings in America,* 14–15.

25. *People's Unrivaled Family Atlas of the World* (Chicago: People's Publishing Company, 1886). Similar types of charts continued to be published into the twentieth century. For one example, see the chart in *Maury's New Complete Geography* of 1906, https://c1.staticflickr. com/3/2253/2228668286_5216064f44.jpg, accessed September 20, 2015.

26. I am using the word "race" advisedly in this context rather than "ethnicity" in order to better recapture the sense of struggle over difference as it occurred in the early years of the twentieth century. For a history of that struggle, and one to which the following synopsis is indebted, see Matthew Frye Jacobson, *Whiteness of a Different Color* (and I am following Jacobson here in his usage of "race"). The substitution of "ethnicity" for race, Jacobson argues, has obscured the way in which white difference was understood during the period in question. David R. Roediger presents a detailed genealogy of the transition from "race" to "ethnicity" in *Working Toward Whiteness: How America's Immigrants Became White* (New York: Basic Books, 2005), 3–34. The context in which such differences are studied also affects how they are perceived. David Nasaw, in his study of public amusements in the United States between 1880 and 1920, emphasizes the acceptance of new immigrants relative to Asian Americans and (especially) African Americans due to admissions and seating policies in theaters, dance halls, nightclubs, amusement parks, and other such venues. David Nasaw, *Going Out: The Rise and Fall of Public Amusements* (New York: Basic Books, 1993), 47–61. For an example of "race" used in music industry discourse to refer to different white races, see "Creating Sales Among the Foreign-Born: Securing the Confidence of New Comers to Our Shores Requires Study of Their Preferences, Says H. L. Wasserman, Live Dealer," *TMW,* July 15, 1924, 19.

27. One could understand the period discussed in chapters 2, 3, and 4 of this book as being bounded by two important pieces of legislation that attempted to control the movement of raced bodies either into the United States or within it: Plessy v. Ferguson of 1896, which inaugurated the Jim Crow era, and the Johnson-Reed Act of 1924.

28. Nothing could better illustrate the shifting meanings of the word "Caucasian" than an ad that relied on the earlier meaning, referring specifically to people from the Caucasus Mountains. This ad ran in the December 15, 1923, issue of *TMW* for the Edward B. Marks Music Corporation for a song titled "Caucasian Love," "by the Russian-American Lehar Joseph Chernlavsky" (172). For more on the concept of ethnicity and American cultural politics during the 1930s, see Michael Denning, *The Cultural Front: The Laboring of American Culture in the Twentieth Century* (London and New York: Verso, 1997). For a musical study of a piece exemplifying the transitional notions of race and ethnicity in the late 1930s, see Lisa Barg, "Paul Robeson's *Ballad for Americans*: Race and the Cultural Politics of 'People's Music,'" *Journal of the Society for American Music* 2, no. 1 (2008): 27–70.

29. The history of racism following the 1920s makes it clear that distinctions based on visuality persisted even if they were discounted in scholarly and journalistic circles. At times during the period preceding the 1920s, these races of "new immigrants" were allied with African, Asian, and Native Americans against "old stock" whites, and, at other times, granted a kind of provisional whiteness in opposition to nonwhite races. Matthew Frye Jacobson describes the notion of the "three great divisions of mankind" as the dominant racial paradigm emerging in the United States in the 1930s and 1940s (see the chapter "Becoming Caucasian, 1924–1965") in *Whiteness of a Different Color*, 91–135. Regional difference, however, could often play an important role in the understanding of race. While Henry Cabot Lodge in 1891 found Slovak immigrants to be interchangeable with Chinese in Colorado, proslavery forces in California during the 1870s were not above using "Celts" in their battle against Chinese immigration (ibid., 5, 42, 46).

30. This is a point that both Matthew Frye Jacobson and especially David R. Roediger (to whom I owe the notion of "in-between-ness") are at pains to make. See Matthew Frye Jacobson, *Whiteness of a Different Color*, and David R. Roediger, *Working Toward Whiteness*, especially 57–130.

31. William Howland Kenney, *Recorded Music in American Life*, 65–66.

32. See Charles Hiroshi Garrett, *Struggling to Define a Nation*, 130–32, 149–52.

33. See Josh Kun, *Audiotopia: Music, Race, and America* (Berkeley and Los Angeles: University of California Press, 2005), 69. For more on the history of Jewish humor in the United States, see Esther Romeyn and Jack Kugelmass, *Let There Be Laughter! Jewish Humor in America* (Chicago: Spertus Press, 1997); and Henry D. Spalding, "Dialect Stories," in *A Treasure Trove of American Jewish Humor*, ed. Henry D. Spalding (Middle Village, NY: Jonathan David Publishers, 1976), 63–72.

34. Liner notes to *Jewface* (Reboot Stereophonic, 2006).

35. William Howland Kenney discusses the shift in "Hebrew-Yiddish" recordings in similar terms in *Recorded Music in American Life*, 82–83.

36. For more on the *freygish* scale, see Mark Slobin, *Tenement Songs: The Popular Music of the Jewish Immigrants* (Champaign-Urbana: University of Illinois Press, 1996), 184, 187; and Joshua S. Walden, "The 'Yidishe Paganini': Sholem Aleichem's *Stempenyu*, the Music of

Yiddish Theatre and the Character of the *Shtetl* Fiddler," *Journal of the Royal Musical Association* 139, no. 1 (2014): 107–8.

37. Matthew Frye Jacobson explores the continuity of New World and Old World Jewish stereotypes and cultural practices in the context of Jewish immigration to the United States in "Looking Jewish, Seeing Jews," in *Whiteness of a Different Color,* 171–87.

38. See ibid., 171–99.

39. *TMW,* July 15, 1924, 89. A dealer for Columbia lists thirty-two languages in an ad from a few months earlier (*TMW,* January 15, 1924, 137).

40. "Oakland Phono. Co. Enlarges: Addition of Thirty Demonstration Rooms Follows Taking on of Sonora Line," *TMW,* June 15, 1923, 135. Other articles also discussed sales strategies for foreign records, many of which focused around speaking the native tongue of the customer or communicating via foreign-language newspapers. See "Creating Sales Among the Foreign-Born" and "Advertising for Foreign Trade at Home: The Great Percentage of the Population in the Larger Cities May Be Reached Through Publicity in Foreign Language Newspapers," *TMW,* July 15, 1923, 45. The Columbia ad mentioned earlier confirms that this mode of communication was already in place: "Columbia advertising is appearing in one hundred leading foreign language periodicals published in twenty-one different languages" (*TMW,* July 15, 1924, 89).

41. *TMW,* November 15, 1920, 77. For a history of "His Master's Voice" (the Victor logo) as embedded in colonial practice, see Michael Taussig, *Mimesis and Alterity,* 193–211. And indeed, as William Howland Kenney notes, Victor had been extremely active in searching even the most far-flung parts of the globe for new musical material (*Recorded Music in American Life,* 67–73). See also Michael Chanan, *Repeated Takes,* 29–31. Also interesting in this respect is the autobiography, cited in the epigraph of this chapter, of the "chief recorder and talent scout" of the Gramophone Company (soon to become Victor) during this period, Frederick W. Gaisberg. Even the brief quote in the epigraph conveys a sense of how Gaisberg's approach to business and aesthetic sensibility was shaped by colonial attitudes.

42. Frank E. Parsons, "How Recognition of the Pride of Race Will Increase Record Sales," *TMW,* March 15, 1918, 4. Seven years later, this type of homological thinking still persisted, as evidenced from the title of another article, "Pushing Records That Fit Your Trade: You Can't Sell Italian Records to a Norwegian, So Why Try—Analyze Your Customers' Desires and Give 'Em What They Want," *TMW,* June 15, 1925, 24.

43. The quote is from Jonathan Sterne, *The Audible Past,* 177.

44. Jack Kapp, "Reasons for Popularity of Certain Selections and Their Effect on Sales," *TMW,* March 15, 1923, 162a, 162b; and "Creating Sales Among the Foreign-Born."

45. "Some Thoughts on the Foreign Record Trade," *TMW,* November 15, 1923, 80. On "Chinese musicality" and the laundry trade, see also Frederick W. Gaisberg, *The Music Goes Round,* 64.

46. T. W. Adorno, "The Curves of the Needle," in *Essays on Music,* ed. Richard Leppert, trans. Thomas Y. Levin (Berkeley and Los Angeles: University of California Press, 2002), 274. Originally published in 1927 and revised in 1965.

47. This was expressed in countless publications from this time, perhaps most famously in the third chapter of Sigmund Freud's *Civilization and Its Discontents* (London: Penguin, 2002), written during the period under discussion here. See also Cecil Sharpe,

"Introduction," in *English Folk Songs from the Southern Appalachians* vol. 1, ed. Maud Karpeles (London and New York: Oxford University Press, 2012), xxi–xxxvii, originally published in 1917.

48. James Humphris, "How the Talking Machine Gives Reality to Musical History" (pt. 1), *The Talking Machine Journal*, March 1920, 14; and "How the Talking Machine Gives Reality to Musical History" (pt. 2), *The Talking Machine Journal*, April 1920, 45.

49. "Advancing the Cause of Music in America," *TMW*, June 15, 1920, 8.

50. Ibid.

51. This assertion is based on the following quote: "How music brings the foreigner into accord with American sentiment was demonstrated at the Sunday concert recently, at which many distinguished visitors from Washington and New York were present. The concert was opened by playing 'The Star-Spangled Banner' on the Victrola, and instantly there arose and stood at attention 20,000 immigrants, who showed marked reverence for our national anthem, and for the country that is so democratic as to begin at its very doors to welcome the strangers who desire to make America their home." "Talking Machine a Vital Aid in Americanization," *TMW*, November 15, 1920, 77.

52. Lisa Gitelman discusses how the music industry viewed the gramophone, even in the early years of the century, as a mechanism for uniting diverse groups of people while simultaneously reconfirming ideas about racial hierarchy. Particularly fascinating is an ad from 1908 that brings together ideas about the gramophone as performance simulacrum and uniting agent of the nation. Lisa Gitelman, *Scripts, Grooves, and Writing Machines*, 136–37.

53. "According to the census figures for 1920, New York City had a total population of 5,839,738 of which 4,294,629 were of foreign birth or the children of foreign-born parents" ("Advertising for Foreign Trade at Home"). See also "Creating Sales Among the Foreign-Born." Another article from the same period affirms the utility of the foreign record buyer because, unlike "the average purchaser of records in the English tongue or compositions that may be classed as American lets up on his buying as a rule," the "foreign-born citizen . . . stays pretty close to home and keeps right on buying those things which appeal to him." "No Seasonal Lull with Foreign Records," *TMW*, September 15, 1924, 11. This article pegs the foreign-born population of many cities at over "50 per cent of the total population." For articles that demonstrate the shift in the discourse on foreign music to a gradual emphasis on the thriftiness and reliability of foreigners as customers, see "Ad: Columbia *New Process* RECORDS for all Nations," *TMW*, July 15, 1924, 89; and especially "How Goran Brothers Cater to Foreign-Born: David Goran Points Out Reasons Why Foreign-Born People Make Excellent Prospects and His Methods of Securing Their Trade," *TMW*, November 15, 1924, 14.

54. For the importance of phonographs to new immigrants, and the use of recordings to consolidate group identification, see Lizabeth Cohen, *Making a New Deal: Industrial Workers in Chicago, 1919–1939* (New York: Cambridge University Press, 1990), 105. On the use of the phonograph simultaneously to unite the nation and transcend nationality, see Jonathan Sterne, *The Audible Past*, 213.

3

Forward to the Past

Race Music in the 1920s

Let us begin with a story of origins. In February 1920, after almost ten years spent touring in vaudeville shows, hustling his songs, and angling for an opening in the rapidly changing world of popular recorded music, Perry Bradford finds a sympathetic ear with Fred Hager, recording chief at the General Phonograph Company, also known as OKeh. Hager's responsibilities include seeking any possible advantage for OKeh to disrupt the near-hegemonic status of the two industry giants, Victor and Columbia. Hager is thus more receptive than executives at those companies to the sales pitch of Bradford, an African American, who would not normally be given the time of day by a white businessman. Bradford proposes that his original compositions be recorded by an African American female singer, Mamie Smith, a preposterous idea according to the common wisdom of the day, but one that Hager begins to consider once plans to record Bradford's songs with Sophie Tucker, a well-known white singer, fall through. Mamie Smith's first recording, "That Thing Called Love" backed with (b/w) "You Can't Keep a Good Man Down" is a modest hit, and her second recording, Bradford's "Crazy Blues" b/w another Bradford tune, "It's Right Here for You (If You Don't Get It . . . 'Tain't No Fault of Mine)," becomes the surprise success story of the year for the U.S. recording industry. "Crazy Blues" inaugurates a craze for classic blues, and the birth of race music—that is, music recorded largely by, and putatively for, African Americans— soon follows.[1]

"Crazy Blues" has been discussed countless times, and forms the beginning of virtually every history of race music, yet this recording has rarely been considered within a genealogy of musical categorization. Considering race music within such a genealogy changes the frame in which it is studied away from a history that would look at race music in isolation and find historical causes for the effects of African American popular music in the present. Rather, the approach here will be to place "Crazy Blues" within a musical network existing in the early decades of the twentieth century in which the concept of race music emerged in dialogue with the other categories and concepts circulating in the popular music field. The quasi-autonomy of the musical practices employed by the recordings of the period are understood and analyzed as impulses and responses that are reciprocal to the cultural and historical dynamics of the period.

WHO HAD THE BLUES BEFORE 1920?

The discussion of categories and genres around 1920 in the previous chapter introduced (albeit in passing) two terms associated now and then with African Americans: "blues" and "jazz." The profusion of post–World War II discourse on blues and jazz has somewhat obscured the manner in which these terms circulated, their connotations for performers and audiences, the musical style characteristics, if any, that may have been associated with them, and their role in struggles around cultural hierarchies and group identifications.[2] The term "blues," in particular, can seem particularly reified in current usage, as it is frequently associated with a specific musical-formal pattern, rhyme scheme, lyric content, and approach to melody and harmony—a usage that contrasts with the vast range of ways that it was employed when it began to circulate.[3] Blues histories tend to place country blues artists at a site of origin predating their recordings (which began in the mid-1920s) with perhaps a cursory nod to the classic blues. Oral accounts of the origins of the blues are traced back to the turn of the century, but these tend to rely on accounts recorded after 1930.[4]

Jazz history, if anything, has become even more standardized than the history of the blues, having established a much firmer foothold in academia and the undergraduate textbook market. Students of jazz will be familiar with the early recordings of Louis Armstrong and Jelly Roll Morton, and will have perhaps been exposed to the 1917 recordings of the Original Dixieland Jazz Band (ODJB) in addition to absorbing the founding narratives placing the birth of jazz in New Orleans. During and subsequent to its birth, so the standard historical account goes, jazz acquired certain musical practices such as swing, improvisation, the use of blue notes, et cetera, from whence issued historical genres such as swing, bebop, cool jazz, hard bop, and free jazz.[5]

These standardized historical narratives pay little attention to the usages of the terms "jazz" and "blues" in music industry discourse, and utterances made by musicians, journalists, and scholars of the period are similarly given short shrift.[6] Such histories tend to rely on an unexamined opposition between art and commerce, in which folk or traditional music occupies the pole of art, which at least partly explains, in turn, the relative paucity of studies exploring the commercial background for the irruption of blues-associated recordings (both folk and otherwise) by African American artists during the 1920s. The privileging of a type of folk authenticity over debased commercial musical products aligns with familiar associations between aesthetic prestige and gender. Here the authentic, virile tradition of folk (or country, as it is usually referred to) blues sung by men is placed at the point of historical origin, while the debased commercial (and technologically mediated) form of the blues sung by women is seen as derivative, even though the first country blues was recorded six years after Mamie Smith waxed "Crazy Blues."[7] The analysis of the assumptions that form the basis of such histories is central to a genealogy of blues and jazz. Because these terms were central to the formation of the race music category, it is crucial to restore some sense of the struggle over them that took place at this time.

W. C. Handy and the Tin Pan Alley Blues

What emerges from a study of the discourse surrounding the terms "jazz" and "blues," as well as from recordings that predate 1930, is that these terms (and "ragtime," for that matter) were often used interchangeably, and frequently referred rather loosely to ways of producing music that shared certain musical practices, rather than to distinct genres or standardized formal patterns. At their most tangential, the terms were used in song titles as advertisements in the manner of brand names (as in "Ching-a-Ling's Jazz Bazaar" mentioned in chapter 2) or merely because the lyrics alluded to "having the blues."[8] One example of this tangential approach, "Chinese Blues," was written and first recorded in 1915, eventually becoming the most popular blues hit of the year. A recording of the song made by Irving Kaufman (a prolific early recording artist) in 1918 presents the stereotypical East Asian musical and lyrical tropes prevalent then—woodblocks, parallel fourths—and the lyrics open with "Chinaman, Chinaman, wash 'em laundry all day / Chinaman, Chinaman, smoke 'em pipe they say," thereby combining clichés about the disposition toward certain professions and opium addiction. Twelve-bar forms, aab rhyme schemes, and blue notes are nowhere to be found, although the lyrics do inform us that the song's protagonist has the "Chinese Blues."

This song makes it bracingly clear how techniques of othering found in minstrelsy, coon songs, Hawaiian music, and songs about Chinatowns and immigrants were effortlessly combined with public fascination with "the blues," often overriding any sort of musical-stylistic connection.[9] This othering was present in the vaudeville novelty effects (exaggerated trombone slides, "whoopee" whistles, interjected percussion breaks on woodblocks, cymbals) in recordings that combined jazz and blues, as in "Some Jazz Blues" by the Memphis Pickaninny Band in 1917.[10] The use of these novelty effects, constituting a kind of musico-racial stereotyping, clarify that such songs are novelties rather than vehicles for the expression of the sentimental feelings indicative of serious affect in many popular songs of the period.

Examples such as "Chinese Blues" and "Some Jazz Blues" notwithstanding, many published and recorded blues prior to 1920 did include some of the now-stereotypical features of blues musical form and lyrics, occasionally even repeating floating musical phrases and lyrics from song to song. This matching of genre name ("blues") with music and lyrics, though inconsistent and haphazard, suggests that certain tropes were already circulating within musical communities—both literate and illiterate, as well as black and white—prior both to the first published blues to experience widespread commercial success, as well as to the song that arguably commenced the blues craze (that is, published songs with "blues" in the title) of the 1910s, W. C. Handy's "Memphis Blues." Handy published "Memphis Blues" in 1912, although he claims to have composed it initially in 1909 as "Mr. Crump's Blues."[11] "Memphis Blues" features a twelve-bar opening chorus replete with stereotypical harmonic scheme, blue notes, (what would now be described as) ragtime-based syncopations, a contrasting sixteen-bar B section, and a blues-based closing section that is a variant of the opening. Handy's work resembles that of several other blues published in the years from 1908 to 1912, such as Antonio Maggio's "I Got the Blues" (1908, an instrumental), even sharing certain musical phrases (such as the alternation of flat and natural third scale degrees, and an opening twelve-bar section with stereotypical blues harmonic progression and ragtime-based syncopation) and setting the tone for much of the classic blues that would be recorded in the 1920s.[12]

Tin Pan Alley blues such as "Chinese Blues," "Memphis Blues," and "I Got the Blues" (the subtitle of which references two other genres, ragtime and the two-step) relied not only on sound recordings and sheet music for dissemination. Rather, in the words of Lynn Abbott and Doug Seroff, during the 1910s, "the compositions of W. C. Handy and other blues writers were repeatedly performed in street parades and on circus lots in countless locations throughout every inhabited part of the United States and much of Canada."[13] In other words, these commercialized blues were as much if not more accessible through live performances, including traveling vaudeville acts, minstrel companies, and circus sideshows, than they were through recordings. These descriptive accounts attest to how the sound of the Tin Pan Alley blues permeated both domestic and public space.

It is worth pausing to discuss Handy's own conception of the blues, which has subsequently been re-cited frequently enough to participate in the myths that inhabit the widely accepted narratives of blues history as well as in much of the recent cultural analysis of early blues and race records.[14] In terms of affect, in most of his published utterances, Handy didn't go into much detail about the unique features of the blues other than specifying a slow tempo and (in folk-blues) "the employment of humor for the expression of misery" in the lyrics as what distinguished blues from ragtime or coon songs. On the other hand, he could occasionally be more specific when discussing formal features, as when he stated in one publication that "the earmarks of the genuine blues . . . are numerous," and include three-line stanzas in aab form, the use of blue notes, and especially the twelve-bar section length, which can "stand alone."[15]

In his autobiography, *Father of the Blues*, Handy recounts how the idea of refashioning a more down-home, folk form of the blues came to him: while waiting for a train in Tutwiler, Mississippi, around 1903, he heard an itinerant musician playing slide guitar and singing what (according to Handy's description) we would now call a blues. It struck Handy that this song contained a vital essence that would have enormous communicative power if harnessed to the more refined musical technique in which he had been trained. Eventually, after several other reminders of the transformative power of this type of music, some of them humiliating (due to Handy's inability to produce the music demanded by the folk), Handy began to create arrangements of blues and work songs. At last, in 1909, he composed "Mr. Crump's Blues," which would eventually be published as "Memphis Blues."

Whenever Handy discusses the music of the musically illiterate folk, he is careful to emphasize his distance from them. This folk music is beautiful in its naturalness, and totally adequate as raw source material for a trained musician. But Handy, as a college-educated man and former educator at the college level, classically trained and musically literate, clearly belongs to another social stratum, even if he hailed from small-town Alabama himself.[16] Handy occasionally employs the background of his childhood experiences to locate his compositions in a pre-commercial notion of tradition, as when, for example, he traces the main strain of "St. Louis Blues" (published in 1914) back to a preacher he heard in Florence, Alabama.[17]

But Handy's main apprenticeship came, as it did for many of the other professional African American musicians at the time, neither in college nor from absorbing tradition from his childhood surroundings, but in one of two alternatives: minstrel shows (in the case of Handy) and vaudeville.[18] In the minstrel show, he developed a sense of what the public, white and black alike, wanted, and how to entertain an audience. Through extensive travel, he became aware of the latest developments in popular music, including both learned styles such as ragtime as well as a wide range of vernacular musics, including, one assumes, the blues in nascent form. These peripatetic experiences enabled him to assert that certain tunes, such as "Got No More Home Than a Dog," were "sung around 1890 by the Negro quartet in Florence" (Alabama, Handy's hometown) and that he "heard it played by mandolin and guitar as far west [and North] as Evansville, Indiana"— observations attesting to the broad circulation of musical tropes that formed the matrix of black musical practices at that time.[19]

At the same time, professional survival was more important to Handy than remaining faithful to an elevated aesthetic. In other words, he was willing, in what amounts to a recurring refrain among movers and shakers in the music business, to give the public what they wanted. His epiphanies included not only rustic blues, but other types of music based on repetition and rhythm:

> Art, in the high-brow sense, was not in my mind. My idea of what constitutes music was changed by the sight of that silver money, cascading around the splay feet of a Mississippi string band. Seven years prior to this, while playing a cornet solo, Hartman's *Mia,* on the stage in Oakland, California, I had come to the conclusion, because of what happened in this eleven minute solo, that the American people wanted movement and rhythm for their money.[20]

Handy doesn't always clearly describe the listeners or dancers in these settings, although he often states or provides clues that suggest the audiences were white. The clues, which include a request for him to play some of his "native music," also strongly imply that the audience had a prior familiarity with these infectious rhythms.[21]

The period described by Handy occurs during a period that Karl Hagstrom Miller has described as a shift from a "minstrelsy-based" paradigm—in which identification with black music was understood as primarily performative (or, to use Georgina Born's terms, "imaginary")—to a folklore-based model in which different demographic groups were understood as clearly separate, as were the cultural productions that were associated with them (approaching Born's homology model). Handy's comments were published in 1926 (by his amanuensis, Abbe Niles), and in his autobiography in 1941, after folkloristic ideas, according to Hagstrom Miller, had already come to dominate discussions of African American music. The writings of other African Americans such as James Weldon Johnson that traverse the period in question bear witness to a shift in attitudes among African Americans about their relationship to the music associated with them.[22]

The idea that the music of the black folk had a kind of vitality that literate black musicians could draw upon was firmly established by the end of the 1910s and shared by many of the leading African American musicians and intellectuals of the time.[23] This vitality lay in the realm of rhythm primarily, but also in expressive pitch bending, blue notes, and a wide range of nonstandardized timbres—in other words, in precisely those parameters that subsequent writers have identified with African American musical difference in general.[24] For example, here are statements about rhythm from Handy himself, James Reese Europe (the most successful African American bandleader of the 1910s), and the famed African American literary figure and songwriter James Weldon Johnson: "Negroes react rhythmically to everything. That's how the blues came to be. Sometimes I think that rhythm is our middle name" (Handy); "The negro musically is always a worshipper of rhythm; often he is a rhythmomaniac, and 'jazz' arises from his rhythmic fervor, combined with a peculiar like for strange sounds" (Europe, as reported by

Grenville Vernon); "Ragtime music was originated by colored piano players. . . . These men did not know any more about the theory of music than they did about the theory of the universe. They were guided by their natural musical instinct and talent, but above all by the Negro's extraordinary sense of rhythm" (Johnson).[25]

By the 1920s Handy was publicizing that most of the blues themes in his compositions were borrowed from folk sources, but at the same time allowing that the finished works required him to arrange these melodies for public consumption and to add melodies of his own invention.[26] What might seem to be Handy's attempt to have it both ways is indicative of debates among Harlem Renaissance writers of the time, who recognized that even as the homological relation to African American music created a sense of ownership, it reified African American music as well, freezing this newly authenticated music into a kind of primitivistic frame.[27] Handy was thus at pains to emphasize his status as a creative artist, not a mere conduit of preexisting folk matter.

An Ethnography of the Early Blues?

Another picture of the state of African American music at that time comes from Howard Odum's ethnography of musical practice published in 1911.[28] Odum describes many songs that may fit contemporary definitions of the blues, but it's difficult to ascertain the precise nature of the material due to vague descriptions and the lack of musical transcriptions, meaning that conclusions about the relation between what he describes and current classifications of the sounds he heard are necessarily conjectural. He presents many songs featuring three-line stanzas, some of which repeat one line three times (what Odum calls "one-verse songs," 263), others of which have an aab rhyme scheme, for example:

GOIN' BACK TO SWEET MEMPHIS, TENNESSEE
Well, if that's yo' man, you'd better buy a lock an' key, O babe!
Well, if that's yo' man, you'd better buy a lock an' key, O babe!
An' stop yo' man from runnin' after me-e-e. (282)

In addition to songs, the rhyme scheme of which recalls that of the blues, Odum details what he calls "knife songs" that feature slide or bottleneck guitar technique (261) as well as floating verses, musical and lyrical improvisation, and use of the phrase "I got the blues" in several songs (e.g., "Look'd Down de Road," 272)—all musical-lyrical practices subsequently associated with the blues. He also mentions how collectors might be influencing what the singers produce and the ubiquity of current popular hits and coon songs (259, 262), thus calling into question the folkness of these folk sources, how much of an objective snapshot this study provides, and whether something called the blues was ever separate from contemporary commercial popular music practice.[29] The "knife-song" brings several proto-blues tendencies together, including the use of bottleneck technique and the line "I got de blues." Odum declares that "many songs are sung to this music," perhaps alluding to how many of these proto-blues in fact do rely on similar harmonic-melodic patterns. The topic of this song, "the wanderer and his love-affairs," also matches that of many early blues recorded by African Americans.[30]

What is clear from the discussion of Odum's work and early published blues is that the blues, as it developed and circulated in the first two decades of the twentieth century, was the product of performances, publications, and recordings by black and white professional musicians working primarily in vaudeville, minstrelsy, and traveling circuses. The term "blues" circulated as a description for a mood prior to 1900, but it was not associated with specific musical practices until around 1910, and even then, this association was not consistent. Although several musicians remembered hearing blues or blues-type songs in the latter decades of the nineteenth century, many of these memories were recorded well after the blues had been established as a commercial genre, and after the recording of country blues artists began in the late 1920s.[31] The obverse of the situation, in which songs with "blues" in their title included no musical characteristics now associated with the blues, exists in cases in which musicians may have been playing what we would now call the blues but didn't use the term to refer to the music; thus we have to rely on the accounts of recollections of musicians after the fact to make this connection. For example, W. C. Handy, in a discussion of Phil Jones's song "Got No More Home Than a Dog," commented, "It was a blues, but the word formed no part of its title. What we now call blues, to the folk musicians meant a *kind* of song."[32]

Blues as African American Music

These accounts and practices (that is, the publication, performances, and recordings of blues by whites and blacks) also suggest that blues and early jazz were formed, at least in part, within a matrix of black and white interactions and relations that were ongoing in a racially integrated musical context (for example, Antonio Maggio, the composer of "I Got the Blues," was white). This, however, in what may seem like a paradox, had little or no effect on the perception of jazz and blues as irreducibly African American forms of music (recall the injunction for Handy that he play some of his "native music"). Nor does it imply that the music performed and created by African Americans was solely a matter of catering to white taste, or of refashioning white forms. Lynn Abbott and Doug Seroff convincingly argue for the relative autonomy of black performance networks—that is, of African Americans performing for other African Americans, forming a tempting analogy with the negro baseball leagues that also took shape in the decades following the turn of the century. They portray a world in which musical practices were pursued that found favor with African American audiences, sometimes to the chagrin of performers and critics who had high cultural ambitions.[33] Such performance networks played a crucial role in spreading the popularity of the Tin Pan

Alley blues (blues of the sort composed by Handy and recorded by Kaufman et al.). And such accounts underscore an important aspect of musical identification discussed in chapter 1: individual examples of people and music tend to escape clear categorization. The early blues offers an example of how music industry categories and public conceptions of certain genres often imply a tight and unwavering connection, a one-to-one mapping between musical styles and demographic groupings, while at the same time listening practices, as well as the repertoire choices of musicians, never map so neatly.

Such originary forms of hybridity-in-practice help explain, for example, the parallel shifts in entertainment music from minstrelsy and coon songs to blues, ragtime, and jazz among both white and black Americans. These parallel transformations in musical fashion also indicate that African Americans and Euro-Americans had already developed shared notions about high and low aesthetics, and the value of folk authenticity.[34] And even an emphasis on the interactions between black performers and black audiences barely begins to suggest the heterogeneity of that audience at any given show. That is to say, some audience members, like many of the musicians, preferred "refined" entertainment: classically trained musicians playing classically influenced, or classical, music. An analysis of this moment only in terms of the white reception of black music comes to emphasize a top-down approach that doesn't explain why some stereotypes and social connotations of genres became widely shared across demographic groups and others did not. As with the discussion of Jewish music in chapter 2, the legibility of first the blues, and then of race music, could only be attained via the gradual assembling together of musical sounds, the social connotations of performers and audience, and a shared sense of affect and physical movement that cut across demographic divisions, along with a term or concept that could function as a label.

Another related issue has to do with disentangling the diversity of consumption practices within a social group from what specific musical categories or genres may have signified at a particular moment. This challenge highlights the articulative role of genre in the iterative quality of identification discussed in chapter 1. That is, if identificatory labels refer to a subject position that is in the process of coming into being, then genres that are associated with particular groups are part of how that process works. The situation of the blues in the 1910s is in some respects similar, then, to that of minstrelsy in the nineteenth century (or Jewish music in the early twentieth century, for that matter). If blues, like minstrelsy, reminded audiences, black and white, of some aspect of musical blackness, then this phenomenon is a separate issue from whether the origins of these genres can be traced to a location purely within the African American community (this is the tenor of some anti-essentialist arguments that debunk the notion of black music because of its impure origins). Thus, when Marie Cahill begins her recording of "Dallas Blues" (1917) with an anecdote with all the marks of a story of origins—in this case, a creation myth replete with religious imagery—and claims to be only a conduit for what she "heard a darkey sing . . . down in Texas," she is simultaneously recon-firming an association that would have already been familiar to an audience and offering an explanation of how a white woman would know a song that is in twelve-bar blues form throughout, featuring blue notes and verses with an aab rhyme scheme. Never mind that the song was published by two white vaudevil-lians, Bert and Frank Leighton, in which they took the melody of a song by the same name, published by another white man, Hart A. Wand, in 1912, and com-bined it with the stuttering effect introduced in "Negro Blues" by the white min-strel man Leroy "Lasse" White in a song published in 1913. How else, listeners probably wondered, could a white woman know the liberating powers of repeti-tion, if she had not learned them from a real African American? Recordings such as Cahill's, like those of Kaufman discussed earlier, also continued not only the use of black-associated forms by white performers, but the conventions of vaudeville, minstrelsy, and the coon song as well.[35] The popularity of these recordings played off the same dynamic of desire and disavowal that had saturated the public response to minstrelsy, presenting a vision of uncontaminated nature that was as attractive as it was inadmissible except through a mask.[36] Whether or not this music was produced and consumed solely by African Americans is beside the point. To the vast public, this music *signified* African American–ness.

In addition to minstrel-derived material, spirituals made up a significant por-tion of the modest number of recordings made by African Americans prior to 1920. Just as touring companies of African Americans singing spirituals found large audiences that crossed social divisions, so did recordings of groups such as the Fisk Jubilee Singers constitute a large portion of the music recorded by African Americans prior to the advent of race records. This body of work stands as the socio-aesthetic counterweight to minstrel-derived performances on the one hand—which featured hits such as "The Whistling Coon" (1891) by George John-son (who was equally expert at whistling and *laughing*: his recording of the "Laugh-ing Coon" [1894?] is widely believed to be the most popular song of the 1890s)—and to the syncopated dance music performed by outfits led by musicians such as Europe and Handy on the other.[37]

Recordings of spirituals, early blues, ragtime, jazz, and black-performed min-strelsy were not part of a separate category of popular music prior to 1920, prima-rily because the music industry did not direct these recordings toward a black audience. Rather, they were slotted in alongside similar recordings by white artists and marketed toward what was assumed to be a white, Northern, urban audience. This lack of a separate conceptual category also helps explain the dominance in early recordings by black artists of coon songs and other minstrel-based material: the people in charge of recording companies and the assumed audience for record-ings expected certain musical representations of blackness, regardless of the racial identity of the performer. The arrival of black artists recording this material did, however, evoke anxiety on the part of white, bourgeois listeners, as already alluded to in the discussion of the reception of early sound recordings in chapter 2.[38]

RECORDING THE BLUES

White Female Singers Had the Blues

Two white female singers during the 1910s have been strongly connected with African American–associated styles, such as ragtime, the coon song, blues, and jazz: Marion Harris and Sophie Tucker, the latter known for her "coon" shouting (she even billed herself as a "Revelation in Coonology"[39] and was the first singer scheduled to record Perry Bradford's songs, as mentioned at the outset of this chapter). Both of these singers trumpeted their connections to, and apprenticeships with, African American musicians: Tucker via coaching by black musicians on how to perform coon songs and minstrel material (that is to say, a white woman coached by African Americans on how to perform material largely written by white people in styles created by white people who thought they were mimicking black people), and Harris though her putatively Southern provenance (she claimed to be from Kentucky but was actually born in Indiana). As with Odum's folklore studies, early blues sheet music, and descriptions of blues performances, a search for racial origins reveals a tangled and fascinating web of creative miscegenation.

Tucker recorded the song with which she was most closely identified, "Some of These Days," in 1911. The song was the work of an African American songwriter, Shelton Brooks, and, so the story goes, she was persuaded to give the song (and Brooks) an audition by her African American maid.[40] Many elements of this performance share much with then-current conventions of minstrel performance. Her singing is unusually full-bodied for the time, and she performs the song's syncopations with verve, albeit a bit stiffly from the perspective of post-1920 jazz and blues performances and recordings. For example, at 2:00 her rendering of the line "You'll miss your little da-ad, da-ad, da-ad, da-ad, daddy, some of these days" (musical example 4) shows her approach, with a mild ragtime-based syncopation in the first measure ("You'll miss your") and a more complex series of off-beat micro-inflections of the pulse in the third measure, which are set off by the dramatic pause on the downbeat following the regular accents of measure 2.

MUSICAL EXAMPLE 4: Sophie Tucker, "Some of These Days"

Tucker's 1919 recording of "Everybody Shimmies Now" shows her keeping up to date with more recent genres evoking African American–ness. Accompanied by the Five Kings of Syncopation, a group whose approach recalls that of the ODJB, Tucker enacts and proclaims the attributes of a current dance craze. This recording features Tucker with the same kind of instrumental-accompanimental texture that would appear a year later in Mamie Smith's "Crazy Blues." Interestingly enough, the minor-key passages recall the passages in Yiddish minor from popular contemporaneous Yiddish recordings (00:58), as does the beginning of the second section of "Some of These Days" (00:54).

Marion Harris worked in a similar vaudeville-based, coon song–dominated milieu as Sophie Tucker, yet presented a different musical sensibility. The obvious minstrel-inspired dialect-isms are minimized and Harris's accent seems more like a generic Southern accent, or a white Southern accent that comes and goes in her recordings but which could plausibly be her own. Several of her recordings make use of minstrel-inspired imagery, picturing the South as "paradise," as in "Paradise Blues," but gone are the grotesque caricatures of African Americans found in coon songs. The lyrics of many of her songs celebrate African American–associated genres such as blues, ragtime, and jazz, although occasionally these lyrics echo the condescension typical of the period. So, while she can in one breath proclaim, "Honey don't play me no opera / play me some blue melodies" (in "Paradise Blues," 1916), in "When I Hear That Jazz Band Play" (1917) she can announce that "you'll hear them very soon / they play all out of tune."[41] "Jazz" is associated with the body, movement, and, by implication, sex: "Say what you will, you can't keep still while they're playing / you can't resist, you've got to twist, while you're swaying / hear that trombone, with that peculiar moaning / hear that saxophone with that peculiar groaning" ("When I Hear That Jazz Band Play," 1917); and "there's something in the tone of the saxophone / that makes me do a little wiggle all my own" ("Jazz Baby," 1919). Harris (or the songwriters of these songs), like Dave Chappelle in his skit eighty-five years later, associates *instruments* (saxophone, trombone) with *genres* (jazz) with *kinesthetic responses* ("a little wiggle") with *affect* (moaning and groaning). The type of people associated with jazz are, for the moment, implied but not stated.

Harris comes closer to current conceptions of African American musical practice than a singer like Tucker with the fluent use of blue thirds, slurs, falsetto whoops, sense of rhythmic flexibility, and swing. The syncopations in the music are indebted to ragtime, which the lyrics in "Jazz Baby" make clear, as Harris (via the lyricist of the song) traces her own artistic lineage: "My daddy was a ragtime trombone player / my mammy was a ragtime caba-rayer / they met one day at a tango tea / there was a syncopated wedding and then came me." This song illustrates the full incorporation of ragtime rhythmic devices into the pop music of the time, with the various syncopations marked by an *x* and *y* in musical example 5.[42]

Measure 2 of this example shows the use of the blue third, while the subtle vocal inflections on the seventh scale degree in measure 5 also illustrate a melodic practice now associated with blues singing. Although some similarity with Tucker's performance of "Some of These Days" is evident (the alternation of measures of non-syncopated eighth notes with syncopations), the range of syncopation, both in the tune and in Harris's inflection of the melody, is much greater.

A month before Harris's 1919 disc, the most famous African American band of the time, led by James Reese Europe, made its own recording of "Jazz Baby." Europe had just returned from service in World War I, where he had directed a regimental band. Upon his return he made a conscious decision to incorporate more jazz and blues influences into his work, which he accompanied with statements about the importance of African American music.[43] The vocal, by C. Creighton Thompson (who sings in a style very similar to that of Europe's main vocalist of the time, Noble Sissle), displays interesting divergences from Harris's (see musical example 6). Overall, Thompson creates syncopation more through rhythmic displacement than through the micro-rhythmic inflections favored by Harris. In terms of pitch, Thompson adds a turn around the syllable "jazz" in "jazz-in'" and a glissando on the word "jazz" in the first measure—both calling attention to the word "jazz," and both devices that would become popular among vocalists in the 1920s—but uses fewer blue note inflections than Harris. Overall, the Europe recording is at a significantly quicker tempo, meaning that Harris has more space for precise rhythmic articulation than Thompson; the slower tempo also allows Harris to develop a more nuanced persona in relation to the words. Harris appears to be enacting a "Jazz Baby" persona, while Thompson applies a popular vocal approach to the song without necessarily adapting to the character of the song.

The comparison of the Harris and Europe-Thompson recordings does not produce a clear sense in which the Europe-Creighton recording seems more "African American" than Harris's, either in contemporary terms or in the musical devices then associated with blues and jazz—genres which, in turn, clearly signified blackness in the U.S. social imaginary at the time. Although Europe made his recording one month before Harris, it is difficult to know if Harris heard Europe's recording and could have thus been influenced by it, or to what degree the arrangements (which are very similar) and vocal performances of both recordings were developed in response to the sheet music and the pitches of song pluggers. Thus, we lack markers that indicate whether one recording was building off the other, or if connotations of race played a significant role in marketing these recordings for different audiences. In fact, the music industry did not recognize an African American market for recordings at this time, which may account for the similarity of approach at this moment between black and white singers and arrangers.

Another possible example for exploring how African American musical difference might have signified during the period is the song "Everybody's Crazy 'Bout

MUSICAL EXAMPLE 5: Marion Harris, "Jazz Baby"

Note: x = syncopation through displacement; y = syncopation through polyrhythmic accent. Horizontal arrows indicate micro-rhythmic inflection.

MUSICAL EXAMPLE 6: C. Creighton Thompson / James Reese Europe, "Jazz Baby"

Note: Thompson's vocal has been transposed up a perfect fourth to allow for easier comparison with Harris's recording.

the Dog-Gone Blues but I'm Happy," which was recorded by Marion Harris and by the African American clarinet virtuoso Wilbur Sweatman. However, because Sweatman's is an instrumental recorded at a much quicker tempo, and a recording that referred to a different genre (the type of up-tempo novelty jazz popularized by the ODJB), it becomes more difficult to tease out which differences might have signaled different identificatory associations, as these differences are subsumed by the generic differences. A particularly striking feature of Sweatman's recording from a historical perspective is Sweatman's apparent improvisations over the tune from the latter half onward, using techniques heard clearly in his earlier "Down Home Rag" from 1916, which predated—as did many recordings of Europe's band—the first recordings of the ODJB, a significant point in light of the usual chronology of the jazz canon. How, and whether, Sweatman's recording signified musical blackness at the time is influenced by the fact that it was included in a category with other instrumental recordings in which the assumed audience was white. That is to say, such differences were not yet significant to the cultural gate-keepers of the music industry, for whom the recordings by African Americans based neither on minstrelsy nor on spirituals were of little interest, and thus recordings such as "Down Home Rag" could not be allied with a category representing black musicians and consumers. The significance of the musical tropes of blackness circulating at the time differed from the significance that would arise with the formation of race music in the next decade because the assemblage of musical sounds, demographic associations, et cetera into an institutionalized category such as race music were to assume the legibility of a category across demographic divisions.

Nevertheless, musicians and audiences did make distinctions based on race, and no white musician of the era seems to have earned the respect of black musicians more than Harris.[44] The respect came evidently not only from her ability to distance herself musically from other white vaudeville performers of the time, but also from her championing of African American songwriters.[45] The story may be apocryphal, but legend has it that Harris left Victor for Columbia because Victor refused to let her record what was destined to be the first vocal version of Handy's "St. Louis Blues" in 1920. Oddly enough, Harris's performance in the twelve-bar "A" sections of her Columbia recording of "St. Louis Blues" seems restrained and somewhat stiff compared to some of her earlier recordings such as "Jazz Baby." However, she increases her intensity during the famous Habanera-inflected "B" section, and lets loose an inspired whoop at the end of the first phrase of the second "A" section (at ca. 2:22). The accompaniment, which also seems quite genteel during the opening "A" sections, becomes more animated after the middle sections, with many ragtime-based fills and flourishes, and even some gutbucket flutter tonguing toward the end. The recording of this song, while it may have been read as an intervention in the struggle for civil rights, did not therefore intervene significantly in the performance practice or racial connotations of the blues.

Attempts to construct Harris as a representative of musical whiteness, or as a foil to African American musicians of the period, are further complicated by the fact that Marion Harris had already achieved a kind of honorary black status. Her singing struck African American commentators as a passable facsimile of the style that they were accustomed to. What contrasts might be extracted between Harris and Europe-Thompson and Sweatman suggest that an African American approach to musical performance distinct from a performer like Harris remained at this point outside the realm of commercial recording. By the mid-1920s, these contrasts became more obvious, as can be observed by comparing the opening of Harris's "St. Louis Blues" with Bessie Smith's canonical version recorded five years later. Harris's recording now sounds rhythmically and melodically stiff next to Smith, who employs a much wider range of pitch bending and other inflections (particularly notable in her approach to the third scale degree) and a more flexible and supple rhythmic sense. Did this difference signify some sort of absolute difference between perceptions of an African American singing the blues and a white person influenced by African American music singing the blues? Or did it reflect how notions of what constituted African American singing had changed between 1920 and 1925? It is possible that what struck listeners as a strong rendering of African American vocal style in a mainstream forum in 1920 (as produced in Harris's recordings) had already begun to seem outmoded by 1925, after the public had had five years to become accustomed to recordings by African American women.

Enter Mamie Smith

What should be clear from the discussion of Tucker and Harris is that the idea of a (white) woman singing songs identified as blues, jazz, or ragtime had been well established by 1920. As the examples of C. Creighton Thompson and Noble Sissle (the main singer for Europe's band) indicate, a precedent also existed for recording African Americans singing non-minstrel and non-spiritual material, although the practice was still rare. The novelty of Mamie Smith's recording of "Crazy Blues" derived from an *African American* woman singing a blues on record. In other words, the overwhelmingly vast majority of vocal music recorded by African Americans prior to Smith's OKeh recordings was either very dignified and not officially presumed to be entertainment (spirituals), or music that treated black people like buffoons (coon songs). Even Europe-Thompson's "Jazz Baby" was clearly a novelty number.[46] None of these genres provided a context in which African Americans could express interiority, emotions associated with human relationships, or responses to particular social situations that might be taken seriously. African Americans on record possessed either timeless dignity or ephemeral silliness and debauchery, but little in between.

Mamie Smith's first two recordings in February 1920 of two Perry Bradford compositions, "That Thing Called Love" and "You Can't Keep a Good Man Down," would have been unlikely to strike listeners as particularly innovative or controversial if they had not known the racial identity of the singer. Accompanied by what Bradford later called Fred Hager's "ofay orchestra," these compositions are very much in the mode of other popular jazzy material of the time, with some polite chromaticism and a few blue thirds.[47] The orchestra does indeed sound similar to those heard on Harris's Victor recordings, and Smith sings in a style not radically different from Harris.

That "Crazy Blues" presented a significant departure from these was evident from the first notes of the introduction. The raucous polyphony of the all–African American band was something new, far wilder than anything produced by the likes of the ODJB or even Sweatman's jazz recordings, for that matter, the relaxed sense of rhythm lending some credibility to Bradford's reminiscences of the band members' partying that preceded the recording session.[48] The song is set in a key

MUSICAL EXAMPLE 7. Mamie Smith, Climactic Phrase of "Crazy Blues"

that pushes Smith's voice into a higher register than the songs from her previous recording session, resulting in some raspy timbres at moments of melodic climax that are strikingly different from her previous recordings. Particularly notable are passages such as those occurring at 1:33 and 2:58 (see musical example 7). Smith combines many melodic and timbral devices and techniques to produce figures in this passage that would become blues clichés for many blues singers to follow (and that were already clichés for blues and jazz instrumentalists). Based largely around the major pentatonic in F, Smith enriches this with the use of the blue seventh in measure 1, and blue thirds in measures 2 and 4. Range and vocal color play a large role in the effect of this passage, as she pushes her chest voice up to a high F, and then produces a descending figure with a blue seventh and melisma on the blue third in the second measure to produce a melodic figure that, when combined with a raspy timbre, would come to be identified as archetypically African American with its reiteration by numerous other blues and gospel performers (and which probably already resonated with connotations of African American identity). Smith's vocal delivery also results from entrainment (grooving, or feeling a common pulse strengthened by numerous minute anticipations and delays with the beat) with the band, participating in a feedback loop that echoes and helps to generate the rhythmic relaxation of the instrumentalists.

A point of further interest is the extent to which this passage may have been improvised; a comparison with the same measures in the sheet music reveals very few points of melodic resemblance (musical example 8). Did Smith improvise this passage out of floating melodic tropes to fashion the striking climax of the song? The presence of Perry Bradford as the de facto producer and arranger of the recording session, which was preceded by extensive rehearsal of Bradford with Smith, raises the possibility that Smith's performance decisions may have resulted from collaboration with Bradford. At any rate, it is clear that Smith's performance habits significantly reshaped the melody of the song, giving her a role in the authorship of the recording (if not actual credit for the songwriting or access to the royalties) and injecting vernacular musical practices into—what is on paper—a fairly typical Tin Pan Alley blues. Smith's vocal line also added considerable interest to what is otherwise a composite of pentatonically based melodic ideas that lacked a strong identity on their own.

MUSICAL EXAMPLE 8. Comparison of Mamie Smith's Recording of the Melodic Climax of "Crazy Blues" with Published Sheet Music

The connection to what we now consider to be the blues is also interesting. The song reveals its indebtedness to ragtime form, with a complex multi-thematic structure consisting of four discrete sections (see table 3). One of these strains is twelve bars long with the harmonic movement associated with the blues; the variation of this strain (B' at 1:50 and 2:16) includes a striking unison passage between band and singer during the first two measures. This kind of complex embedding of blues form within a song titled the blues was, as we have already seen, a common procedure in commercially published blues dating back as far as Maggio and Handy, and includes the previously discussed "St. Louis Blues."

The lyrics of "Crazy Blues" are for the most part a collection of clichés associated with the blues, but a striking pair of lines occurs at the high point of the final refrain, beginning at the melodic climax at 2:58 paralleling the passage noted in musical examples 7 and 8. When Bradford penned the lines "I'm gonna do like the Chinaman go and get some hop / get myself a gun, and shoot myself a cop," he wasn't mimicking blues clichés, but rather associating his hoped-to-be hit with another popular genre: songs about Chinamen who smoked hop and then committed random acts of violence.[49] These lines lend themselves to many possible interpretations. If Bradford were a solitary artist, cut off from the mainstream of popular music, we could even view this as a precursor of gangsta rap.[50] It is true that the idea of the bad-man character was already well established among African American storytellers and songsters, as in the Staggerlee song and tale, but the connection with the numerous songs about Chinatowns and Chinamen from the

TABLE 3 Form of "Crazy Blues"

Section	Intro	A (aba')	B	C	B'	B'	C	Coda
Measures	4	16 (8+4+4)	12	16	12	12	16	1+
Timing	0:00–0:10	0:10–0:47	0:47–1:14	1:14–1:50	1:50–2:16	2:16–2:41	2:42–3:14	3:14–3:18
Other Features of Interest	introduces raucous, carnivalesque atmosphere	complex internal form; contrasting minor section	blues form	begins with "Now I've Got the Crazy Blues"; features climax at 1:33	blues with striking unison passage at beginning	repeat of last section with new words	similar to previous C section; second climax at 2:58	rubato

period is too strong to ignore.[51] Bradford was nothing if not a commercial musi-cian, albeit one working in a specifically African American milieu.

Following the success of "Crazy Blues," now the shoe was on the other foot, so to speak, and Mamie Smith's recording influenced not only numerous African American women to sing the classic blues (even as Smith simultaneously opened the door for these women to record), but also influenced the approach of white singers such as Sophie Tucker, who, as already mentioned, had been recording African American–associated material for more than ten years. By 1922 Tucker was recording for OKeh, the same company producing Smith's records (and one of the leaders in the development of race records), and her "High Brown Blues" from that year presents a prime example of Smith's influence. Sung from the male per-spective, the song's persona laments his treatment at the hands of the song's name-sake, and shows Tucker adding stylistic traits that accord with contemporary con-ceptions of the blues.

Mamie Smith's "Crazy Blues" shifted the playing field in terms of how the blues would be understood. I have earlier indicated the subtle nature of what was inno-vative about this recording in terms of the social identities of the performers and the elements of its musical styles. It is worth pausing for a moment to consider this recording within the sonic and discursive field of popular music circa 1920.

WHAT'S IN A NAME? THE COALESCENCE OF RACE MUSIC

African American Popular Music Before Race Music

This extended discussion of the genealogy of jazz and blues and the examination of how these ideas circulated in the popular music of the 1910s and early 1920s sets the stage for the emergence of the race music category. The recordings of George John-son, the Fisk Jubilee Singers, James Reese Europe, Wilbur Sweatman, and even Mamie Smith had not by themselves led the music industry to create an entire cat-egory dedicated to African Americans. Mamie Smith's recording, however, did rep-resent something new that would force the music industry to adjust its conceptual framework. Not only had the door been opened for African Americans to enact everyday situations and express their subjectivity in the lyrics of popular tunes, but "Crazy Blues" also revealed that a large audience of blacks and whites existed for recordings with these novel musical and lyrical dimensions. The newfound audibil-ity of music made by, and presumably for, a distinct race (notwithstanding the crossover success of "Crazy Blues") echoed the conditions already established for foreign music and Hawaiian music, suggesting the need for a new category.

Before black popular music had its own category, however, the music industry nevertheless did classify the scant number of African American–associated record-ings that were released into preexisting categories. A brief survey of these classificatory acts hints at widely held attitudes about the social position of these recordings. The most common genres of black popular music, blues and jazz, were inevitably placed prior to 1920 into either the vocal or dance categories (bearing in mind that these recordings were invariably performed by white artists, and that these categories represented the de facto mainstream). The same applied to the few recordings made by African Americans appearing in the lists of upcoming record releases, in which recordings such as those by James Reese Europe's band appeared in Pathé's "Dance" section. As for artists that now feature in the jazz canon, Columbia placed recordings by the ODJB in an August 15, 1917, ad in the category of "Dances—Greatest Ever!" Coon songs were so standard in the 1910s that they were routinely included in "Vocal Records" and "Novelty," or in other categories referring to comedy or humor.

As mentioned earlier, the two options for the representation of black identity on recordings before 1920 were either the alternately ridiculous or menacing buffoon found in the coon song, or the noble bearer of the folk tradition found in the spiritual. Spirituals, in fact, provided the only music industry category prior to the 1920s in which African American identity was explicitly recognized in the title of the category, and the only type of African American–associated music (unlike the coon song, or blues and jazz for that matter) produced exclusively by African Americans. For example, Columbia veered away from the coon song genre (if not the minstrel show in its entirety) in the October 15, 1917, issue of *Talking Machine World* by featuring categories for "Regular Old Negro 'Spirituals'" (featuring the Fisk University Jubilee Quartet) and "Old Negro Folk Songs" (recorded by Harry C. Browne, Henry Burr, and J. Malachy White).[52] The songs recorded in this category ranged from spirituals such as "Jordan Am a Hard Road to Travel" by Browne, to "Sing Me Love's Lullaby" by Burr, to "The Minstrel Boy" by White.

Discussions in the late 1910s and early 1920s of African American artists in *Talking Machine World* adopted a kind of language designed to obscure the racial identity of performers directed to white readers who might have been uneasy about buying a recording made by an African American, even as ads and articles still employed tropes about race and rhythm. For example, during the period in which Pathé enjoyed enormous success with the recordings of James Reese Europe, copy for an advertisement read (with the source of the quotation within the ad identified as that of "one of the boys of our office [who] went to war"):

> The French and British bands would play and one would say to himself, 'what beautiful music!' But when Europe's Band came along, no one, whatever his race, could keep still. There was that pep, that something of life and animation that made everybody want to do something.[53]

That "something" that "everybody wanted to do" was presumably left up to the imagination of the reader, although in this context it could have meant something like "go out and shoot a German."[54]

Ads such as those quoted above and categories such as "Old Negro Folk Songs" appear sui generis within the larger sweep of how categories were discussed and used by recording companies at this time, and more often than not, various types of African American–associated (be it by genre or by the identity of the artist) recordings were folded into other categories. None of these ways of labeling African American music, however, indicated that black people had a voice as (in the literal sense) performers or as customers. As I've been arguing, however, these recordings and the way in which they were understood by the music industry did create part of the context for the emergence of race records. The confluence of the blues craze, instrumental recordings by African American ensembles, and the scattered vocal recordings of spirituals, minstrel-based material, and the occasional novelty—all these set the stage for Perry Bradford's fateful visit to Fred Hager.

Yet the release of "Crazy Blues" did not automatically lead to the formation of a new category, even if it provided the impetus. "Crazy Blues" appeared in the list of upcoming record releases in *Talking Machine World* in the October 15, 1920, issue, described as a "Popular 'Blues' Song" ("blues" always appears in quotes in *Talking Machine World* during this period, suggesting that the use of it as a genre marker was not yet widely accepted). In a display of the importance of "Crazy Blues," OKeh took out a full-page advertisement with Smith pictured in profile, proclaiming her as a "singer of 'Blues'—the music of so new a flavor." OKeh continued to aggressively promote Smith while experimenting with different approaches. In the ad that appeared for Smith in the next issue of *Talking Machine World* (November 15, 1920), "Mr. Public Opinion" appears in blackface to deliver a pitch for "Crazy Blues" in dialect: "I's heard Blues, but I's telling you Mamie's beats 'em all."

The implications of this are difficult to reconstitute. Is the ad attempting to place "Crazy Blues" within the lineage of the minstrel show and coon song in order to disguise the novelty of an African American performer recording material that emanated from black vaudeville rather than the minstrel show—that is to say, a type of material directed toward a black rather than a white audience? Or is it based on the assumption that this is how people interested in this type of music addressed one another? Vestiges of blackface imagery continued to appear in both advertisements and the song lyrics of nascent race music (e.g., expressing nostalgic feelings about domestic life in the South) up through the mid-1920s.

While new recordings by Mamie Smith continued to be listed in *Talking Machine World's* "upcoming record releases" and promoted in advertisements, a sign in late 1920 that an awareness of this type of recording might be spreading can be glimpsed in an article titled "What the Talking Machine Has Done to Aid the Cause of Music in America." The author champions the cause of more refined demographic research while alluding to its difficulties: "It is difficult for us to allocate a distinct type of music to a certain section of the country. 'Blues' have a relatively larger sale in the South, but, aside from this, distribution is about equal in the various sections of the country."[55] This relatively newfound interest in geography was to influence previous notions of identity that had structured the music industry up to this time, as the 1920s progressed and the conception of identity-category relations expanded. The difficulties encountered in assigning a type of music to a type of people spurred greater efforts in demographic research, as revealed by the articles about foreign music from 1923 and 1924 in which retailers began tabulating information about specific consumer groups based on language, race, and precise location.

The appearance of competition to OKeh provided an even clearer sign that the value of this as-yet-unformed category was recognized than the musings of the previously cited article about the relation between place and taste. Other labels quickly caught on to the idea of a new category dedicated to black popular music, and Arto, Columbia, Emerson, Pathé, and Gennett all released blues recordings sung by African American women during 1921, with the recordings of Lucille Hegamin for Arto representing the fastest response to the success of "Crazy Blues." These iterations of musical gestures and lyrical tropes, articulated to particular identifications, began to summon the race category into being. Arto released two recordings by Hegamin that were listed in the February 15, 1921, issue of *Talking Machine World*: "The Jazz Me Blues," and "Everybody's Blues," which was described as a "fox-trot." However, Arto categorized Hegamin's next recording as a "Colored Vocal Record" in what amounted to the first attempt in *Talking Machine World* (March 15, 1921) to classify a recording made by an African American and aimed at African American listeners with its own identification-marked category. This recording, "Arkansas Blues" b/w "I'll Be Good but I'll Be Lonesome" was a huge hit, with the A-side rapidly covered by other African American artists, and eventually became the most successful blues recording of the year.[56] In terms of musical style, Hegamin's recordings resemble white vaudeville more closely than does a recording like "Crazy Blues."[57]

OKeh began producing a separate numerical series for their catalog (their 8000 series) in the summer of 1921 devoted to African American artists, paralleled by their production of a brochure describing releases of recordings by African Americans.[58] Yet the terminology in OKeh's brochures and catalogs was no more consistent than that used in the pages of *Talking Machine World*, borrowing Arto's practice of referring to these recordings as their "colored catalog." The term "race" did appear in music industry articles and advertisements directed toward an African American audience during this time, but these appearances serve more as examples of slippage in the use of the term than as consistent usages heralding a new musical category. As early as December 3, 1921, OKeh employed the term "race" in an ad for Mamie Smith in the African American newspaper, the *Chicago Defender*, proclaiming that "The Greatest Race Phonograph Star can be heard only on OKeh Records." From this context it is unclear whether this usage simply referred to Smith as a raced person or to a whole category for a type of music. Other references to African American artists by companies most active in recording classic blues, such as Paramount, followed OKeh's lead throughout 1922 and the first half of 1923, and clarify the usage of the term "race." "Race music," in other words, was not yet used as a categorical label; rather, music performed by African Americans is advertised as "music by great race musicians," with "race" referring to the identity of the performers.

The Stabilization of a Concept

In the labeling practice of the United States music industry, from the beginning of 1921 to the end of 1924 the usage of "race music" gradually gained in frequency until it reached a tipping point, picking up a growing cohort of record companies that were becoming aware of the audience for contemporary music performed by African Americans until the term became the default label for black popular music. In addition to advertisements, record company catalogs, and feature articles, the industry-wide search for a categorical label was waged in the "Upcoming Record Releases" section of *Talking Machine World*. Table 4 displays the genealogy of this category during the period from March 1921 to November 1924. This chart illustrates the uncertain hesitations as Arto and OKeh traded off in 1921, and a few companies joined in in 1922, only to be followed by a gap of six months in which no company used a distinctive categorical label to alert distributors to these recordings. Then, beginning in July 1923, OKeh seems to have hit on a label with the usage of "race records" (highlighted in bold type in table 4), although "race records" as a categorical label only stabilized in the November 15, 1923, issue, when three companies (OKeh, Pathé, and Aeolian) began to use it simultaneously. This pattern continued as more and more companies adopted "race records" from that point on through to the end of 1924, culminating when one of the two majors, Columbia, finally capitulated in November 1924. It thus appears that the idea of using "race music" as a categorical label really took hold between July and November 1923, with the ground being laid by the increasingly frequent use of "race" as a term to describe African American artists in the preceding three years.

Table 4 shows vividly how a category, uniting a type of music and an audience, is formed within the music industry while circulating within pertinent segments of the public. In this case, African Americans who enjoyed listening to recently created songs in a contemporary style were accorded the same status as the multitude of white racial categories (and Hawaiian music) that had been catered to since the early years of the twentieth century in the category of foreign music. This status was not granted without a struggle. The idea that music recorded by African Americans for African Americans might be commercially viable caught the industry by surprise, as this was a group that was not supposed to have the means (or perhaps the interest?) to participate as consumers in the industry. Also, it must be

TABLE 4 The Stabilization of "Race Music" in *Talking Machine World*

Date	Arto	OKeh	Black Swan	Globe	Pathé	Brunswick			
Mar. 15, 1921	Colored Vocal Records								
Apr. 15, 1921									
May 15, 1921	Colored Vocal Records								
June 15, 1921	Colored Vocal and Dance Records								
July 15, 1921	Vocal "Blues" Records								
Aug. 15, 1921									
Sept. 15, 1921	(1) Colored Vocal; (2) "Blues" Records								
Oct. 15, 1921									
Nov. 15, 1921									
Dec. 15, 1921									
Jan. 15, 1922		For the Colored Catalog							
Feb. 15, 1922									
Mar. 15, 1922									
Apr. 15, 1922									
May 15, 1922		For the Colored Catalog							
June 15, 1922									

(continued)

TABLE 4 *(continued)*

Date	Arto	OKeh	Black Swan	Globe	Pathé	Brunswick								
July 15, 1922														
Aug. 15, 1922		(1) Mamie Smith Records; (2) For the Colored Catalog	Blues	Instrumental "Blues" Records										
Sept. 15, 1922														
Oct. 15, 1922														
Nov. 15, 1922			Blues	Instrumental "Blues" Records										
Dec. 15, 1922			Blues Records											
Jan. 15, 1923														
Feb. 15, 1923														
Mar. 15, 1923														
Apr. 15, 1923														
May 15, 1923														
June 15, 1923														

Date	Arto	OKeh	Black Swan	Globe	Pathé	Brunswick	Aeolian/Vocalion	Emerson	Columbia	Regal		
July 15, 1923		(1) **Records by Race Artists;** (2) Special "Blues" Records			Negro Vocal							
Aug. 15, 1923						Records for the Colored Catalog	Vocalion **Race Bulletin:** (1) Vocal; (2) Dance					
Sept. 15, 1923												
Oct. 15, 1923					**Race Records**		Vocalion **Race Bulletin**-Vocal					
Nov. 15, 1923		**Race Records**			**Race Records**		**Race Records:** (1) Vocal; (2) Dance					
Dec. 15, 1923		**Race Records**					**Race Bulletin**	**Race Records**				
Jan. 15, 1924							Vocalion **Race Bulletin:** (1) Dance; (2) Vocal					
Feb. 15, 1924		**Race Records**			**Race Records**		**Race Records** (Dance)					
Mar. 15, 1924		**Race Records**			**Race Records**				April Negro Records			
Apr. 15, 1924		**Race Records**					**Race** (Vocal)		Negro Records			

(continued)

TABLE 4 *(continued)*

Date	Arto	OKeh	Black Swan	Ajax	Pathé	Brunswick	Aeolian/Vocalion	Emerson	Columbia	Regal	Banner	Domino
May 15, 1924		**Race Records**					**Race** (Dance)	**Race Records**		Vocal Blues Records	Vocal Blues Records	
June 15, 1924					**Race Records**		**Race**: (1) Dance; (2) Vocal		July Negro Records	Vocal Blues	Vocal Blues	
July 15, 1924		**Race Records**					(1) Dance-**Race**; (2) Vocal-Race		Negro Records			Vocal Blues Records
Aug. 15, 1924		**Race Records**					(1) **Race** (Vocal); (2) Dance - **Race**		Records by Colored Artists	Vocal Blues Records	Vocal Blues Records	
Sept. 15, 1924		**Race Records**			**Race Records**		**Race** (Dance/Vocal)	**Race** (in ad)				
Oct. 15, 1924							Vocal-**Race**					
Nov. 15, 1924		**Race Records**		Blues Records			**Race**-Vocal		**Race Records**	Vocal Blues Records	Vocal Blues Records	Vocal Blues Records

clarified that, almost from the beginning, African Americans as a separate demographic did not attract the attention of music industry gatekeepers. Rather, the success of singers in the early 1920s such as Mamie Smith, Ethel Waters, and Bessie Smith depended on their appeal to white consumers and thus represented an early form of crossover success.[59] The proliferation of companies using a distinct category for the music also reflects the vast increase in the number of recordings that might be classified as race records. At least part of the struggle revolved around the allocation of resources, as the creation of a category dedicated to African American–associated music meant that funds for production and promotion that would otherwise have been devoted to mainstream popular music were shifted to race records.

The search for a generic label that I've been describing recalls the proprietary conflicts described by Rick Altman in the film industry's process for arriving at genre names. Initially a company may seek to maintain a paternalistic control over a particular type of recording linked specifically with their company. However, the other companies have precisely the opposite goal, which is to remove the link between a popular category of music and a particular company. The relatively late arrival of Columbia and Victor (neither of which established a race catalog until July 1928) in establishing their own race records divisions confirmed their ability to ignore fine-tuning their categories, and indicated their position of power in the industry. The lack of concern of the two music industry powers asserted that they had no pressing need to find new audience niches to exploit.[60]

Not surprisingly, the discourse around race music expanded in mid-1923, when the labels began to recognize its importance through the use of a distinctive category, which also responded to an increase in the number of releases corresponding to this category. OKeh began using the term "race records" to clearly denote a musical category in advertisements in *Talking Machine World* in the April 15, 1923, issue ("A Complete Stock of OKeh Race Records—Always Awaiting Your Orders") and in the *Chicago Defender* in the issue for May 5, 1923. Their headlining phrase— "The World's Greatest Race Artists on the World's Greatest Race Records"—brings together the demographic description with the newly born categorical label.[61] The trope of homological relations between cultural production and race was already reassuringly familiar at this point. Thus, when the Aeolion Company initiated a new "list of race records," the accompanying article (appearing two months after the OKeh ad, in July 1923) acknowledged the following truism: "It has been recognized for some time that the negroes had their own favorites among artists of their own race and that records by such artists, particularly of 'blues,' had a much stronger appeal than similar records made by white singers." The article continued with advice for retailers that also invoked ideas about imaginary relations and crossover marketing when it added, almost as an afterthought, "Incidentally, the records are expected to appeal to a large portion of the white race."[62] OKeh, in turn, was happy to be the follower as well as the leader if it meant that it could call attention to the vast audience for this music, echoing the Aeolian ad the following month: "The growing tendency on the part of white people to hear their favorite 'blues' sung or played by famous colored 'blues' artists, added to the already immense demand by the colored race for such records, has made the Negro Record field more fertile than ever before."[63]

The recognition of the booming success of race records, and their surprising appeal across racial lines, appeared in a spate of articles, as retailers hoped to cash in, and music industry reporters observed the rapid increase in the number of race music divisions as record companies rushed to jump on the bandwagon.[64] At the same time, the race of the audience could be varied, while that of the performers remained fixed (as the OKeh ad quoted in the previous paragraph stated, these recordings were "sung or played by famous *colored* 'blues' artists"). The pride of Columbia, Bessie Smith, figured prominently in these discussions. Shortly after her first recording session in February 1923, Smith achieved rapid success of a sort that activated the crossover trope more than any previous race artist and destabilized the homological link between the race of the artist and that of the consumer. Already by the summer of 1923, her tours were attracting notice and contributing to a breakdown in audience boundaries. *Talking Machine World* reported favorably on a performance in Atlanta that Smith gave "exclusively for white people." In a concert with the title "Midnight Frolic," the event served a "double purpose": "an evening's entertainment and an opportunity for white people to see the progress made by the colored performers." Although the author of the article confided that such performers were already "an institution" in New Orleans, the white theatergoers in Atlanta had thus far lacked opportunities to experience them in such a setting.[65]

The emergence of race music, although often described with excitement in the music press, also received a less benign reception. More than a whiff of panic could be detected in many of the moral assessments of recordings falling into this new category. In a discussion that took many forms—most notably in the profusion of articles from the late 1910s and 1920s on the degeneracy of jazz—race records (including both blues and jazz) were believed to be the source of a range of mental and physical infirmities on the basis of irrefutable scientific proof. Writing in the pages of *Billboard* in early 1921, Anne Faulkner Oberndorfer bemoaned the vulgarization of spirituals that had resulted in the newfound popularity of blues and jazz. She maintained that the music was rooted in the practices of the "lowest type of Negro," those "who, half crazed by sensuality and beastiality [*sic*], sought to invoke the voodoo by means of a weird incantation of strange sounds and odd, unreal syncopated rhythms." These, she said, "were the originators of jazz in America." Oberndorfer averred that "scientific research has proven that the tones and accents of jazz produce an evil effect on the brain balance of the human being."

That the spiritual, one of the two forms of African American music prior to 1920 to be widely accepted, should be upheld as the noble ideal against which popular forms would suffer by comparison comes as little surprise. This point of view displayed remarkable longevity, and spirituals continued throughout the decade to be opposed to contemporary black popular music as the one "good" form of African American music.[66]

The formation of race records also contributed to ongoing discussions about technology, aesthetics, and domesticity. An article from the end of 1923 in *Talking Machine World* notes the rather astonishing interdependence of performer, sound reproduction technology, and recording company promotion, as this description of Mamie Smith's act makes clear:

> Miss Smith's act opens with a huge phonograph in the center of the stage, bearing a legend about Okeh records, for which Miss Smith is an exclusive artist. Miss Smith steps out of the phonograph and starts the act with several of the popular blues numbers that she has recorded for the Okeh library.[67]

In an extension of the phenomenon noted in chapter 2, in which the phonograph comes to stand in for earlier modes of domestic amateur performance, here the human performer is actively identified with the machine, the performer's aura now synchronized with mechanical reproduction, not only extending the phenomenon noted earlier but in effect reversing the use of the gramophone in the parlor as a substitute for a human performer. Now the human replaces the use of a machine in a riotous confusion of conceptual categories: of mimesis with originality, in the substitution of the original for the copy, and in the association of the performer with modernity to the point where it glories in the simulacrum. As also observed earlier in chapter 2, the sense of the realness of the live performance depended on the existence of recorded versions of the same songs, that is, the idea of a live performance could only now make sense in terms of a prior understanding of the absolute difference between recording and live performance. At the same time (as we will see in the next chapter), live performances were promoted in terms of their ability to reproduce recordings. If live performances relied on recordings, the same could not be said for recording companies and performers. Few events marked the lack of reciprocity between artist and recording company more than the cancellation of Mamie Smith's contract with OKeh during the period in which this tour was taking place.[68]

Race Music in the Chicago Defender

An examination of the *Chicago Defender*, the weekly publication with the largest circulation among African Americans during the 1920s, presents a rather different picture from that found in *Talking Machine World, Variety,* and *Billboard,* and helps us understand the role of the intended audience in the categorization of popular music. Most obviously, the sheer number of advertisements in the *Defender* for recordings made by African American artists relative to the other publications discussed here reveals the centrality of the assumed connection between artist and audience based on demographics. Some record companies, such as Paramount, which ceased listing in *Talking Machine World* before they began a race records division, advertised actively in the *Defender*—a necessity given that Paramount became OKeh's greatest competitor as the decade progressed, with Paramount artist Alberta Hunter counterpoised to OKeh's Mamie Smith in the competition for Queen of the Blues in the early 1920s.

In fact, a battle over who could claim the mantle of the first company with a race records division broke out between the two companies. By May 1923, other major companies, such as Columbia (the label of Bessie Smith), attempted to horn in on the success of OKeh and Paramount in a belated effort to compete.[69] Black Swan, the only African American–owned record company, also tried vigorously to match the efforts of OKeh and Paramount in the *Defender* by touting the racial solidarity of the company as a whole with the newspaper's readership:

> Only bonafide Racial Company making talking machine records.
> All stockholders are Colored, all artists are Colored, all employees are Colored.
> Only company using Racial Artists in recording *high class* song records. This
> company made the only Grand Opera Records ever made by Negroes. All others
> confine this end of their work to blues, rags, comedy numbers, etc.[70]

This advertisement also recalls the earlier discussion about a high-low divide within the world of African American music, with spirituals and Western art music on one side, and blues and jazz on the other. The attempt to appeal to consumers through an aesthetic discourse founded on cultural hierarchy stems from the raison d'être of Black Swan, which was based on the notion of cultural uplift.[71] This ad proved to be a swan song of sorts for Black Swan, as the company issued its last recordings in the summer of 1923.

Advertisements in the *Defender* also provide a more panoramic view of the emerging category of race music. Because of this, one can see a subtle shift in the wording of advertisements for singers such as Mamie Smith and Alberta Hunter when compared to two singers who burst onto the race records market in 1923. While Smith and Hunter were praised with terms like "fun" and "pep" (a frequent adjective in descriptions of early classic blues and jazz—recall the ad for James Reese Europe discussed earlier), Paramount's Ida Cox, the "Uncrowned Queen of the Blues," was touted for the "real feeling in her songs" and "her Blues whinin' voice," while Bessie Smith was lauded for her "moaning" voice that "drips feeling."[72] This rhetoric closely anticipated the early ad copy for the first appearance of what would later be recognized as a country blues artist. Paramount's announcement for Blind Lemon Jefferson's debut amplified the language used for Bessie

Smith and Ida Cox, promoting Jefferson's recording as "a real, old-fashioned Blues by a real, old-fashioned Blues singer. . . . With his singing, he strums his guitar in real southern style—makes it talk, in fact."[73] This rhetoric of "real feeling" and a sound rooted in the past ("old-fashioned") at the site of the music's origins ("real southern style") also referred to a slow shift in sound from the vaudeville blues of Mamie Smith and Alberta Hunter, with their quicker tempos, multi-thematic forms, more "legit" sound, and "pep"; through Bessie Smith and Ida Cox, with their slow tempos, heavier sound, increased use of bent and "blue" notes and twelve-bar forms; to Blind Lemon Jefferson, a self-accompanied street singer with unpredictable phrasing and a rough vocal tone that could only come from the soul of the folk. This stylistic spectrum was also understood as a mapping of class divisions within African American audiences, recalling the varied response to blues performers in the black vaudeville of the 1910s.[74]

"'Bama Bound Blues," the song touted in the *Defender* ad for Ida Cox, exemplifies the musical shift in classic blues from "Crazy Blues" that had occurred in only three years. Even a look at the first vocal chorus (musical example 9) reveals an approach that stands in stark contrast to both Harris-Thompson on the one hand, and Mamie Smith on the other. This is most clear in the element of rhythm and phrasing, with its almost complete avoidance of downbeat and on-beat accents (and the transcription does not begin to represent the large degree of microrhythmic inflection in the performance). The only on-beat accident also occurs on the downbeat (of measure 10), in which Cox delivers the musical punchline of the chorus with a scoop up to the fifth scale degree and one of most sustained pitches of the tune, emphasizing that her *man* is "'Bama Bound."

The contrast of "'Bama Bound Blues" with the earlier examples of blues occurs also in the element of pitch inflection, particularly evident here in the play with the third scale degree (previously noted in Bessie Smith's recording of "St. Louis Blues"), and with the fifth scale degree, evident in the third phrase, measure 10, making that measure stand out both rhythmically and melodically in contrast with the rest of the song. Cox's "'Bama Bound Blues" continues the melodic basis in the pentatonic scale also found in the passage of "Crazy Blues" discussed earlier (a basis not found in previous Tin Pan Alley Blues such as "Memphis Blues" or novelties such as "Jazz Baby") and further restricts the melodic background to focus on three pitches or pitch areas: B-flat, D-flat/D-natural, and F. In terms of its overall sound and texture, "'Bama Bound Blues" is worlds away from Mamie Smith's "Crazy Blues," and from the vaudeville basis of other early classic blues singers such as Hegamin and Alberta Hunter, in which the stripped-down sound of the solo piano accompaniment on Cox's recording presents a contrast to the full-band arrangements of popular dance and vocal tunes of the time.[75] The lyrics, too, show a shift in their representation of the South: they reference going "back to Alabama," but only because the singer's persona is following her man (a point that

MUSICAL EXAMPLE 9. Ida Cox, "'Bama Bound Blues"

Cox's performance ensures that we don't miss), not because the South is a prein-dustrial paradise, as in Marion Harris's "Paradise Blues." Compared to the multi-thematic forms of the Tin Pan Alley blues, "'Bama Bound Blues" sticks resolutely to a twelve-bar form throughout. The break from ragtime is also complete in the approach to syncopation.

By the time Blind Lemon Jefferson released his first recording, "Booster Blues," the recording featured in the Paramount advertisement discussed earlier, record-ings by singers such as Cox and Bessie Smith had introduced an approach to race records that now signifies as more down-home than the early classic blues. "Booster Blues" (musical example 10) is also based on the major pentatonic like "'Bama Bound Blues" and the passage of "Crazy Blues" transcribed in musical example 7. This restriction of pitch material (centered around three pitches in "'Bama Bound Blues," four pitches in "Booster Blues") and use of pendular thirds might have conjured up the idea of folk music and primitivism even as it shifted the emphasis to microtonal inflections in the melody that conveyed an increased sense of extemporaneity.[76] Jefferson's occasionally slurred diction (relative to the classic blues singers) also contributes to his rustic aura, although certain words and phrases emerge with clarity at moments of particular musical significance (especially the rhyming line "I just can't stay here long").

In terms of rhythm and phrasing, the transcription may make the melody of "Booster Blues" seem simpler and less syncopated than "'Bama Bound Blues," but the transcription does not capture the almost constant anticipation of the beat of most of the attacks notated on the beat. Exceptions to this occur in measures 6 and 10, where the attacks occur squarely on the beat, with an emphasis created in meas-ure 6 by the doubling of the vocal melody with bent guitar pitches an octave higher

MUSICAL EXAMPLE 10: Blind Lemon Jefferson, "Booster Blues"

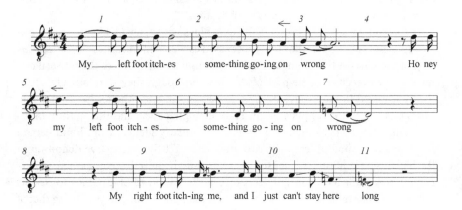

(is this how Jefferson makes his "guitar talk," as per the ad?). This rhythmic empha-sis again, as in the Smith and Cox examples, highlights the variability in the third scale degree. The larger rhythmic texture also has an impact in the perception of rhythm when comparing the Cox and Jefferson examples. Cox is accompanied by Lovie Austin on the piano, who plays with a steady pulse that in itself provides an intriguing cross between the then-recent African American musical past, in the form of ragtime, and African American piano styles yet to come. The steadiness of the piano's pulse throws Cox's rhythmic nuances into relief. Jefferson accompanies himself on the guitar, in a part that sounds semi-improvised and includes frequent shifts in texture and slight irregularities in meter and tempo, rendering the vocal melody's departure from the underlying pulse more ambiguous.

. . .

A male singer by the name of Papa Charlie Jackson released his first recordings in 1924. A perusal of the music industry discourse around race music in the early 1920s makes it clear that self-accompanied male blues singers were a novelty at this time, and that while male blues singers achieved more prominence beginning in 1926 with the emergence of Blind Lemon Jefferson, by the end of the decade women still dominated the field, with only Jefferson, Charlie Patton, and few oth-ers having established themselves. Paramount's copy for Papa Charlie Jackson suc-cinctly sums up what is at stake:

> Papa Charlie Jackson—the famous Blues-singing-Guitar-playing Man. Only man living who sings, self-accompanied for Blues records. . . . Be convinced that this man Charlie can sing and play the blues even better than a woman can. (*Chicago Defender*, August 23, 1924)

With each of the three sentences in the advertisement referencing Jackson's gender, it comes as a small surprise that blues was considered anything but a manly form of music at the time of the ad's publication.

A recording such as Jackson's "Salty Dog Blues" (1924) again, like the numerous examples of the Tin Pan Alley blues discussed earlier, demonstrates the capaciousness of the blues at that point in time, containing almost none of the musical elements now perceived to be part of the form (although they were already abundantly featured in recordings by Cox, Bessie Smith, and others). Jackson's banjo (not guitar, in this case) playing, his relaxed singing style, and the ragtime-influenced melody and harmonic progression are similarly a far cry from Blind Lemon Jefferson's recording of less than two years later. Yet the retroactive definition of the blues as a tradition has focused overwhelmingly on self-accompanied, guitar-playing male singers, from Jefferson to Charlie Patton to Skip James to Robert Johnson, whose mode of playing the blues is then understood as preceding that of the female artists who recorded before them, even though the move toward a more folk-oriented blues had already begun with the recordings of female artists such as Bessie Smith and Ida Cox (who further continued a trend away from the vaudeville paradigm begun by Marion Harris and Mamie Smith). Again, the virile tradition of folk blues triumphs over the commercially debased and technologically mediated form of the blues sung by women, which is then viewed as derivative of the music that it preceded. Celebrated early collections of late-1920s music such as Harry Smith's *Anthology of American Music* (originally issued in 1952) enshrine this version of history, installing an aesthetic preference in place of producing a cross section of the music that circulated the most during the period. Subsequent blues historians and directors of reissues of recordings reinforced this aesthetic predilection. The rise of blues-influenced rock music in the mid- to late 1960s further consolidated this vision of history, which has persisted to the present day, in which aesthetics, gender, and musical form intermingle.[77] It is thus hard to escape the conclusion that, as time moved forward in the 1920s, the site of the origin of the music called blues—and the music industry category called "race"—receded further into the past.

NOTES

1. Versions of this narrative may be found in the following (among many others): Robert M. W. Dixon and John Godrich, *Recording the Blues* (1970), reprinted in *Yonder Come the Blues: The Evolution of a Genre* (Cambridge: Cambridge University Press, 2001), 25–52; William Howland Kenney, *Recorded Music in American Life: The Phonograph and Popular Memory, 1890–1945* (New York and Oxford: Oxford University Press, 1999), 114–15; Perry Bradford, *Born with the Blues* (New York: Oak Publications, 1965), 114–29; Kyle Crichton, "Thar's Gold in Them Hillbillies," *Collier's*, April 30, 1938, 26–27, reprinted in David Brackett, ed., *The Pop, Rock, and Soul Reader: Histories and Debates* (New York and Oxford:

Oxford University Press, 2014), 28–32. For two accounts that complicate this story of origins, see Adam Gussow, "'Shoot Myself a Cop': Mamie Smith's 'Crazy Blues' as Social Text," *Callaloo* 25, no. 1 (2002): 8–44; and Karl Hagstrom Miller, *Segregating Sound: Inventing Folk and Pop Music in the Age of Jim Crow* (Durham, NC, and London: Duke University Press, 2010).

2. Although a recent surge of interest in these topics is addressing this lacuna. See Karl Hagstrom Miller, *Segregating Sound*; Richard Middleton, *Voicing the Popular: On the Subjects of Popular Music* (New York and London: Routledge, 2006), 37–90; Lynn Abbott and Doug Seroff, "'They Cert'ly Sound Good to Me': Sheet Music, Southern Vaudeville, and the Commercial Ascendancy of the Blues," *American Music* 14, no. 4 (Winter 1996): 402–54; Peter C. Muir, *Long Lost Blues: Popular Blues in America, 1850–1920* (Champaign: University of Illinois Press, 2010); and Susan McClary, "Thinking Blues," in *Conventional Wisdom: The Content of Musical Form* (Berkeley and Los Angeles: University of California Press, 2000), 32–62.

3. The entry of "blues" into public discourse is charted by Lynn Abbott and Doug Seroff in *Out of Sight: The Rise of African American Popular Music* (Jackson: University of Mississippi Press, 2002).

4. For examples of these stories of origins, see Alan Lomax, *Mister Jelly Roll: The Fortunes of Jelly Roll Morton, New Orleans Creole and "Inventor of Jazz"* (New York: Pantheon 1993); and W. C. Handy, *Father of the Blues: An Autobiography* (New York: Da Capo Books, 1969). Classic histories of the blues include Samuel B. Charters, *The Country Blues* (New York: Da Capo Press, 1975); Paul Oliver, *Blues Fell This Morning: Meaning in the Blues* (Cambridge: Cambridge University Press, 1990); and Robert Palmer, *Deep Blues* (New York: Viking Press, 1981). For scholarship focused on the classic blues, see Hazel Carby, "It Just Be's Dat Way Sometime: The Sexual Politics of Women's Blues," *Radical America* 20 (June–July 1986): 9–22; Daphne Duval Harrison, *Black Pearls: Blues Queens of the 1920s* (New Brunswick, NJ: Rutgers University Press, 1988); and Angela Y. Davis, *Blues Legacies and Black Feminism: Gertrude "Ma" Rainey, Bessie Smith, and Billie Holiday* (New York: Pantheon Books, 1998).

5. For critiques of this standard jazz history, see Scott DeVeaux, "Constructing the Jazz Tradition: Jazz Historiography," *Black American Literature Forum* 25, no. 3 (Autumn 1991): 525–60; and David Ake, *Jazz Cultures* (Berkeley and Los Angeles: University of California Press, 2002). For an essay that proposes alternatives to the standard narrative about the origins of jazz, see Jeffrey Taylor, "The Early Origins of Jazz," in *The Oxford Companion to Jazz,* ed. Bill Kirchner (New York: Oxford University Press, 2000), 39–52.

6. A collection such as *Keeping Time: Readings in Jazz History,* ed. Robert Walser (New York: Oxford University Press, 1999), by offering contemporary reportage about jazz, makes available a possible corrective to this tendency.

7. Andreas Huyssen has written about the connection between this historiographical move and other alignments between forms of "low" mass cultural production and woman; see his "Mass Culture as Woman: Modernism's Other," in *After the Great Divide: Modernism, Mass Culture, Postmodernism* (Bloomington: Indiana University Press, 1986), 44–64. A growing literature that analyzes the relationship between gender and jazz historiography includes the following: Sherry Tucker, "Big Ears: Listening for Gender in Jazz

Studies," *Current Musicology* 71–73 (Spring 2001–2): 375–408; Nicole T. Rustin and Sherrie Tucker, eds., *Big Ears: Listening for Gender in Jazz Studies* (Raleigh, NC: Duke University Press, 2008); Sherry Tucker, "Deconstructing the Jazz Tradition: The 'Subjectless' Subject of New Jazz Studies," *Jazz Research Journal* 2 (2005): 31–46; and David Ake, "Regendering Jazz: Ornette Coleman and the New York Scene in the Late 1950s," in *Jazz Cultures*, 62–81.

8. On this point, see Abbe Niles's introduction to *Blues: An Anthology*, ed. W. C. Handy (Bedford, MA: Applewood Books, 1926): "Of the songs in this section [on the blues] some, in spite of their titles, contain no 'blues' as the word was originally understood, but show musically a blue influence. Some use a blues as introduction or 'verse' but depart from type in the chorus; some reverse the process" (31). Peter C. Muir refers to songs that are "blues in name only" as "titular blues." Peter C. Muir, *Long Lost Blues*, 2.

9. For more background on "Chinese Blues" see Peter C. Muir, *Long Lost Blues*, 18. The song's combination of popularity and un-bluesiness prompted a bemused comment from Abbe Niles in *Blues: An Anthology*, 19.

10. The racial identity of this group is unclear. Tim Brooks includes this track in his anthology *Lost Sounds: Blacks and the Birth of the Recording Industry, 1891–1922* (Archeophone, 2005), but admits that he is uncertain whether the group was black or white. What is clear is that this was a transparent attempt to capitalize on the sensational success of the ODJB. See also Tim Brooks, *Lost Sounds: Blacks and the Birth of the Recording Industry, 1890–1919* (Urbana and Chicago: University of Illinois Press, 2004), 518.

11. W. C. Handy tells the story of the transformation of "Mr. Crump's Blues" to "Memphis Blues" in *Father of the Blues*, 93–102. See also Abbe Niles, "Introduction," in *Blues: An Anthology*, 13–14.

12. Lynn Abbott and Doug Seroff recount the history of the early publication of blues in "'They Cert'ly Sound Good to Me,'" 406–7. Notwithstanding the search for the first *published* blues, Handy claims that "Memphis Blues" was the first *recorded* blues. W. C. Handy, *Father of the Blues*, 99.

13. Lynn Abbott and Doug Seroff, *Ragged but Right: Black Traveling Shows, "Coon Songs," and the Dark Pathway to Blues and Jazz* (Jackson: University of Mississippi Press, 2007), 207.

14. For examples of this work, see also Eric Porter, *What Is This Thing Called Jazz? African American Musicians as Artists, Critics, and Activists* (Berkeley and Los Angeles: University of California Press, 2002), 20–26; and Karl Hagstrom Miller, *Segregating Sound*, 148–52, 254–57.

15. Abbe Niles, *Blues: An Anthology*, 31; W. C. Handy, *Father of the Blues*, 99. See also Lynn Abbott and Doug Seroff, "'They Cert'ly Sound Good to Me,'" 418.

16. W. C. Handy, *Father of the Blues*, 71–88.

17. Lynn Abbott and Doug Seroff, "'They Cert'ly Sound Good to Me,'" 406.

18. African American vaudeville and minstrelsy are detailed in Lynn Abbott and Doug Seroff, *Ragged but Right*.

19. Abbe Niles, *Blues: An Anthology*, 30.

20. W. C. Handy, *Father of the Blues*, 77.

21. Ibid., 76–77; Abbe Niles, *Blues: An Anthology*, 12. This passage is discussed in detail by Eric Porter, *What Is This Thing Called Jazz?*, 21.

22. See Karl Hagstrom Miller, *Segregating Sound*, especially 131–37, 249–53, for a discussion of how these ideas spread from minstrelsy through folklorists and the recording industry to become the "truth" of black music for, first, black and white inhabitants in the urban Northeast, and then, rather quickly, in the rural South as well. Ronald Radano argues that a conception of black music indelibly associated with hot rhythm also coalesced in the early decades of the twentieth century. Ronald Radano, *Lying Up a Nation: Race and Black Music* (Chicago: University Press of Chicago, 2003).

23. Handy had written in the late 1910s about the genesis of the blues prior to his collaboration with Niles in 1926, describing the blues as related to, or perhaps even the equivalent of, works songs and spirituals; in other words, his usage of the term provided no more musical consistency than did the published blues of the period. See W. C. Handy "The Blues," *Chicago Defender*, August 30, 1919; and W. C. Handy, "The Significance of the Blues," *The Freeman*, September 6, 1919, cited in Lynn Abbott and Doug Seroff, "'They Cert'ly Sound Good to Me,'" 423–24. And then there is the canonical moment of attributing this kind of vitality to slave songs in W. E. B. DuBois, *The Souls of Black Folks* (New York: Bantam Books, 1989).

24. The bibliography on this topic is huge, but for a sample of some of the most influential writings, see the following: Richard Alan Waterman, "African Influence on the Music of the Americas," in *Mother Wit from the Laughing Barrel: Readings in the Interpretation of Afro-American Folklore*, ed. Alan Dundes (Jackson: University Press of Mississippi, 1990), 81–94; Richard Alan Waterman, "Hot Rhythm in Negro Music," *Journal of the American Musicological Society* 1 (1948): 24–37; Olly Wilson, "The Significance of the Relationship Between Afro-American Music and West African Music," *Black Perspective in Music* 2 (Spring 1974): 3–22; Portia Maultsby, "Africanisms in African-American Music," in *Africanisms in American Culture*, ed. Joseph E. Holloway (Bloomington: Indiana University Press, 1990), 185–210; Samuel A. Floyd, *The Power of Black Music: Interpreting Its History from Africa to the United States* (New York: Oxford University Press, 1995).

25. W. C. Handy, *Father of the Blues*, 82; James Reese Europe as told to Grenville Vernon, "A Negro Explains 'Jazz,'" in *Keeping Time: Readings in Jazz History*, ed. Robert Walser (New York: Oxford University Press, 1999), 12 (first published in 1919); James Weldon Johnson, "Preface to *The Book of American Negro Poetry*," in *Voices from the Harlem Renaissance*, ed. Nathan Irvin Huggins (New York: Oxford University Press, 1995), 283 (first published in 1922). For a commentary of the rise of the rhythmic trope in the discourse around African American music, see Ronald Radano, *Lying Up a Nation*, 276.

26. W. C. Handy, *Father of the Blues*, 137–51.

27. See Eric Porter's summary of the debate as it occurred in the 1910s and 1920s and involved a host of figures associated with the Harlem Renaissance, such as Langston Hughes, James Weldon Johnson, Zora Neale Hurston, and Alain Locke, in Eric Porter, *What Is This Thing Called Jazz?*, 11–26.

28. Howard W. Odum, "Folk-Song and Folk-Poetry as Found in the Secular Songs of the Southern Negroes," *Journal of American Folk-Lore* 24, no. 93 (July–September 1911): 255–94. Subsequent citations will be made in the text followed by page numbers.

29. Karl Hagstrom Miller presents a detailed description of how folklorists shaped their collections according to their preconceptions about what constituted the music of the folk in *Segregating Sound*, 241–82.

30. Howard W. Odum, "Folk-Song and Folk-Poetry as Found in the Secular Songs of the Southern Negroes (Concluded)," *Journal of American Folk-Lore* 24, no. 94 (October–December 1911): 362–63. I am using the term "proto-blues" here as a reminder that neither Odum nor his informants used the term "blues" to refer to this music.

31. Charles Keil strongly disputes the notion of blues as folk music, instead hypothesizing that the blues arose primarily as an "urban phenomenon, . . . a white idea about blacks, and . . . most influential . . . as a recorded or mass-mediated form." Charles Keil, "People's Music Comparatively: Style and Stereotype, Class and Hegemony," in *Music Grooves: Essays and Dialogues,* ed. Charles Keil and Steven Feld (Chicago and London: University of Chicago Press, 1994), 200. On the history of "blues" as a term for a mood, see Peter C. Muir, *Long Lost Blues,* 80–103.

32. W. C. Handy, *Father of the Blues,* 143.

33. Lynn Abbott and Doug Seroff, "'They Cert'ly Sound Good to Me,'" 414–15. This modification of one's ambitions also clearly applies to Handy, who adapted his highbrow musical preferences to please audiences, black and white.

34. As I have been at pains to point out, however, by the mid-1920s an emphasis on cultural homology had obscured similarities in favor of differences. Embedded in a series of helpful hints on blues performance, these comments by Handy and Niles underscore how racial difference could produce a sense of musical alterity: "A note on blues at the piano: (1) they should be played slowly; (2) but in meticulous time; (3) for a while at least, the white man should play them exactly as written—that his subsequent improvements (if any) may be in character." Abbe Niles, *Blues: An Anthology,* 30–31.

35. Muir asserts that "Negro Blues" (aka "Nigger Blues"), the song that forms the basis for Cahill's recording of "Dallas Blues," is one of the few out of 456 (!) songs published with "blues" in the title between 1912 and 1921 that are based on a twelve-bar form throughout, and which rely so heavily on "floating verses." Peter C. Muir, *Long Lost Blues,* 38–39.

36. The idea of minstrelsy driven by a dynamic of disavowal and desire is adapted from Eric Lott, *Love and Theft: Blackface Minstrelsy and the American Working Class* (New York: Oxford University Press, 1993).

37. Tim Brooks discusses the career of George Johnson in *Lost Sounds,* 15–71.

38. Lisa Gitelman, *Scripts, Grooves and Writing Machines,* 133–37.

39. See Will Friedwald, "The First of the Red Hot Mamas," October 15, 2009, http://online.wsj.com/article/NA_WSJ_PUB:SB10001424052970203440104574400902110126532.html, accessed August 22, 2010. And see Susan Ecker and Lloyd Ecker for the some sixty-six different monikers she employed between 1906 and 1922 before settling on "The Last of the Red Hot Mamas" in 1923 (liner notes for *Sophie Tucker: Origins of the Red Hot Mama, 1910–1922* [Archeophone, 2009], 22–23).

40. Competing versions of this story exist; the most credible asserts that Tucker met Brooks some five months after recording "Some of These Days," during a courtesy call in which Brooks thanked Tucker for making the song a hit. Susan Ecker and Lloyd Ecker, liner notes for *Sophie Tucker,* 29–30. See also Tucker's own account in Sophie Tucker (in collaboration with Dorothy Giles), *Some of These Days: The Autobiography of Sophie Tucker* (Garden City, NY: Doubleday, Doran and Company, 1945), 114; and Armond Fields, *Sophie Tucker: First Lady of Show Business* (Jefferson, NC: McFarland, 2003).

41. This assertion of "subcultural capital" (a kind of slumming, or mockery of high culture and assertion of preference for blue melodies) could be a reference to blues as "colored folks' opera." See Lynn Abbott and Doug Seroff, "'They Cert'ly Sound Good to Me.'" The term "subcultural capital" comes from Sarah Thornton, who derived it from Pierre Bourdieu's "cultural capital," meaning a conjunction of economic class and educational training. See Sarah Thornton, *Club Cultures: Music, Media and Subcultural Capital* (Hanover, NH, and London: Wesleyan University Press, 1996); and Pierre Bourdieu, *Distinction: A Social Critique of the Judgement of Taste* (Cambridge, MA: Harvard University Press, 1984).

42. For a typology of ragtime syncopations in early jazz, see Brian Harker, "Louis Armstrong, Eccentric Dance, and the Evolution of Jazz on the Eve of Swing," *Journal of the American Musicological Society* 61, no. 1 (Spring 2008): 67–121.

43. Maurice Peress, *Dvořák to Duke Ellington* (New York: Oxford University Press, 2004). See also F. Reid Badger, *A Life in Ragtime: A Biography of James Reese Europe* (New York: Oxford University Press, 1995). For an example of Europe's statements about African American music, see the quotation from earlier in this chapter ("A Negro Explains 'Jazz'").

44. For example, see the following quote from Abbe Niles (and W. C. Handy): "As to the singing of the blues, it would seem necessary, first, to be a colored contralto—except for the fact that Marion Harris is white" (Abbe Niles, *Blues: An Anthology*, 31); and "Marion Harris . . . sang blues so well that people hearing her records sometimes thought that the singer was colored" (W. C. Handy, *Father of the Blues*, 199–200). Muir, for one, also notes the difference between Harris and other blues and ragtime recording artists of the 1910s (Peter C. Muir, *Long Lost Blues*, 96–97).

45. W. C. Handy, *Father of the Blues*, 199–200.

46. Although it is interesting to note that the Europe band's recorded repertoire showed other signs of moving beyond the coon song/minstrel/spiritual paradigm as well, with several songs alluding to the band's experience serving overseas in the military, as well as other novelty songs along the lines of "Jazz Baby" (such as "Jazzola").

47. Perry Bradford, *Born with the Blues*, 119.

48. Ibid., 125.

49. See Charles Hiroshi Garrett, *Struggling to Define a Nation: American Music and the Twentieth Century* (Berkeley and Los Angeles: University of California Press, 2008), 121–64, and the discussion of the use of Asian stereotypes in the popular music of the 1910s in chapter 2.

50. Adam Gussow has taken this approach, writing about "Crazy Blues" as a kind of protest song and as gangsta rap avant la lettre; the line "Shoot Myself a Cop" even forms part of the title of his *Callaloo* article. In contrast to my argument above, which emphasizes the intertextual relation with other popular music texts circulating at the time, Gussow relies on a more literal interpretation (Adam Gussow, "'Shoot Myself a Cop'"). Oddly enough, a Marion Harris recording, namely, "They Go Wild, Simply Wild Over Me" (1917), provides a stronger connection with a contemporary hip-hop persona than does "Crazy Blues," with lines such as "No matter where I'm at, all the fellows thin or fat / the small ones, the tall ones, I grab them off like that. . . . I meet so many funny men, no matter where I go / they're waitin' in a row / they seem to love me so." "They Go Wild" brings to mind nothing so much

as these lines from "My Humps" (2005) by the Black-Eyed Peas: "I drive these brothers crazy / I do it on the daily / they treat me really nicely / they buy me all these ices [diamonds]. . . . They say I'm really sexy / the boys they wanna sex me / they always standing next to me / always dancing next to me."

51. For the classic discussion of the history of Staggerlee, see Greil Marcus, *Mystery Train: Images of America in Rock 'n' Roll Music* (New York: Plume, 1990), 65–95; and for an analysis of the Staggerlee myth as an example of oral poetry/storytelling and toasting, see Roger Abrahams, *Deep Down in the Jungle: Negro Narrative Folklore from the Streets of Philadelphia* (Chicago: Aldine Publishing, 1970).

52. The racial identities of these performers are difficult to ascertain. Browne was probably African American (Tim Brooks describes him as a "minstrel man" in *Lost Sounds,* 168), while Burr and White were almost certainly white. Tim Brooks, *Lost Sounds,* 511.

53. Pathé ad, *Talking Machine World* (hereafter *TMW*), June 15, 1919, 81.

54. The ideas of "pep" and "that certain something" recur during this period to describe the exotic and ineffable in both race and old-time music, as will be seen in discussions later in this chapter and in chapter 4.

55. "What the Talking Machine Has Done to Aid the Cause of Music in America," *TMW*, December 15, 1920, 19.

56. Robert M. W. Dixon and John Godrich, *Recording the Blues,* 250–53.

57. Robert M. W. Dixon and John Godrich, in their overview of early blues recordings, contend that Hegamin's "The Jazz Me Blues" and "Everybody's Blues" "could be considered the first real blues disc" (*Recording the Blues,* 251).

58. Ibid., 257.

59. The African American–owned Black Swan record company provided an exception, in that initially the company did not overtly seek crossover success. Black Swan's exceptionalism in this regard will be discussed.

60. Rick Altman, *Film/Genre* (London: British Film Institute, 1999), 49–68. Perry Bradford comments on Columbia and Victor's lack of interest in race records because of their prestigious position in *Born with the Blues,* 115–16.

61. So noteworthy was the full-page ad in the *Defender* that the May 15, 1923, issue of *TMW* called attention to it with the following headline: "Unusual OKeh Publicity Drive: Well-Known Colored Record Artists Featured in New Advertising Campaign of General Phonograph Corp. of New York" (150). See also May 15, 1924: "Emerson Co. Adds 'Race' Records to Its Catalog" (106).

62. "Aeolian Co. Announces First List of Race Records," *TMW,* July 15, 1923, 137. An early article about Bessie Smith also discusses her popularity with white audiences: "Bessie Smith, Colored Blues Singer, Now Exclusive Columbia Record Artist," *Phonograph and Talking Machine Monthly,* January 16, 1924, 42.

63. *TMW,* August 15, 1923. Also interesting in this context are Perry Bradford's comments about the popularity of race music with white audiences in *Born with the Blues,* 117, 126.

64. See for example "Colored Singers and Players to Fame and Fortune by Discs," *Variety,* August 9, 1923, 3; "Race Record Album Offers Dealers Big Opportunity for Boosting Sales Volume," *TMW,* November 15, 1924, 94; and the ad for "Ajax: The Quality Race Record," *TMW,* March 15, 1925, 132.

65. "Bessie Smith Scores Success: Columbia Artist Appears in Atlanta Theatre—Novel Performance Attracts Attention," *TMW*, August 15, 1923, 116. See also "Bessie Smith Renews Contract: Popular Colored Singer Renews Columbia Exclusive Contract—Records Enjoying Wide and Steadily Increasing Popularity," *TMW*, January 15, 1924, 158. Michelle R. Scott examines Bessie Smith's popularity within the larger trajectory of U.S. and African American history in *Blues Empress in Black Chattanooga: Bessie Smith and the Emerging Urban South* (Urbana and Chicago: University of Illinois Press, 2008).

66. Anne Faulkner Oberndorfer, "The Sources of American Music," *Billboard*, February 5, 1921, 45, 93. For a later example, see "'Negro Spirituals' Are Classics, States Advertisement of Droop Music House: Advertisement Devoted Exclusively to 'Negro Spiritual' Recordings by Paul Robeson Gives Interesting Information on This Type of Music and the High Plane It Occupies," *TMW*, September 15, 1926, 28. For a sampling of statements about the morally degenerate nature of jazz in the 1910s and 1920s, see Robert Walser, ed., *Keeping Time*.

67. "Mamie Smith on Extensive Tour," *TMW*, December 15, 1923, 59.

68. Evidently Mamie Smith was not the only classic blues singer to step out of a piano. Kathy Ogren notes how Ma Rainey performed a similar routine in *The Jazz Revolution: Twenties America and the Meaning of Jazz* (New York: Oxford University Press, 1992), 101.

69. OKeh ad, *Chicago Defender*, May 5, 1923, 7; Paramount ad, *Chicago Defender*, June 16, 1923, 20; Columbia ad, *Chicago Defender*, May 26, 1923, 2. Paramount definitely acceded to the race music label by December 15, 1923, with an ad featured in boldface at the bottom of the page: "Paramount: The Popular Race Record" (12).

70. *Chicago Defender*, June 2, 1923, 7. Emphasis in original.

71. For more on Black Swan and their founding policy of cultural uplift, see David Suisman, *Selling Sounds: The Commercial Revolution in American Music* (Cambridge, MA: Harvard University Press, 2009), 204–39.

72. Ad for Ida Cox, *Chicago Defender*, August 4, 1923, 8; ad for Bessie Smith, *Chicago Defender*, June 30, 1923, 2.

73. *Chicago Defender*, April 3, 1926, 7.

74. For an eyewitness account of how notions of audience and aesthetics could affect musical practice among African American performers in the early 1920s, see Ethel Waters (with Charles Samuels), *His Eye Is on the Sparrow* (New York: Da Capo Press, 1992), 146–47. David Suisman discusses how Black Swan's emphasis on cultural uplift led them to reject "down-home" singers such as Bessie Smith in favor of the vaudeville stylings of Ethel Waters, Trixie Smith, and Isabelle Washington in *Selling Sounds*, 221–23.

75. The piano player on this recording was Lovie Austin, a female pianist celebrated in her own right, as even the ad copy and photo in the advertisement for "'Bama Bound Blues" makes plain. For more on Lovie Austin in the context of the history of jazz piano in the 1920s, see Jeffrey Taylor, "With Lovie and Lil: Rediscovering Two Chicago Pianists of the 1920s," in *Big Ears: Listening for Gender in Jazz Studies*, ed. Nicole T. Rustin and Sherrie Tucker (Durham, NC: Duke University Press, 2008), 48–63.

76. The Cox and Jefferson examples show the use of the "pendular thirds" described by Samuel Floyd Jr. in his discussion of continuities in African American music. Samuel Floyd Jr., "Ring Shout! Literary Studies, Historical Studies, and Black Music Inquiry," *Black Music Research Journal* 11, no. 2 (Fall 1991): 265–88; and Samuel A. Floyd, *The Power of Black Music*.

On African American music as a long-range historical discourse, see Guthrie Ramsey Jr., *Race Music: Black Cultures from Bebop to Hip-Hop* (Berkeley and Los Angeles: University of California Press, 2003).

77. *Anthology of American Music* (Folkways Records, 1952; reissued by Smithsonian Folkways Recordings in 1997). Other anthologies reflecting this historical preference include CD reissues such as *Race Records on OKeh/Paramount/Columbia*. Revisionist blues histories do exist; prominent among them is Elijah Wald, *Escaping the Delta: Robert Johnson and the Invention of the Blues* (New York: Amistad, 2004).

4

The Newness of Old-Time Music

Let us continue with another story of origins. In 1923, three years after the recording of "Crazy Blues," the recording industry falls into a slump, and a former assistant of Fred Hager's at OKeh, Ralph Peer, takes the lead in developing another category of music that targets a heretofore-neglected segment of the popular music audience. In search of Southern talent, black or white, Peer consults with an Atlanta furniture salesman named Polk Brockman, who has become OKeh's top distributor. Brockman alerts Peer to the popularity of "mountain music" among both city dwellers and recent transplants from the surrounding countryside, and is particularly impressed by the talents of Fiddlin' John Carson, a featured performer and prizewinner in Atlanta Interstate Fiddlers' Conventions. Peer and Brockman set up a makeshift studio in a vacant warehouse in Atlanta and record, among other things, Carson playing his fiddle and singing "The Little Old Log Cabin in the Lane" b/w "The Old Hen Cackled and the Rooster's Going to Crow" —performances filled with drones, heterophony, and a timbral approach to the voice and fiddle that would undoubtedly have sounded rough or rustic to urban, bourgeois listeners of the time. Peer can't believe his ears but presses five hundred copies to humor Brockman without giving the recording a serial number or a place in OKeh's catalog. Brockman sells out his copies of the recording instantly and Peer, more interested in commerce than in reconfirming his sense of taste, assigns Carson's recording a serial number in OKeh's popular series, presses more copies, and old-time or hillbilly music is on its way.[1]

The history and trajectory of music made largely by and for white people from rural areas in the southern United States is closely bound to that of race music. Like race music, this music—in the 1920s called by various publications "Mountain

Music," "Old-Time Tunes," "Special Records for Southern States," "Special Southern Records (Fiddling)," "Square Dance Records," "Hill Country Music," and "Familiar Tunes"—could boast a prehistory of sorts, with recordings made since the early years of the century that evoked the rural South but were directed toward an urban, bourgeois audience (the mainstream). One of these, Alma Gluck's "Carry Me Back to Old Virginny," was recorded in 1914 in the dominant popular style of the day, with singing influenced by legit (i.e., classical) technique, and was described by Joel Whitburn as "the fourth reported million-seller in history."[2] The early 1910s also featured efforts such as those by Charles Ross Taggart, who called himself the Old Country Fiddler, and who recorded two songs with Victor. The recordings, titled "Rural Monologue with Violin Specialty" and "Violin Mimicry," consist of comic skits using the violin as a prop.[3]

Preceding Peer's story of the miraculous birth of this category, an anomalous event in the history of music industry categories occurred with the release in 1917 by Columbia of "Old Zip Coon" b/w "Arkansas Traveler," described in *Talking Machine World*'s "Upcoming Record Releases" as "Violin Solo, piano acc. Don Richardson." Little biographical information is available about Richardson. His rendition of "Arkansas Traveler," however, was accompanied by piano (not an instrument typically found in string bands), and his tone is somewhat cleaner from a classical point of view than later recordings of the tune. If Richardson's tone is cleaner, his approach is not so distant from later country recordings so as to present a classicized arrangement adapted for middle-class audiences. Although exceptional with respect to the generic conventions of the time, Richardson's recording did not qualify as old-time music, as it was not made within the context of an ongoing industry-wide discourse that recognized this recording as part a distinct category of music separate from the mainstream. The same is true of the other welter of "comic derivatives and 'concert improvements' of folksong . . . [that] were available on cylinder or disc dating back to the 1890s."[4] As with early recordings of spirituals and coon songs by African Americans, these recordings were not enough to establish a separate category of popular music.

In a parallel between the early recording history of country music and the previous discussion of blues, jazz, and race music, historiographical orthodoxy of the last fifty years has somewhat obscured the struggle over terminology that accompanied the early years of country music. The profusion of names given in the second paragraph of this chapter indicates how agreement over an appropriate label for this music was far more problematic than that for race music. Particularly striking are the conflicting usages of the term "hillbilly" during the period, which histories of country music have often installed as the de facto term used by participants in this music during the 1920s.[5] This chapter will explore the struggle over the naming of this category, pausing along the way to analyze the history of important recordings such as "Arkansas Traveler" and "The Wreck of the Old 97" and artists such as Vernon Dalhart and Fiddlin' John Carson.

A FEW EARLY RECORDINGS AND A WELTER OF NAMES

The story of the emergence of early country music as a category (with many names) resembles that of race music. As with race music, country music was already marked by difference from the mainstream even as it lacked a conceptual term to mark its difference. A good example of this markedness is provided by what is often given the prize for first country music recording avant la lettre: Eck Robertson's recording session in 1922 of a set of fiddle tunes made both solo and in a duet with Henry Gilliland, which included another version of "Arkansas Traveler."[6] The contrast between Robertson's and Gilliland's "Arkansas Traveler" with Richardson's is stark. Richardson takes an extremely fast tempo, playing variations that become increasingly virtuosic, as if he were competing in a fiddling contest. The understated piano accompaniment only increases the prominence of the fiddle. In terms of the relationship of the two performances to "common-practice" tonal conventions, although Richardson makes some use of drones during the A section of the tune (thus emphasizing fiddling, rather than common practice, conventions), the piano provides stable functional-harmonic backing that is particularly clear in the B section when the melody ascends to a higher register and the drone ceases. Measures 6 and 8 even provide an example of contrary motion between the bass (played by the piano) and the melody, adding to the sense of "functional" tonal centricity (see musical example 11). The sound of the Robertson-Gilliland duet, on the other hand, is dominated by drones and heterophonically produced dissonance, which heighten the sense of modal tonality (see musical example 12). This would surely have struck the ears of mainstream listeners inculcated by vaudeville numbers, show tunes, and fox-trots played by dance orchestras such as Paul Whiteman's as bizarre (had they heard it), and far stranger than the race music being recorded and released at that time, the sound of which still bore a strong resemblance to the mainstream. Robertson's famed solo recording of "Sallie Gooden" comes from the same set of recording dates. This recording also highlights Robertson's tendency to create a harmonic context based on pentatonic modality, heightened in this case by the almost constant use of the A and E strings of the violin to create a drone.[7]

The position of these pre-1923 recordings is similar to that of the 1920 recordings of Mamie Smith, however, in that they were illegible within the categorical frames existing at the time, with a significant difference being that Smith's recordings were immediately popular enough to inspire company executives to attempt to capitalize on her success. Richardson's recording made (apparently) little

MUSICAL EXAMPLE 11. Don Richardson, "Arkansas Traveler" (0:03–0:35)

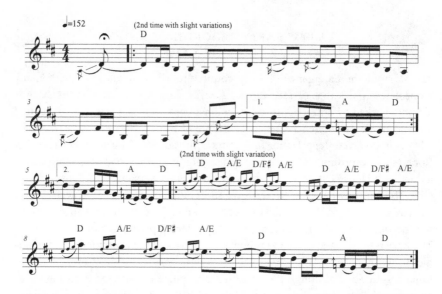

impression, Victor evidently considered Robertson's recording a one-off, and other artists recording during the rest of 1922, 1923, and the first half of 1924 who would later form part of the early history of country music were all assimilated into other dominant music industry categories. Robertson's recording lay dormant for almost a year before it was released in April 1923, at which time it was placed in the most mainstream and non-descriptive of categories—that of "Vocal and Instrumental Records."[8]

As already stated, the emergence of what would eventually be called old-time tunes (among other things) by mid-1924 was intertwined with the emergence and stabilization of race music. Up until 1923, race music had been largely an urban phenomenon, recorded by singers based in northern areas (or who performed as part of traveling vaudeville units) and sold largely to consumers in those same regions. As it became apparent that race music had staying power, the record companies who were most involved with it began to look outside urban areas for more talent. In addition to creating the model for a popular music category based on a formerly neglected segment of the (non-foreign) population, race records influenced the emergence of old-time music in another way as well: as mentioned in the opening of this chapter, the search for race artists in (what was assumed to be) their native habitat led indirectly to Fiddlin' John Carson's first recording session.

TABLE 5 Timeline of Early Country Recordings, 1923–24[10]

Date of Recording	Artist	Song Recorded at the Session	Recording Company
1. June 14, 1923	Fiddlin' John Carson	"Little Old Log Cabin in the Lane"	OKeh
2. December 10, 1923	Henry Whitter	"The Wreck of the Old Southern 97"	OKeh
3. March 7–8, 1924	Riley Puckett and Gid Tanner	"Little Old Log Cabin in the Lane"	Columbia
4. April 1924	George Reneau, the Blind Musician of the Smoky Mountains	"The Wreck of the Old Southern 97"	Vocalion
5. April 22, 1924	Samantha Bumgarner and Eva Davis	"Big-Eyed Rabbit"	Columbia
6. April 26, 1924	Ernest Thompson	"Wreck of the Old Southern 97"	Columbia

In contrast with, and perhaps because of, race music, "old-time music" spread more quickly from OKeh (again the innovator) to other companies. Race music and foreign music provided models for how to apply ideas about homology to the formation of musical categories—that is, to connect types of music to narrowly targeted segments of the population—leading to the relatively rapid acceptance of old-time music as an industry category even as imaginary identifications with these categories continued to proliferate. Before 1923 ended, OKeh made more recordings with Fiddlin' John Carson and also recorded a harmonica-playing guitarist-vocalist from Virginia named Henry Whitter. By April 1924, Columbia had recorded two duos, Riley Puckett and Gil Tanner, and (the first female country artists to record) Samantha Bumgarner and Eva Davis, as well as a solo artist, Ernest Thompson. Vocalion recorded Blind George Reneau from Tennessee and "Uncle Am" Stuart the same month (see table 5). Columbia was particularly active, mounting an assault (in relative terms) on OKeh's prior position of dominance.

In addition to the sudden burst of activity in March and April 1924, a notable feature of table 5 is that three of the six artists on this list recorded a disaster ballad, "The Wreck of the Old Southern 97," and, in a similar vein, Puckett and Tanner "covered" Carson's "Little Old Log Cabin in the Lane." "The Wreck of the Old 97" proved particularly influential, and will be discussed in more detail later in this chapter. For now, suffice to say that these recordings, with the possible exception of Reneau's, hail from the same sound world as Fiddlin' John's "Little Old Log Cabin in the Lane," making few concessions if any to the vocal tone and instrumental arrangements then prevalent among the popular dance bands and in studio recordings of leading vocalists. These artists, as the advertising copy made plain, sound as if they were plucked out of the backwoods of North Carolina,

TABLE 6 Significant Signposts for the Adoption of a Popular Music Genre Label Referring to Southern, Rural, White People as Found in *Talking Machine World*

Date	Recording Company	Label
July 15, 1924	Vocalion	Special Records for Southern States
August 15, 1924	Vocalion	Fiddling Records
	Columbia	Fiddle, Banjo and Guitar
	OKeh	Square Dance Records
September 15, 1924	Vocalion	Special Southern Records (Fiddling)
	Columbia	Old-Time Records
October 15, 1924	Vocalion	Southern Records
November 15, 1924	Vocalion	Southern Records—Vocal; "Fiddling"
	OKeh	Hill Country Music
January 15, 1925	Vocalion	Southern Vocal Record
	OKeh	Old-Time Tunes
	Columbia	Old Familiar Tunes

Georgia, or Tennessee, a sound forming an integral part of the alterity of the public image of the old-time artist as it began to circulate throughout North America.

The battle over naming the category unfolded in terms that were both rather low-key and inconclusive relative to what transpired with race music. Table 6 illustrates how Vocalion struck first with a distinctive category in *Talking Machine World*'s "Upcoming Record Releases" in the July 15, 1924, issue with "Special Records for Southern States." Columbia followed in the September 15, 1924, issue with a "Fiddle, Banjo and guitar" series, and in the same issue OKeh countered with "Square Dance Records."

By October 1924, Columbia had switched its labeling of this as-yet-undefined music to "Old-Time Records" while Vocalion had settled on "Southern Records." OKeh then began to oscillate between "Hill Country Records" (in their advertisements) and "Old-Time Tunes" (in the record releases).

In some respects, Columbia moved more quickly than OKeh to consolidate this category, as by November 1924 they had produced a catalog supplement titled *Familiar Tunes on Fiddle, Guitar, Banjo, Harmonica, and Accordion,* featuring musicians "whose names are best known where the square dance has not been supplanted by the fox-trot."[11] Columbia started its own numerical series for "Familiar Tunes" in January 1925, the 15000-D series, meant to parallel its 14000-D race series.[12] The activity at other companies in the months that followed attests to the growing importance and familiarity of "familiar tunes." OKeh produced a brochure in January 1925, the *"Old-Time Tune" Records* (which the company promoted as equivalent to its *Foreign Language Records* and *Race Records* special catalogs), and began its 45000 old-time series later in 1925.[13] Victor, the powerhouse in the world of commercial sound recording, jumped in with a splash in November 1924 with its "Olde Time Fiddlin' Tunes" series. In fact, it was a recording made for Victor by Vernon Dalhart of "The Wreck of the Old 97" b/w "The Prisoner's Song" in October 1924 that would create a national presence for old-time tunes, similar to that of the race music of the preceding few years, even if the relation between label and sound in early country music was unstable compared to that produced with race music.

That "Certain Something" of the South

In the introduction to this chapter I stated that historians have retroactively installed the term "hillbilly" at the origin of country music. Before "hillbilly" entered the music industry discourse of the era, however, an active conversation was already taking place around the music for which none could utter (or agree upon) the name. The discourse found in articles and advertisements ran almost in tandem with the process of naming found in the "upcoming record releases" section of *Talking Machine World*. Roughly coterminous with the first announcements of Fiddlin' John Carson's recording sessions came a newfound interest in farmers as a potential market. A concern with recording the farmers' consumption habits, musical preferences, and comfort level with technology revealed that rural dwellers as far north as Malone, New York, preferred "jigs, reels, and old-time songs," preferences that were noted with statistical precision.[14] The discovery of the potential of farmers as consumers paralleled a revitalized interest in the South and the recurrence of tropes in which the South was a repository of natural musical talent, warmth, conviviality, and illiteracy.

Many of these tropes occurred most clearly in descriptions of the old-time musicians' first visits to New York for recording sessions (despite Fiddlin' John's first session in Atlanta, it was far more common during the early days of country music recording for artists to come to studios in the city). In fact, it was nothing other than Fiddlin' John Carson's first visit to New York for his second recording session that prompted the first of these observations. Evidently, "there were several things that did not meet with his approval. There was too much city and not enough 'country' to suit his taste and he was glad to return to the sunny South."[15] Such a focus on the South as a paradise of innocence and the province of rubes and hicks continued with the sharp uptick in the number of country recordings in mid-1924 and the arrival of George Reneau from Tennessee in New York for his first sessions with Vocalion. Here, Reneau—billed as "George Reneau the Blind Musician of the Smoky Mountains"—did not express an urge to escape the bewildering metropole, but rather impressed observers with his finely tuned natural instincts, which were heightened by his blindness. During a tour of the usual tourist attractions, Reneau "at his own request was taken to the top of the Woolworth Building, where, though blind, he declared he could feel the sensation of height." At almost the same time, Columbia brought the first two female old-time musicians, Samantha Bumgarner and Eva Davis, to New York to record. Their visit revealed their demure sensibilities as well as their lack of worldliness, in that this visit "was a big event in their lives as well as a pleasant one for Columbia officials."[16]

Even when the rube-like qualities of country musicians did not merit notice on their own, their natural musicianship, springing from the warmth of their native environment, attracted attention. When OKeh announced the first recordings of Fiddlin' John Carson, they referred to him as a "Picturesque Southern Mountaineer" and remarked that he "sings the numbers in his own quaint way."[17] Quaintness and natural talent could at times merge with the novelty of blind musicianship and the prevalent stereotype at the time of Southern illiteracy. Ernest Thompson, who like Reneau was blind, began to record for Columbia in April 1924 and possessed a particularly appealing blend of disability and astonishing musicianship: a "unique character . . . he plays more than two dozen instruments and plays them well."[18] The same month featured a blurb for George Reneau. Like Thompson, Reneau made his living playing on street corners, and like Whitter and Thompson, he played guitar and harmonica at the same time. The praise for Reneau's musicianship was restrained compared to that for Thompson, but his authenticity was never in question, for when he sings "an occasional verse of the folk melodies of his native mountains, . . . [he] gives to those melodies a rendition that is characteristic."[19]

But this very naturalness also made it difficult to understand the music's appeal, especially when it seemed to attract listeners from outside the South. A growing awareness of the crossover appeal of the music was explained by recourse to the ineffable, clarified in this introduction to yet another artist who made his debut on Vocalion at this time, "Uncle Am" Stuart, of Morristown, Tennessee:

> Although this old fiddler cannot read music, he knows all the tunes associated with Southern barn dances "befo' th' wah," and can play them all. His records for Vocalion have that *inimitable touch* associated with the country fiddler of the type who glories in playing "The Arkansas Traveler" with variations.[20]

"Uncle Am" may not be blind, but he can neither read (music) nor pronounce English properly. He's a musical illiterate, which reinforces the sense that he, like Carson, Thompson, and Reneau, is abundantly blessed with natural talent.

The ineffable and broad appeal of hill country music was already evident in the recordings of Gid Tanner and Riley Puckett a month before "Uncle Am's" inimitable touch made itself felt: "No Southerner can hear them and go away without them. And it will take a pretty hard-shelled Yankee to leave them. The fact is that these records have got that '*something*' that everybody wants."[21] Ernest Thompson also had it, whatever "it" was: "In his recordings Mr. Thompson is specializing in old Southern songs, dances and ballads, with that *stirring something* on banjo and guitar that makes these instruments favorites."[22] The "stirring something," as is made clear by the rest of the article, was made all the more miraculous by Thompson's blindness. That "inimitable touch," that "certain something," that *je ne sais quoi*: the writers are struggling to find a vocabulary to communicate what this music is, how it sounds, why it appeals to people.

At times that undefinable something could cause startling effects in listeners, unleashing their inner primitive. A "well-known radio reviewer" wrote after hearing "Uncle Am" fiddle that it made him "feel reckless the rest of the evening." The ad claimed somewhat more modest effects for other listeners, reporting that his playing "makes 'em all pat their foot."[23] The recourse to "that certain something" as an explanation for the appeal of country music beyond an audience of rural Southerners speaks to the power of the homological model in the U.S. social imaginary of the time, inculcated through years of marketing foreign music and race music, as well as to the rise of what Karl Hagstrom Miller calls the folkloristic mode of authenticity. Despite the inconsistencies noted in earlier chapters, in which the fit between the identities of producer and consumer was not as tight as assumed, market research and advertising up to that time for marginal musics had been predicated on the belief of a one-to-one correspondence between musical and demographic categories. The porousness of the hillbilly's identity (a white Protestant, and thus part of the mainstream, but from a special region, and thus also marginal) spilled over into the reception of the music, to audiences who felt an affinity for it without identifying with the particularity of those producing it. At the same time, publicity for the music relied on conveying a sense of difference in the music's origins as a way of promoting its universality. The monotony of the recourse to the idea of "that certain something" in marketing for old-time music can be expressed in the following formula: marginal music + "that certain something" = mainstream audience.

Recalling the efflorescence of race music about a year earlier, the competition for the role of discoverer of old-time music began in earnest in the June 15, 1924, issue of *Talking Machine World,* an issue that represented a coming of age of sorts for country music. Both OKeh and Columbia placed ads boasting of their location at the origin of the music as a music industry category. Stressing the breadth of country music's appeal, OKeh linked the discovery of it with other, prior discoveries, without, however, spelling out what it was they had discovered in the past: "The craze for this 'Hill Country Music' has spread to thousands of communities north, east and west as well as in the south and the fame of these artists is ever increasing. And this again gives OKeh Dealers *another* new field discovered, originated and made possible by the manufacturers of OKeh Records."[24] The other new fields discovered and made possible by OKeh are not mentioned here, but surely the main referent would be race records, with the flurry of attention devoted to that field the previous summer still fresh on retailers' minds. Columbia's claims, by way of contrast, were more modest: "Columbia leads with records of old-fashioned southern songs and dances."[25] Even if they could not claim the thrill of discovery or access to the origin, they nonetheless were now the leaders (and, indeed, table 6 makes plain their effort in attempting to take the lead).

The two advertisements illustrate the different claims made by OKeh and Columbia, and the different rhetorical means used to substantiate these claims. The Columbia ad seeks to illustrate its leading position by overwhelming with sheer numbers: five musicians are pictured in this ad, as opposed to the two featured in OKeh's. The pictures also demonstrate the variety of their artists, from the wild lack of inhibition displayed by Gid Tanner, to the inner concentration of Riley Puckett, to the very proper yet rustic profiles of Samantha Bumgarner and Eva Davis, to the stoic, multi-instrumental virtuosity of Ernest Thompson. OKeh counters by emphasizing the thrill of discovery embodied by their label's innovative recording projects. In this ad, Carson plays the proper Southern gentleman, while Whitter's posture closely duplicates that of Thompson in the Columbia ad.

As the debate about which company had sired old-time music simmered and new ways of publicizing this music were tried, OKeh published a full-page ad for Fiddlin' John Carson that succinctly wove these threads together: "His OKeh records were the very *first of their kind* ever offered. And here are some other facts worth noting. . . . The most surprising and important part of it is, that many of these requests come from territories which ordinarily are supposed to have no market for 'Fiddlin' records."[26] This observation regarding the gap about the assumptions of a homological audience and how this music is giving rise to imaginary identifications reinforces the claim made by Columbia in the headline of the advertisement discussed earlier that the "Fiddle and guitar craze is sweeping northward!"[27] The months that followed consolidated the increase of interest in "fiddlin'" records (even as it claims paternity in this ad, OKeh can't seem to decide what to call the music) with the dedication of numerical series for the music by OKeh and Columbia. The launching of brochures by OKeh, Columbia, Victor, and Vocalion to further focus attention on this newfound group of recordings indicated that it seemed to require a separate category even as it resisted easy labeling and continued to appeal to mainstream audiences.

TWO RECORDINGS AND TWO ARTISTS
"The Prisoner's Song": Old Familiar Music

In retrospect, the difficulty in finding a name for the emergent category of rural, white, Southern music was curious, yet it is debatable whether this difficulty impeded its formation. The conditions of the category's iterability relied not on finding a single designation, but rather on a bundle of distinctive sonic, visual, and discursive resources that could be referred to by a variety of labels. Here again, however, as with blues, jazz, and race music, one must distinguish between presentist and historicist uses of the terms applied.[28] This is especially true of the term "hillbilly," which, as a retrospective designator for the category, bears its own story of miraculous origins. A young string band from Virginia led by Al Hopkins made a recording for OKeh in January 1925. When asked by Ralph Peer to provide a name for the group, Hopkins hesitated, seemingly stumped. Finally, Hopkins replied, "Call the band anything you want. We are nothing but a bunch of hillbillies from North Carolina and Virginia anyway." The six tracks made at the session later appeared credited to the "Hill Billies." And thus, so the story goes, hillbilly music was born.[29]

This anecdote undoubtedly participated in a general flow of discourse around old-time music and the music with which it was associated. A study of the circulation of the term "hillbilly," however, reveals a complicated tale about how this name came to be associated with the music that was eventually hailed as country. The term "hillbilly" appeared primarily during this time (the practice of Al Hopkins and his peers notwithstanding) in the guise of commentary by urban writers, usually in a quasi-sociological context as a way of explaining the music as a pathological phenomenon. This particular fascination with early country music was initiated in large part by the spectacular popularity of "The Prisoner's Song," a song recorded by Vernon Dalhart in August 1924.

By late 1925 the success of "The Prisoner's Song" was undeniable, and entertainment industry publications responded with incredulity and wonder before eventually conceding its role in the popular music field. The particular form of success helped further establish a pattern, already begun by foreign and race music, that would be repeated over and over again in subsequent years as marginal musics attracted mainstream consumers. Yet, in addition to citing a nascent crossover effect, at least part of the interest of "The Prisoner's Song" for journalists was its almost magical properties of attraction for consumers. Stupefied by the "weird funereal" qualities of the "The Prisoner's Song" and other disaster ballads that had become popular during the previous year (such as "The Wreck of the Old 97," the song that graced the other side of Dalhart's "The Prisoner's Song"), a writer for *Talking Machine World* speculated in December 1925 that the "simplified song form" of such recordings offered a contrast for listeners to the "over-arranged jazz offerings" and the "overproduction of songs of the fox-trot order." Not only their simplicity, but also the timeless appeal of such "sob songs of several generations ago" prompted the "revolt" of the public.[30] Nevertheless, at least this writer fared better in his quest for an explanation than Riley Barnes, a writer for *Liberty* magazine charged with writing an article on "The Prisoner's Song." Barnes also pondered the song's popularity, asking "Why in this sophisticated age, should we take to our hearts this melancholy ditty, which has none of the musical merit of even such super-sentimental ballads of the past . . . but which is as popular today as were any of them in their hour?" This question, however, refused to yield its secrets, and Barnes, apparently dumbfounded, could provide no answers.[31] That certain ineffable something that had animated the earliest old-time recordings appeared to perpetuate itself in a recording that confirmed once and for all the appeal of this music beyond the usual territories for fiddlin' records.

Other writers felt that the appeal of the "The Prisoner's Song," which appeared to provide an antidote to that which ailed the listening public, lay not only in its simplicity but in its timelessness, a quality shared with other recordings of its type. Indeed, the names given to country music also trade on the belief that the songs are old, that is, that their appeal transcends the transience of modern, "manufactured," commercial music. These are, after all, "old-familiar," or "old-time" tunes that conjure up the past in the present as a remedy to the fast pace of modernity and the contrived complexity of popular music. As we have already seen, advertisements in 1924 for Fiddlin' John Carson and other early country artists already relied on this idea, juxtaposing ideas about Southern-ness, crudeness, and quaintness and (not for the last time) announcing boldly that these were "genuine songs of the Southern mountaineers."[32] Almost a year later, a bulletin for Victor proclaimed that "these songs are more than things for passing amusement: they are chronicles of the time, by unlettered and never self-conscious chroniclers." By 1928, Columbia Records added to the praise of this unconsciously produced art, using rhetoric in their catalog that would remain more or less consistent in the promotion of country music up through the 1940s, promoting as it did notions that their recordings of "folk ballads and dance tunes . . . spring from the hearts of the people."[33] Here, or so it would seem, was an expertly crafted song that had sprung from the souls of the folk.

At other times, music industry publications contented themselves with chronicling the remarkable popularity of "The Prisoner's Song" in numerical terms. *Variety,* in an article titled "'Prisoner's Song' Gold Mine," called the song "an old-time ballad" and reported on its sales, which at that point totaled "590,000 copies of sheet music, [and] over 250,000 records on Victor." That the music industry still recognized sheet music sales as the most important barometer of popularity can be seen from the identification of the song in this article as belonging to the Shapiro-Bernstein music company, the song's publisher, rather than associating it with Vernon Dalhart, the singer of the most popular version. Only one month later, Elliot Shapiro himself (the Shapiro in Shapiro-Bernstein), in another *Variety* article, revised this estimate upward, stating, "It has gone 800,000 copies so far and over 1,000,000 in records" and estimating that "the song will reach 3,000,000 copies in total sales."[34]

Even if the music press valued sheet music more than recordings, record companies bent over backward to give special attention to Dalhart, who seemed to be single-handedly reviving the slumping fortunes of the industry. Regal Records in the January 15, 1926, issue of *Talking Machine World* presented a whole category in the "Upcoming Record Releases" section called "Vernon Dalhart Records," while

Dalhart's popularity prompted Edison to include a special listing of "Mountaineer and Rural Ballads" in their catalog.[35] Dalhart biographer Jack Palmer sums up this activity in terms that make the quantitative impact of "The Prisoner's Song" clear: "By the time the frenzy ended, Dalhart had recorded the song eighteen times for twelve different companies. It was ultimately issued on fifty-three labels in the United States."[36]

Observers at the time seemed split on whether "The Prisoner's Song" was in fact inaugurating a trend—a point of view shared in general by subsequent historians of country music—or a sui generis hit with special, ineffable qualities. Those taking the latter view emphasized how little effort had gone into producing and promoting the song, recalling the causal chain initiated by the *je-ne-sais-quoi* factor discussed previously. Early in 1926, *Variety* appeared to think that the recording was "starting the hilly-billy and old-fashioned song vogue" by virtue of its "being a natural." *Billboard* chimed in some eight months later, questioning not the song's naturalness, but rather its status as a trendsetter. In words that could well be used to explain the unexpected popularity of cultural artifacts in general, the article offered that "'The Prisoner's Song' was a natural hit. . . . It was not made popular thru any one person or group of orchestra leaders introducing it, but grew of its own accord." The article then concludes that the "Hill Billy song cycle" has faded much the same way as last year's fashions because "after hearing the number to its heart's content, the public had its fill of this type and wanted no more, hence the expected and hoped-for cycle died at its birth." Oversaturation of "The Prisoner's Song" had thus exhausted the public's desire for "this type" and it was now clearly time to move on, although the staff of *Billboard* and *Variety* quite patently did not seem to know toward what. *Billboard*'s dour forecast may have primarily reflected the publisher's point of view; the same article elaborates elsewhere that "Shapiro, Bernstein & Company, Inc., publishers of the prison number, managed to convert 'The Death of Floyd Collins' into a fairly good seller, but no other publisher produced anything of this type which resembled a near hit."[37]

Dalhart's Advantage

Vernon Dalhart had, in fact, been uniquely positioned to convert disaster ballads into popular hits, combining as he did the qualities of cultivated refinement and the rawness of the folk. Born in southeastern Texas and taking his professional name from two towns in the vicinity (Vernon and Dalhart), he trained as a classical singer in Dallas and made his way to New York in 1910 while in his mid-twenties. Opportunities to record proved elusive initially, but he managed to forge a career as a tenor in operettas. He made several attempts to impress Thomas Edison and earn a chance to record light classical repertoire for Edison's company, all of which failed. Then, on one auspicious day in 1916, fate smiled on Dalhart when he sang a coon song, "Can't Yo' Heah Me Callin' Caroline," into Edison's ear trumpet

(Edison was famously hard of hearing). Some ten years after the historical event, Dalhart recounted the experience for the writer Bob Dumm: "Time and again I sang opera into that horn while the old man listened, only to be turned away. Then one day I forgot all my high-falutin ideas of singing and going back to my Southern accent, and sang 'Can't Yo' Hear Me Callin', Caroline?' into his trumpet."[38] Thus did Dalhart throw off the yoke of over-refinement and return to his "true" self, voluntarily abandoning the cultural capital he had so painstakingly accumulated. Yet it was perhaps the failure (or inability) to divest himself of artifice that ultimately supplied the most providential stroke of all.

Over and over again, the Edison Company in their promotional literature returned to the idea of the naturalness of Dalhart's accent based on his Southern origins as a characteristic that set him apart from other interpreters of the coon song literature. Even as Jim Crow raged in the South, strenuously asserting absolute racial difference in the legal and social codes of the day, Dalhart (in interviews) and Edison (in the company's advertisements) sought to blur racial difference in the service of establishing Dalhart's authenticity. This mode of performance and accent was not something that Dalhart had to acquire artificially, and, not for the first or last time, proximity (be it imaginary, claimed, or lived) to African Americans was found to have its uses. As he put it himself:

> "Learn it?," he said. "I never had to learn it. When you are born and brought up in the South your only trouble is to talk any other way. All through my childhood that was almost the only talk I ever heard—because you know the sure 'nough Southerner talks almost like a negro, even when he's white.[39]

Two years later, Victor could promote him as "one of the best light tenors in America" and in the next breath attest to the naturalness of his performance of dialect songs, claiming that "There is no burlesquing in Mr. Dalhart's singing of negro songs. To quote his own words, he simply imagines he's 'back home' again and sings as the spirit and his experiences dictate."[40] In a later interview, Dalhart's portrayal of this delicate balancing act between refinement and authenticity would shift, leading him to downplay his training, thus creating another kind of authenticity-by-association narrative (in addition to the white-proximity-to-African American narrative) that has proven useful to the popular music industry ever since: "I've ridden horses all my life. I've punched cattle and I've picked bales and bales of cotton."[41]

In addition to the depth of his authenticity, Dalhart's training, even when disavowed, gave him an indisputable edge when it came to recording country material compared to other early country recording artists such as Fiddlin' John Carson and Henry Whitter. His vocal timbre and technique resembled that of other popular singers of the era, and his versatility honed by years of rapidly learning new repertoire for recordings meant that he could offer something different yet the same that would tickle the mainstream audience's appetite for novelty without confronting them with the unassimilable alterity of musicians such as Carson and Whitter.

"The Wreck of the Old 97": The Song of the South as Disaster Ballad

If histories of country music with a long teleological arc tend to credit Eck Robertson's recording sessions in June and July 1922 with having produced the first country music recordings, then historical accounts focusing on the formation of old-time music as an industry category tend to look elsewhere. The honor of initiating the institutional embrace of old-time music frequently falls to Fiddlin' John Carson, as is clear from the many anecdotes dating back to the late 1930s that refer to Carson's sessions in Atlanta with Ralph Peer and Polk Brockman as the origins of hillbilly music (such as the one recounted at the beginning of the chapter).[42] Carson's first recording, "The Little Old Log Cabin in the Lane" b/w "The Old Hen Cackled and the Rooster's Going to Crow" bears some similarity to Robertson's recordings of the previous year in the prominence given to the fiddle. An important difference is that the fiddle is used in these songs as accompaniment to vocal numbers rather than as the focal point of virtuosic instrumental numbers, as in Robertson's recordings. The tempi are therefore considerably more moderate, and the focus falls more squarely on Carson's voice, which is aptly described by Malone as "a style suggestive of rural hymn singing."[43]

OKeh evidently thought highly enough of Carson's commercial potential to bring him to New York some five months after his initial session in Atlanta, although, as we have seen, during this visit not everything was to Carson's liking.[44] He did manage to record eleven songs in November 1923, one of which was his take on a tune recorded by Robertson, "Sallie Gooden," which Carson called "Old Sallie Goodman." Carson again accompanies his own singing, although this time he uses more space to demonstrate the fiddling technique that won him numerous contests in and around the Atlanta area. Meanwhile, OKeh found another musician, Henry Whitter from Fries, Virginia, and decided to record him in December 1923.[45] One of the recordings made at that time—"The Wreck on the Old Southern 97"—was to play a major role in the formation of old-time music.

On "The Wreck on the Old Southern 97," Whitter sings and accompanies himself on guitar and harmonica, and even within the aesthetic context of old-time singing in the early 1920s, Whitter's singing seems to lack the subtlety and timbral variety of a singer like Fiddlin' John Carson.[46] That said, Whitter's performance was sufficient to disseminate this song in a particular stylistic modality that found a large enough audience to interest other recording companies and artists in recording it.

As the old-time category coalesced, Carson's rustic hymnody and Whitter's restricted nasality gave way to something more difficult to place. Very quickly, "old-time" vocal style meant to offer a vocal approach that was both trained and rustic, seamlessly blending artifice and authenticity. Blind George Reneau, the mountain man from Tennessee, was paired in his 1924 recordings with Gene Austin, later of "My Blue Heaven" fame, and now known to students of popular music for his innovative exploitation of the possibilities of the electric microphone in recording and for the development of the crooning vocal style a few years after his work with Reneau. Recording "The Wreck of the Old 97" four months after Whitter in April 1924, the Reneau-Austin duo demonstrate that this blend—what later writers have often viewed as a compromise of authentic Southern roots—already existed in a form that could be cited, or reiterated. When Dalhart made his second recording of the tune for Victor in August 1924 in the same session that yielded the biggest-selling version of "The Prisoner's Song" (originally the B-side of Dalhart's "The Wreck of the Old 97"), listeners could hear the song in the highest-fidelity sound available at the time, with the words perfectly enunciated and enriched by just the hint of a Texas drawl.

This particular old-time sound, polished yet raw enough, would dominate the public circulation of country music in the 1920s. For example, celebrated authentics such as Buell Kazee studied voice and music in college and majored in English literature, and Charlie Poole, a canonized folk artist, claimed that his biggest influence was the Jazz Singer himself, Al Jolson.[47] The notion that old-time singing should refer to the approach of Dalhart and Austin can be heard in other rustics such as Gid Tanner and His Skillet Lickers, who in their 1927 recording of the "The Wreck of the Old 97" cite aspects of Dalhart's recording, such as the vocal vibrato on sustained high notes as well as some train-whistle sound effects.

What can we glean from table 7? First of all, several elements held steady throughout the first five versions of the song, principally the instrumentation of harmonica and guitar, and the use of harmonica during the introduction and most of the instrumental interludes. All six versions use the same five verses that outline the song's tragic narrative. The first three versions all feature a guitarist playing the harmonica simultaneously. The first two versions, by Henry Whitter and George Reneau the Blind Musician from the Smoky Mountains (Gene Austin was uncredited), use the same formal scheme, with the minor change of one less harmonica chorus at the end of Reneau's. Ernest Thompson introduces the practice of alternating sung verses with instrumental choruses, a practice followed by subsequent versions with minor alterations. Finally, Dalhart's version introduces the idea of additional instrumental variety, with guitar solos in his Edison recording, and a whistling solo in the second.

The Skillet Lickers' recording is the outlier in many respects, and is included here to illustrate the long-reaching legacy of the stylistic identity achieved in the 1923 and 1924 recordings of "The Wreck of the Old 97." Their 1927 recording brought together many of the elements of the earlier recordings, following Thomp-

TABLE 7 Comparison of Different Recordings of "The Wreck of the Old 97"

Artist	Date (Record Company)	Instrumentation	Sound Effects	Form	Vocal Style	Other Musical Features
Henry Whitter	December 1923; released March 1924 (OKeh)	guitar, harmonica	none	AAA – harmonica AAAAA – vocal AAA – harmonica	baritone, rustic, lack of timbral variety	metrically irregular interludes; key of C
George Reneau, Gene Austin	April 1924 (Vocalion)	harmonica, guitar, harmonica accompaniment during singing	train whistle	AAA – harmonica AAAAA – vocal AA – harmonica	tenor range, clean diction, timbral variety, pop sound + country inflection	faster tempo than Whitter; key of F
Ernest Thompson	April 1924 (Columbia)	guitar, harmonica	none	alternates harmonica solos with sung verses	tenor range; rustic, but with more nuance than Whitter	key of E
Vernon Dalhart (version 1)	May 1924 (Edison)	guitar, harmonica	none	AA – harmonica AA – vocal A – guitar A – harmonica AA – vocal A – guitar A – harmonica A – vocal AA – harmonica	baritone; pop vocal tone with Southern inflections	slower tempo than other recordings, key of D, rhythm à la polka
Vernon Dalhart (version 2)	August 1924 (Victor)	guitar, harmonica, whistling	train whistle	AA – harmonica AA – vocal A – harmonica A – vocal A – whistling solo AA – vocal A – harmonica	similar to Edison recording	cleaner recording than Edison, even more careful enunciation

(continued)

TABLE 7 *(continued)*

Artist	Date (Record Company)	Instrumentation	Sound Effects	Form	Vocal Style	Other Musical Features
Gid Tanner and His Skillet Lickers	March 1927 (Columbia)	fiddle(s), banjo, multiple singers	train whistle and crash	brief intro – fiddle AA – vocal A – fiddle A – vocal A – fiddle A – vocal A – fiddle A – vocal	baritone, pop music influence in vocal, ends on high note	key of D, slower tempo, folkloric quality

son's formal alternation of vocal and instrumental, while introducing fiddle inter-ludes and a richer texture overall with banjo added to guitar and multiple vocalists replacing the solo vocal of previous versions. Reneau introduced the train-whistle effect that Dalhart added to his second recording with Victor, and which the Skil-let Lickers enhanced further with a crash sound effect introduced at a strategic moment in the song. Looking across the different versions, one notices a variety of keys, vocal ranges, and tempi. Overall, however, one can see how Dalhart's second (Victor) recording created a template by synthesizing several aspects of the earlier recordings. From Whitter came the idea of using the harmonica; from Reneau and Austin the train whistle effect and pop-influenced singing; and from Thompson the alternation of vocal and instrumental. Dalhart then further modified these elements by introducing a slower tempo and expanding the variety of instruments used. The Skillet Lickers retained Dalhart's synthesis and modifications, and intro-duced further textural and timbral variety.

This emphasis on continuity and gradual transformation is not to deny that a difference can be heard between Henry Whitter's recording and Vernon Dalhart's, but rather to show that the recordings in table 7 can be heard as citations of one another that, taken collectively, created a common frame of reference that acquired the label of old-time music. In terms of the polished-but-rough-enough vocal sound that came to dominate early country music, my argument is that no clear demarcation existed between pop singing and old-time singing during the 1920s. The two bled into one another and at the same time depended on one another for their meaning. The challenge is to develop a typology of the different modes of singing that together contributed to the formation of the old-time category. In other words, legit singing technique did not exist in a position exterior to the cat-egory, but rather was constitutive of it.

Dalhart vs. Carson

To take another example of how the process of slight but constant modifications of the sound of earlier recordings contributed to the emergence of the category, in early 1925 the record companies tried to capitalize on the success of "The Wreck of the Old 97" with a string of other disaster songs. "The Death of Floyd Collins" was written in 1925 and offered first to Fiddlin' John Carson and then to Vernon Dal-hart, both of whom recorded it.[48] Carson's approach differs little from that used on "Little Old Log Cabin in the Lane": he accompanies himself on the fiddle in a style marked by drones and implicit harmonic movement and function. His singing, as on his other recordings, resembles that of the Sacred Harp Singers recorded dur-ing the 1920s. Metrically, he suggests a compound meter of 6/8, but seems less assured than on the earlier recording as indicated by the variable meter of the transcription, which, while approximate, is an attempt to represent the metrical freedom of this performance (see musical example 13). Perhaps Carson found it

MUSICAL EXAMPLE 13. Fiddlin' John Carson, "The Death of Floyd Collins" (0:03–0:18)

MUSICAL EXAMPLE 14. Vernon Dalhart, "The Death of Floyd Collins" (0:24–0:37)

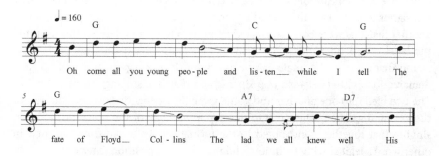

difficult to adapt to the practices and regimens of popular performance, which required the ability to learn newly written songs rather quickly. That said, Carson does establish a metrical pattern that he then follows throughout the recording: a measure that fits fairly easily into 6/8 is then followed by a shorter measure.

Dalhart, on the other hand, evidently encountered no such problems. Superbly adapted to popular performance practice, his recording seems almost jaunty next to Carson's and is clearly in 4/4 meter (see musical example 14). In contrast to Carson's fiddle drone and bare whiff of tonic-dominant movement at the cadences, Dalhart's recording clearly situates the tune within a common-practice tonal space, replete with dominants and applied dominants. Dalhart's renowned Southern accent comes and goes a bit, but was apparently convincing enough to continue his appeal to the core audience of old-time fans. It is the element of rhythm that reveals the starkest differences, especially as the rhythm is presented here in staff notation. The extreme simplicity of Dalhart's rhythm relative to Carson's may have had many sources, most notably the strong pulse projected by Dalhart's guitarist accompanist as opposed to Carson's self-accompaniment on the fiddle. But it is tempting to speculate on a reciprocal process deriving from the two musicians' very different training. Dalhart, with the ability to read Western staff notation, thus produced performances of old-time music that were extremely easy to notate. Carson, lacking experience in the musical gestures prescribed by notation, produced performances not readily assimilable to the even, arithmetic divisions of phrase and beat demanded by Western notation.

"The Death of Floyd Collins" also demonstrates that notions of popular song cycles and instrumental, melodic, and lyrical hooks were already firmly in place. Dalhart's recording reprises both the viola accompaniment that distinguished "The Prisoner's Song" and the harmonica accompaniment that figured prominently in most of the recordings of "The Wreck of the Old 97" made in 1923 and 1924, while Carson's recording seems likely to have been aimed at the same audiences who bought "Little Old Log Cabin in the Lane," reproducing the basic sound, texture, and affect of that earlier recording.[49]

Dalhart's advantage over Carson when it came to recording popular music had sources other than his vocal training and professional experience in a variety of genres. He also had the uncanny ability to sound like a gramophone, honed through years of participation in the Edison Tone Tests. The Edison Tone Tests were performances in which musicians would alternate renditions of a song with a recorded version of the same song. The idea was to impress upon the audience that the sound of the Edison recording was indistinguishable from the sound of the live performance (recall also the discussion from chapter 2 of an advertisement for Edison picturing an audience rapturously in thrall to the performance of the talking machine). Performers would practice emulating the sound of their own recordings in order to succeed in duplicating them, often beginning the song on stage, and then gradually reducing their volume in semidarkness while the gramophone's volume increased. The "real" performer would then leave the stage, and the audience would be stunned to discover when the lights came up that they had been listening to a talking machine rather than a singing human.

Of the artists who participated in the Tone Tests, Dalhart was among the most successful. Touring almost constantly for three or four years with a talking machine and accompanist, Dalhart traversed the United States promoting the high fidelity of Edison recordings. The similarity of the recording and live performance depended not only on a prior understanding of their absolute difference, and the idea that technology was mediating (and capable of mediating) human performers, but also on the validity of comparing the two practices. Audiences were convinced that listening to a gramophone was somehow equivalent to listening to a live performance, and the mediation of an "authentic" performance thus acquired its own authenticity. Little wonder, then, that when called upon, Dalhart could produce

FIGURE 4. Vernon Dalhart
Performing an Edison
Tone Test.

an old-time recording that sounded just the way such a recording *should* sound
(see figure 4).[50] From another perspective, Dalhart's success with the tone tests
relied on an aesthetic that anticipated its own mechanical reproducibility. In other
words, mechanical reproduction, in the form of sound recording, emerged in
response to performance styles such as Dalhart's, in which a performance appeared
as if it were already a mechanical reproduction of an earlier performance.[51]

"HILLBILLY": THE OTHER WITHIN

Although it is true that the music industry did not use the term "hillbilly" for a
category of music in the 1920s in catalogs, advertisements, or lists of upcoming
record releases, the earlier discussion of "The Prisoner's Song" clarifies that the
term did find its way into articles describing this music in the music industry press.
Most of the time it was used as a general descriptive term, synonymous with "old-

time," "old familiar," and any of the other labels that occurred in more official business forums. An early example of this usage of "hillbilly" appears in the title of a
December 15, 1925, *Talking Machine World* article: "What the Popularity of Hill-
Billy Songs Means in Retail Profit Possibilities: The Widespread Vogue of the Funereal Type of Songs Is Attested by Publishers and Record Manufacturers—Is It of
Significance as Indication of Public Taste?" As in this article, by far the most common usage in the pages of *Talking Machine World*, *Variety*, and *Billboard* during the
following year had to do with commenting on the "hill-billy" song vogue or, as
another article put it, "the craze for mountaineer music" (the term "hillbilly" was
invariably hyphenated at this point, and was occasionally ornamented with an
extra *y*, as in "hilly-billy"). Writers marveled at how this popularity occurred "without any exploitation," and wondered how such songs might be reproduced "professionally," although, as we have already seen, this process was well under way with
singers such as Vernon Dalhart and his songwriting, guitar-playing accomplice
Carson Robison. This vogue extended not only to "Southern mountain" territory
as might be expected, but into urban areas as well.[52]

By the end of 1926 it was time to reflect and take stock of the situation. In summarizing the year just concluded, a writer for *Variety* recognized the similarity
between "'race' records and the 'blues'" and "novelty records, hill-billy records,
standard and nationalistic numbers" as part of a "freak yen by the public."[53] Yet these
descriptive modes, relying as they did on the lighthearted use of negative terms
("craze" for "mountaineer music," "freak yens," and the term "hill-billy" itself), were
brought into focus by more overtly xenophobic comments in which the racial
thinking of the early twentieth century was applied to regional and urban-rural
distinctions. This racialized thinking in which Northern urban attitudes toward
Southern rural whites were explicitly articulated to the emergent category of early
country music appears most clearly in the writing of Abel Green, an editorialist for
Variety. In an oft-quoted article titled "Hill-billy Music" that appeared in the
December 29, 1926, issue of *Variety*, Green began with a description of the consumer of this music:

HILL-BILLY MUSIC. This particular branch of pop-song music is worthy of treatment on its own, being peculiar unto itself. The "hill-billy" is a North Carolina or
Tennessee and adjacent mountaineer type of illiterate white whose creed and allegiance are to the Bible, the Chautauqua and the phonograph.

The talking machine's relation to show business interests most. The mountaineer
is of "poor white trash" genera. The great majority, probably 95 percent, can neither
read nor write English. Theirs is a community all unto themselves.

Illiterate and ignorant, with the intelligence of morons, the sing-song, nasal-
twanging vocalizing of a Vernon Dalhart of a Carson Robison on the disks, reciting
the banal lyrics of a "Prisoner's Song" or "The Death of Floyd Collins" (biggest hillbilly song-hit to date), intrigues their interest.

Green, however, observed that the recording industry was able to recuperate the deficiencies of the hill-billy for its own gain. These "ignoramuses" inadvertently created "a bonanza" for dealers, in that they would buy "as many as 15 records at one time of a single number." This was necessary, in that the hill-billy tended not to come down from his "mountain perch" for weeks at a time, and would wear out his favorite records, hence needing multiple copies.

The hill-billy's fanatical behavior did have its drawbacks: "In Knoxville is a local edict that no hill-billy song can be played in a phonograph store within earshot of the market-place. It has been found that as soon as a hill-billy hit is turned loose, the market merchants lose their prospects. It attracts the natives to the source of the music like flypaper." But said merchants had discovered a way to deal with the problem of these insect-like nuisances: "The surest chaser is the turning on of a regular popular song record. That's the cue to the h.-b.'s that they're no longer welcome and they disperse with alacrity."[54] Despite assuming the rhetorical stance of an expert, Green failed to distinguish between professional, New York–based performers such as Dalhart and Robison and the "h.-b.'s" described in his article. He also seemed unaware of or uninterested in the evidence that had been published in his magazine and other music industry publications about the diversity of musical interests among listeners in the rural South and the appeal of old-time music across demographic boundaries.

Green was fond of these anecdotes and repeated them several times over the next couple of years; he was particularly enthralled by the number of copies of a single recording that hillbillies purchased in a single shopping trip. Whether describing the growing preference among mountaineers for homegrown singers rather than citified counterfeits, thereby illustrating their newfound ability to distinguish the authentic from the copy, or explaining the advent of radio programs catering to rural, Southern folk, Green continued to return to the apparently attention-grabbing activity of buying "six to fifteen disks" at a time of the same song.[55]

Were Green's views unique? Green assumed editorship of *Variety* less than five years after writing "Hill-billy Music," a development that could attest to the congruity between his views and those of the magazine.[56] Furthermore, that *Variety* saw fit to publish Green's thoughts on the subject at the time provided tacit approval, anticipating that such ideas would provoke no protests from the readership, and thus suggesting that this particular position was within the range of acceptable public discourse at the time for the imagined audience. Green's basic point of view, in which race, musical style, and aesthetics intermingled, was shared by music industry journalists, notably William Braid White, editorialist for *Talking Machine World* and author of the recurring column "Featuring the Musical Possibilities of the Talking Machine."[57] At the same time, no other music writer of the day appears to have so vociferously produced such xenophobic stereotypes as did Green. His pronouncements were extreme, but they nonetheless merely amplified the attempts found in other music business publications at producing lighthearted renditions of the same stereotypes.

Curiously enough, none other than Vernon Dalhart furnished commentary reminiscent of Green's, even if his condescension lacked a comparable level of vitriol. In a conversation with the publisher Elliott Shapiro, relayed to the public by *Billboard*, Dalhart (described by Shapiro as "the father of hill-billy songs") contended:

> "The Prisoner's Song" just happened to contain the kind of maudlin sentiment which stirs the hearts of mountaineers. To them the character in a song is just as attractive and interesting to them as some famous actor. And they never tire of hearing the song. When one record of any favorite hill billy number wears out or is broken, the mountaineers purchase another.[58]

Evidently both Green and Dalhart relied on the same informants for this striking aspect of hillbilly behavior, although given Dalhart's oft-cited status as a participant-observer (i.e., his authentic renditions of old-time tunes were based on his experience), he may have simply been recounting events from his life growing up in the South.[59]

Dalhart was indeed the "father of hill-billy songs," because this classically trained recording veteran combined a newly written song in a traditional style ("The Prisoner's Song") with a song about twenty years old in a traditional style ("The Wreck of the Old 97") in a way that assembled a new music-audience relationship. The audience was indubitably "hillbilly": unimaginable apart from its commercial context, it arose as a relational construct with mainstream popular music, race music, and foreign music. Dalhart talks in a confessional tone to the *Billboard* writer, creating an "us" of the professional, urban music world against the "them" of the "mountaineers" (it is worth noting that Dalhart only uses the term "hill billy" as an adjective to describe a recording, not as a noun to refer to a group of people). Like Abel Green, Dalhart remarks on the strange dependence of the hillbilly on mechanical reproduction and repetition, which, owing to the primitive state of the commodity form, represents the realization of a capitalist fantasy.[60]

Part of the difficulty of naming the "hillbilly" formation may have had to do with precisely the difficulty in delimiting this group from the majority. The iterability of hillbilly identity proved particularly unstable due to the overlap of racial, religious, and linguistic characteristics with white non-hillbillies. The violence of the language used in describing the "hillbilly" in Abel Green's 1926 article thus displaced the fear of similarity. Another factor was that, unlike "race"—a term that was used with pride by African Americans in the 1920s—"hillbilly" was a highly contested term, one that rural, white Southerners might use among themselves (as in the Al Hopkins anecdote), but which they did not appreciate when used by Yankees. Thus, the term was unlikely to be adopted across the range of people who were involved in using it, including both urban-dwelling music business professionals and hill-country mountaineers.

Archie Green's conclusion in his oft-cited 1965 article "Hillbilly Music: Source and Symbol" anticipates some of the psychoanalytically influenced observations of a writer such as Eric Lott in his writings about blackface minstrelsy. Lott termed the dynamic created by the simultaneous impulses of desire and disavowal internalized by white people toward cultural productions associated with African Americans "love and theft." Archie Green speculates that white Americans outside the South needed (and need) the South to experience both sentimental feelings of nostalgia and feelings of revulsion toward ignorance and unrefined primitivism— desire for a past that never existed, and disavowal of feelings, such as racism, that those outside the South could imagine as residing only in the South. For the white, urban, Northern bourgeois, the "white trash" possessed (or possess) a status very similar to the African American. Like African Americans, increasing numbers of poor white Southerners were migrating to urban areas in the North during this period, becoming another example of the "other" within.[61] Another similarity between Abel Green's treatment of the hillbilly and the psychodynamics of minstrelsy exists in Green's Jewish background. New white immigrants in the North were often the most active participants in minstrelsy, precisely because of the need to assert their difference from African Americans and their solidarity with other Euro-Americans. It does not require a stretch of the imagination to see a similar dynamic at work with new immigrants (and their descendants) and white, rural Southerners.

. . .

The years 1920 to 1925 saw an increasing concern in the music industry with population. Thus did recording executives, musicians, and consumers trade ideas about the viability of marketing-as-census, a process that concerned itself with targeting ever-finer segments of the population, dividing these segments into ever-finer taste groups, matching musical characteristics with definable demographic groups, and identifying new groups, geographical regions, and activities. Groups identified with geographical isolation of some sort, such as farmers, indigenous minority groups, or immigrants who lived in urban ghettos, were targeted by means of the print media specific to them, or by individuals who surveyed their tastes and spending habits, meticulously recording these as a means to increase sales. The existence of a foreign records category dating back to the earliest days of recording suggests the importance of narrowcasting as a constitutive feature of the recording industry, but the 1920s revealed an emphasis on finer distinctions and new methods of surveillance.

The early years of the decade also featured the emergence of two new categories that have figured centrally in the discourse of the U.S. popular music industry ever since. Race and old-time music were both defined by an explicit sound identified as authentic (that is, as exterior to the commercial processes that brought them into being). In the case of race music, however, this sound began with close similarity to mainstream pop and then diverged increasingly from dance-vocal-popular (mainstream) music, while old-time began at a distant remove from the mainstream and then adopted certain elements (particularly vocal style) from it. Old-time increasingly relied, in what might seem to be a contradiction, on a sound associated with folk music even as ever more of its songs were being newly composed by professional songwriters.

By the later months of 1924, the major record companies shared a new vision of the popular music field. And not only the popular music field—this vision included "All the Music of All the World," as a Columbia Records ad from September 1924 boasted. The ad listed Columbia's leadership not only in "dance orchestras," "song-hit artists," the "old-time novelty field," the "foreign language record field," and its "race record stars," but in the "classical field," "lighter music," and "educational records for children" as well. OKeh followed with an ad in November 1924 of "The Fastest Selling Numbers of the Moment," in which individual recordings were divided into the categories of dance, vocal, old tunes, race, Irish, and sacred. The following month OKeh was more concise, focusing on "Blues by Popular Negro Artists," "Dance and Popular Song Hits," "Hill Country Music," and the "List of All Foreign Languages." Not to be outdone, Emerson in the same month (December 1924) listed "Latest Songs," "Dance Hits," "Race," and "Foreign," among others, including "Operatic," and "Hawaiian" (still sometimes listed separately from "Foreign").[62] These ads taken together show the emergence of a four-pronged popular market consisting of dance and popular song hits (the mainstream), race, old-time, and foreign records.

Through the end of the decade, sales and marketing people at record companies continued to refine their techniques and reformulate their ideas about how homological relations between listeners and musical categories could be exploited and reinforced. In early 1928, Jack Kapp, one of the more astute music industry people when it came to using musical categories to build large audiences, reformed marketing at Vocalion to focus on three categories: popular records, race records, and old-time tunes.[63] The three-year lag between Vocalion's marketing categories and those formed by Columbia, OKeh, and Emerson at the end of 1924 points to the uneven adoption of this model within the industry, to the difference between the innovators and the others, and to the novelty of some of these categories, especially those such as race records and old-time tunes, which many probably suspected would disappear quickly.

Such was the rapidity with which new categories of music were appearing that new understandings of old terms seemed the order of the day. Not for the last time would folk music appear as a form of popular music: when the Tenth Recreation Congress met in early 1924 to honor songs as folk songs, two "comparatively recent songs" were selected. *Talking Machine World* commented, "It isn't often that a song attains the dignity of being a folk song within the lifetime of its own composer, but that is what has happened to both of these."[64] This type of malleable thinking, in which tradition could be embodied in the newly created, anticipated the move in early country music toward an increased reliance on professional songwriters and newer songs, even as the music continued to be perceived as a kind of folk music.[65] Thus did the newness of old-time music reflect modernism's urge to find value in the ever novel even as it registered the nostalgic yearning to embrace the last vestiges of the preindustrial.

"Hillbilly" did eventually gain acceptance, however, as a music industry term, but only after the flurry of attention that occasioned its emergence had subsided. OKeh identified its 45000 series as "Hill Billy" in 1933, and Decca issued several *Hill Billy Records* catalogs in 1935. Despite this, achieving the industry-wide consensus of the "race" label remained elusive for country music, and the rest of the companies continued to use their own terminology until the late 1940s (the subject of chapter 6).

A new feature of music industry publications as the decade of the 1920s waned was the emergence of the first popularity charts that did not appear as part of publishing or recording companies' advertisements, but rather as "gathered from the reports of sales made . . . by the leading music jobbers and disk distributors in the territories designated." This "table," as it was called, appeared in *Variety* in the November 13, 1929, issue and listed the six top-selling sheet music songs in New York, Chicago, and Los Angeles, and the top six records in each of these markets for Brunswick, Columbia, and Victor. A third table listed the top three songs nationwide for fifteen different publishers. Most of the sheet music hits came from current musicals, and the vast majority of the recordings were the type of vocal and dance numbers that participated in the mainstream at that time, featuring artists such as Al Jolson, the Ted Lewis Orchestra, the Paul Whiteman Orchestra, and Rudy Vallee. Yet musical utterances from the margins did appear as well: Vernon Dalhart's "Farm Relief Song" was listed as Columbia's number one hit in New York, while the African American singer Ethel Waters's version of "Am I Blue" topped Columbia's chart for Chicago. A recording of "Ain't Misbehavin'" (associated with and composed in part by Fats Waller) by Bill "Bojangles" Robinson, a famous African American song-and-dance man, was listed as Brunswick's number four recording in both New York and Chicago.[66]

Popularity charts perform several functions, and they assumed an increasingly important role in the decades that followed. For our purposes here, their significance is that this early appearance of a chart, which was only to recur fitfully, signaled that markets across the United States had become sufficiently synchronized to make a reporting of sales useful to music industry personnel.[67] The marginal segments of the popular music field—foreign, race, and old-time—were still too disorganized, their development still too uneven, to merit the sort of large-scale surveillance and coordination being lavished on the mainstream.

What, then, about the label around which much discussion of this chapter centered? Old-time music, as a term in the 1920s, can now be understood as activating both homologous and imaginary identifications at the same time. The assumed audience for the music was rural, white Southerners, but as we have seen, the category of old-time music was not recognized as such by the music industry until it involved members of social groups other than the assumed target audience. The music was widely perceived to form a homology with white people from the rural South, but that very group of people used a name for themselves and the music, "hillbilly," that they resented when used by people who were perceived as not belonging to their demographic group. The struggle over the name speaks to the difficult and unspoken negotiations between urban, white Northerners and rural, white Southerners in finding a label that could be used to communicate about this music across social divisions.

NOTES

1. The uncertainty, and thus the struggle, over what term to use for old-time and hillbilly music was more intense than that around race music. I will use "old-time music" as the default term for reasons that will become clear. The story about the origins of old-time music probably assumed something like the form described above based on an interview given by Ralph Peer to Kyle Crichton in 1938; see Kyle Crichton, "Thar's Gold in Them Hillbillies," *Collier's*, April 30, 1938, 26–27. For other accounts, see Archie Green, "Hillbilly Music: Source and Symbol," *Journal of American Folklore* 78 (July–September 1965): 204–28; Bill C. Malone, *Country Music U.S.A.* (Austin: University of Texas Press, 1985), 36–39; William Howland Kenney, *Recorded Music in American Life: The Phonograph and Popular Memory, 1890–1945* (New York: Oxford University Press, 1999), 135–48; Colin Escott, "The Talking Machine: How Records Shaped Country Music," in *The Encyclopedia of Country Music*, ed. Paul Kingsbury (New York and Oxford: Oxford University Press, 1998), 465–69; and Karl Hagstrom Miller, *Segregating Sound: Inventing Folk and Pop Music in the Age of Jim Crow* (Durham, NC, and London: Duke University Press, 2010), especially 187–240.

2. Joel Whitburn, *Pop Memories, 1890–1954* (Menomonee Falls, WI: Record Research, 1986), 175.

3. The following account of early country recordings is much indebted to Archie Green's "Hillbilly Music: Source and Symbol" and Bill C. Malone's "The Early Period of Commercial Hillbilly Music" in *Country Music U.S.A.*, 31–75.

4. Archie Green, "Hillbilly Music: Source and Symbol," 207. Karl Hagstrom Miller discusses this repertoire and underscores its connections to minstrelsy in a section titled "The Common Roots of Hillbillies and Minstrels," in *Segregating Sound*, 142–47.

5. The conflicting usages of "hillbilly" in this context are part of a larger cultural history of the term in the U.S. media, a history told in fascinating detail by Anthony Harkins in *Hillbilly: A Cultural History of an American Icon* (New York: Oxford University Press, 2004).

6. Perhaps no one is more responsible for producing the emergent canon of country music than Bill Malone, who, with his magisterial work *Country Music U.S.A.* and liner notes for *The Smithsonian Collection of Classic Country Music,* almost single-handedly (along with a few others such as Archie Green and Charles Wolfe) established country music as a scholarly field.

7. Robertson's "Sallie Gooden" can claim to participate in the canon of country music through its inclusion in Bill Malone's first Smithsonian collection.

8. For more on Robertson, see Bill C. Malone and Judith McCulloh, eds., *Stars of Country Music: Uncle Dave Macon to Johnny Rodriguez* (Urbana: University of Illinois Press, 1975), 12. Robertson's recording only came about, apparently, because he had traveled to New York and convinced Victor to record him.

9. Transcription by Laura Risk.

10. Discographical information comes from Tony Russell, *Country Music Records: A Discography, 1921–1942* (Oxford and New York: Oxford University Press, 2008).

11. *Talking Machine World* (hereafter *TMW*), November 15, 1924, 51.

12. Columbia went on to release more old-time recordings than any other label. Charles Wolfe documents how Columbia's superior production and distribution system also meant that Columbia's old-time recordings played a particularly important role in the dispersion of old-time recordings across North America. Central to this system were the two pressing plants operated by Columbia in Bridgeport, Connecticut, and Oakland, California. Charles Wolfe, "Columbia Records and Old-Time Music," *JEMF Quarterly* (Autumn 1978): 118–25, 144.

13. This information comes from Archie Green, "Hillbilly Music," 211.

14. These preferences assumed the following proportion: "Jigs, reels and old songs, 50 per cent; dance records (popular), 40 per cent; classical records, 10 percent." The tripartite division is also worth noting here, as is—in what may contradict previous assumptions about a strictly homological form of identification—the range of the farmers' musical tastes. See "Rural Dwellers Make Excellent Prospects: Farmer's [*sic*] Mode of Living and Isolation Favor the Sale of Talking Machines and Records—Successful Methods of a Live Dealer," *TMW*, December 15, 1923, 26. See also, from the previous month, "Radio Opportunities in the Rural Sections: Survey of the Farming Districts Made for the Radio Corp. of American Indicates That Rural Dwellers Will Represent an Important Part of the Retail Radio Sales Field," *TMW*, November 15, 1923, 30. For a discussion of sales in the South that reinforces this sense of diverse listening practices within a particular socially recognized demographic group, see "Dealer Tie-Ups with Visiting Artists Create a Satisfactory Record Demand," *TMW*, June 15, 1924, 156. In addition to the predictable (according to the homology model) popularity of Gid Tanner and Riley Puckett, opera records and the mainstream bandleader Vincent Lopez are mentioned.

15. "OKeh Artist Visits New York," *TMW*, December 15, 1923, 52.

16. "Young Blind Musician Records for Vocalion: George Reneau from Tennessee Mountains Makes Several Characteristic Recordings Which Prove Distinctly Popular in South," *TMW*, June 15, 1924, 46; "Two New Columbia Artists from Carolina: Samantha Bumgarner and Eva Davis, Who Have Achieved Fame in the South as Musicians, Visit New York to Make First Records," *TMW*, June 15, 1924, 26.

17. "Fiddlin' John Carson Joins OKeh: Picturesque Southern Mountaineer Makes OKeh Record—Is Fiddling Champion of the South," *TMW*, September 15, 1923, 30.

18. "Ernest Thompson Signed as a Columbia Artist," *TMW*, June 15, 1924, 57 or 58.

19. "Young Blind Musician Records for Vocalion: George Reneau from Tennessee Mountains Makes Several Characteristic Recordings Which Prove Distinctly Popular in South," *TMW*, June 15, 1924, 46.

20. Italics added. "'Uncle Am' Now Fiddles for the Vocalion Red Records," *TMW*, June 15, 1924, 181.

21. Italics added. Columbia ad, *TMW*, May 15, 1924, 153.

22. Italics added. "Ernest Thompson Signed as a Columbia Artist: Prize-Winning Musician of Carolina Makes First Records for Columbia Co.," *TMW*, June 15, 1924, 59. It's worth recalling that similar language was used in Pathé's advertisement to describe the music of James Reese Europe, as noted in chapter 3.

23. Vocalion ad for "'Uncle Am' Stuart: Champion Fiddler of Tennessee," *TMW*, August 15, 1924, 53.

24. OKeh ad, *TMW*, June 15, 1924, 66. My italics.

25. Columbia ad, *TMW*, June 15, 1924, 17.

26. *TMW*, September 15, 1924, 59. My italics.

27. Columbia ad, *TMW*, June 15, 1924, 17.

28. For an alternative analysis of this moment, see Richard Peterson's "system of production" approach based on recording, radio, touring, song publishing, and songwriting in *Creating Country Music: Fabricating Authenticity* (Chicago and London: University of Chicago Press, 1997), 17–25.

29. Bill C. Malone, *Country Music U.S.A.*, 40.

30. *TMW*, December 15, 1925, 177. An almost precisely contemporaneous article in *Billboard* noted the success of "wreck," "death," and "funeral ditties": "Land O' Melody," *Billboard*, December 26, 1925, 21.

31. Riley Barnes, "The Prisoner's Song," *Liberty*, May 15, 1926.

32. Victrola ad, *New York Times*, October 3, 1924.

33. *New Victor Records*, November 1, 1925, cited in Jack Palmer, *Vernon Dalhart: First Star of Country Music* (Denver: Mainspring Press, 2005), 142; and "Familiar Tunes Old and New," Columbia Record Catalog, 1928 (cited in Jack Palmer, *Vernon Dalhart*, 210).

34. "'Prisoner's Song' Gold Mine," *Variety*, December 16, 1925, 47; "Land O' Melody," *Billboard*, January 23, 1926; "Inside Stuff on Music," *Variety*, February 17, 1926.

35. "Mountaineer and Rural Ballads," Edison Blue Amberol Records catalog, February 1926 (quoted in Jack Palmer, *Vernon Dalhart*, 125).

36. Jack Palmer, *Vernon Dalhart*, 125. Elsewhere Palmer furnishes further evidence for Dalhart's numerical triumph. Three years earlier, during a period in which other writers have described his career as being in decline, Dalhart's numbers were apparently even more impressive: "In 1923, Dalhart's recording career finally took a big jump, even though the record business was still doing poorly. . . . Even so, during the year Dalhart made 102 sides for fourteen different companies during at least fifty-eight recording sessions. The recordings were issued on 32 different labels and under eight other names besides Dalhart" (91). Palmer reports similar lists of numbers fourteen times in four different chapters. The

spectacular prolixity of Dalhart's recordings can be gauged by the fact that his recordings take up fifty-one pages in Tony Russell's discography of early country music recordings (Tony Russell, *Country Music Records,* 242–92). And this is only Dalhart's country recordings. In Palmer's biography of Dalhart, his entire discography runs to eighty-three pages (280–362). In his study of Columbia's "Old and Familiar" series, Charles Wolfe points out that between 1924 and 1928 Dalhart made one third of all sides in the series. Meanwhile, as Anne Cohen and Norm Cohen make clear, Columbia was only one of ten companies for which Dalhart recorded old-time tunes. Charles Wolfe, "Columbia Records and Old-Time Music," 120; Anne Cohen and Norm Cohen, "Folk and Hillbilly Music: Further Thoughts on Their Relation," *JEMF Quarterly* 13, no. 46 (Summer 1977): 56.

37. "Inside Stuff on Music," *Variety,* February 17, 1926; "Land O' Melody," *Billboard,* October 9, 1926, 21. See Richard Peterson on the production of "The Death of Floyd Collins," which relied on a partnership between the entrepreneur Polk Brockman and the blind old-time songwriter-performer Andrew Jenkins, in *Creating Country Music,* 24.

38. Bob Dumm, "Two Men Who Sell New Songs for Old," *Farm and Fireside Magazine* (May 1927), cited in Jack Palmer, *Vernon Dalhart,* 41. It was true that Dalhart had been making Edison records "ever since" his first sessions for them in 1916, but due to differences in how recording contracts were structured, it was possible for an artist to also record for other companies simultaneously, an option Dalhart availed himself of quite promiscuously during his heyday in the mid-1920s.

39. "Vernon Dalhart and the Negro Dialect," *Edison Amberola Monthly* (December 1918), cited in Jack Palmer, *Vernon Dalhart,* 47. Narratives based on white proximity to African Americans can be found in the earliest stories associated with blackface minstrelsy. For the most thorough analysis of this narrative see Eric Lott, *Love and Theft: Blackface Minstrelsy and the American Working Class* (New York and Oxford: Oxford University Press, 1993).

40. "Dalhart, Vernon, Tenor," *1920 Catalogue of Victor Records* (published 1919), quoted in Jack Palmer, *Vernon Dalhart,* 80.

41. Bob Dumm, "Two Men Who Sell New Songs for Old."

42. See especially Kyle Crichton, "Thar's Gold in Them Hillbillies."

43. Bill C. Malone, *Country Music U.S.A.,* 44.

44. Readers may recall that "there were several things that did not meet with [Carson's] approval." "OKeh Artist Visits New York," *TMW,* December 15, 1923, 52.

45. Some versions of this story (including Whitter's own) have Whitter making a test recording for OKeh in March 1923, which was then unearthed after Carson's success, leading to Whitter's December 1923 sessions. Recent scholars have not been able to confirm this earlier session. Tony Russell, *Country Music Records,* 954. A version of the story may be found in Bill C. Malone, *Country Music U.S.A.,* 36.

46. Whitter's singing has come in for much criticism over the years, and, indeed, it is interesting that when he teamed with George Banman (G.B.) Grayson a few years later, in the duo in which he found the most success, Whitter confined himself to accompanying Grayson's singing and fiddle playing, implying that Grayson, Whitter, and the people recording them preferred Grayson's voice. Bill C. Malone sums up the opinions of many when he describes Whitter as a "mediocre singer at best." Bill C. Malone, *Country Music U.S.A.,* 36.

47. Bill C. Malone, *Country Music U.S.A.*, 56–57. A good history of the various recordings of "The Wreck of the Old 97" may be found in Jack Palmer, *Vernon Dalhart*, 101–7.

48. Richard Peterson describes the role of Polk Brockman in creating this early attempt to systematize the country music industry in *Creating Country Music*, 24–25.

49. Another axis of comparison that could be used in contrasting the styles of Dalhart and Carson lies along what Richard Peterson has called the "hardcore-softshell" opposition in country music. While Peterson does mention Dalhart as a pioneering softshell artist, and refutes notions of teleology and tradition, he finds the 1920s dominated by the hardcore aesthetic (within which we could include Fiddlin' John Carson), with softshell rising to dominance in the 1930s. Richard Peterson, *Creating Country Music*, 137–57.

50. On the tone tests, see Jonathan Sterne, *The Audible Past: Cultural Origins of Sound Reproduction* (Durham, NC, and London: Duke University Press, 2003), 261–66; Emily Thompson, *The Soundscape of Modernity: Architectural Acoustics and the Culture of Listening in America, 1900–1933* (Cambridge, MA: MIT Press, 2004), 237–39; and Emily Thompson, "Machines, Music, and the Quest for Fidelity: Marketing the Edison Phonograph in America, 1877–1925," *Musical Quarterly* 79 (Spring 1995): 131–71. On Dalhart's involvement with the tone tests, see Jack Palmer, *Vernon Dalhart*, 57–78.

51. This argument is derived from Jacques Rancière's reversal of Walter Benjamin's argument about the relation between technology and art. Rancière contends that mechanically reproduced art could only appear with the production of art that already relied on an aesthetic that could be mechanically reproduced. Jacques Rancière, *The Politics of Aesthetics: The Distribution of the Sensible,* trans. and with an introduction by Gabriel Rockhill (London: Continuum, 2004), 32.

52. "What the Popularity of Hill-Billy Songs Means in Retail Profit Possibilities," *TMW,* December 15, 1925, 177. "Hill-billy song vogue" was mentioned in "Inside Stuff on Music: 'Hilly-Billy' Records Growing," *Variety,* February 24, 1926, 48; and "Melody Mart Notes," *Billboard,* March 27, 1926, 21. The success without "exploitation" is discussed in "Inside Stuff on Music: More 'Hill Billy' Songs," *Variety,* March 3, 1926, 39. The "craze for mountaineer songs" comes from "Melody Mart Notes," *Billboard,* July 10, 1926. The spread of hillbilly music to urban areas comes from "Inside Stuff on Music: 'Hilly-Billy' Records Growing." Anthony Harkins offers an exemplary analysis of the circulation of the hillbilly trope both preceding and during this period across various media in *Hillbilly,* 47–101.

53. "The New Year in Records," *Variety,* December 15, 1926, 45, 54.

54. "Hill-billy Music," *Variety,* December 29, 1926, 3, 72. This use of mainstream popular music to disperse hillbillies anticipates the contemporary use of classical music to disperse gangs, a technique widely utilized at bus and train terminals. See "Classical Music Still Effective at Dispersing Loitering Teens," *Los Angeles Times,* April 4, 2011, http://latimesblogs.latimes.com/culturemonster/2011/04/classical-music-still-works-at-dispersing-loitering-teens-.html, accessed September 30, 2014.

55. "Inside Stuff—Music," *Variety,* July 11, 1928, 47; Abel Green, "Radio Review," *Variety,* July 31, 1929, 57. A similar anecdote forms the topic of "Inside Stuff—Music: Hagen's Cowboy Songs," *Variety,* October 10, 1928, 53.

56. Some twenty-nine years later, Abel Green featured as the quasi-anonymous author of "A Warning to the Music Business," one of the more obvious signs of the moral panic that

greeted the early examples of rhythm and blues crossover recordings, thus making him the unwitting patrolman of socio-musical boundaries separated by almost thirty years. *Variety,* February 23, 1955, 2, reprinted in David Brackett, ed., *The Pop, Rock, and Soul Reader: Histories and Debates* (New York: Oxford University Press, 2014), 98–99.

57. See for example William Braid White, "Featuring the Possibilities of the Talking Machine," *TMW,* September 15, 1923, 166; and W. B. White, "New Era in Record Development," *TMW,* December 15, 1923, 158.

58. "Hill Billy Numbers Spring from Incidents of Life," *Billboard,* January 22, 1927, 24.

59. This is unlikely, however, if we map the events of Dalhart's biography against the development of talking machine technology, given that he left Texas (not really hillbilly country in any event) in 1910, well before these putative listening and consumption habits came into existence.

60. Articles on farmers in *TMW* also reinforce and anticipate this idea, discussing how rural dwellers are excellent consumers of recordings.

61. Abel Green, "Hillbilly Music," 223; Eric Lott, *Love and Theft.* For more scholarship on early country music and the provenance of the term "hillbilly," see D. K. Wilgus, *Anglo-American Folksong Scholarship Since 1898* (New Brunswick, NJ: Rutgers University Press, 1959); and Anne Cohen and Norm Cohen, "Folk and Hillbilly Music."

62. See "All the Music of All The World" (Columbia ad), *TMW,* September 15, 1924, 18–19; "The Fastest Selling Numbers of the Moment" (OKeh ad), *TMW,* November 15, 1924, 59; "A Very Profitable Proposition" (OKeh and Odeon ad), *TMW,* December 15, 1924, 96; "Emerson Solves the Problem" (Emerson ad), *TMW,* December 15, 1924, 163. Emerson never really entered the old-time market.

63. "Jack Kapp, Vocalion Sales and Recording Director, Inaugurates New Policies: Newly Appointed Executive Makes Complete Change in Development of Vocalion Line— Records to Be Merchandised in Specific Classes Which Will Be Released Separately," *TMW,* February 15, 1928, 94.

64. "Selected as Folk Songs: Tenth Recreational Congress Selects Two Widmark Numbers as Worthy of That Title," *TMW,* January 15, 1924, 149.

65. This turn to professional songwriters was partly attributable to the realization on the part of some music industry agents, especially Ralph Peer, that copyrighted old-time tunes were extremely profitable. See Benjamin Filene, *Romancing the Folk: Public Memory and American Roots Music* (Chapel Hill and London: University of North Carolina Press, 2000), 37–39; and Richard Peterson, *Creating Country Music,* 37.

66. "Monthly Music Survey," *Variety,* November 13, 1929, 71.

67. This notion of market synchronization as necessary for the appearance of popularity charts is derived from Philip Ennis, *The Seventh Stream: The Emergence of Rocknroll in American Popular Music* (Hanover, NH: University Press of New England, 1992).

5

From Jazz to Pop

Swing in the 1940s

1947 began on a strange note for Count Basie. On January 3, he and his orchestra recorded "Open the Door, Richard," a novelty song that had recently been creating a stir on the West Coast in a version recorded by the saxophonist Jack McVea. Basie's career had suffered a bit of a downturn in the wake of World War II, as had many of the most successful swing bands. Little could he have guessed, however, that he was about to enjoy the greatest commercial success of his career, as "Open the Door, Richard," released in late January, zoomed to the top of *Billboard*'s charts for "Best-Selling Popular Retail Records" and "Records Most-Played on the Air."

This anecdote raises a host of complicated questions about popular music historiography as well as the relationship between (what was still at that point called) race music and mainstream popular music. How could Count Basie, the urcanonical jazz pianist and bandleader, have topped the charts in 1947 with "Open the Door, Richard," a recording clearly based in vaudeville featuring a skit performed in broad African American dialect that evoked nothing so much as minstrelsy? How might the existence of this recording, never mind its success, enter into the various historical narratives in which Count Basie regularly participates, such as the history of jazz, the history of swing, and the history of popular music?

In the course of considering such questions, the story of "Open the Door, Richard" can serve as a vehicle to illuminate shifts occurring during the 1940s in the larger music industry categories of (mainstream) popular music and race music. Swing and jazz were not themselves music industry categories, but rather what I refer to in chapter 1 as critic-fan genres. Recalling the discussion of scale and level in chapter 1, such genres are not simply subsumed by music industry categories, but rather interact with them and participate in their transformation as much as these genres are influenced by changes in music industry categories. Swing and jazz recorded by African Americans played an important role in facilitating crossover between race music and the mainstream at the beginning of the decade, even as other race records marked out a territory associated exclusively with African Americans. The success of swing and the creation of a more stable network for the circulation of race music led to greater music industry prominence for music associated with African Americans over the course of the decade, which in turn led to broader public access to the music. These transformations within the music industry, along with changing conceptions of race in U.S. society at large, contributed to the renaming of the category for black popular music to rhythm and blues in 1949.[1] Yet the arc that leads from a recording like Basie's "Jumpin' at the Woodside" (a minor mainstream hit in 1938) to the success of "Open the Door, Richard" cautions us that the story of African American popular music in the 1940s might not be one of ever-increasing mainstream success—or, perhaps, that such success comes with a price.

One way to begin examining this arc is to address, first of all, the relationship between the three terms in the title of the chapter. "Swing" is conventionally the name given to the type of music played by the big bands that dominated popular music between the years 1935 and 1945. "Swing" is also the name given to a type of rhythmic groove associated with jazz both before the big band era and after. In the words of Amiri Baraka, swing went from being a verb (to swing) prior to 1935 to a noun (the music known as swing).[2] Swing, in its form as a noun, played a complicated role in what was then understood as jazz, forming a subcategory of jazz at the outset of the 1940s that dominated popular music, but becoming embroiled in a debate about the essence of jazz after the war as its influence waned in the mainstream.

The interaction of jazz, pop, and swing tells only part of the story, however. The conclusion of chapter 4 described the emergence of the notion of nationwide tracking of popularity. The fact that "Open the Door, Richard"—a recording by a single artist (as opposed to the idea of the song as an abstract template embodied in sheet music)—could be recognized as popular in both record sales and for radio play in charts that represented nationwide popularity speaks to a sea change in several related arenas: how the texts of the popular song were defined; social and technological changes in the playback of recorded music; the synchronization of music distribution across large geographical expanses; refinement in the tracking of audiences; technological and legal shifts affecting record production and radio; and changes in the recognition and understanding of constellated communities related to the different music industry categories.

JAZZ HISTORY, POPULAR MUSIC HISTORY

Popular music histories tend to assert that swing bands died after the war. I will not argue that this is false per se, although a few big bands did manage hits, and swing-influenced music was very much alive and well. After all, one could say that Count Basie's band was big, that it played swing, and, in "Open the Door, Richard," that it definitely had a hit. Jazz histories are similarly not wrong about the life cycle of the big bands, so much as overly simple when examined in light of a survey of the recordings with the greatest circulation during the period 1939 to 1947, and a perusal of popularity charts such as those published in *Variety* or *Billboard*. If these histories agree that the big bands died and were superseded by small combos playing bebop, then they tend to ignore the continued activity of bands led by canonical figures such as Basie and Duke Ellington, as well as the non-canonical white swing bands that persisted and occasionally even flourished, such as Woody Herman's and Stan Kenton's. And, as Scott Deveaux observed more than twenty years ago, this postwar moment in jazz historiography is marked above all by the emphasis on symbolic capital (i.e., the approval of musicians by other musicians and critics) and the consequent denigration of economic capital (i.e., approval by the mass public and financial success), and on evaluations of authenticity based on race.[3] Bebop musicians succeeded in creating a type of music that would be evaluated on its artistic merits, not on how it performed in the marketplace. In what amounts to a recurring refrain (recall the discussion of blues histories in chapter 3), the consecration of jazz artists in subsequent historical texts (and to some extent in previous jazz histories, though they were few and far between) therefore depended on an inversion between artistic merit and commercial success, meaning that many jazz historians were suspicious about the artistic credentials of artists who were too successful.

It's no wonder then, that Count Basie's "Open the Door, Richard" would not figure in histories of either jazz or popular music.[4] The late 1940s and early 1950s tend to be a lacuna in popular music histories anyway, as the mainstream is seen as marking time between the efflorescence of the big band era and the irruption of rock and roll.[5] If the usual narratives assert that the instrumental and vocal recordings of the big bands (i.e., a form of jazz understood in the broadest sense) were supplanted by crooners singing ballads accompanied by studio orchestras (i.e., not a form of jazz by anyone's reckoning), then, to reiterate a point made earlier, my argument is not that this narrative is incorrect, but rather that its simplicity obscures as much as it elucidates.

The very terms in which I have been discussing African American artists such as Count Basie and Duke Ellington as part of the transformation of the popular music mainstream already suggest an articulation of musical style and identification. The position of their recordings in by-now-conventional historical narratives points to the interconnections between style, identification, and prestige, in that these artists are routinely recognized as upholding the core values of jazz (principally swing, improvisation, and African American identity) even though they occupied a position within the orbit of mainstream popular music (albeit at the periphery) during their commercial height from the late 1930s to the mid-1940s. Jazz critics and aficionados of that era celebrated them because of the recalcitrance of their recordings with respect to mainstream success, a failure to achieve complete commercial acceptance that both forms and anticipates an implicit rationale for their inclusion in subsequent jazz histories.

This tension between symbolic capital and economic capital, already in its nascent form in jazz criticism of the time, and an opposition that has guided jazz history ever since, forms the backdrop for an examination of the fortunes of jazz and swing from the late 1930s to the late 1940s. The history of that period begins here by examining the interrelationship of institutional structures, music transmission technologies, and aesthetics; moves to an analysis of the instrumental swing number "Tuxedo Junction" (first recorded by the African American bandleader Erskine Hawkins and then covered by the Euro-American bandleader Glenn Miller); surveys the shifting relationship between racial and musical categories in the mid-1940s; and concludes with the commercial triumph of "Open the Door, Richard." Basie's hit provides an opportunity for analyzing mainstream popular music, jazz, and black popular music at the end of the 1940s. Drawing on previous homological relations, the notion of black popular music retained the power of homology through its transformation via the acquisition of new stylistic elements and audiences. Successive musical iterations categorized within the rubric of race music referred back to previous conventions even as they synthesized these with other musical elements. At the same time, the emergence of swing music during the mid-1930s (and carrying over to the beginning of the period discussed in this chapter) as a black-identified form afforded a new range of imaginary identifications as well.

As indicated in chapter 3, something approaching a contemporary notion of which sounds and musical practices might be identified as African American began to take shape during the early decades of the twentieth century, spurred on by the growing importance of commercial sound recording and the increasing dominance of homologous musical identifications, occurring not only with African American music, but with old-time and foreign music as well. All the now-familiar elements were already in place in discourse about African American music in the 1920s, including a swinging rhythmic sense, distinctive vocal and instrumental timbres, a particular approach to dissonance and pitch inflection, and improvisation (and its affective correlate, spontaneity)—practices associated with genres such as blues, jazz, and gospel.

Yet the relationship between race music and the mainstream did not exist solely on the plane of musical style, or even only on the articulation of style with racial identity, but must be understood within a broader and more abstract struggle. For race music faced structural, institutional impediments that slowed the recognition of its economic and symbolic capital. The very terms in which musical popularity and aesthetics were understood within the popular music industry devalued the musical components most associated with black popular music as well as the technological forms used to transmit it, rendering the music almost illegible from a mainstream perspective.

POPULAR MUSIC AND THE WORK CONCEPT

The source of the structural resistance to black popular music lies in a series of interconnected conflicts that dominated this period in popular music history, and which affected the circulation of popular music in virtually every medium of transmission. The struggle revolved around the terms in which debates about popularity would be conducted, with the "work concept" (the song as the unit, measured by sheet music sales, radio plugs, et cetera) derived from Western art music aesthetics representing one pole, and the sound recording, offering the nuances of performance, representing the other.[6] Whereas the song-as-text emphasizes structure and fixed identity (of the work), which could then be reproduced either on a recording or in amateur performances at home, the recording-as-text inscribes the marks of spontaneity, of individualized, embodied gestures, that are unique to a particular recorded performance.[7] In this context, improvised, non-notable musical components could only begin to figure in the construction of musical categories if recordings (or performances) were considered a viable format for the measurement of popularity.

In the late 1930s, recordings did not factor into the construction of popularity charts, which consisted solely of noting the number of times *which* song was played on the radio, not *who* played it or *how* it was played (the playing of specific recordings on the radio was not charted until 1945). Tabulations of the number of times a song was heard were counted in the category of song plugs, a measurement used by music publishers to gauge the success of their attempts at popularizing their product. Live performances were not factored directly into measurements of popularity, but were discussed solely in reviews of particular bands or nightspots.

The alignment of the work concept with institutional power and dominant social groups appeared unmistakably in music industry discourse, affecting everything from evaluations of performances and recordings to which songs and recordings received the most attention for their apparent popularity. At the same time, an emerging discourse during this period, which tentatively recognized recordings as texts, created a conflict with the dominant aesthetic, as the music associated with African Americans, whites from the Southern states and rural areas, and immigrants became strongly affiliated with (what I am calling) the sonic aesthetic. This emerging discourse, found in music industry trade publications, argued for the economic viability of the music associated with these marginal populations, yet the dominance of the work concept created a temporary indifference to this source of potential profit. To understand how the culture industry could malfunction in this manner requires a better grasp of the distinctions between these two competing conceptions of the musical text.

The argument here does not assert an absolute difference between the opposed textual categories of the work concept and the sonic aesthetic. In other contexts, one could understand notated scores, embodying the work concept, as inscribing marks of spontaneity, in that the more-or-less spontaneous creative process of the composer or arranger brings those marks into existence. By the same token, recordings, embodying the sonic aesthetic, could be understood as having a more fixed structure than notated compositions, in that the musical details of a recording are repeated exactly from one instantiation to the next, while the musical details of different realizations of musical scores vary. Another wrinkle to this argument is created by the notion of an aural tradition, in which sound recordings (rather than notated scores) become a template for later interpretations and performances. The sonic aesthetic extends to the performance of notated music (as do the concepts of oral and aural tradition), the recognition of the value of which has encountered many of the same obstacles in the institutional structure of the music industry, copyright law, and academic discourse as non-notated music.

This sonic aesthetic, based on the unique qualities of sound associated with particular performers and performances, could only circulate beyond a specific performance space on radio broadcasts or mechanically reproducible recordings. Sheet music could not communicate subtle timbral differences, let alone the micro-rhythmic nuances responsible for different grooves (easily felt by dancers but elusive for transcribers) or the pitch inflections that enliven melodies with otherwise-limited pitch content (easily hummed along with by well-trained listeners but not amenable to even-tempered notation). The circulation of these musics, associated with marginal elements of the population, which had thrived in the 1920s and almost disappeared during the early years of the Depression, began a vigorous comeback with the launching of the swing era in the mid-1930s. The recording's gradual usurpation of pride of place from sheet music as the primary means of musical circulation figured prominently in a debate in the public sphere between competing aesthetics and different concepts of the musical work. This debate was foreshadowed, as we have already seen in the discussions in chapters 2 and 4 about the effect of mechanical reproduction on the music industry and the popularity of recordings such as "The Prisoner's Song."

The debate uniting musical value and demographic categories with notions of the work concept and the sonic aesthetic arose against the background of a titanic struggle between competing interests in the music industry. On one side lay the well-established publishing rights organization the American Society of Composers and Publishers (ASCAP), and, to a lesser extent, the American Federation of Musicians (AF of M). On the other side lay the relative upstarts: the record companies, coin-machine (jukebox) operators, and promoters and producers (in both the creative and the business sense) of the marginal categories of music. The song-as-text aesthetic embraced by ASCAP emphasized melody, craft, and tradition, whereas the sonic aesthetic, as one might expect, stressed the importance of spontaneity, originality, and the transference of personality (or aura) from live performance to the medium of recording.

Song Pluggers and Coin Machines

The arena in which this battle was waged ranged across several different strands of music industry discourse. The most subtle and seemingly objective strand transpired in the presentation of musical popularity. In the late 1930s, *Billboard* and *Variety*, the two leading publications of the U.S. music industry, both presented popularity primarily through two charts, one for "Best-Selling Sheet Music" and one for "Most Radio Plugs." These charts both spoke to the interests of the publishing industry and to the notion of song-as-text. In the case of "Best-Selling Sheet Music" this connection requires little explanation, but "Most Radio Plugs" references a concept that has since fallen out of favor. In this case, "plugs" referred to the promotion of newly copyrighted songs to either bandleaders or advertising executives who were responsible for choosing the songs that would be played on one of two different types of network radio programs: sustaining broadcasts, made late at night and featuring a leading band from a remote ballroom location, or sponsored shows built around a star performer, and usually named after the show's sponsor (e.g., "The Chesterfield Hour," "The Lucky Strike Hit Parade"). Three networks—CBS, NBC, and Mutual—dominated national broadcasting with a station in every major market in the country. Shows on these networks, therefore, reached far more people than broadcasts on local, independent stations.[8]

Yet the broadcasters and publishers did not exist in a state of perfect harmony. Broadcasters resented the demands of ASCAP for "performance rights" payments, and ASCAP felt as if broadcasters could always do more to promote the sale of sheet music and wanted to increase the fee for performance rights, which had remained the same for many years. Both sides geared up for battle on the eve of the expiration of their contract, which was scheduled for 1940. The broadcasters responded by forming their own publishing rights organization, Broadcast Music Incorporated (BMI). Although on one level about the flow of capital, this conflict and the developments that sprang from it were also bound up with notions about aesthetics, demographics, and the policing of social boundaries.[9]

That ASCAP's aesthetics were strongly allied with the work concept derived from Western European art music has already been stated if not implied. Their relationship with radio was predicated on the belief that the music publishers could recognize the best songs, which, if played enough, would translate directly to sheet music sales. By the late 1930s, however, it had become clear that domestic music making, usually in the form of playing Tin Pan Alley–produced songs on a keyboard instrument, was in a state of irreversible decline, resulting in a concomitant decline in the sales of sheet music. Song pluggers, bandleaders, and advertisers were all rewarded financially for the number of plugs a song received, but the number of plugs no longer transferred to what mattered most to publishers: sheet music sales. Bandleaders resorted increasingly to playing strings of truncated versions of songs in order to plug them, thereby inflating the songs' rankings on the charts, often in instrumental versions, which negated whatever benefit such plugs might have for music sales.[10]

Another development threatened the industrial-aesthetic-material trifecta constituted by music publishing, the work concept, and sheet music: a rapid increase of record sales and the spread of coin machines (jukeboxes), which were responsible for 60 to 75 percent of all record sales by the late 1930s.[11] ASCAP's main objection to coin machines was that it received limited mechanical royalties from the public playback of recordings on them. A debate ensued in music industry publications that exposed the aesthetic and sociological implications of the rift between publishing and the world of network radio plugs on the one hand, and sound recordings and coin machines on the other. For it soon transpired that many of the songs featured on recordings that were not allied with ASCAP—songs labeled as race, hillbilly, foreign, or other novelty recordings—were often quite popular on coin machines even though the song-plugging apparatus did not promote them. Another factor in this split was the emergence of swing as a dominant genre of mainstream popular music. Many of the most popular swing bands wrote their own (non-ASCAP) material, and many swing musicians embraced musical values that diverged from those of ASCAP.

The difference between the work concept and the sonic aesthetic made itself felt in ways that were subtle, such as in the presentation of musical popularity, and in the increase in discourse around sound recordings in the music industry press. In April 1938 *Billboard* began featuring a "Record Buying Guide" (henceforth RBG). This guide—a commentary on the expected success of recordings on coin machines—appeared in the back of the magazine in the "Amusement Machines" section, well separated from the music section, implying, perhaps, that music circulating primarily via the jukebox had not earned the right to be called music. Although the RBG was not a numerical ranking, *Billboard* divided recordings according to four categories: "Going Strong—Keep Them In," "Coming Up—Better Stock Them," "Operators' Specials," and "Going Down—Not Worth Pushing." From the outset, the RBG listed songs recorded by, or in a style associated with, African Americans (such as "Jumpin' at the Woodside," "Hold Tight!" and "Tain't What You Do" in early 1939) that were either ignored entirely by, or ranked very low in, the sheet music and radio plugs charts. The presence of these recordings in the RBG occurred despite the fact that the RBG was already in part determined by the same forces that dominated the sheet music and radio plugs charts. As a notice at the beginning of the RBG put it, "Tabulation is based upon radio performances, sheet music sales and record releases of the week. Reports from music publishers as to the relative importance of certain songs in their catalogs are also considered, as well as information received each week from prominent operators."[12] While influenced heavily by the interests and tastes of music publishers, the RBG deviated through its inclusion of "information . . . from prominent operators"—a deviation that was slight, yet significant.

The drift toward factoring in revenue derived from recordings, be it from coin machines or actual sales, continued during 1940. On July 27, 1940, *Billboard* combined all previous means of presenting popularity (radio plugs, sheet music bestsellers, and "Most Popular on Music Machines") on a single page, and added a new list of "National and Regional Best Selling Retail Records." Now the popularity of texts based on both the work concept and the sonic aesthetic could be compared side by side. At almost exactly the same time, *Variety*, which tended to give more space to the trials and tribulations of music publishing than *Billboard*, recognized the validity of measuring the sales of sound recordings. *Variety*'s "10 Best Sellers on Coin-Machines" chart debuted in the same issue that the magazine dropped its listing of network song plugs. Like *Billboard*, *Variety*'s coin-machine rankings gave newfound prominence to African American artists.[13]

An aspect of the perceived difference between music on coin machines and music on network radio was the idea that the coin machine operators, because they were not music industry insiders, were closer to the taste of the people. A populist thread arose that opposed the force-feeding of music by the radio networks to the liberation of audience taste performed by the "poor man's orchestra," the name given to the coin machine by one writer for *Billboard*. Whether explanations cited the musical illiteracy of coin machine operators or their closeness to the people, most agreed that the boom in coin machine business was "due to the public's discovery that on records it can get a style and quality of entertainment that is not readily available in radio." The fact that the coin machine operators were musically illiterate could even be spun as an advantage for them, because, as Walter W. Hurd of *Billboard* informed his readers, "a musical education actually narrows the range of musical enjoyment, so that those who profit by music should be grateful that the masses of the people have a much wider range of taste than the musicians and critics."[14]

In 1939 *Billboard* began to feature a counter-discourse on popularity in which coin machine operators from across the United States would write in to relay to readers which records were doing well in their regions. This counter-discourse, titled "What the Records Are Doing for Me," focused entirely on the economic value of recordings, thus sidestepping the aesthetic discourse produced by publishers that implicitly legitimated their product. Coin machine operators noticed a disjuncture between the preferences of their clientele, which they could measure precisely based on the number of nickels deposited for each tune, and the music that formed the core of *Billboard*'s discourse on music. This disjuncture could even result in requests to apportion coverage in order to parallel more closely the sources of their revenue. Frank Hanosh of the Dot Music Co. of Detroit thought, "It would be a good idea if *Billboard* would devote more space to this [race music] like the hillbilly and foreign records sections" because the "colored locations . . . turn in more money than any white spots."[15] Hanosh, in keeping with the practice of his fellow operators, did not advocate for a type of music based on its quality, but rather for purely pragmatic reasons. This suggests, however, that the reason for the disjuncture between the coverage given to mainstream music by *Billboard* and *Variety*, and the popularity of race and hillbilly music among coin machine patrons, lay in an aesthetic ideology: Why else would these publications ignore music that could benefit the music industry financially?

Several articles that appeared in a special issue of *Billboard* devoted to coin machines, published in September 1939, furnish plentiful examples of what was at stake in the debates between ASCAP and music industry professionals with interests other than publishing. In one of these articles, Jack Robbins, a Tin Pan Alley veteran of the publishing business, adopts a paternalistic stance as he compares "the music publishing business with the younger music machine industry." Robbins advocates against employing a scattershot approach to marketing. Music publishers, evidently, at one time threw the equivalent of musical mud at the wall and hoped that some of it would stick, the approach (according to Robbins) that coin machines operators now employ, and one that they would be well advised to modify. For music publishers, having learned to "rely on their own judgment, sharpened by years of experience," are now more discriminating and have isolated certain stylistic features that will ensure the success of popular songs. Robbins identifies two elements: the first of these, melody, the publishers discovered "was the basic compound of a commercial song." The second element required by a popular song was a "good lyric," which consisted of "not merely the wedding of pretty phrases, but [the telling of] a picturesque story that would attract the attention of the listener." Robbins also offers a corrective to those who might have attributed the success of swing to original tunes composed by band members that were based on riffs. Rather, "these same disciples of hot jazz have had their best selling platters on *melody* songs" [my emphasis]. The connections between the interests of the music publishers, aesthetics, and genre become clearer as the article proceeds. Novelty tunes such as "A-Tisket A-Tasket," "Beer Barrel Polka," and "Hold Tight!" represent "the most dangerous form of music speculation," and "a close touch on the public fads and fancies is necessary." However, "it must remain for the [coin machine] operators to take seriously [the] recommendations" of music publishers, because the music publishers "are in a better position . . . to feel the public pulse."[16]

Robbins does not mention that novelty tunes such as "A-Tisket A-Tasket" and "Hold Tight!" both presented swinging forms of dance music identified with, and originally recorded (and written) by, African Americans, based on riffs (i.e., songs not emphasizing melody according to Western art music conventions) and lyrics that decidedly did not tell a picturesque story (although this would depend, perhaps, on one's idea of the picturesque).[17] "Beer Barrel Polka," an instrumental written by the Czech songwriter Jaromír Vejvoda, was the biggest coin machine hit of the spring and summer of 1939, with a recording by the German accordionist Will Glahe as its biggest-selling rendition (it was originally classified as both a foreign and an international recording before crossing over to mainstream success).

In the same issue of *Billboard*, almost diametrically opposed positions were produced by Irving Mills, a music publisher and promoter associated with African American musicians such as Duke Ellington and Cab Calloway, and Joe Glaser, a promoter who managed Louis Armstrong and Billie Holiday, among others. Echoing the rhetoric about race and old-time music from the 1920s that celebrated the ineffable, Mills mentions "Hold Tight!" and "Beer Barrel Polka" as among the songs possessing "that unbeatable something." And of what might this "something" consist? "These songs. . . . had an individuality all their own that made them so different from the songs usually heard over the air waves." The trope of the coin machine as the facilitator of choice in listeners, and the radio as a medium that force-feeds audiences a product that they don't necessarily desire, is reiterated here: "When a person listens to the radio he is forced to sit back and take what is given him with a grain of advertising. But when this same individual plays a tune on a phono in his local tavern he is digging down in his pocket for something he really wants to hear." Mills does not stress the elements of musical style that might contribute to the formation of a new aesthetic, but he does mention what recordings can do that sheet music cannot: bring to listeners the sound of a tune being played by the people who created it. Thus, according to Mills, listeners prefer "the original recording" of bands who rely on "special material" written by themselves, thereby further disturbing the smooth functioning of the Tin Pan Alley production system.[18]

Although Mills does not raise the issue of race explicitly, two other articles discuss the role of race in terms of originality and the transference of aura from live performance to recordings. Glaser amplifies Mills's assertions about originality: "Since race artists record their original compositions for the most part, their recordings have a better opportunity for a longer life than those in the 'hit parade' category that changes in public favor from week to week." The fact that the recording of originals possesses greater symbolic prestige—"it's an art," according to Glaser—also seems to be responsible for the longevity of these recordings' popularity. Another article, "Personality on a Platter," attributes a kind of presence to the recordings of African American entertainers, given that they possess "the happy faculty of being able to add improvisations into any available material." This happy faculty results in the transference of "visual personality" from live performance to the recording, a "glowing example" of which is Ella Fitzgerald, who "does indescribable things which exemplify her personality to a song with her voice and insures the operator of a hit nine times out of ten." The same quality is possessed by the Four Ink Spots, Edgar Sampson, Fats Waller, and Louis Armstrong—all African Americans.[19]

The differing arguments of Robbins, Mills, and Glaser, taken together, clarify what was at stake in the emerging institutional prestige of coin machines. Jukebox technology gave newfound emphasis to consumer choice. The machines were serviced by industry middlemen who responded to the popularity of their products with fewer preconceived notions about "good" music than those involved with music publishing, an attitude that in turn expanded the musical categories now demanding attention. Robbins's fear of the "dangerous speculation" of coin machine operators, couched in the language of cultural uplift, thus comes to appear tied to a fear of losing control of the marketing and distribution of popular music.

The Aesthetics of Swing

I have included this rather lengthy discussion of the impact of coin machines because of their important role in effecting a transition between the work concept and the sonic aesthetic in popular music. This transition relied on the intertwining of technology with music industry structure, so that a move toward recognizing the commercial importance of sound recordings also created an opening for categories of popular music—such as those associated with African Americans, rural white Southerners, and immigrants—that had hitherto been relatively neglected. This shift to new technology and a revamped industrial structure also occasioned new aesthetic discussions around sound recordings, as the number of published record reviews increased dramatically in the late 1930s. Moreover, the shift toward the sonic aesthetic, however slight, opened the door further for musical practices such as improvisation, distinctive vocal and instrumental timbres, and pitch and beat inflection that were associated with jazz, swing, and race music in general.

The record reviews of this period provide fertile turf for teasing out an aesthetic discourse that articulated elements of musical style to genre and to performers whose musical strengths and weaknesses seem to cluster together almost miraculously based on their race. Musical elements that attracted attention included not only melody but intonation, volume, rhythmic intensity, the amount and type of repetition, and the degree of spontaneity, among others. Two examples from late 1939 will suffice. The September 13 issue of *Variety* reviewed Ernie Field's Orchestra, an African American band. The band was described as "not being ready for big time competition" because of it was "weak from the angle of arrangements." Although the "most solid section of the outfit is its rhythm," the brass and saxes "give out in badly intonated manner." Further criticisms cite the profusion of improvised soloing and poor material due to the use of "few popular numbers."

A month later, Coleman Hawkins, flush from the coin machine–driven success of "Body and Soul," received a review in the same column. While praising the inventiveness of his soloing in "Body and Soul," the review criticizes his eight-piece band as "not comparable to his talents." The rhythm section is "hard driving" but "indifferent" and "occasionally goes off intonation." The drumming is "monotonous" and the "continual loudness" of the band "causes even the tables to vibrate." The band's tendency in material to rely on "good oldies" such as "Body and Soul" "will have to be remedied, and will be, as the outfit is to go on the air from here."[20] Many other performance and recording reviews of artists such as Benny Carter, Lionel Hampton, Erskine Hawkins, Jay McShann (an early employer of Charlie Parker), Count Basie, and Duke Ellington repeat the criticisms of at least some of the same musical elements: lack of melody, overuse of original material, overemphasis on rhythm, excessive volume, poor intonation.[21]

But then (as with Dave Chappelle), every experiment needs a control. A review of a performance of (the white bandleader) Les Brown's "Band of Renown" from November 1940 offers musical and visual praise, as the writer finds the band both "clean looking and clean playing." In addition to this, the band "interprets smart arrangements," and is "well rehearsed," demonstrating its "excellent taste"—praise that rarely occurred in conjunction with African American artists. Brown's band's achievements do overlap at times with African American bands in that the band "swings out with a wealth of drive." The band's young vocalist, Doris Day, also receives abundant approval as the "good-looking possessor of a nifty voice and style."[22]

The interests of ASCAP are represented above in how the approval of bands depended on the degree to which a certain form of ASCAP-approved melody was present, and on the reliance or lack thereof on ASCAP material. The debate could also take the form of the advocacy of the swing subgenre of sweet jazz over hot jazz. This advocacy occasionally made the racialized terrain of the debate quite unmistakable, and in late 1939 and early 1940, the drum roll for the ascension of sweet jazz over hot jazz began:

> Swing—in the blaring ear-bending style that has been generally associated with the word for the past several years—is nearing extinction. The public is again melody conscious. It has indicated in various ways lately that it would "Like to Recognize the Tune." What probably will eventually be evolved from the trend away from accented brass will be a white man's style of swing, retaining the Negroid bounce but coupling it to more respect for the melody, a distinct departure from the recent method of aping colored bands and instrumentalists. Latter style was the one universally copied at the beginning of swing.[23]

Few quotes could better summarize the conjuncture of musical style, genre, and race. The values of mainstream popular music as supported by ASCAP emphasized melody, arrangement, low volume, and whiteness, to which might be added a discreet "Negroid bounce." The triumph of sweet over hot may have been little more than wishful thinking at this point, but the frequency of such predictions eventually transitioned into reports. The full impact of a transition away from hot jazz and big swing bands, however, would take several years to be truly felt.

TWO STOPS AT "TUXEDO JUNCTION"

This narrative of generic and aesthetic transformation forms the backdrop for an analysis of one of the biggest hits of the period, "Tuxedo Junction." The recordings of "Tuxedo Junction" by Erskine Hawkins and Glenn Miller exemplify how differences in musical style were often correlated with how the recordings were classified, the fluidity of their circulation, the size of their audience, and their access to various modes of dissemination.

The bandleader and trumpeter Erskine Hawkins cowrote "Tuxedo Junction" and recorded it with his band in 1939. Hawkins's band was one of the few African American ensembles to be featured regularly on radio broadcasts, an advantage accorded by virtue of a long-running engagement at Manhattan's Savoy Ballroom, which had a wire pickup (i.e., his performances were transmitted regularly by radio). This sustaining broadcast gave Hawkins a forum for self-promotion not quite at the level of the most successful white bands, but one that undoubtedly played a role in the unusual popularity of this recording and the type of attention it received.

"Tuxedo Junction" is a medium-tempo, riff-based number derived from a simplified form of "I've Got Rhythm" (see musical examples 15 and 16—melodies of both the intro and "A" section are based on short riffs, labeled "riff 1" and "riff 2").

The stripped-down harmony and texture, which looks forward to (what are now recognized as) the jump blues and rhythm and blues of the mid-1940s, allow for an abundance of superimposed riffs and bluesy improvisations. The trumpet and clarinet soloists both improvise full thirty-two-bar choruses, revealing an awareness of contemporary hot soloing trends.

Credited to Hawkins, and the saxophonists Bill Johnson and Julian Dash, the song (as composed structure) would not have been promoted by the apparatus then dominant in the U.S. music industry, wherein song pluggers attempted to persuade bandleaders to record and, most importantly, play their songs on radio broadcasts. The reliance on non-notatable musical elements, and the creation of the song outside of the circuits of Tin Pan Alley, rendered Hawkins's recording of "Tuxedo Junction" unattractive to song pluggers. All of the factors previously mentioned about the preeminent role of the publisher in the presentation of, and discourse around, popularity meant that Hawkins's recording of "Tuxedo Junction" would generate little commentary in the music industry press, which would be incapable of perceiving its popularity or lack thereof.

MUSICAL EXAMPLE 15: Erskine Hawkins, Intro to "Tuxedo Junction"

MUSICAL EXAMPLE 16: Erskine Hawkins, "A" Theme to "Tuxedo Junction"

Hawkins's recording did receive some attention at the back of *Billboard*, that is, by the segment of the industry interested in coin machines, and coin machine operators often found that many of the same people who liked Glenn Miller's band, the most popular ensemble of the period, also liked Hawkins's. One jukebox operator reported to *Billboard* in "What the Records Are Doing for Me" in the December 30, 1939, issue: "As for bands, Glenn Miller seems to grow more and more popular along with Erskine Hawkins, the latter going like a house afire in the colored neighborhoods" (150). After a few weeks of attention, Hawkins's recording seemed to sink without a trace in the pages of *Billboard*, only to reappear several weeks later. Although initially mystified, *Billboard* quickly put two and two together:

Erskine Hawkins, who wrote the tune, recorded it some weeks ago and it enjoyed a slight measure of phono [i.e., jukebox] popularity. Glenn Miller then picked the song up and began to feature it on his radio programs, with the result that requests flooded in for him to record it. The Miller version of the number has already created such excitement that his disk is practically certain to be another "In the Mood." Be prepared for a big thing here. (February 24, 1940, 72)

Subsequent issues of *Billboard* noted that Hawkins's recording had experienced a resurgence of interest in jukeboxes after the appearance of Miller's, which became one of Miller's biggest hits, ranking with previous recordings of his, such as "In the Mood."

It is interesting to speculate on just how exactly Miller managed to "pick the song up." Hawkins and Miller shared a pre-Christmas gig on December 2, 1939, at the Savoy Ballroom, soon after the release of Hawkins's recording and a mere two weeks before the first recognition of the song's popularity in *Billboard* in the December 16, 1939, issue. It is not wild speculation to imagine that Miller heard the Hawkins band perform it, saw the positive crowd response, and realized that it could be a vehicle for the type of arrangement he had just used for "In the Mood."[24]

Miller and the arranger Jerry Gray considerably rearranged the tune, using a slower tempo and a heavier approach to groove. The most striking difference is formal, however: Miller adds a new introduction, and then takes the AABA form of the original and reduces it to only one eight-measure "A" section, followed by the eight-measure "B" section. Two solo sections follow over the harmonic progression of "A," after which his own intro figure returns.

Table 8 illustrates how Miller transforms Hawkins's riff tune, a vehicle for improvisation, into what is essentially a through-composed chart. Miller compresses what he borrows from Hawkins into the first minute and a half of his recording. Miller's only complete statement of the "A" theme is combined with Hawkins's intro, an arranging idea that he borrowed from Hawkins's last statement of the "A" section in his recording.

In the "B" section, Miller retains the call-and-response format of Hawkins's recording, transcribing for an entire saxophone section (with a few rhythmic simplifications) what sounds to be the improvised responses of the alto sax in Hawkins's version (musical example 17).

Finally, for the first of only two eight-measure "A" sections to feature improvisation, Miller recycles Hawkins's bluesy backing riff. For the second, Miller uses the "A" theme itself as the background for a muted trumpet solo, as in the first "A" section of Hawkins's fourth chorus.

Following the muted trumpet solo, Miller's intro reappears. This intro provides the most striking aspect of Miller's recording, featuring as it does Miller's unique approach to the trombone section of the big band, what Gunther Schuller called his "gorgeous velvety sound and texture."[25] This reappearance of the intro appears

TABLE 8 Comparison of Form in Two Versions of "Tuxedo Junction"

Hawkins (tempo: q=ca. 154)	Miller (tempo: q=ca. 115)
Intro	**Intro**
bass/harmonic progression of "A" section (eight bars), trumpet melody	fade-in (eight measures)
	Chorus 1
Chorus 1	A: combines intro figure with theme "A" as in last
A: (eight bars)	A section of Hawkins's chorus 4
A: repeat	B: as with Hawkins
B: melody with obbligato (eight bars)	A: trumpet solo, same background as "A" section
A: repeat of A	of Hawkins's chorus 2
	A: muted trumpet solo, background is Hawkins's
Chorus 2	melody A
Trumpet solo	
AABA	**(1:25) Coda**
	Intro returns (eight bars), extended with shouting
Chorus 3	brass (+ 2 measures)
Clarinet solo	(1:46) A: (four bars), shouting brass continues as
AABA (different backing riff for "A" sections)	background leading to "reveille" interruption
	(four bars)
Chorus 4 (partial)	(2:03) Intro + extension (new brass chord riff) +
Muted trumpet	A/interrupted
A: solo over melody of first chorus	Intro + extension (shouting background again) +
A: trumpet plays intro figure over diminuendo	A/interrupted (two measures) + tag (ca. two
(Miller's "A" theme)	measures)

to lead back, via "shouting" trumpets," to a restatement of the "A" theme. The recap, however, is interrupted by trumpets playing what sounds like a bugle performing reveille. This device, repeated several times, eventually reveals itself to be the coda of the song (see musical example 18).

Miller's formal rearrangement results in transforming the song so that it refers clearly to two popular genres: swing, and one of the most durable mainstream genres of the era, the novelty number. As such, the continual interruptions function as a commercial hook for the song altogether lacking in Hawkins's version, and seem tailor-made to fit Theodor Adorno's scathing critique, published at almost exactly the same time, of the use of novel effects to create "pseudo-individualization" (Adorno's term) in popular songs.[26] Form is significant here, because Hawkins's recording, which is more standardized than Miller's in the Adornian sense, is actually more poorly adapted to commodification, contradicting Adorno's theory about the relation between standardization and commodification in popular music. That is, Hawkins's version features a thirty-two-bar AABA form, the sine qua non of formal standardization in the popular music of the era, while Miller's form is very irregular (see table 8). Yet that very irregularity produces the

MUSICAL EXAMPLE 17. "B" Section of Erskine Hawkins's "Tuxedo Junction"

hook-gimmick that can then recur a maximum number of times, as the interrupted coda occupies almost two-thirds of the recording (see musical example 18).
The formal regularity of Hawkins's version provides a backdrop for the improvised
solos, which in turn produces a kind of variety lacking in the Miller version.[27] The
interruptions of Miller's "Tuxedo Junction" resemble closely those used in "In the
Mood" (the Miller band's most recent big hit), in which the formal interruption is
used in two different ways: first, to cut off the flow of an improvising soloist, and
second, to create suspense during the long fade-out at the coda, the device re-
created in "Tuxedo Junction." This formal device had thus become a kind of trademark for Miller, not unlike the way a 1939 Ford Deluxe might distinguish itself
from a 1939 Studebaker Champion by the size and shape of its front grille.[28]

Although the through-composed form on Miller's recording is sui generis, and
thus arguably nonstandardized, on another level one could argue that soloistic
improvisation in Hawkins's recording actually destandardizes the moment-to-
moment experience of the recording. While Miller's formal irregularities must be
repeated as closely as possible from one performance to the next, locking the band

MUSICAL EXAMPLE 18. Glenn Miller, "Tuxedo Junction," First Reappearance of Intro Figure / Partial Recap of "A"/Reveille (1:25)

into endless restagings of their recording, the improvised thirty-two-bar choruses of Hawkins's recording make literal repetition unlikely, as well as not particularly desirable from either the listening or the performing standpoint. As stated earlier, sheet music not only had copyright law and a whole apparatus for measuring popularity on its side, but the idea of the song, or a through-arranged song that mimicked the unique form of a through-composed piece of art music, was also in line with the aesthetic values enshrined in the Western art music canon and the work concept. Heavily arranged versions of songs such as Miller's thus benefited in public discussions of musical aesthetics when compared to versions such as Hawkins's, in which sectional form served as a generic frame in order to facilitate improvisation.

Indeed, one of the most general differences between the recordings lies in the role of improvisation, a musical component that is also crucial in differentiating race music from the mainstream. Improvisation permeates popular race records of the time in a way that transcends common understandings of it as soloistic melodic invention. Thus improvisation is found not only in solo sections, but even in the construction of the song itself, where, as in "Tuxedo Junction," songs are blues- or riff-based and therefore created out of "floating" musical tropes that were recombined in an endless variety of ways from song to song. Composition itself thus comes about often through a performative, improvisatory approach.

The reception of the Hawkins and Miller bands and "Tuxedo Junction" unites the foregoing observations about the respective recordings of the bands with the discussion earlier in this chapter about the racialized aesthetics of the period. Miller's band was widely recognized as the most successful band between 1939 and 1942, and, as such, his recording of "Tuxedo Junction" placed that song within a prominent public discussion of popularity. The attention paid to Miller overflowed and spilled onto Hawkins, leading writers to inquire about the origins of "Tuxedo Junction." An account in *Down Beat* emphasized the role of improvisation in the tune's genesis: apparently, the main theme in "Tuxedo Junction" had served as a stock device for providing a transition between bands at the Savoy Ballroom in Harlem: "One band, finishing a set, would swing into the simple phrase, picked up by the relief band as it moved on to an adjoining bandstand to take over." One evening, however, when Chick Webb's band was scheduled to follow Hawkins's, the tardiness of the diminutive bandleader forced Hawkins to "improvise around the phrase for four minutes." This improvisation led to the creation of a new introduction and a "16-bar middle to the principal phrase," which Hawkins remembered when he went to record the tune.[29] "Tuxedo Junction" juxtaposes opposites: urban and sophisticated musical techniques with off-the-cuff improvisations and down-home riffs; and the creation of the tune in the North and verbal references to the South ("Tuxedo Junction" was a jazz and blues club in Birmingham, Alabama, Hawkins's hometown). This combining of opposites exemplifies what Guthrie Ramsey Jr. has termed "Afro-Modernism," a trope that became prominent in African American cultural practices during the 1940s.[30]

This anecdote highlights the close association between the use of floating phrases that were then in circulation and shared by many African American swing bands and the development of riff-based melodies from improvisations that were repeated, remembered, and gradually assumed a standardized form. "Tuxedo Junction" in this way epitomized precisely what ASCAP-based publishers were railing against when they complained about the increased use of un-pluggable originals by hot swing bands.

Miller, contra Hawkins, stressed elements other than improvisation in his descriptions of his band's musical values. The title of one profile, made just as his version of "Tuxedo Junction" was released, almost says it all: "Rhythm Section Is My Only Worry." This self-penned article in *Down Beat* reveals that Miller "stresses ensemble work," and that "some nights the band thrills [him] with its precision, intonation, and other qualities every leader seeks." Unless, of course, those bandleaders were Benny Carter, Lionel Hampton, Erskine Hawkins, Jay McShann, or Count Basie, all bandleaders who seemed to be thrilled by other musical qualities. The qualities that critics praised in these bands—namely rhythm and improvisation—proved to be those that Miller either "worried about" or downplayed; after all, the ensemble was more important to him than having a band "featuring terrific [i.e., improvising] soloists." A month later, Miller went even further, claiming, "I haven't a great jazz band, and I don't want one." Now, instead of ensemble work, Miller stressed the importance and his mastery of "harmony," which resulted from his "years of serious study" with "legitimate teachers." This training enabled him "to write arrangements, employing unusual, rich harmonies, many never before used in dance bands." With unusual, rich harmonies came that other element so prized by publishers: "By giving the public a rich and full melody, distinctly arranged and well played, all the time *creating* new tone colors and patterns, I feel we have a better chance of being successful" [emphasis in original].[31]

The celebration of Miller's harmony, intonation, and ensemble, and the concomitant downplaying of the importance of his rhythm section, supported the comments of ASCAP representatives such as Jack Robbins as well as one of the editorial projects of *Down Beat* of the period: the search for an authentic form of white jazz. In addition to "not wanting a jazz band" and not particularly valuing great soloists, Miller admitted that "a dozen colored bands have a better beat than mine." The general discourse of white inferiority filling the pages of *Down Beat* amplified this idea, as when one author observed that "Glenn Miller's band would probably fall off the stand if it heard itself swing a note."[32] This sense of inferiority manifested itself in advocacy for a white jazz that would be free of black influence. This advocacy ranged from bemoaning "that we are not doing much to develop a jazz which is essentially 'white' in character" to celebrating how "for the first time in four years, the brass section [in *Down Beat*'s All-American 1939 Band] does not include one or more of the great colored stars" to wondering wistfully what white jazz might have been "if Bix and Tesch had lived." Some writers, for instance Marvin Freedman, even referred to the practice of promoting white jazz as a cause, which could become a litmus test of racial loyalty.[33]

A discourse on the economic reality of black musicians inverted the advocacy of the development of a white jazz. Statements such as "The truth is that the public will absorb only a very limited number of Negro bands" were presented as though they were a fait accompli. Other articles addressed the material and practical exigencies facing black bands. One asked: "Are there too many good bands kicking around? Has the public turned to white schmaltz?"[34] What this discourse implied everywhere but did not state was that these musicians would all be successful "if [their] conditions were identical with those [of white musicians]." Others offered specifics rather than questions, especially in forums other than *Down Beat.* After providing a list of the most prominent African American popular musicians of the time, most of whom had flirted with mainstream success in the late 1930s, Irving Kolodin, writing in *Harper's,* argued that even though these performers "are names with a familiar echo" to the public, "they are almost never to be encountered in a prominent hotel, and never on a commercial radio program." Kolodin contrasts the fate of these musicians with none other than Glenn Miller, who shot to fame in 1939 after prominent engagements in major New York hotels and ongoing sustaining broadcasts, which in turn led to a lucrative string of one-nighters and a well-paid contract for network-sponsored broadcasts with Chesterfield.[35]

Despite the disparity in the reception of Hawkins and Miller and their recordings of "Tuxedo Junction," and the ways in which institutionalized attitudes about race and genre influenced the circulation of these recordings, the two bandleaders remained partners throughout the early 1940s in the public imagination, or at least in the segment of the public that produced and read *Billboard* (see figure 5). Such was the popularity of "Tuxedo Junction" that it produced an enduring association several years after the heyday of their recordings.

The Popular Music Field and Race Records, 1940

One of the striking aspects of popular music during this period is how musical practices associated with African Americans saturated the fabric of mainstream popular music, even as performed by white musicians. This is not a paradox. The whole premise of an imaginary identification with genre is that the dominant social connotations of a type of music quite often do not match the primary social identification of the performers. Such imaginary identifications also apply to listeners, who do not necessarily restrict themselves to listening only to recordings projecting social connotations that match their demographic classification, this being one of the primary factors in enabling crossover recordings.

One point follows from this claim about crossover that is particular to this relatively brief historical moment: the manner and frequency with which white musicians were adopting certain African American musical practices was generating new effects. For example, when Glenn Miller's band recorded "Tuxedo Junction," even though soloistic improvisation diminished compared to Hawkins's version, it didn't disappear altogether, and bands such as Miller's evoked other musical

*Here's **Glenn Miller's** new one—
A hot side
and a blue one!*

VICTOR 20-1536 { **BLUE RAIN**
CARIBBEAN CLIPPER
—*Glenn Miller and his Orchestra*

Glenn does BLUE RAIN very sweet and slow, with Ray Eberle singing the dreamy vocal. Then Glenn sends 'em with CARIBBEAN CLIPPER—solid jive, with Maurice Purtell on the drums. No hep nickel will miss this one!

*Ain't that trumpet grand?
It's **Erskine Hawkins'** band!*

BLUEBIRD 30-0813 { **DON'T CRY, BABY**
BEAR-MASH BLUES
—*Erskine Hawkins and his Orchestra*

In DON'T CRY, BABY, Jimmy Mitchell does a swell vocal, then Erskine scorches up the place with his hot horn. BEAR-MASH BLUES is in drag tempo, with a haunting tune you can't get out of your mind. Strictly a jack-pot proposition, men.

YIPPEE—HERE'S MONTANA SLIM AND HIS GEE-TAR!

BLUEBIRD 33-0505 { **THE PRISONER'S SONG**
WE'LL MEET AGAIN IN PEACEFUL VALLEY
—*Montana Slim (The Yodeling Cowboy)*

Montana Slim puts his heart into that sad old favorite, THE PRISONER'S SONG, then brightly yodels his own romantic tune, WE'LL MEET AGAIN IN PEACEFUL VALLEY. That's gold in that thar platter, pardner!

To help us make New Victor and Bluebird Records for you, sell your old ones to your distributor.

FIGURE 5. Glenn Miller and Erskine Hawkins, Together Through the 1940s.[36] Advertisement is reproduced courtesy of Sony Entertainment.

practices associated with African Americans at the time, such as swing rhythmic feeling and a certain approach to timbre.

Another sign of the ubiquity of African American musical practices can be found in the boogie-woogie craze that swept the country in the early 1940s, derived from African American pianists such as Pete Johnson and Albert Ammons, and from singers such as Joe Turner. White bandleaders Will Bradley ("Beat Me Daddy Eight to the Bar," 1941), and Freddie Slack ("Cow Cow Boogie," 1942) enjoyed immense success for a few years with music that approximated some of the rhythm and blues and jump blues that would arise later in the decade, and which popularized sounds otherwise confined to the world of race music. Their popularity was such that even the Andrews Sisters, those mainstream barometers of crossover success, scored with "Boogie Woogie Bugle Boy" in 1941.

From the standpoint of the political history of racial relations, even more significant than the use of these musical tropes by white musicians was the increased social circulation of swing-based music by African American artists, which meant that African Americans, not only African American–associated sounds, found a larger audience than they had since the classic blues craze of the 1920s, and more than they would again until the breakthrough of rock 'n' roll in the mid-1950s. The musical practices of blackness were consumed by the mainstream audience, whether performed by black or white musicians, and could be understood as part of that mainstream without having their symbolic capital diminished (i.e., trivialized) through their presentation as a novelty or through the invocation of the desire and disavowal that characterized minstrelsy and post-minstrel musical performances of black identity.[37] Yet for a mainstream to be perceived, and for crossover to be meaningful, a marginal category must exist from which a recording can cross over. In this case, the category of race music figured as the opposing pole to the mainstream most pertinent to the current chapter.

Many African American artists led flourishing performing and recording careers during 1939 and 1940, and yet were never mentioned in *Billboard,* never appeared in a popularity chart, and were rarely mentioned in black newspapers such as the *Chicago Defender.* These artists—including Tampa Red, Washboard Sam, the Golden Gate Quartet, Blind Boy Fuller, and Peetie Wheatstraw—each recorded more than thirty songs during this two-year period, demonstrating that the record companies found their music profitable even if their popularity was not measured in a fashion comparable to mainstream popular music.[38] One might ask, then, what characteristics did these artists have in common with each other that were not shared with crossover hits such as Hawkins's "Tuxedo Junction"? By the same token, what linked "Tuxedo Junction" to other mainstream hits?

In general, and not too surprisingly, one finds intensification in the non-crossover race records of those musical characteristics identified with African American music at the time (and more generally from the 1920s to the present).

This is a tautological process, admittedly, as the recordings that were represented as having only an African American audience turn out to be those most strongly marked with African American musical characteristics. The most striking difference, however, has not to do with musical practices related to pitch and rhythm, but with audible traces of raced bodies within the recordings.

The sounds of the body are conveyed most directly by the voice—both the way it sings and how it sounds. That is to say that it isn't only the singing style that differentiates race records, but the *type* of voice that sings, and what's more, the racial connotations of that voice. Count Basie, Duke Ellington, Jimmy Lunceford, Erskine Hawkins, and Coleman Hawkins could all cross over from 1938 to 1941, but almost none of their biggest hits featured black vocalists. The biggest successes—Basie's "One O'Clock Jump" and "Jumpin' at the Woodside," Ellington's "I Let a Song Go Out of My Heart" and "Take the 'A' Train," and Coleman Hawkins's "Body and Soul"— were instrumentals, and most of them (with the exception of Coleman Hawkins's recording) shared the basic sound and texture of the most successful white bands of the era. Thus, black vocalists were almost totally absent from crossover recordings,[39] and white listeners could listen to recordings of black bands without being reminded that they were listening to African American musicians. In this sense, the ways in which categorical boundaries were inscribed recall those that existed at the beginning of the 1920s, when the main novelty of "Crazy Blues" was the fact that the singer, Mamie Smith, was African American. In 1920, as in 1940, musical tropes associated with African Americans were already circulating in mainstream popular music as played by either white or black musicians, yet as sung mostly by white singers. African Americans, through the impulses propelled by swing grooves and hot improvisations, may have moved the bodies of white listeners, but without a voice, they had more difficulty accessing white souls and were allowed few opportunities to project the romantic sentiments of mature, thoughtful adults.

Taking the recordings of Tampa Red, Washboard Sam, et al. as a broad sample, one finds that, in addition to vocal style and timbre, instrumentation and lyrics form a major point of departure from mainstream popular music. Most non-crossover race records of the period featured a solo singer accompanied by either a guitar or a piano, or by a small ensemble that typically included guitar, piano, harmonica, and washboard. Techniques such as bent notes and use of bottleneck slide on the guitar, or instruments such as harmonica, washboard, and kazoo, resided in an alternate aesthetic universe from that of the big bands. The lyrics of the songs also departed from mainstream conventions in the use of African American slang and non-Hollywoodesque depictions of male-female relations. The relationships between race music, race-to-mainstream crossovers, and the mainstream are represented in figure 6.

As stated earlier, and somewhat contrary to the most entrenched stereotypes about black music, rhythm is not one of the most obvious differentiating factors.

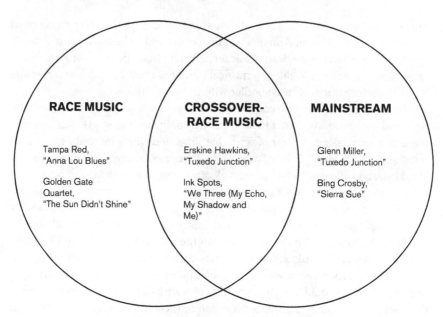

FIGURE 6. The Circular Logic of Race-Mainstream Crossovers ca. 1940.

"Swing" music, after all, swung at least some of the time, even when played by white bands, and a shuffle or swing groove also dominates race records of the time.

FROM "JUNCTION" TO "RICHARD"

Although many of the style characteristics that identified the distinctiveness of race music would remain separate from the mainstream, by and large, until the 1950s, changes in the status of African American musicians and the growing presence of musical practices associated with African Americans were recognized by the music industry at the time. The following quote from the January 2, 1943, issue of *Billboard* explicitly connects the shift away from a minstrel-based paradigm for African American music to the popularity of swing:

> The biggest break Negro performers received . . . has been the recognition of Negroes as first-rate jazz musicians. The craze for swing music suddenly put the spotlight on Negro musicians as creative artists and did much to live down the typical presentation of Negro entertainers as carefree, banjo-plucking cotton pickers continually grinning and shouting jazzy spirituals. . . .
>
> Negro name band leaders have held their own thru the years because they presented a brand of music whites could not easily duplicate.[40]

Even as these words appeared in print, however, the status of swing—and thus, to some degree, of African Americans within the popular music mainstream—was declining. A variety of factors contributed to the shift, although, as with any change in mass taste, cause and effect are difficult to determine. Wartime shortages of fuel made the travel between one-nighters, so essential for the livelihood of big bands, considerably more expensive. Large numbers of young men were conscripted, disrupting the heterosexual rituals so essential to filling ballrooms with dancing couples. In addition to the ongoing ASCAP-BMI struggles, the AF of M went on strike in 1942, limiting the amount of recording available to instrumentalists. While interfering with a source of income for big bands, this last development also encouraged the circulation of recordings by non-union musicians, which included many who participated in the marginal categories of race, hillbilly, and foreign music, a change that would lead to dramatic changes in the status of those categories.

The Harlem Hit Parade, Covers, and Crossovers

Thus far, this chapter has focused on swing and jazz, and their interaction with the mainstream and race categories. The institutional alliance between mainstream popular music and the work concept meant that certain aesthetic values were promoted in a variety of ways: via the greater circulation of mainstream recordings, through greater prominence in music industry discourse, and through the privileging of popularity charts for mainstream music, particularly those that emphasized the song as published artifact. The growth in record sales, abetted by the greater distribution of coin machines, attracted the attention of the music industry, resulting in a greater emphasis in the tracking of the popularity of recordings. These developments created an infinitesimal shift toward the sonic aesthetic as well as toward the types of music, such as race music and hillbilly music, that relied on this aesthetic. The interest in African American popular music as a realm separate from the mainstream increased the subtlety of the mechanisms used to articulate music style to identification, resulting in a number of new popularity charts and an increase in discourse around race music. The following section deals with a new level of complexity in the relationship between musical style, musical categories, and identity that only became possible because of these new tracking mechanisms and attention to recordings. This may take us rather far from Count Basie and "Open the Door, Richard," but such an account of the relationship between race music and the mainstream will throw into relief the changes that occurred during the 1940s, and will help make sense of the strange event that was the success of "Open the Door, Richard."

Perhaps due to the causes listed at the end of the last section, the number of big band recordings in charts such as *Billboard*'s "Best-Selling Retail Records" (hereafter BSRR) diminished during the war years, and, in what may seem to confirm the standard popular music historical narrative, the number of sentimental songs crooned by solo singers backed by orchestras and choruses increased. At the same time, as if to compensate for the decrease of African American–associated music in the mainstream, *Billboard* began, albeit in a tentative fashion, to produce a representation of the popularity of race records. This development showed that race music had achieved a level of commercial importance such that the music industry felt it advantageous to track it in some fashion. The chart, dubbed the "Harlem Hit Parade" (hereafter HHP), "based on sales reports" from a variety of record shops (in African American neighborhoods, one assumes),[41] continued from October 1942 until February 17, 1945, when it was replaced by a "Most Played Juke Box Race Records" chart.

The HHP possessed several properties that historians of black popular music might find a bit counterintuitive. The first of these was the sheer number of white artists who appeared on the chart, including Bing Crosby, Tommy Dorsey, Harry James, Glenn Miller, and Dick Haymes, none of whom hold prominent places in historical accounts of race music.[42] Bing Crosby's "White Christmas" even topped the HHP in the December 19, 1942, edition, and held the top position for the following two weeks. A possible rationale for this state of affairs might be that the HHP reported sales in selected record shops, not pre-filtering their tabulations according to notions of what constituted race recordings. These non-race recordings sold well in these locations because of their ubiquity on the radio (almost no race recordings would have circulated via radio during this period) and their superior distribution networks ("White Christmas," for example, became the best-selling recording of all time following its release in 1942). Very few recordings were produced during the war years anyway, and therefore few releases of race records existed that could compete with commercial powerhouses such as "White Christmas." The popularity of recordings by white artists on the HHP produced what could be termed a reverse crossover effect that could lead to at least two different conclusions: that these crossovers illustrated the diversity of tastes and imaginary identifications among African American consumers and the overlapping of tastes between marginal and mainstream populations, or that people can be persuaded to consume almost any type of music if they hear it enough and have few other choices.

A second observation that emerges from a study of the HHP is the popularity of African American artists such as the Ink Spots, the Mills Brothers, and Ella Fitzgerald. These artists all recorded for a major label, Decca, and their most popular recordings during this period did not project stylistic elements with strong associations of African American popular music.[43] Their material was derived from ASCAP-related sources and recorded with mainstream production values, and featured at most a discreet "Negroid bounce," little instrumental improvisation, clean vocal timbres and enunciation, lyrics with picturesque stories, et cetera. The recordings by these artists often rose to the top of the mainstream charts such as the "Best-Selling Retail Records" (BSRR) and "Most Played on Juke Boxes," and cover versions by white artists rarely supplanted them in these listings. Their recordings were sometimes more popular on the mainstream charts than on the HHP, and often appeared simultaneously on both charts, thus not following a typical crossover pattern. It is clear from following the chart performance of these artists that they were accepted as both mainstream and race artists.

Although cover versions of songs recorded first by the Mills Brothers, the Ink Spots, and Ella Fitzgerald did not overtake the originals, the same cannot be said of another group of recordings. Table 9 shows the performance on both the HHP and the BSRR of recordings made by African American artists such as Duke Ellington, the King Cole Trio, Louis Jordan, and Lionel Hampton that were then covered by white artists. It demonstrates the process of white artists covering recordings by black artists that then resulted in greater success for the cover version. The original recordings, after first achieving sustained success in the HHP (or the jukebox race records chart that succeeded it) were routinely overtaken in the BSRR chart by recordings that were stylistically adapted to mainstream conventions and recorded by artists better known to mainstream audiences. The process of covers surpassing the mainstream success of recordings initially identified with African Americans is usually identified with the period in the 1950s leading up to rock 'n' roll but was clearly already full-blown in the mid-1940s.

Louis Jordan is the outlier in table 9, as his "Is You Is or Is You Ain't (My Baby)" is only matched by the Bing Crosby and Andrews Sisters' cover version in the BSRR, and Jordan's version ranks higher in the BSRR than the HHP. Jordan, as has been often noted, was the most successful African American performer during the mid-1940s among mainstream audiences. Jordan had preceded "Is You Is or Is You Ain't (My Baby)" with "G.I. Jive," a huge hit that made number one on both the HHP and the BSRR and outpaced the cover version by Johnny Mercer. In a pattern that would be repeated for the next forty years, up through Motown and Michael Jackson, Jordan gained entrée to the popular mainstream through a distinctive idiolect that did not (or could not) necessarily transfer to other African American artists. "G.I. Jive," for example, featured Jordan's humorous patter style applied to lyrics with timely topical resonance: the travails of an infantryman in the U.S. armed forces.

The success of "G.I. Jive" paved the way for Jordan's success over the next few years. Jordan's sound became a kind of brand name marker for the mainstream audience, facilitating the success of his subsequent efforts, which in effect cited his previous crossover success. Jordan's infectious vocal style also proved difficult to duplicate. By way of contrast, Duke Ellington's style, already well known to mainstream audiences due to his popularity during the swing era, failed to inoculate him from the imitative efforts of Woody Herman and Harry James, probably due to his identity as a bandleader and instrumentalist rather than a vocalist with a style that could be assimilated to the novelty category (indeed, the style of Ellington and Basie had been prey to the likes of Charlie Barnet earlier during the

TABLE 9 Comparison of Cover Versions of Race Records, 1944–46

Recording	HHP/MPJBRR	BSRR	Cover Version	BSRR
Duke Ellington, "Do Nothin' Till You Hear from Me" (January 1944)	#1	#10	Woody Herman	#7
King Cole Trio, "Straighten Up and Fly Right" (April 1944)	#1	#9	Andrews Sisters	#8
Louis Jordan, "Is You Is or Is You Ain't (My Baby)" (June 1944)	#3	#2	Bing Crosby and the Andrews Sisters	#2
Duke Ellington, "I'm Beginning to See the Light" (January 1945)	#4	#6	Harry James[i]	#1
Louis Jordan, "Caldonia Boogie" (May 1945)	#1	#6	Woody Herman	#2
Lionel Hampton, "Hey! Ba-Ba-Re-Bop" (March 1946)	#1	#9	Tex Beneke / Glenn Miller Band	#4

HHP: Harlem Hit Parade

MPJBRR: Most Played Juke Box Race Records

BSRR: Best-Selling Retail Records

[i] The history of "I'm Beginning to See the Light" is more tangled than most, however, as Harry James was listed as one of the song's cowriters, along with Duke Ellington, Johnny Hodges, and Don George.

swing era). The humor of Jordan's recordings, and its faint evocations of minstrelsy, also facilitated the grouping of his recordings under the novelty label, a factor in many crossover race recordings of the 1940s. Even an early advertisement for Jordan during his initial breakthrough success emphasized the novelty elements of his performance style with photos of Jordan featuring funny glasses, broad grins, bug eyes, and captions such as "1942's Most Amazing Musical Personality!" and "They Clown! They Sing! They Swing!"[44]

As already stated, numerous white artists appeared in the HHP because this chart lacked presorting by categorical assumptions. Among these artists were a few whose recordings were treated as if they were crossovers by black artists. The aforementioned boogie-woogie craze of the late 1930s and early 1940s figured in many of these recordings, the most prominent of which were by pianist Freddie Slack and a vocalist who began her career with Slack, Ella Mae Morse. Recordings such as Slack's "Mr. Five by Five" (1942, featuring a vocal by Morse), and Morse's "Shoo-Shoo Baby" (1943) followed the same path etched by the recordings of Louis Jordan and the King Cole Trio, in that they first achieved a high degree of prominence on the HHP, which, after a sustained period at or near the top of the HHP, was followed by a listing on either the mainstream retail records chart (BSRR) or the jukebox records chart.[45] Musically, these recordings relied either on the sound of black boogie-woogie pianists and singers and followed the template established by white bandleaders such as Tommy Dorsey in his 1938 recording "Boogie Woogie" and Will Bradley in his 1940 recording "Beat Me Daddy Eight to the Bar" (a recording that featured Slack on the piano) or on the sound of the hot black swing bands, like Count Basie's. Morse in particular was treated discursively as if she were African American, as can be seen in the review of her 1944 recording of "The Patty Cake Man" b/w "Invitation to the Blues": "A rhythmic jingle in jive setting, Miss Morse rocks the verse as a slow blues, stepping up the pace as she hits the choruses to create an even greater degree of heated piping."[46] This type of rhetoric was ubiquitous in *Billboard*'s descriptions of race records of the period, as will be detailed a bit later in this chapter.

Indeed, the ways in which the popularity of these recordings was represented in *Billboard* and their relationship to cover versions by white artists resembled that of the race records shown in the table 9. For example, Slack's "Mr. Five by Five" reached number one on the HHP and number ten on the mainstream BSRR, while Harry James's cover version reached number one on the BSRR. In a similar vein, Morse's "Shoo-Shoo Baby" achieved the top ranking on the HHP and number four on the BSRR, but was overtaken by the Andrews Sisters' cover, which ascended to number one on the BSRR.

Somewhat less frequent in appearance on the HHP than black and white cross-overs were recordings of non-crossover race artists. This category includes artists such as Sonny Boy Williamson and, once again, Tampa Red, whose recordings were occasionally discussed in the record reviews section of *Billboard* and other publications such as *Down Beat*, but never appeared in any mainstream chart. When these artists were discussed, record reviews inevitably appeared with advice for jukebox operators about the suitability of these recordings "for race locations only," or with other descriptors such as "Harlemese ditty," "a jump number," or "race blues shouting/chanting/wailing."[47] A few examples from early 1945 will suffice. First, a review of Sonny Boy Williamson's "Win the War Blues" b/w "Check Up on My Baby Blues":

> The excited blues shouting and ranting of Sonny Boy Williamson for his own songs are right in the race blues register. With the harmonica heated, piano, guitar, and traps, the spinning is smoky all the way.[48]

And now for a review of Tampa Red's "Lulu Mae" b/w "The Woman I Love":

> Singing the race blues laments of the back-biting women, Tampa Red is highly effective for both of these sides. Not shouting or growling, singing it from way deep down to strike a sympathetic response.[49]

"Race blues" seems to be the term reserved for recordings that *Billboard*'s reviewers believed bore the strongest stamp of African American identity. In terms of musical style, these recordings resembled those discussed earlier from 1940, with the more frequent addition of electric guitar and drums.

The consolidation of a race records "mainstream" in the form of jump blues coincided with a shift in the representation of the popularity of black popular music. The replacement of the HHP with the "Most Played Juke Box Race Records" (MPJBRR) in February 1945 effected a subtle but significant shift. The naming of the chart indicates some of the factors involved. Unlike the "Harlem Hit Parade," which recorded sales from selected record stores without presorting them according to category, the MPJBRR already assumed a categorical unity in the identity of the contents of the charts in "race records." The mainstream white artists who had formerly populated the HHP in the form of reverse crossovers were consequently vanquished, and more space was now given to non-crossover race records.

Overall, during the years 1942 through 1945, if we were to begin with the assumption that the mainstream equaled white music and race music equaled black music, then the way in which identity functioned in the categories in practice was clearly more complex. Certain African American artists such as the Ink Spots, the Mills Brothers, and Ella Fitzgerald achieved mainstream success, and thus may have been coded as almost white even though the public was never unsure of their demographic classification. By the same token, white artists such as Ella Mae Morse and Freddie Slack were coded as almost black. Nevertheless, as with jazz and blues in the 1910s, the ability of certain musicians to perform an identity that did not match their demographic classification did not negate how certain musical genres signified race in a manner that was widely recognized across social divisions.

At the same time, the increasing precision with which recordings were tracked and classified resulted in a decrease in mainstream opportunities for African American artists playing music with strong associations of black identity. This structural change in the industry was accompanied by a reduction in instrumental mainstream hits, which also worked against African American musicians, although, as we have seen, white cover versions tended to surpass in popularity songs that were initially recorded by African Americans. Louis Jordan provided the exception to the rule, an exception that lay in the realm of novelty.

Jazz, Race, and the Mainstream

Even as modes for the representation of popularity and race underwent considerable reshuffling, the status of jazz vis-à-vis the mainstream continued to provoke discussion among journalists in the well-documented "moldy figs versus modernists" debate.[50] The opposition of economic versus symbolic capital initially lay at the heart of this discussion, with commercialized swing representing the debased pole of economic capital and hot jazz representing the pure, authentic pole of symbolic capital. The discussion was complicated by many factors, one of which was the identity of hot jazz itself: Should it be confined to revivals (or continuations) of New Orleans, 1920s-style jazz, or should it include small group recordings featuring improvisation by contemporary swing artists? With the emergence of what would eventually be called bebop at the end of the war, race also became an explicit factor in this discussion.

In another example of the distance between presentist and historicist approaches to the writing of history, music journalists focused much of their attention during the immediate postwar period on the small group recordings of white bandleaders such as Benny Goodman, Harry James, and Tommy Dorsey, which have now been written out of the historical record. The response to bebop was ambivalent at best. At the same time, these writers recognized that bebop represented a new kind of specialist music that revolved around the creative efforts of African American musicians.

The splintering of jazz was both a response to and a factor in its relationship to the mainstream. Whereas in the early 1940s swing dominated both the discourse around jazz and the recordings in the popular mainstream, the understanding of the identity of jazz had become more complex during 1945 and 1946, even as the influence of swing on the mainstream waned. Jazz had more or less divided into black jazz and white jazz, thus weakening the effect that had obtained during the swing era, when elements of musical style associated with African Americans had entered the mainstream via swing. Now, swing's influence began to decrease even as more black jazz musicians moved away from the swing style. In 1946, therefore, the white swing bands of Harry James, Woody Herman, Les Brown, and Tex Beneke had hits; black artists in a mainstream style (Ella and the Ink Spots, King Cole Trio) had hits; and artists who produced songs that were legible within the category of novelty (Louis Jordan, Count Basie with "Mad Boogie") had hits. Yet swing, the music that in 1943 had enabled "Negro name band leaders" to hold "their own" because it "presented a brand of music whites could not easily duplicate," now found itself represented almost entirely within mainstream popular music by white bands. African American popular music was increasingly dominated by jump blues, while the most adventurous black jazz musicians gravitated toward bebop, which held only a tenuous relationship to swing or jazz as it was conceived by journalists at the time. Neither jump blues nor bebop lent themselves immediately to easy duplication, but swing, as an example of an "emergent identification," now became increasingly identified with white musicians.

ONE DOOR OPENS, ANOTHER ONE CLOSES

Thus we arrive back where this chapter began. It is definitely true that after the war the status of the big bands and swing music had changed, but in a way that the usual narrative of the decline of the swing bands only begins to suggest. Due to the decrease in swing, African American–ness became, rather than a sound woven into the fabric of popular music, something that could only be performed literally by the corporeality of black voices on recordings that signaled a revitalization of racialized tropes, including those that resembled nothing so much as the trope of the "carefree, banjo-plucking cotton pickers" mentioned in the passage quoted from *Billboard* from 1943. This revitalization was found, in a more general sense, in a wide proliferation of novelty recordings during this period, most of which invoked the simultaneous desire and disavowal that comes with the process of stereotyping. Unlike minstrelsy, novelty recordings thus formed a genre with the advantage of being adaptable to nonwhite others of all denominations. The words of a tune such as "Managua, Nicaragua" (a hit for Freddy Martin in early 1947) exemplify exotic images of female sexuality, travelogues, colonial trade, and imperialism all melding together seamlessly to create a novel sense of humor. The second verse begins, "Managua, Nicaragua is a heavenly place / you ask a señorita for a 'leetle' embrace," while the third begins, "Managua, Nicaragua what a wonderful spot / there's coffee and bananas and a [*sic*] temperature hot."

In addition to novelty numbers, medium- to up-tempo swing tunes played by big bands still occasionally put in an appearance, although these tended to reside solely at the Glenn Miller end of the swing spectrum. Musical style elements derived from the big band era continued to permeate the sound of the mainstream, even when performed by studio orchestras, or by sweet bands such as Freddy Martin's and Sammy Kaye's, which often featured novelty numbers. Without the interaction of these bands with the music of contemporary African American artists, however, either as models for recordings or collaborators, the associations of swing with African Americans weakened. This is also because African American musical tropes were mutating and becoming associated with other genres, such as jump blues on the one hand and bebop on the other, or even with some of the country music of the late 1940s, such as that recorded by Hank Williams or the Delmore Brothers.

Phillip Ennis writes compellingly about the synchronization of media—records, jukeboxes, radio, all based on the recording as the most important unit of exchange—necessary for the formation of a black popular music field that could achieve visibility within the larger music industry, and that would eventually create crossovers (again) beyond the sphere of the novelty record.[51] With the development of forums such as the HHP and the MPJBRR in publications such as *Billboard* for tracking and producing the popularity of recordings among African American consumers, a realm of black popular music separate from the mainstream was reinforced. As if the tentative mainstream introduction of black musical tropes by swing bands and the boogie-woogie craze of the early 1940s constituted an intolerable threat, the riffs, grooves, and blues notes of the early 1940s were figured as an absence in the remaining vestiges of swing that could only appear somewhere else in the popular music field—that is, in another category with its own apparatus for the evaluation of economic capital, such as race music or rhythm and blues (the music industry name for race music after 1949). Black musical tropes after the war thus formed a constitutive outside to a mainstream aesthetic in which nonwhite others would, for the time being, only function as novelties.

This is where the curious tale of "Open the Door, Richard" comes in. One of the few recordings by an African American artist (or, more accurately, artists) in the years immediately following the war to be heard on network radio, it could also be found in record stores and jukeboxes outside of black neighborhoods. A brief account of the song's tangled history provides a great example of a text without an origin.[52] An African American vaudeville comedian, Dusty Fletcher, learned a routine in the 1920s from a comedian named John Mason, who had, in turn, learned it from another black comedian, Bob Russell (a comedian on the African American blackface minstrel circuit who, we presume, learned it from someone else).[53] This routine describes the plight of a man named Richard who is locked out of his apartment in a somewhat inebriated condition. A saxophonist named Jack McVea, who was playing primarily on Central Avenue in Los Angeles, worked with Fletcher when they both toured with Lionel Hampton's band in the early 1940s. When McVea began touring with his own band up and down the West Coast, playing shows from Southern California to Oakland to Seattle, he started to feature a version of the skit, to which he added a memorable chorus. McVea recorded it in September 1946 in Los Angeles and the recording quickly became popular regionally. As the recording was about to break out into a national hit, the major record companies rushed to put out their own versions, as did independents specializing in race records. Fletcher's own two-sided version came out early in 1947, and the race was on.[54]

In a portent of things to come, even the first discussion of the song in *Billboard*, on January 25, 1947, put the versatile potential of the title to good use: a headline reading "Open the Door, Richard, and Let All the Lawyers In" referred to a dispute raging between McVea and Fletcher, while the brief review of the disc in the same issue instructed jukebox operators to "open the door to the jukes and slip these platters onto the changers" (18).[55] Soon the floodgates opened, and radio listeners were treated to versions by (among others) the Three Flames, the Pied Pipers, the Charioteers, Louis Jordan, Bill Samuels and the Cats 'n' Jammer Three, Tosh (One-String Willie) and His Jivesters, Walter Brown and Tiny Grimes, the Merry Macs, Big Sid Catlett, the Hot Lips Page Orchestra, and Hank Penny as well as the afore-mentioned recording by Count Basie.[56]

A riot of different versions saturated the market, with Basie scoring the biggest hit. Unlike the example of "Tuxedo Junction" and countless other instances of crossover recordings, this is an example of a recording by a black artist, covered largely by other black artists (of the fourteen recordings listed above, at least ten are by African Americans).[57] Deemed a novelty by music industry publications, and undoubtedly received as such by mainstream listeners, the song displayed a remarkable ability to adapt to a wide range of situations. In addition to becoming punch lines for comics of all stripes, a common greeting for door knockers everywhere, and a torment for anyone unfortunate enough to be named Richard, the song was recorded by hillbilly artists and calypso artists, and in Yiddish, Spanish, Swedish, French, and Hungarian. Moreover, the many recordings of "Richard" fit in effortlessly with a newfound abundance of novelty recordings that, as I already mentioned, relied on stereotypical others for their punch lines.

In the African American community, however, another debate erupted. Was "Richard" an embarrassing reminder of minstrelsy, an evocation of Uncle Tom–like behavior? This view, probably the first to come to mind to someone contemplating the song today, was held by many in the African American community seeking to gain respectability and distance from a history of degrading caricatures. To some younger, more radicalized black listeners, however, "Richard" became a call to arms: "In 1947 students from Georgia colleges marched to the state capital demanding the resignation of segregationist governor Herman Talmadge, carrying banners reading 'Open the Door Herman.'" The *Los Angeles Sentinel,* the city's black newspaper, ran an editorial entitled "Open the Door Richard" calling for political representation at City Hall and an end to discriminatory housing practices.[58]

Figure 7 displays, when compared with the early graphic in figure 6, both the shift in the relationship between race music and mainstream popular music from 1940 to 1947, and how race music recordings that crossed over to the mainstream charts were required by 1947 to cite the conventions of the novelty genre. Such a dependence on novelty addresses the growing distance between race music and the mainstream, spurred in part by the decline of big bands—a forum that had enabled African Americans to participate (albeit semi-invisibly) in the realm of instrumental music. The new mainstream styles relied, on the one hand, on the centrality of a single vocalist, a development less hospitable to African Americans, revealing, as it tended to, the social identity of the vocalist who could project an "adult" persona endowed with subjectivity, an option rarely available to African Americans at this time. On the other hand, the rise in novelty recordings either used the stereotypes of nonwhite others as the subject of the lyrics, thereby discouraging African American participation and identification, or revived minstrel practices. African American–associated musical practices, including improvisation in performance and song construction, drained out of the mainstream and into the semiautonomous realm of race music, a category that grew in commercial importance by leaps and bounds after 1945. The focus on solo singers did pay dividends for a small number of African American singers, however, as vocalists such as Nat King Cole and Billy

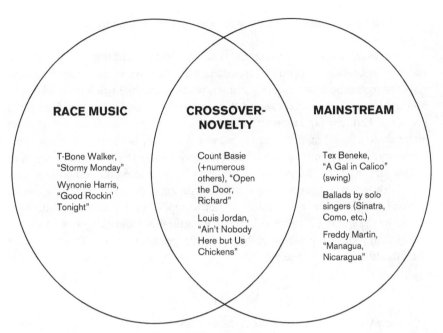

RACE MUSIC

T-Bone Walker,
"Stormy Monday"

Wynonie Harris,
"Good Rockin'
Tonight"

**CROSSOVER-
NOVELTY**

Count Basie
(+numerous
others), "Open
the Door,
Richard"

Louis Jordan,
"Ain't Nobody
Here but Us
Chickens"

MAINSTREAM

Tex Beneke,
"A Gal in Calico"
(swing)

Ballads by solo
singers (Sinatra,
Como, etc.)

Freddy Martin,
"Managua,
Nicaragua"

FIGURE 7. The Circular Logic of Race-Mainstream Crossovers, ca. 1947.

Eckstine gave improbable voice to expressions of true love that had not previously had access to a large audience.[59]

. . .

The period that forms the focus of this chapter provides an excellent opportunity to analyze what was at stake in the formation and re-formation of musical categories. The 1940s began with swing as an integral part of mainstream popular music, spreading forms of improvisation and groove associated with African Americans among heterogeneous audiences. Whether or not swing was a type of jazz was hotly debated among critics and jazz connoisseurs, but swing's participation in the mainstream was not open to debate. By 1947, while swing had not completely disappeared from the mainstream, what remained deemphasized improvisatory practices and lost much of its association with African Americans. As far as the debate over the meaning of jazz went, big band–based swing was no longer a factor. Instead, within the realm of mainstream popular music, African American–ness appeared as a stereotype grouped with stereotypes of assorted Others, while jazz and soloistic improvisation were exiled either to a more connoisseur-oriented form of jazz, or to the increasingly semiautonomous field of black popular music. Due in part to these changes, the "outside" of mainstream popular music acquired greater cohesion with the increased stability of country and rhythm and blues.

An examination of terms such as "jazz" and "swing" and their relationship to race music (later rhythm and blues) and mainstream popular music has the potential to reorganize our sense of jazz history, which since the 1950s has favored evolutionary models, excluded music that was overtly commercial, and ascribed greater authenticity (and more value) to music made by African Americans. Close attention to a broad range of music that was circulating at the time can also reorganize our sense of popular music history, which tends to look at music from 1940 to 1955 for how it anticipates rock 'n' roll, but often overlooks the complex interactions between style, category, and identity occurring at the time. Finally, a focus on a broad range of music, canonical or not, complicates our notions of the role played by the shifting allegiances between identifications and categories, in which, rather than confirming a sense of their stability, we gain a renewed appreciation of their fluidity and contingency.

NOTES

1. Jerry Wexler claims to have coined the term "rhythm and blues" as a label for a music industry category when he worked for *Billboard*; see Jerry Wexler and David Ritz, *The Rhythm and the Blues: A Life in American Music* (New York: St. Martin's Press, 1993), 62–63. As I have argued throughout this book, however, such terms cannot take hold unless a prior discursive practice exists that makes such a label legible. The terms "rhythm" and "blues" had been connected previously when referring to black popular music, even before they were conjoined as a label for a music industry category. See for example "RCA Changes Terms for Catalog Items," *Billboard*, September 28, 1946, 109.

2. Amiri Baraka (aka Leroi Jones), *Blues People: The Negro Experience in White America and the Music That Developed from It* (New York: William Morrow, 1963), 142–65.

3. The classic theoretical formulation about the relationship between economic and symbolic capital may be found in Pierre Bourdieu, "The Field of Cultural Production," in *The Field of Cultural Production: Essays on Art and Literature* (New York: Columbia University Press, 1993), 29–73. See Scott DeVeaux, "Constructing the Jazz Tradition," *Black American Literature Forum* (1990): 525–60. For DeVeaux's later reflections on related issues, see his "Core and Boundaries," *Jazz Research Journal* 2 (2005): 15–30. See also David Ake on the exclusion of popular figures such as Louis Jordan in *Jazz Cultures* (Berkeley: University of California Press, 2002), 42–61; and Sherrie Tucker, on the exclusions of gender performed by the conventional framing of jazz historiography, in *Swing Shift: "All-Girl" Bands of the 1940s* (Durham, NC, and London: Duke University Press, 2000), 1–29. For other accounts of the struggle for critical and aesthetic prestige between pre-swing jazz (New Orleans or Chicago jazz), swing, and bebop, see Bernard Gendron, *Between Montmartre and the Mudd Club: Popular Music and the Avant-Garde* (Chicago and London: University of Chicago Press, 2002), 121–42; and John Gennari, *Blowin' Hot and Cool: Jazz and Its Critics* (Chicago and London: University of Chicago Press, 2006), 61–115.

4. Nor does this recording seem to merit discussion in Basie's autobiography (although he does mention that he recorded it), or in other biographical literature about him, receiving at best a passing mention. See Count Basie (as told to Albert Murray), *Good Morning Blues: The Autobiography of Count Basie* (New York: Random House, 1985); Stanley Dance, *The World of Count Basie* (New York: C. Scribner's Sons, 1980); and Raymond Horricks, *Count Basie and His Orchestra: Its Music and Its Musicians* (London: Victor Gollancz, 1957).

5. Though for a recent attempt to address this lacuna, see Albin Zak III, *I Don't Sound Like Nobody: Remaking Music in 1950s America* (Ann Arbor: University of Michigan Press, 2010). For broader histories that do not give this era short shrift, see Elijah Wald, *How the Beatles Destroyed Rock 'n' Roll: An Alternative History of American Popular Music* (New York: Oxford University Press, 2009); and Philip Ennis, *The Seventh Stream: The Emergence of Rocknroll in American Popular Music* (Hanover, NH, and London: Wesleyan University Press, 1992).

6. For more on the work concept in Western art music, see Lydia Goehr, *The Imaginary Museum of Musical Works: An Essay in the Philosophy of Music* (Oxford: Oxford University Press, 1992).

7. A body of scholarly literature exists that argues for the recording as the referential text for post–rock 'n' roll popular music. For examples see Theodore Gracyk, *Rhythm and Noise: An Aesthetics of Rock* (Durham, NC, and London: Duke University Press, 1996); and Albin Zak III, *The Poetics of Rock: Cutting Tracks, Making Records* (Berkeley: University of California Press, 2001). Zak, in *I Don't Sound Like Nobody,* extends the dichotomy of song-as-printed-artifact versus song-as-recorded/sonic-experience back to the late 1940s.

8. For an excellent and concise account of the synergy and conflicts between broadcasters and publishers, see Philip Ennis, *The Seventh Stream,* 42–70.

9. This period in popular music history is richly documented. See Philip Ennis, *The Seventh Stream,* 105–9, 165–68; John Ryan, *The Production of Culture in the Music Industry: The ASCAP-BMI Controversy* (Lanham, MD: University Press of America, 1985); and Russell Sanjek and David Sanjek, *American Popular Music Business in the 20th Century* (New York and Oxford: Oxford University Press, 1991), 58–78. For an argument about this period in terms of the ascension of a new technological-industrial model, see Tim J. Anderson, *Making Easy Listening: Material Culture and Postwar American Recording* (Minneapolis: University of Minnesota Press, 2006), 3–47.

10. Anecdote related from Philip Ennis, *The Seventh Stream,* 118–20.

11. On the popularity of jukeboxes, see Chris Rasmussen, "'The People's Orchestra': Jukeboxes as the Measure of Popular Musical Taste in the 1930s and 1940s," in *Sound in the Age of Mechanical Reproduction,* ed. David Suisman and Susan Strasser (Philadelphia: University of Pennsylvania Press, 2010), 181–98.

12. "Record Buying Guide," *Billboard,* January 7, 1939, 62.

13. "Music Publishers Frown Upon Spread of 'Hit Parade' Idea Via Platters," *Variety,* March 6, 1940, 41; "Drop 'Most Played' Box Pro Tem," *Variety,* December 4, 1940, 41.

14. Arthur E. Yohalem, "Poor Man's Orchestra: The Story of the Automatic Phono," *Billboard,* January 3, 1942, 70–72; Ben Bodec, "Boom on Wax," *Variety,* January 4, 1939, 165; Walter W. Hurd, "Popular Records," *Billboard,* January 27, 1940, 70.

15. "What the Records Are Doing for Me," *Billboard,* June 17, 1939, 78.

16. Jack Robbins, "Picking Hit Songs," *Billboard,* September 23, 1939, 7, 45.

17. While "A-Tisket, A-Tasket" was written, recorded, and popularized by Ella Fitzgerald with the Chick Webb orchestra, the Andrews Sisters recorded the most popular version of "Hold Tight!" although their version was preceded, according to a 1942 retrospective, by a "colored male trio's disk" (the first recording was in fact credited to Sidney Bechet and His Orchestra with vocals by the "The Two Fishmongers"); this statement is followed by the author making a comparison between the racialized nature of the relationship between original and cover and the success of "Hold Tight" and "Tuxedo Junction," which was released later in 1939. The author, Arthur E. Yohalem, once again has recourse to the idea of "that certain something" in explaining the difference between original and copy, which in this case revolves around the success of the white cover version: "Sometimes bands and vocalists are able to impart a certain intangible something to recordings that will make successful nickel-nabbers where others' efforts failed." "Poor Man's Orchestra," *Billboard*, January 3, 1942, 70–72.

18. Irving Mills, "Prospecting for Hit Tunes," *Billboard*, September 23, 1939, 11, 32, 44. Mills fails to mention that many of the musicians he celebrates in this article are managed by him. A similar point of view about the coin machine as the facilitator of the people's choice appeared in an article published several months earlier: Ben Bodec, "Boom on Wax," *Variety*, January 4, 1939, 165.

19. Joe Glaser, "Race Artists Bring Profits," *Billboard*, September 23, 1939, 14, 36, 37; "Personality on a Platter," *Billboard*, September 23, 1939, 10, 32.

20. "Band Reviews," *Variety*, September 13, 1939, 36; "Band Reviews," *Variety*, October 11, 1939, 49. This criticism of the use of "oldies" in relation to "going on the air" references the need to plug recently copyrighted tunes on radio broadcasts.

21. For a representative sample of record reviews, see "Record Reviews: Benny Carter," *Variety*, May 15, 1940, 44; "Record Reviews: Lionel Hampton," *Variety*, June 12, 1940, 34; "Record Reviews: Lionel Hampton," *Variety*, August 21, 1940, 50; "Band Reviews: Jay McShann," *Variety*, November 13, 1940, 48; "Record Reviews: Duke Ellington," *Variety*, December 4, 1940, 48; "Record Reviews: Duke Ellington," *Variety*, December 18, 1940, 42; and "Record Reviews: Count Basie," *Variety*, February 26, 1941, 43.

22. "Band Review: Les Brown," *Variety*, November 13, 1940, 48.

23. "SWING KNOCKED ITSELF OUT: Modified, Varied Styles Coming In," *Variety*, January 24, 1940, 35.

24. See "Miller, Hawkins, Cooper Score at Savoy Xmas Eve," *Chicago Defender*, December 30, 1939, 17.

25. Gunther Schuller, *The Swing Era: The Development of Jazz, 1930–1945* (New York and Oxford: Oxford University Press, 1989), 671. Another largely sympathetic reevaluation of Miller can be found in Gary Giddens, "Stride and Swing: The Enduring Appeal of Fats Waller and Glenn Miller," *The New Yorker*, May 31, 2004, 85–87.

26. See Theodor Adorno (with the assistance of George Simpson), "On Popular Music" (1941) reprinted in *Essays on Music*, ed. Richard Leppert (Berkeley and Los Angeles: University of California Press, 2002), 437–69.

27. Of course, Adorno believed all jazz improvisations to be themselves predigested, but this seems to be a rather famous instance of how his assumption of an identical reception context for Western art music and the popular music of the period actually dulls the force of his argument. Adorno never analyzed jazz improvisation in any detail. Within his overall

focus on composition, however, Adorno believed that the hook would reside in the "pseudo-individualized" melody rather than the form—in a notated element rather than one appearing in the act of performance.

28. This reference to the difference in car models in the context of a discussion about Adorno takes its cue from Bernard Gendron, "Theodor Adorno Meets the Cadillacs," in *Studies in Entertainment: Critical Approaches to Mass Culture*, ed. Tania Modleski (Bloomington and Indianapolis: Indiana University Press, 1986), 18–36. The arranging device of the interrupted ending was striking enough to attract attention in the first mention of "In the Mood" in *Billboard*: the song features an "arrangement twist near the finish that is bound to entertain and amuse." "Record Buying Guide," *Billboard*, October 7, 1939, 68. Schuller also refers to Miller and his arranger's reliance on a "half-dozen or so Miller Sounds," of which the trombone section (including four trombones) playing softly with plunger mutes (as heard on "Tuxedo Junction") was one. These sounds "provided that distinctive quality, instantly recognizable and very memorable, which Miller had known to be the key to the *kind* of success he strove for." In other words, these "sounds" also functioned as advertisements. Gunther Schuller, *The Swing Era*, 671–72.

29. Artie Atlas, "'Tuxedo Junction' Was Originally a Sign-Off!" *Down Beat*, April 1, 1940, 17. The middle section is actually eight bars long, as per the conventions of AABA songs during this period.

30. Guthrie Ramsey Jr., *Race Music: Black Cultures from Bebop to Hip-Hop* (Berkeley and Los Angeles: University of California Press, 2003), especially chapters 3 and 5. The concept of Afro-Modernism, which encompasses migration narratives and the contrast between the recent African American past in the South and the present in the North, could be fruitfully applied to much of the music discussed in this chapter, including the jump blues of Louis Jordan, bebop (both discussed by Ramsey), and "Open the Door, Richard."

31. Glenn Miller, "'Rhythm Section Is My Only Worry'—Miller," *Down Beat*, January 1, 1940, 2; Dave Dexter Jr., "'I Don't Want a Jazz Band'—Glenn Miller," *Down Beat*, February 1, 1940, 3, 18.

32. Dave Dexter Jr., "'I Don't Want a Jazz Band'"; Marvin Freedman, "Black Music's on Top; White Jazz Stagnant," *Down Beat*, April 1, 1940, 7, 20, reprinted in *The Pop, Rock, and Soul Reader: Histories and Debates*, ed. David Brackett (New York: Oxford University Press, 2014), 15–17.

33. As seen in the following remark: "Even a great musician like Harry James forsakes the white cause, and carries out the ideas of colored musicians." Marvin Freedman, "Black Music's on Top," 7. The other quotes in this paragraph come from the following articles: Paul Eduard Miller (PEM), "Jazz—Not for Morons Only," *Down Beat*, February 1, 1939, 20; and "11 Leaders on Down Beat's All-American 1939 Band," *Down Beat*, January 1, 1940, 12. This last article also notes that Charlie Christian, "a young Oklahoma Negro, is the only 'dark horse' to win this year."

34. "Sidemen Are Revealed in New Bands and Jenney 'Shakeup,'" *Down Beat*, April 15, 1940, 6; R. L. Larkin, "Are Colored Bands Doomed as Big Money Makers? Negro Leaders Could Make More Money Running a Rib Joint," *Down Beat*, December 1, 1940, 2, 23.

35. Irving Kolodin, "The Dance Band Business: A Study in Black and White," *Harper's Magazine* (June 1941): 78–82, reprinted in *The Pop, Rock, and Soul Reader*, 18–20. For an excellent comparison of the material conditions for black and white bands during the late

1930s and early 1940s, see Scott DeVeaux, *The Birth of Bebop: A Social and Musical History* (Berkeley and Los Angeles: University of California Press, 1997).

36. *Billboard,* July 17, 1943, 64.

37. See Eric Lott, *Love and Theft: Blackface Minstrelsy and the American Working Class* (New York: Oxford University Press, 1993). The range of the psychodynamics of minstrelsy are quite vast, however, and undoubtedly active in the performances of musical blackness by Miller, Bradley, and Slack noted above.

38. Discographic information from Robert M. W. Dixon, *Blues and Gospel Records: 1890–1943* (Oxford: Oxford University Press, 1997).

39. Of course many exceptions can be found to this assertion, most clearly in several recordings of the Duke Ellington orchestra, featuring singers such as Ivie Anderson and Herb Jeffries.

40. Paul Denis, "The Negro Makes Advances: Edging Into Radio, Films; Bigger Than Ever in Music; and Despite Many Obstacles," *Billboard,* January 2, 1943, 28. The *Chicago Defender,* not prone to commenting on black popular music during this period, weighed in on the growing popularity of the blues around the same time; see "'B' not 'I' Has It Because the Latter Is Swing Not the Blues," *Chicago Defender,* February 19, 1944, 8.

41. *Billboard,* October 24, 1942, 25.

42. In comments that resonate eerily with the phenomenon just described, none other than Duke Ellington gave the following opinion in a December 1942 interview: "The trouble . . . is that in a place like Harlem, a place where they have a chance to give impetus to original Negro compositions and an idiom already established, they turn to accepted Tin Pan Alley creations. Listen to any Harlem jukebox and you'll find the latest Hit Parade tunes, with an occasional song that details Negro musical expression. . . . It means that until the time comes when the colored race takes its own music seriously, Negro music will remain undeveloped and for the most part unearthed." "Ellington on Negro Music," *Variety,* December 9, 1942, 37.

43. Albin Zak III makes a similar observation in *I Don't Sound Like Nobody,* 125–26.

44. General Amusement Corporation ad, *Billboard,* December 26, 1942, back cover.

45. Slack had a hit earlier in 1942 with "Cow Cow Boogie," which featured Morse's singing, a hit on the BSRR before the HHP came into existence, leading to the hypothesis that it would have followed the same pattern as "Mr. Five by Five" had the HHP existed. Despite her unusual identificatory position vis-à-vis genre, little has been written about Morse. For an exception, see Nick Tosches, *The Unsung Heroes of Rock 'n' Roll: The Birth of Rock in the Wild Years Before Elvis* (New York: Harmony Books, 1984), 64–68.

46. *Billboard,* August 12, 1944.

47. "Jump" was frequently used as an adjective during this period, and jump blues has retroactively become accepted as a genre. During the late 1930s and 1940s, many tunes included "jump" in their titles, and it is possible to describe a group of musical style traits that most of these songs use (bands such as Louis Jordan's were also referred to as "jump bands"). Gena Caponi has written about jump as a genre and its connection to other African American cultural practices during this period. See her *Jump for Joy: Jazz, Basketball and Black Culture in 1930s America* (Amherst: University of Massachusetts Press, 2008), especially chapter 5, "The Joint Is Jumping."

48. *Billboard,* February 3, 1945, 65.

49. *Billboard,* March 24, 1945, 63.

50. On this debate, again see Bernard Gendron, *Between Montmartre and the Mudd Club,* 121–42.

51. See Philip Ennis, *The Seventh Stream,* 161–92.

52. The following is a summary of the account in RJ Smith, "Richard Speaks! Chasing a Tune from the Chitlin Circuit to the Mormon Tabernacle," in *This Is Pop: In Search of the Elusive at Experience Music Project,* ed. Eric Weisbard (Cambridge, MA: Harvard University Press, 2004), 75–89.

53. A video of a 1945 performance of Fletcher performing this skit may be viewed at http://archive.org/details/open_the_door_richard, accessed February 26, 2013.

54. The *Chicago Defender* gave another account of the transformation of "Open the Door, Richard" from vaudeville skit to popular recording. Referring to Dusty Fletcher as "our favorite comedian," the *Defender* locates the crucial moment at a 1946 run that Fletcher made at the Club Zanzibar on Broadway in New York. The composer Ned Sparks is given credit for the idea of adding a chorus. "Popularity of 'Open the Door Richard' Good Proof That Music Is the Thing," *Chicago Defender,* February 1, 1947, 19.

55. This legal dispute reflects the uncertain status of non-notatable elements with respect to copyright law, and refers back to questions around the legibility of different sorts of musical texts with respect to the music industry. The sound of a recording, and the *way* in which a song was performed, were not protected in the same way that the notated melodic-harmonic matrix of a song was. See also George Frazier, "Jocks, Jukes and Disks," *Variety,* January 29, 1947, 38; and "'Richard' Opens Door to Top Money for McVea," *Down Beat,* February 12, 1947, 2.

56. The CD *Open the Door, Richard! The Story of a Showbiz Phenomenon* (Acrobat, 2012) presents an exhaustive collection of recordings: sixteen different versions plus eight answer records.

57. *Down Beat* reviewed three versions of "Open the Door, Richard" (placing them in the novelty category)—by Basie, Lips Page, and the Pied Pipers—declaring Basie's "the best, both swinging and lacking the Uncle Tomism that makes some of the other versions offensive." "Diggin' the Discs with Mix," *Down Beat,* February 26, 1947, 19.

58. RJ Smith, "Richard Speaks!" 83. Other articles in the black press blamed "Open the Door, Richard" and its sequel, "The Key's in the Mail Box," for an uptick in crime. The *Chicago Defender* reported that "In Los Angeles, Calif., the police chief has been broadcasting on the radio, pleading with householders to stop leaving their keys in their mail boxes," because "burglars have been entering homes by the simple procedure of taking the key out of the mailbox and putting it back when they leave with the loot." "Race," *Chicago Defender,* April 26, 1947, 15.

59. On Billy Eckstine, see Scott DeVeaux, *The Birth of Bebop.* On African American crooners, see Vincent Stephens, "Crooning on the Fault Lines: Theorizing Jazz and Pop Vocal Singing Discourses in Rock," *American Music* 26, no. 2 (Summer 2008): 156–95.

6

The Corny-ness of the Folk

Rapidly following on the heels of "Open the Door, Richard," a hillbilly novelty, "Smoke! Smoke! Smoke! (That Cigarette)" conquered the "Honor Roll of Hits." Signaling public awareness of the negative effects of tobacco consumption years before it would become a hot political issue, the song presented a humorous portrait of the perils of nicotine addiction. The chart-topping triumph of the recording was the climax of years of flirtation between country music and the mainstream.

Although it appeared on an even footing with novelty race recordings such as "Open the Door, Richard," the position of "Smoke! Smoke! Smoke! (That Cigarette)" within the historical trajectory of country music is nonetheless quite different. It is true that many of the same conditions that affected the circulation, legibility, and impact of black popular music affected country music as well. The dichotomy between the work concept and the sonic aesthetic also applied to the reception of country music, which was by the early 1940s called hillbilly, folk, or occasionally even country music in the music industry press.[1] The media industry forces embodied in network radio, song plugging, and ASCAP presented as much of a barrier to the wide circulation of hillbilly music as they did to race music.

Yet the differences between the histories of country music and race music are striking. Unlike race music, which was embedded within the mainstream in the form of swing at the beginning of the decade, hillbilly music existed in a position of greater exteriority. In the years immediately preceding 1940, and in contrast to swing and boogie-woogie, no subgenre of hillbilly music had been incorporated into the mainstream to the extent that non-hillbilly performers would devote themselves to it; few elements of rhythm, phrasing, melody, or instrumentation related to hillbilly music had influenced the mainstream; no dance crazes related to hillbilly had become media sensations; and no mainstream performers admitted to being influenced by hillbilly performers in the way that white big band leaders were obviously indebted to Duke Ellington, Count Basie, and Fletcher Henderson. The relation of hillbilly music to the mainstream at the outset of the 1940s, then, resembled that of non-crossover race music, with a few exceptions. Hillbilly music thus lacked the internal differentiation of the race music field in terms of the relation of crossover to non-crossover material. This situation was to change by the end of the decade.[2]

The relative lack of public interaction between hillbilly music and the mainstream did not mean, however, that no contact existed, or that no interpenetration of the two fields occurred. In contrast to the situation of race music, which shared swing as an important stylistic feature with the mainstream, country music circa 1940 appeared in the mainstream in the form of cover versions, a few hits by singing cowboys, and the occasional crossover blockbuster. The displacement of swing bands by novelty numbers after the war, however, along with a rapid shift in the commercial importance of folk/hillbilly music, resulted in a startling transformation of possibilities. If the realm of otherness that was the novelty tune created a new type of opening in the mainstream for artists such as Count Basie, a similar opening occurred for novelty tunes associated with country music.

ONE EARLY JUKEBOX HILLBILLY HIT

At the dawn of the 1940s, however, country music was all but ignored in music industry publications, with the main exception to this neglect being the column "What the Records Are Doing for Me" (WTRADFM) in *Billboard*. The music machine operators' lack of musical literacy—already extolled in chapter 5 when it enabled them to appreciate the commercial potential of African American swing bands and race music—also attuned them to the popularity of country music. A few operators in 1939 were quick to note the spectacular popularity of hillbilly recordings, especially in the case of the biggest country hit of the year, Cliff Bruner's "It Makes No Difference Now."

The reports from "WTRADFM" on country music tended to focus around Bruner's recording throughout 1939 and well into 1940, and they came in from Amarillo, Texas; Stephenville, Texas; Natchez, Mississippi; North Little Rock, Arkansas; Danville, Illinois; Spokane, Washington; Tolar, Texas; and Kansas City, Missouri. While these reports were concentrated in the South, the expected geographical center of hillbilly music, the success of this recording in Washington state and Illinois indicates that the popularity of the music was not limited to the area associated with the music by most homologically based stereotypes. An awareness, however faint, of the discrepancy between the public connotations of the audience for hillbilly and the diverse experiences of its consumption appeared in discussions of the term "hillbilly" itself, as when the radio producer George C. Biggar, writing for *Billboard* in April 1940, argued that "there are limitations to this name because so many city folks as rural people listen to the programs and patronize personal appearances."[3]

"It Makes No Difference Now" featured prominently in the non–numerically ordered listing of "Hillbilly and Foreign Record Hits of the Month" that began appearing in the March 25, 1939, issue of *Billboard*. This list—which *Billboard* published erratically, beginning with once or twice a month before finally settling into an every-other-month pattern—included Bruner's version of "It Makes No Difference Now" in every iteration until the November 25, 1939, issue. The recording then reappeared on January 27, 1940, before finally disappearing for the March 30, 1940 listing.

One of the great challenges posed to the beliefs and values of music industry agents by Bruner's "It Makes No Difference Now" was its sonic particularity, a challenge related to struggles between the work concept and the sonic aesthetic discussed in the last chapter. One operator reported that he "tried replacing it with Jimmy Davis' version and others only to have to change back to Bruner's the next trip round my stops."[4] At other times, especially in locations outside the South, contributors to "WTRADFM" seemed to seek cover versions of the song, or else to fantasize that a cover version by an artist such as Bing Crosby would come into existence. Although it would take more than a year for a version by Crosby to materialize, a faux-Crosby recording soon came about as an answer to operators' dreams: late in 1939, reports from New York City and Buffalo, New York, both applauded the success of a recording of the song by Dick Robertson, a crooner in the mold of Crosby.[5]

"It Makes No Difference Now" facilitated different sorts of identifications simultaneously. These identificatory effects varied depending on the location of the observer, a mutability that may have been one of the keys to the tune's popularity. At times, the recording was associated by coin machine operators with other marginal musics—for instance the race recording "Hold Tight!" or the smash foreign hit "Beer Barrel Polka"—while at other times it was understood as reinforcing a boundary between country music and race music.[6]

An important aspect of the negotiations over genre-audience relations in which "It Makes No Difference Now" participated consisted of a dialogue between musicians. The genealogy of Bruner's own style illuminates the role of this dialogue in the production of genre. Cliff Bruner was a fiddle player who began his career with western swing pioneer Milton Brown and His Musical Brownies. After Brown's death and the subsequent dissolution of the Brownies, Bruner formed his own group, the Texas Wanderers, with similar instrumentation to that of Brown's band: amplified steel guitar, a second fiddle, guitar, bass, piano, and amplified mandolin.

With one foot in the traditional sound of a Southern string band, Bruner's band also had much in common with the western swing of bands like Brown's and Bob Wills's, and anticipated, in both music and the focus of the lyrics, what would come to be known as honky-tonk in the late 1940s.

The stylistic hybridity of western swing is evident in "It Makes No Difference Now" in Dickie McBride's crooned vocals (which would not have been out of place in a mainstream pop recording, as they lacked any obvious regional accent) and Bob Dunn's pioneering steel guitar work, underpinned by Moon Mullican's bar-relhouse piano playing and the steady two-beat rhythm provided by the bass and guitar.[7] The stylistic blend in Bruner's recording (and in western swing more generally) in many respects continued the flamboyant impurity of popular 1920s old-time recordings, with their merger of instrumentation with rural connotations, aspects of groove and arrangement affiliated with mainstream swing, and legit singing style.

Discovering the Country Audience

The success of Bruner's recording alerted mainstream performers who might wish to record a cover version of his song and would only have to drop the steel guitar and add big band instrumentation to convert it into an innocuous novelty number. The previously mentioned "WTRADFM" reports from Buffalo and New York City make it clear that Dick Robertson's big band arrangement of "It Makes No Difference Now" had become identified with the song in locations inhospitable to Bruner and the Texas Wanderers. The discussions in "WTRADFM" of Robertson and Crosby clarify that songs such as "It Makes No Difference Now," when recorded by these artists, were grouped with other novelty numbers signifying some sort of racial or ethnic difference (recall the earlier association of "It Makes No Difference Now" with "Beer Barrel Polka"). One report discussed the Western-themed "My Little Buckaroo" in the same breath as the Hawaiian songs "Blue Hawaii" and "Sweet Lelani" and the Mexican setting of "Mexicali Rose" as enduring successes by Robertson and Crosby.[8]

The attempts to understand the makeup of the hillbilly audience transcended the interest in "It Makes No Difference Now," regardless of how significant that recording might have been. While discussion occasionally reaffirmed the notion of geographical homology, reports that contradicted the stereotypical homology were more numerous. On one matter, however, most could agree: hillbilly music and taverns went together like a hand and glove.[9] As 1940 turned into 1941, the spread of hillbilly music outside of an exclusively white, rural, Southern audience gathered momentum, and record companies correspondingly "upp[ed] the number of hillbilly tunes recorded."[10]

These discussions of the audience for hillbilly music raise a topic that is familiar from previous chapters: how to deal with the apparent difference between the widely held and shared public connotations of a homogeneous audience for country music with the accounts of listeners from diverse demographic backgrounds. And, in an apparent inversion, another question follows: how to deal with the diversity of taste within the core, stereotypical audience. After all, not even all "real" hillbillies liked the same type of music. This topic, which was touched upon in chapters 3 and 4, is related to one of the main focal points of Karl Hagstrom Miller's *Segregating Sound,* to wit, that mainstream popular music had been already well known, even in rural areas of the South, since the mid- to late nineteenth century. Following from this observation, the idea of consistent, homogeneous taste within the audience for either country or race music might appear to be a myth created by Northern entrepreneurs and academics with a vested interest in propagating this belief. As I argued in chapter 3, however, if this idea were in fact a myth, it nevertheless resonated enough with a sense of reality shared by diverse social groups that it presented itself as the truth. In other words, if a particular articulation of categorical label and musical style could be comprehended as legible, then it might appear to create its own reality.

The example of the hillbilly music audience also functions as a reminder of the impurity of popular music categories in general. Chapter 4 discussed how the emergence of the music industry category of old-time music was bound up with its production within a commercial matrix and its citation of a variety of other genres. This originary hybridity found echoes in the frustration of folklorists who were required to exhort their informants to play traditional songs that were untraceable to Tin Pan Alley. Richard Peterson, among others, has elaborated at length about how the authenticity and stylistic purity of country music is an effect that at times has required intense labor to be produced, reproduced, cited, iterated, and reiterated.[11] Nonetheless, despite all the contradictions generated by the concept, categories such as country music continued (and continue) to circulate strong connotations of a specific identificatory position.

The reports above from *Billboard* about the non-homological quality of the audience for country music may only indicate the tip of an iceberg. According to Harry Stone, who became the station manager of the Grand Ole Opry in 1930, "Only 15 percent of the 60,000 weekly letters to the station [during the 1930s] came from Tennessee listeners, with at least 20 percent originating from non-Southern states such as Ohio, Michigan, and Pennsylvania."[12]

Hillbilly or Corn?

An important factor in the circulation of the sounds, images, and verbal tropes associated with country music at this moment was the slippage between music produced by performers who identified primarily with country music, and a certain type of novelty music performed by musicians with no particular allegiance to country. The music and performances of this latter group often went by the name of "corn." Because hillbilly music presumably originated in rural, farming regions in which corn, the crop, played a significant role, people associated with the production of corn became associated with novelty music perceived as corny. This slippage appeared in different forums within music industry publications, including "WTRADFM," feature articles, and commentary on the popularity charts.[13]

Such an articulation of musical style, audience, popular slang, geography, and agricultural patterns helps make sense of an article such as the following, which contemporary readers might otherwise interpret as a parody: in the March 4, 1939, issue of *Billboard*, Meyer Horowitz, "who ought to know," claimed that "Jewish and Italian hillbillies usually outshine all others on showmanship," including "real hillbillies," who "rarely have good night club acts." The obsession with identificatory specificity that we observed in the early decades of the twentieth century in chapter 2 is still in full flower here, with Horowitz producing a list of different hillbilly acts he'd hired, with each identified according to his or her race or ethnicity. These include "Spanish-American," "part Indian," "Italian and Irish," "an Irishman," "an Italian," and the otherwise racially unspecified "Freddie Fisher's novel Schnickelfritz Band." This last act is of interest because Fisher's group, like other outfits such as the Hoosier Hot Shots, was known as a corn ensemble: a comedy troupe that wore silly (occasionally hayseed) outfits and played well-known (occasionally traditional) songs replete with novelty sound effects presented in a comic skit format. This article reinforces the impression that novelty corn outfits were equivalent to country musicians, and that the former were more important to urban entrepreneurs, when it dismisses "native-born hillbillies" because "they're short on comedy and showmanship." It follows inevitably, then, that "synthetic hillbillies who rehearsed their Western drawl in Bronx apartments are as a rule more desirable in a night club than the real ones."[14]

A sign of both the low regard in which hillbillies and their music were held, as well as the lack of firsthand acquaintance with the music and the people, is evidenced by reports, such as those by Edgar A. Grunwald in *Variety*, asserting that the "hillbilly and his slicker brother, the Texas cowboy, are radio inventions."[15] A description of Fiddle Bow Bill's Dew Valley Acorns, a novelty band using a "hillbilly scenic background," provides insight into the conflation of hillbilly music with corn and novelty acts, and helps explain why hillbilly music appeared to be a radio invention to music industry observers.[16]

If hillbilly musicians were nothing other than vaudevillians performing a corny novelty act, then why shouldn't the radio have invented them? In some ways this analysis is fairly accurate and speaks to the importance of the variety format of barn dance radio shows (in which musical performances were interspersed with comic skits), though not for the reasons advanced by Grunwald: "hillbilly music" as a category of popular music *was* an invention of the radio, as well as of the gramophone, late-nineteenth and early-twentieth-century touring practices, mass cultural promotional practices, and a discourse counterpoising authenticity to commercialism that is inseparable from cultural production within a capitalist economy. Even conceding this last formulation, however, does not mean that hillbilly musicians recognized by other hillbilly musicians of the time as hillbilly musicians would have recognized all corny novelty performances as hillbilly music.

The substitutability of corn for country music was accompanied by novel genealogies in which the previous history of country music as a commercial category was forgotten. Grunwald, in addition to proposing that hillbillies were a radio invention, also emphasized the amateurishness of country performers, their lack of musicianship, and their inability to read music. Recalling Abel Green's assessments from some fourteen years earlier, Grunwald concluded with descriptions of hedonistic activities in which only lazy illiterates seem to indulge: hillbilly musicians were "village idlers who did nothing at all but drink corn likker and crave dancing." Once again, however, perhaps because of the consumption of "corn likker," the distance between hillbilly music and novelty numbers collapsed; after all, "The audience often likes 'em corny."[17]

The conflation between hillbilly music and corn found its way into what passed at the time as the most objective representation and categorization of hillbilly music, the list of "Hillbilly and Foreign Record Hits of the Month." Here alongside western swing and neo-honky-tonk artists such as Cliff Bruner, Bob Wills, Al Dexter, and Jimmy Davis were found singing cowboys such as Gene Autry and numerous corn novelty artists such as the Hoosier Hot Shots (with "Beer Barrel Polka"), and Freddie Schnickelfritz Fisher (with "Horsey, Keep Your Tail Up").

The Lure of Borderland Romance

Although the music industry press evinced growing interest in country music in the early 1940s, and although much of this interest sprang from country music's transgression of its presumed borders, little crossover effect occurred between country music and the mainstream. While the listing of "Hillbilly and Foreign Record Hits of the Month" acknowledged the growing commercial presence of country music and its utility for coin machine operators, even major hits such as Cliff Bruner's "It Makes No Difference Now" received little coverage or recognition outside the immediate hillbilly milieu and the discourse of coin machine operators. The same could be said of cover versions of the tune, such as the one by Dick Robertson, which remained decidedly low profile. The similarity of the cultural position of country music with foreign music also occasionally attracted attention, as in the conjoining of hillbilly and foreign music in the record listing mentioned above. At other times, covers of hillbilly recordings were grouped with recordings such as Bing Crosby's "Mexicali Rose."

The history of "Mexicali Rose" is worth recounting here. A tale of borderland romance, it began as a Tin Pan Alley song written in 1923, but it really took off in popularity following Bing Crosby's 1936 performance in the movie *Rhythm on the Range* and his subsequent recording of it. It was featured in several movies in which Gene Autry starred as a singing cowboy, including one named after the song in 1939. The trope of the borderland romance, in which a gringo falls in love with an idealized Mexican woman, had remarkable staying power. It surfaced in the folk revival favorite "Spanish Is the Loving Tongue" (which was, in fact, written in 1925 at almost the same time as "Mexicali Rose"), in Marty Robbins's 1959 country hit "El Paso," and even in the Grateful Dead's "Mexicali Blues," which remained a staple of the band's performing repertoire until their demise in 1995.[18] "Mexicali Rose" did not contain any style markers that would connect it to country or foreign music, but the location of its subject matter, focusing as it did on some aspect of otherness (and not just otherness, but exotic otherness at that; and not just exotic otherness, but exotic otherness located in an area contiguous with the southwestern United States), provides the link in the semiotic chain that may have been responsible for the association between the song and country music, even in its guise as a Bing Crosby recording.

The imagined world southwest of the border could lend its allure to the U.S. Southwest itself. Texas, especially southwest Texas, possessed two attributes that made it the nexus of two different trends: it was already a source of numerous country musicians, especially those affiliated with the emergent western swing genre, and with what was sometimes referred to as the western subgenre, and it abutted Mexico. In 1938 Bob Wills, one of the musicians who had played a major role in the formation of western swing, wrote and recorded "San Antonio Rose," a song that brought these trends together. Given the stylistic affinities of Bruner's "It Makes No Difference Now" with western swing, "San Antonio Rose" entered a musical field in which its generic associations provided a point of entry for crossover success.

"San Antonio Rose" boasts a somewhat convoluted history, beginning its life as a different song, titled "Spanish Two Step," recorded in 1935. Following the success of "Spanish Two Step," Wills's producer, Art Satherley, requested something similar. Wills (according to the country music historian Rich Kienzle) "played 'Spanish Two Step' backwards," and "San Antonio Rose" was born.[19] While this description of the relationship between the two songs is not totally accurate, the melody and (especially) the chord changes of "San Antonio Rose" are clearly derived from the bridge of "Spanish Two Step," with the steel guitar melody of "Spanish Two Step" adapted to an idiomatic fiddle part in "San Antonio Rose" (see musical examples 19 and 20). "San Antonio Rose," however, by dropping the A-section of "Spanish Two Step," eliminates the rhythmically irregular phrasing of the first song, which contains bars with six beats (see musical example 21, measures 14–15, 21, 29–30, which are highlighted by brackets). While it is true that in measures 14–15 and 29–30 the two measures of 6/4 could be converted to three measures of 4/4, which would then yield "regular" sections of sixteen measures (as notated, these sections

MUSICAL EXAMPLE 19. Bridge of "Spanish Two Step"

MUSICAL EXAMPLE 20. "San Antonio Rose"

contain fifteen bars), I have divided the measures here to coincide with the harmonic rhythm of the song. Retaining 4/4 meter in these passages would cause the resolution of the V-I cadence to occur in the middle of the measure, an effect that is quite audible (the dotted bar lines show where the measures would begin in 4/4). The same kind of accommodation to common time cannot be made with the measure that I notated in 6/4 in measure 21. Consistent notation in 4/4 meter would leave two beats left over in this phrase.

MUSICAL EXAMPLE 21. "Spanish Two Step," First Section

Although it might be tempting to view these metric variations as the mistakes of untutored musicians, the fact that the band maintains the length of the phrases exactly over the course of numerous repetitions indicates that this approach to rhythm may have been an aesthetic choice. A further regularity occurs in that, during the first section of "Spanish Two Step," each of these metric variations functions to extend the last three (out of a total of four) occurrences of the dominant harmony for an extra two beats before its resolution to the tonic. The dominant harmony thus lasts ten beats instead of the expected eight. Within the larger popular music field of the era, the differences in phrasing and rhythm between the first section of "Spanish Two Step" and "San Antonio Rose" participated in establishing a rustic trope associated with metric irregularity opposed to the unwavering common time of the urban mainstream. While more of a variation on the harmonic progression of "Spanish Two Step" (and a fairly close variation at that) than a backward version, "San Antonio Rose" proved so successful that Wills recorded a version with a vocal in April 1940, renaming it "New San Antonio Rose."[20]

The transformation of "San Antonio Rose" into "New San Antonio Rose" went well beyond the mere addition of lyrics and a vocalist. The instruments that Wills's band shared with the swing bands of the era, principally saxophones and trumpets, become more prominent than the twin fiddles that led the earlier version. The song is arranged so that an instrumental version of the tune becomes the introduction, which is followed by two transitory modulations (a swing band arranging convention of the time) to move the song into the right key for Tommy Duncan, the singer for the Texas Playboys. Duncan sings in a style not far removed from mainstream pop crooning, fulfilling a function in the recording similar to that of Dickie McBride with Cliff Bruner's Texas Wanderers (or Vernon Dalhart, for that matter). Overall the change from "Spanish Two Step" to "San Antonio Rose" to "New San Antonio Rose" is consistent with a bid to incorporate as many mainstream swing stylistic markers as possible.

Recorded in April 1940 and released in August, by November 1940 "New San Antonio Rose" had begun to receive recognition from *Billboard* in various forums, most of which simply identified the recording as a hillbilly tune.[21] A few months later, when the recording began to make mainstream inroads, it was recognized both as possessing "that *certain intangible something*" (recalling the reception of old-time music in the 1920s) and as projecting "the popular corny aura of a free and easy little number." Bob Wills's western swing number, although it could now be "dressed up in all the trappings of a real swing band," was nonetheless revealed to be a hillbilly number at its core and conflated with the easily digestible corn filling the ears of mainstream observers whenever they encountered country music.[22]

While Bob Wills's recording registered in the regional best-selling record chart and the coin machine chart in both *Billboard* and *Variety*, his recording benefited from hitching itself to the coattails of a dominant mainstream figure, somewhat in the same manner as had Erskine Hawkins with Glenn Miller and "Tuxedo Junction." In the case of Wills, the figure providing propulsion into the mainstream was none other than Bing Crosby. Now the recording could be described as a "lilting hillbilly styled number" that's "pretty perfect phono fodder." The popularity of Crosby's recording was such that Wills's recording now appeared in a subsidiary role, with Crosby's recording cited as "largely responsible for putting it ["New San Antonio Rose"] in a position of phonograph prominence with a capable assist from BOB WILLS' disk."[23]

As if in response to the premonitory visions of early commentators, "It Makes No Difference Now" constituted the flip side of Crosby's "New San Antonio Rose" and received some attention on its own. "New San Antonio Rose" remained the focus, however, and it was possible for Crosby's audience to hear the song in terms of a southwestern/cowboy lineage begun with "Mexicali Rose" (released as a single in 1938) that continued with "Alla en el rancho grande" (1939), "Tumblin' Tumbleweeds" (1940), "Sierra Sue" (1940), "Along the Santa Fe Trail" (1940), and "Lone Star Trail" (early 1941).[24] This cycle of Crosby's recordings created its own specific reception context that did not require knowledge or awareness of a distinct country music style and market. The only exception to mainstream ignorance lay in the possible awareness of the "singing cowboy" or "western" subgenre of hillbilly music, as the popularity of singing cowboys on film, recordings, and radio crested in the late 1930s and early 1940s.

Crosby's version of "New San Antonio Rose"—recorded with Bing's brother, Bob, and his brother's band, the Bob Cats—dropped the stylistic markers that identified "New San Antonio Rose" as a western swing number in Wills's recording. Gone are the fiddles and steel guitars, the rhythmic groove, the relaxed, conversational phrasing in the melody, Wills's off-the-cuff interjections, and the blues tonality forming an undercurrent in the song (created by piano and steel guitar). Crosby replaces these stylistic markers of western swing with Dixieland-style clarinets, muted trumpets (perhaps to retain a certain mariachi flavor?), a prominent studio orchestra, and his trademark phrasing, which sounds stiff in comparison to Tommy Duncan. Crosby's version slows the tempo and retains the two-beat bass, albeit with a more discreet backbeat. Crosby's arrangement of "It Makes No Difference Now" follows a template similar to that used on "New San Antonio Rose." Due to Bruner's stripped-down small-ensemble approach, the contrast between Crosby's and Bruner's recordings of "It Makes No Difference Now" is even greater than that between the two recordings of "New San Antonio Rose."

Crosby followed "New San Antonio Rose" with "You Are My Sunshine," thus either (depending on one's point of view) extending the dude-rancher persona established through his cowboy/southwestern themed recordings, or furthering the sense in which his covers of country tunes were starting to become a cottage industry. Along with Decca labelmates the Andrews Sisters—and encouraged no doubt by Jack Kapp, an artists and repertoire man at Decca Records, known for his nose for crossover opportunities—Crosby and the Andrews Sisters systematically canvased the marginal popular music categories of race music and hillbilly for breakaway hits that they could cover. Due to the structural resistance to marketing race and hillbilly records to the mainstream, Crosby and the Andrews Sisters benefited from a type of promotion and ease of circulation that would virtually guarantee greater record sales for their cover versions than the recordings that they were covering, a phenomenon already described in chapter 5 with respect to their covers of race music.

NATIONAL BREAKTHROUGHS AND COVER TUNES

The war years witnessed far-reaching changes to the position of country music within the U.S. music industry, in which a few successful crossover country recordings would offer a stylistic contrast to the cover versions of Crosby and the Andrews Sisters. Even the most successful country recordings, however, could not completely displace these cover versions. The outward signs of an industry-wide shift occurred principally in two ways: massive national hits that received attention for exceeding the previous boundaries of country music, and the expansion of discourse in music industry publications such as *Billboard* and *Variety*. The latter included reviews of recordings, a whole section devoted to country music (often referred to as folk music) in *Billboard,* and an increase in narrative articles interpreting and describing notable events in the world of country music. These articles discussed sub-generic distinctions and continued the debates begun earlier in "WTRADFM" over the nature of the audience. The expansion of the coverage of folk music and the general increase in record reviews extended the trend begun with the "Record Buying Guide" for coin machines and continued with the "Best-Selling Retail Record" chart, of a shift in emphasis from the song-as-text to the recording-as-text, and thus from the work concept to the sonic aesthetic.

The publication of quasi-regular record reviews (directed toward coin machine operators) reveals the emergence of a preliminary aesthetic vocabulary for country music distinct from other types of music. The terms of this vocabulary centered around three main musical and expressive dimensions: rhythm, instrumentation, and affect. One early example, a review of Al Dexter's "Honky Tonk Chinese Dime" (a title merging the obsessions of the 1910s with those of the 1940s?) and "Sundown Polka" (making explicit the bond between hillbilly and foreign musics?) addresses the first two of these dimensions. The first song is "taken at a bright tempo in bounce rhythm, with excellent steel guitar and fiddle." In the same issue, a review of Ernest Tubb's "Time After Time" and "When the World Has Turned You Down" touches on all three dimensions, describing the recordings as "two more sentimental ballads," with "Time After Time" receiving further elaboration as "a lugubrious ditty given heavily sentimental treatment" featuring "excellent string plucking," while "When the World Has Turned You Down" "is delivered at a brighter tempo."[25] In general, these reviews emphasize the sentiment of country recordings and their reliance on various forms of "string pickings" and "pluckings," with an affect alternately bouncy or lugubrious depending on the tempo.

A Few More Words About Corn

Terminological uncertainty about what to call the music continued, with occasional attempts to correlate differences in labeling to music-stylistic differences. Although terms such as "folk" and "country" were increasingly used, with "hillbilly" still active but scaled back a bit, the main terminological issue continued to circle around the slippage between country music as corny and a type of novelty number known as corn. Such slippage could emerge in reviews, where country artists as diverse as Elton Britt and Gene Autry might appear alongside novelty outfits such as the Hoosier Hot Shots and Spike Jones and His City Slickers. Or various forms of country music itself might be referred to as corn or King Korn, as illustrated in articles with titles such as "King Korn Klondike: Hillbilly Troupes Roll Up Dizzy Box Office Scores in One-Day and Repeat Stands."[26]

This slippage could become quite vivid at times, seemingly arising in response to reports of the unprecedented popularity of hillbilly music. One article describes the far-ranging effect of the influx of "Oakies" [sic] into Southern California, and concludes by observing, "One maestro here hopes the current appreciation of corny, race, hillbilly and mountain music continues after the war is won." That "maestro"? Spike Jones, who, with his band the City Slickers, "are the top men on the totem pole, all because the Oakies consider him to have the most to offer."[27] Few historians of country music today would consider Spike Jones to be part of the lineage of country music, and even the preceding quote leaves room for differentiation, making distinctions between "corny, race, and hillbilly and mountain music."

The soundie (an early form of music video) for Spike Jones's most successful record, "Cocktails for Two" (1944), illustrates the sonic difference between hillbilly, western, and corn even as it shows how novelty musicians were aware of the public perceptions of their music. In this soundie, the metaphor becomes literal when Jones (at around 2:00) whips out a giant piece of corn and pretends to play it like a harmonica. The trio at the end is sung by a group of men in drag, indicating that corn might have been associated with the instability or subversion of gender positions.[28] Freudian implications aside, this video provides a glimpse into a world of genre terminology and concepts far removed from the present, in which music that was corny and music that was perceived to be from rural areas could merge. The reflexivity of Jones's performance, which displayed awareness of how fan-critical generic labels could be presented as a physical object, indicates the pervasiveness of these connections at this time.

At other times, corn could function as an umbrella category that encompassed the various genres grouped under "hillbilly." An advertisement from October 1943 illustrates this usage (figure 8). Titled "America'$ Foremo$t Compo$er$ of Corn," the ad lists artists who are elsewhere identified as western or cowboy, such as Roy Rogers. Also included are non-crossover stars such as Ernest Tubb and the Delmore Brothers, as well as Al Dexter, the greatest crossover country artist of the period.

The equation of corn with hillbilly barely scratches the semiotic surface of this advertisement, however. To begin with, it is an ad for music publishers rather than recording companies, revealing the (hoped-for?) market for sheet music sales of hillbilly music. And then there is the substitution of dollar signs for s's in the title

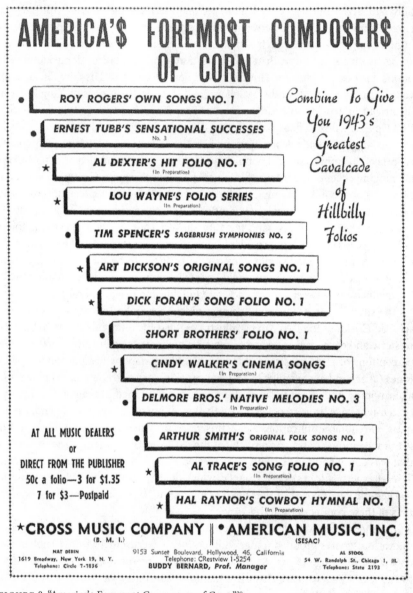

FIGURE 8. "America'$ Foremo$t Compo$er$ of Corn."[29]

in close proximity to "corn": "corn" is more apt than "hillbilly," then, because "corn" in this context explicitly signifies the imbrication of a label (already signifying the union of musical styles, a type of humor, low cultural prestige, and a crop associated with rural areas) within a capitalist network. "Corn" thus exists as a kind of advertisement of itself, so that the ad, with its use of dollar signs, reveals an awareness that it is, in a sense, an advertisement of an advertisement.

Country as Folk

Efforts increased during this period to rebrand country music as folk music. These arose partly to acknowledge internal differences within the category as it functioned within the larger music industry, with participants making distinctions between hillbilly and western or cowboy tunes. At other times, the folk music label connoted a meaning closer to what would now be called traditional music: music transmitted in an oral tradition lacking a defined point of origin or author. Music industry writers debated actively whether country music in toto or merely one subdivision of it could qualify as folk music. Occasionally different types of country music were conflated with black spirituals in an attempt to delineate "the richness and variety of American folk music." The term "hillbilly" features in the title of the article from which the preceding quote was drawn, and "songs of the South and the various types of Western ballads—those from Texas, for example," are offered as examples.[30] This inclusive definition of American folk music was the one eventually employed when the "Most-Played Jukebox Folk Records" chart started in 1944, a category dominated not only by hillbilly and western songs, traditional ballads, and newly written tunes, but one that also initially included African American music of various sorts, as well as other types of traditional music.

The genres of hillbilly and western were often distinguished from one another under the now ever-more-common label of folk music. This distinction appeared in the initial notice in *Billboard* for the recording that would do more than any other to establish the large-scale commercial viability of country music, Al Dexter's "Pistol Packin' Mama." "Pistol Packin' Mama," a "hillbilly" number, was paired with "Rosalita," a "Western couplet."[31] This distinction between hillbilly and western would later be enshrined in 1949, the moment when country music would achieve a new level of institutional recognition with the official rebranding of the category under the rubric "country and western."

The border between the more inclusive folk category and popular music received growing amounts of attention, however, as the number of covers mounted and the occasional crossover hit began to appear. The difference between folk and popular seemed clear. When Bob Wills, in his late 1942 release of "My Confession" and "Whose Heart Are You Breaking Now?" accentuated the pop elements in his already-hybrid style, critics were quick to notice and disapprove. One writer noted, "The band seems to have gone closer to the pop, rather than the folk-music groove.... Wisdom of this is questionable. It's just another band in the pop field, whereas in its own folk music field it's a sensational and outstanding outfit."[32] A review of the irrepressible Dick Robertson's cover of Ted Daffan's "No Letter Today"—a crossover hit for Daffan—identified the musical differences between folk and pop thusly: Robertson's singing lacked the "nasal tang" ("twang"?) of Daffan's original, and the "musical background" of Robertson's recording "spins out in an entire modern and rhythmic pattern."[33]

The fact that, by late 1942, a recording by Bob Wills could be discussed in terms of its relationship to the pop-folk boundary—and that, by late 1943, a pop cover of a country tune had become so commonplace that the writer could assume that the differences between the genres were well known—speaks to the rapid increase in pop covers during this period. The music industry continued to demonstrate an increased interest in tracking the audience for folk music, and a few folk recordings even began to cross over to the pop audience, far transcending the earlier achievement of Bob Wills with "San Antonio Rose" (if not quite equaling Vernon Dalhart's success in the 1920s). Despite the growing respect for the economic viability of folk music, the patronizing rhetoric and conflation of hillbilly music with corn continued. A few remarkable recordings released in 1943, however, started to trouble some of these negative connotations, even as they failed to erase them entirely.

Pistol Packin' Mamas

Throughout 1942 and well into 1943, a new weekly column in *Billboard*, "American Folk Records," recorded the observations of coin machine operators about the popularity of hillbilly disks. According to these reports, which were corroborated by the general discourse in music industry publications, the five biggest hits during this period were Gene Autry's "Tweedle-o-Twill" (1942), Ernest Tubb's "Walking the Floor Over You" (1942), Elton Britt's "There's a Star-Spangled Banner Waving Somewhere" (1942), Al Dexter's "Pistol Packin' Mama" b/w "Rosalita" (1943), and Ted Daffan's "No Letter Today" b/w "Born to Lose" (1943).

Taking their cue from Cliff Bruner's "It Makes No Difference Now" and (especially) Bob Wills's "New San Antonio Rose," these recordings confirmed that success at "country locations" (a phrase frequently used by coin machine operators) and the possibility of crossing over to the mainstream relied on sonic proximity to the dominant mainstream sound. At one extreme lay Elton Britt's "There's a Star-Spangled Banner Waving Somewhere," which featured a muted trumpet quoting "Taps," a boom-chuck two-beat rhythmic groove with bass playing on beats one and three, Britt's quasi-crooner vocal timbre, and patriotic lyrics, with a fiddle the most prominent stylistic marker of country music. At the other extreme resided Tubb's "Walking the Floor Over You," which made almost no concessions to mainstream style in its bluesy electric lead guitar accompanied only by an acoustic guitar, his down-home vocal style with pronounced Southern regionalisms, and lyrics about tormented romantic longing. Somewhat unsurprisingly, this song crossed over less than the others. The songs of Autry, Dexter, and Daffan all adopted aspects of crooner style (with "No Letter Today" featuring close, two-part harmony throughout), two-beat rhythm, and wind instruments such as the clarinet and trumpet, along with accordions, steel guitars, and fiddles. In terms of lyrics, variation among these songs reflects their sub-generic affiliations, with "Tweedle-o-Twill" referencing the rural southwestern routines of the cinematic singing cowboy, "Rosalita" partaking in the borderline romance trope, and "No Letter Today" and "Born to Lose" resembling "Walking the Floor Over You" in their proto-honky-tonk emphasis on romantic longing, torment, and rejection. While "Born to Lose" straightforwardly conveys this proto-honky-tonk pathos ("I'm born to lose, and now I'm losing you" goes the refrain), "No Letter Today" describes a situation that would have become more common during the war: a relationship that hangs on a thread spun by snail mail.

"Pistol Packin' Mama" is the outlier here, neither an ode to the pastoral joys of singing cowboys, nor tormented-proto-honky-tonk rejection, nor jingoistic display of patriotism. In place of these narratives, it provided a comic take on the honky-tonk milieu, with Dexter's vocal style and timbre falling somewhere between Tubb's rustic drawl and Autry's genteel croon. The instrumentation consolidated the post–Bob Wills fusion of string band with swing band. Following hard on the heels of Britt's "There's a Star-Spangled Banner Waving Somewhere," which had only a few months earlier reset the bar for mainstream success, "Pistol Packin' Mama" presented a variation on the old comic routine of a woman who hits her man over the head with a frying pan with the destructive potential of the frying pan exchanged for that of a firearm. Along with "There's a Star-Spangled Banner Waving Somewhere," "Pistol Packin' Mama" provided the catalyst that raised the nationwide profile of country music. Early notices even referred to "Pistol Packin' Mama" as a "ditty [that] may prove to be a sequel to 'There's a Star-Spangled Banner Waving Somewhere.'"[34]

Such characterizations bore more than a grain of truth. Indeed, as we have seen, even before the popularity of "There's a Star-Spangled Banner Waving Somewhere" became evident, a discourse already existed about the audience for country music exceeding its assumed boundaries. Reports about the success of disks such as Tubb's "Walking the Floor Over You" and Acuff's "Tweedle-o-Twill" poured in throughout 1942 in locations spread out over the country from Des Moines to Philadelphia, with this locational specificity occasionally replaced by reports of popularity "thruout [sic] the country."[35] However, a full-fledged discourse of crossover did not emerge until "There's a Star-Spangled Banner Waving Somewhere" breached the (never impermeable) wall separating folk music and the mainstream.

While references to a crossover process frequently took the form of remarking on the popularity of a song such as "Star-Spangled Banner" "thruout the country" or "not only in country locations," at times the descriptions offered greater precision. The best example of this comes from *Billboard*'s "Record Buying Guide" of January 30, 1943, which informed readers that "There's a Star-Spangled Banner Waving Somewhere" "first made a terrific click in the hillbilly field. Then its folksy qualities, abetted by a patriotic motif, carried it helter-skelter into the pop sphere where rapidly it rose to the heights." If this trend continued, then the author would have to commend Britt for having "set some kind of record for capturing two distinct markets of musical appeal" (63).

Here we find that, far from an academic theory about audiences, categories, and musical style, a utilitarian discourse existed that referred to two distinct markets correlated to musical styles and categories. That such statements ignore the abundant evidence about the diversity of audience taste furnished by previous statements in the same publication begs the point raised initially in chapter 1: that widely shared public beliefs about the relationships between categories of people and music do not necessarily correspond to people's everyday experience of these categories.

Initially viewed as a potential sequel to "There's a Star-Spangled Banner Waving Somewhere," Al Dexter's "Pistol Packin' Mama" substituted broad humor that played on popular caricatures of Southerners for the patriotism that had eased the path of "Star-Spangled Banner" to mainstream success. Some even saw "Star-Spangled Banner" and "Pistol Packin' Mama" as the harbingers of a potential wave of hillbilly crossover material, described as but the first in "a long string of other hillbilly numbers appearing on reports with increasing regularity, threatening to nose out [various pop tunes listed]."[36]

Figure 9 displays the relationship between non-crossover folk, folk, and mainstream popular music in late 1943. According to reports in the "American Folk Tunes" section of *Billboard,* Roy Acuff and Ernest Tubb were popular with folk audiences, but seemed to appeal less to non-stereotypical folk audiences. The widespread success of Dexter's and Britt's recordings has already been detailed at length. Crosby's "Sunday, Monday, or Always" and the Mills Brothers' "Paper Doll" were the two most popular songs according to the "Best-Selling Retail Records" chart of late 1943, in addition to Dexter's "Pistol Packin' Mama." Both the Crosby and Mills Brothers recordings show the effects of the American Federation of Musicians ban (discussed in chapter 5), being completely a cappella (Crosby) or almost completely a cappella (Mills Brothers). Both are done at slow tempi, feature crooner vocal styles, and have lyrics reliant on conventional Tin Pan Alley romantic tropes. While Crosby exemplifies the white-identified crooner style, the case of the Mills Brothers is more complicated. As mentioned in chapter 5, they were among a group of African American artists, which also included the Ink Spots and Ella Fitzgerald, who achieved significant crossover success of their own during this period. The Mills Brothers are included here as an example of the mainstream because they were represented as such in music industry discourse of the time.

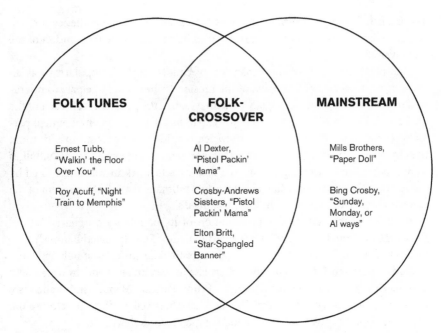

FOLK TUNES

Ernest Tubb,
"Walkin' the Floor
Over You"

Roy Acuff, "Night
Train to Memphis"

**FOLK-
CROSSOVER**

Al Dexter,
"Pistol Packin'
Mama"

Crosby-Andrews
Sissters, "Pistol
Packin' Mama"

Elton Britt,
"Star-Spangled
Banner"

MAINSTREAM

Mills Brothers,
"Paper Doll"

Bing Crosby,
"Sunday,
Monday, or
Al ways"

FIGURE 9. The Circular Logic of Folk Crossover, ca. 1943.

With the dawning recognition of the popular effect of folk tunes came speculation as to the cause. Many reasons were adduced, the first of these being the "longer life" of folk music hits relative to pop band hits. This longer life was due to the way in which "millions upon millions of folk music fans remain true to their favorites for months and even years"; thus folk music was less affected by the shellac shortage caused by the war, because new recordings did not need to be made. The title of another article offered another cause: "Hillbillies Owe Rise to Jukes," argued the author, because the "lack of other recordings forced operators to use mountain music."[37]

Other causes cited for the popularity of folk music ranged from the plausible— "increasing recognition on metropolitan radio," personal appearances by folk artists, cover tunes by "name bands," and newly composed mainstream "tunes that closely approach[ed] the country type"—to the less likely, for instance "increasing recognition in the long-hair press . . . catering to concert-goers who, not long ago, would have sneered at a mere mention of country tunes." Demonstrable support of the war effort, nationalism, and the acquiescence to power also seemed to have been appreciated, with mentions of "Star-Spangled Banner" noting the ability of the "folk-tune field" to come "thru with a large number of patriotic ditties that took the country by storm and splendidly fulfilled the desires of the government."

The main focus of such discussions was the expansion of the audience for folk tunes, stylistic blurring, and thus greater likelihood and public recognition of the crossover effect.[38]

One particular facet of the expansion of country music's popularity was an increase in the geographical reach of the music, attributed in large part to migration to urban areas, although again, as we have seen, the geographical reach of the music seems to have been always already expanding. Changes in employment patterns related to wartime industries, however, provided a new twist. As a location, the city of Baltimore received an extraordinary amount of attention, as hillbillies were reported to be moving to the area in droves to work in war plants. Led by requests for "Pistol Packin' Mama," "Operators estimate that fully 50 per cent of the records most favored here are hillbilly waxings."[39]

In terms of the statistical representation of its popularity on charts, "Pistol Packin' Mama" made much greater inroads than did "Star-Spangled Banner." "Pistol Packin' Mama" reached number one on both *Billboard's* "Best-Selling Retail Records" chart and *Variety's* jukebox chart late in 1943. In an event almost equally striking for a non-mainstream song, "Pistol Packin' Mama" simultaneously reached number two on *Billboard's* "Sheet-Music Best Sellers" list, thus closing the gap in its popularity as song-as-text and song-as-recorded-artifact.

The extraordinary success of "Star-Spangled Banner" and "Pistol Packin' Mama" sparked an awareness, albeit a rather dim one initially, of the institutional barriers to the recognition of country music's popularity. At times this awareness simmered below the threshold of consciousness, as when claims for the inroads made by country music outstripped what the popularity charts actually displayed.[40] However, even as early as the first blush of success for "Star-Spangled Banner," confessions appeared that referenced the structural inequities faced by country music. Although it was a "hillbilly sensation," the anonymous writer for *Billboard's* "Record Buying Guide" admitted, "Elton Britt's disk has been . . . unfairly weighed for its true popularity since it came out in May [1942]." In language evoking nothing so much as the sort of military confrontation that the song itself celebrated, the recording then "invaded the pop fields so strongly that now it forces listing as a Guide item."[41] A week later, the "Record Buying Guide" in *Billboard* allowed that "Star-Spangled Banner" was "worth a lot more to phonos than position here might indicate" (January 16, 1943, 61). The success of "Pistol Packin' Mama" prompted the realization that despite "increasing its popularity each week, . . . [it] holds the same position it did last week . . . because pop tunes by name artists are crowding it out."[42] A similar gap was observed between its sheet music sales and its ranking on sheet music sales charts.[43]

Despite initial obstacles, "Pistol Packin' Mama" did eventually overcome these institutional and structural barriers to the statistical acknowledgment of its popularity and reach number one in the popularity charts of both *Variety* and *Billboard*.

It probably came as a surprise to no one that Bing Crosby and the Andrews Sisters were ready to pounce on "Pistol Packin' Mama," the latest in folk novelties, and cover it. The Crosby-Andrews version charted soon after its release in November 1943 and quickly came to the attention of *Billboard*'s "Record Buying Guide," which noted the generic difference between the cover version and Dexter's:

> Any thought that this hillbilly classic has seen its better days must be now dismissed. In fact, there are still many better days ahead for this *Mama*. She gets young all over again now that Bing Crosby, complimented by the Andrews Sisters, has taken the corn out of the classic and dish [*sic*] it up as a bright rhythmic dish.[44]

The bright and rhythmic Crosby-Andrews dish, as both noun and verb, soon displaced Dexter's in the popularity charts as covers by Crosby and the Andrews Sisters were wont to do with recordings from the race and hillbilly categories.

How did Crosby and the Andrews Sisters take the corn out of the classic? The sound of Dexter's recording is dominated by a muted trumpet, which takes two solos and plays obbligato fills throughout, an accordion that also takes two solos, a steel guitar that takes no solos but accompanies prominently throughout, and a "sock" rhythm guitar accenting beats two and four. As mentioned earlier, Dexter's vocal timbre and phrasing fall somewhere in between Elton Britt's faux croon and Ernest Tubb's rustic drawl. The lyrics of three verses begin with the words "drinking beer in a cabaret," while other verses refer to "dancing with a blonde" (assuredly not the "mama" of the title, who is the narrator's spouse), and close with a reference to Dexter in the third person, who declares "his honkin' [i.e., "honky-tonkin'"] days are done" (see table 10). In terms of form and harmony, the song could not be more straightforward, as it consists essentially of one section, in which the melody is varied slightly between refrain and verse, with the harmony alternating between tonic and dominant in a single key. In an effect reminiscent of Wills's "Spanish Two-Step," rhythmic irregularities occur immediately before verses four and five with a measure of 2/4 interpolated into the otherwise consistent 4/4 meter (noted in table 10).[45]

The Crosby-Andrews version radically transforms the song as heard on Dexter's recording in terms of both the music and the lyrics. For Dexter's proto-honky-tonk ensemble, the Crosby-Andrews recording substitutes a big band arrangement, alternating between a two-to-the-bar and a four-to-the-bar bass swing groove, with no 2/4 measures disturbing the even rhythmic flow. Crosby and the Sisters alternate vocals until they join forces toward the end of the song, with the Sisters providing their trademark three-part vocal harmony. Crosby's vocal interpretation suggests a mocking perspective, as in his "jazzy" interjection of the words "lay that thing [the pistol] down before it goes off and hurts somebody" at the end of the third refrain, and his slurred pronunciation of "pistol" in the fifth refrain (see table 10). The cover version adds a whole new section (labeled "bridge" in table 10) that introduces harmonic variety and several modulations as well as corn novelty effects in the instrumental section.

In addition to these structural changes, the lyrics of the Crosby-Andrews version strikingly alter the character of the song. The three verses beginning with "drinking beer in a cabaret" in Dexter's version are reduced to one, and references to "dancing with a blonde" and to "Al Dexter" and "his honkin' days" are deleted. In place of these lyrics certain substitutions are made, as when, in her solo, Patty Andrews vows to "Bing" that she'll "put her gun away." This change defangs the weapon-wielding mama of the title, whom Dexter, in the parallel verse in his version, implores to "put that gun away" while promising "to be [her] regular daddy" (see table 10). In another verse, Bing is "singing songs in a cabaret" rather than "drinking beer." A new sense of moral propriety enters the picture when later in the same verse he changes the words "until one night she caught me right" to "until one night it didn't seem right" (i.e., instead of changing his ways because he's been caught by his wife doing naughty things, Bing reforms because his conscience informs him that his behavior doesn't "seem right").

New words also accompany the added bridge section of the cover, in which the Andrews Sisters describe themselves as "three tough gals" but lay the blame for the violence at the feet of their "sister Cleo," creating an alternate, yet more complicated, scenario to the narrative of infidelity in Dexter's version. After the instrumental break with corn novelty effects, another new verse is added that describes how "Pappy made a batch of corn." This is a startling revelation, totally inconsistent with the scenario previously established, and one that threatens to render the narrative incoherent. In the end it would be more accurate to say that rather than "taking the corn out of the classic," as described by the reviewer for *Billboard*, Crosby and the Andrews Sisters put the corn *into* the classic while they tone down the references to drinking and extramarital sex. The changes in the musical arrangement and lyrics from Dexter's recording to that of Crosby and the Andrews Sisters produce a verbal-critical trope—corn—that had been associated with folk music but which the practitioners themselves did not employ nor necessarily recognize as being part of the music. Corn, in all its verbal and musical glory, appeared to run in a socio-musical parallel to the musicians and fans who recognized themselves as participants in the field of country music.

Despite the institutional impediments to the representation of its popularity and the habitual critical and musical translation of hillbilly music into corn, Dexter's "Pistol Packin' Mama" capped a string of commercial triumphs of catchy tunes that were classified as hillbilly or western or folk or country that incorporated a few mainstream musical markers. In January 1944, *Billboard* effected a wholesale shakeup of its popularity charts. When the dust settled, a new chart had come into existence. Titled "Most-Played Juke Box Folk Records," this chart was devoted to "Hillbillies, Spirituals, Cowboy Songs, Etc." The number one record?

TABLE 10 Comparison of Two Versions of "Pistol Packin' Mama" by Al Dexter and Bing Crosby and the Andrews Sisters

Al Dexter and His Troopers	Bing Crosby (BC) and the Andrews Sisters (AS)
	BC: [R] Lay that pistol down, babe, lay that pistol down. Pistol packing mama, lay that pistol down.
[V1] Drinking beer in a cabaret and was I having fun, until one night she caught me right and now I'm on the run.	[V1] Oh, drinking beer in a cabaret, was I having fun, until one night she caught me right and now I'm on the run.
[R] Lay that pistol down, babe, lay that pistol down. Pistol Packin' Mama, lay that pistol down.	AS: [R2] Oh, lay that pistol down, babe, lay that pistol down. Pistol packing mama, Lay that pistol down.
[V2] She kicked out my windshield, she hit me over the head. She cussed and cried and said I'd lied and wished that I was dead.	AS (solo): [V4 var.] Oh, I'll sing you every night, Bing And I'll woo you every day. I'll be your regular mama and I'll put that gun away.
[R] Lay that pistol down, babe lay that pistol down. Pistol Packin' Mama, lay that pistol down.	BC: [R var.] Oh, lay that pistol down, babe, lay that pistol down. Pistol packing mama, lay that thing down before it goes off and hurts somebody.
SOLOS (2 x 8 mm.)	
[V3] Drinking beer in a cabaret and dancin' with a blond, until one night she shot out the light—bang! That blond was gone.	[V2] Oh, she kicked out my windshield and she hit me over the head. She cussed and cried and said I lied and she wished that I was dead.
[R] Lay that pistol down, babe, lay that pistol down. Pistol Packin' Mama, lay that pistol down. [+ 2 beats]	AS: [R] Oh, lay that pistol down, babe, lay that pistol down. Pistol packing mama, lay that pistol down.
[V4] I'll see you ev'ry night, babe I'll woo you ev'ry day. I'll be your regular daddy if you'll put that gun away.	[Bridge new] We're three tough gals From deep down Texas way. We got no pals, they don't like the way we play. We're a rough rooting tooting shooting trio but you ought to see my sister Cleo. She's a terror, make no error, but there ain't no nicer terror. Here's what we tell her.

(continued)

TABLE 10 *(continued)*

Al Dexter and His Troopers	Bing Crosby (BC) and the Andrews Sisters (AS)
[R] Lay that pistol down, babe, lay that pistol down. Pistol Packin' Mama, lay that pistol down.	<u>BC</u> [R—new key]: Lay that pistol down, babe, lay that pistol down. Pistol packing mama, [funny pronunciation] lay that pistol down.
SOLOS (2 x 8 mm.)	[band interlude; corn novelty effects]
[V1] Drinking beer in a cabaret and was I having fun, until one night she caught me right and now I'm on the run.	<u>AS</u>: **[V6—new]** <u>Pappy made a batch of corn, the revenuers came, the drought was slow, so now they know you can't do that to Mame.</u>
[R] Lay that pistol down, babe, lay that pistol down. Pistol Packin' Mama, lay that pistol down. [+ 2 beats]	BC & AS: **[R]** Lay that pistol down, babe, lay that pistol down. Pistol packing mama, lay that pistol down.
[V5] Now there was old Al Dexter he always had his fun. But with some lead, she shot him dead. His honkin' days are done.	BC w/AS bg] **[V1 var.]** <u>Oh, singing songs in a cabaret,</u> was I having fun, <u>until one night it didn't seem right</u> and now I'm on the run.
[R] Lay that pistol down, babe, lay that pistol down. Pistol Packin' Mama, lay that pistol down.	BC w/AS [new key, breaks]: **[R]** Oh, lay that pistol down, babe, lay that pistol down. Pistol packing mama, lay that pistol down.
	[tag] Oh, pistol packing mama, lay that pistol down.

Why, none other than "Pistol Packin' Mama," in versions by Bing Crosby and the Andrews Sisters, Al Dexter, and Don Baxter.

FROM "MAMA" TO "SMOKE!"
The Most-Played Juke Box Folk Records Chart

The Most-Played Juke Box Folk Records (MPJBFR) chart presented at first a motley collection of recordings and artists, including the aforementioned versions of "Pistol Packin' Mama" by Bing Crosby and the Andrews Sisters, Al Dexter, and Don Baxter along with other artists mainly identified with hillbilly or western, such as Gene Autry, Ted Daffan, Bob Wills, Floyd Tillman, and Ernest Tubb. The chart also initially included crossover race artists such as Louis Jordan and Lucky Millinder, and from June to July of 1944 the chart was ruled by the King Cole Trio's

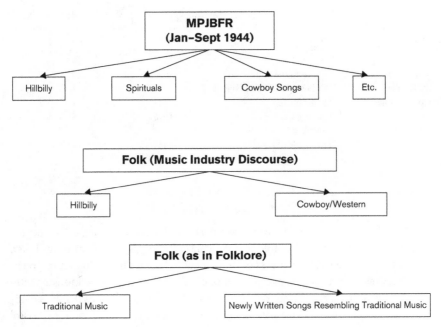

FIGURE 10. Different Usages of "Folk".

proto–jump blues "Straighten Up and Fly Right." The approach to race records on the MPJBFR was riven by contradiction even in terms of *Billboard*'s own implicit rationale for the constitution of its categories, in that some recordings, such as "Straighten Up and Fly Right," topped the MPJBFR chart while others, such as Louis Jordan's "G.I. Jive," featured on the "Most Played Juke Box Records" chart (the mainstream chart) and the "Harlem Hit Parade" but not the MPJBFR, even though his previous "Ration Blues" was ranked on the MPJBFR.

Clearly these charts were meant to say something about audiences, locations, and musical styles and genres, but because of the overlap and lack of synchronization within and between what *Billboard* recognized as different genres, the category of folk was particularly unstable relative to the mainstream and race records.[46] The categorical confusion projected by the MPJBFR can be traced to the multiple simultaneous usages of the "folk" label. The initial listing of the MPJBFR projected an inclusive interpretation of folk that encompassed (potentially) all the marginal categories. In music industry discourse, however, the term tended to have a more restricted usage, usually including only the genres of hillbilly and cowboy (or western) music. Yet at other times, its usage occasionally resembled folkloristic usages of the term "folk." After September 1944 the MPJBFR hewed more closely to the usage of "folk" in music industry discourse (see figure 10).

TABLE 11 Big Folk Hits, 1944–46

Artist	Title	Year	Weeks at #1
Al Dexter	"So Long Pal"	1944	13
Red Foley	"Smoke on the Water"	1944	13
Al Dexter	"I'm Losing My Mind Over You"	1945	7
Spade Cooley	"Shame on You"	1945	9
Al Dexter	"Guitar Polka"	1946	16
Bob Wills	"New Spanish Two-Step"	1946	16
Merle Travis	"Divorce Me C.O.D."	1946	14

Big Folk Hits, 1944–46

The first three years of the MPJBFR was a period of blockbuster hits, as the recordings mentioned in table 11 dominated the charts for long stretches of time. Taken collectively, the stylistic attributes of these recordings, and their citation of preexisting genres, served to consolidate a sense of folk music as a music industry category. Some of these recordings drew overtly on the stylistic features that had characterized successful folk recordings from the previous two years, such as "Pistol Packin' Mama" and "There's a Star-Spangled Banner Waving Somewhere." This connection could be quite direct, as when Al Dexter followed his two-sided smash of "Pistol Packin' Mama" b/w "Rosalita" with "So Long Pal," which retained the sound of "Pistol Packin' Mama" but blended this with lyrics about leaving to go to, and returning home from, the war, thus drawing on the patriotic tone of "Star-Spangled Banner." Dexter also succeeded with his "I'm Losing My Mind Over You," which employed honky-tonk-type lyrics à la "Pistol Packin' Mama." Dexter's last big hit, "Guitar Polka" (number one for sixteen weeks in 1946) signaled a departure in several respects from his previous popular songs, in that the recording really did live up to its title. An instrumental polka led by electric guitar, the song hearkened back to the success of "Beer Barrel Polka," with novelty created by featuring a new sound created by a technological innovation (the electric guitar).

Several of the other huge hits from this period drew on Bob Wills's western swing sound stylistically: Red Foley's "Smoke on the Water" (not to be confused with the 1972 Deep Purple song) cranks the patriotic narrative of "Star-Spangled Banner" into a more triumphalist register, while Spade Cooley's "Shame on You" derives much of its distinctiveness from the deep baritone voice of Tex Williams. Continuing in a similar vein to Cooley, Merle Travis's "Divorce Me C.O.D." used the by-now familiar western swing–based sound enlivened with a novelty lyric and Travis's own distinctive electric guitar playing.

The final recording in this list returns us to a discussion from earlier in the chapter with Bob Wills's "New Spanish Two-Step." This new version blends the music of

"Spanish Two-Step" (which was originally an instrumental) with an approach to lyrics closely related to "New San Antonio Rose," now spiced up with some 1920s-sounding two-step syncopations and mariachi-like trumpets to evoke Spanish-speaking regions south of the border. The lyrics once again tell a tale of borderland romance, while the music, in addition to what was already noted, adds a jazzy electric guitar solo and retains the metric irregularity of "Spanish Two-Step."

None of these tunes, however, despite their citations of previously successful mainstream recordings, crossed over to any significant extent, even though their success as represented within the folk market was comparable to that of "Pistol Packin' Mama." Their extreme longevity at the top of the MPJBFR indicates the restricted number of folk recordings with broad circulation at this time.

In terms of journalistic commentary, the period from 1944 to 1946 largely consisted of a rehash of many of the tropes already discussed earlier: the surprising popularity of folk music in urban areas; the attribution of this popularity to the "flourishing war industries"; attempts to define the difference between "hillbilly" and "cowboy" ("the only real difference . . . is a ten-gallon hat"); and the overlap with corn novelty. And all of this was relayed in language that continued the condescension typical of the preceding years ("The call of the cow-puncher and the melancholy lament of the mountaineer has become a national institution").[47] New explanations were also adduced, including the ubiquity of "folk airshows" and the "fantastic grosses" of live performances of "folkshows."[48] The importance of folk music within the industry found confirmation in the amount of space allotted in *The Billboard 1944 Music Year Book* (forty-six pages) and the periodic cover photos and artist profiles that appeared in *Billboard* during this time featuring the likes of Ernest Tubb, Spade Cooley, Roy Acuff, and Pee Wee King. This increased visibility had a dark side, however, and enthusiasm could tip over toward paranoia. The issue featuring Pee Wee King on the cover included an article titled "Hillbillies Are Hepping to Dollar Sign, Dotted Line and Biz of 'Yours Is Mine.'" This article closed dolefully with "one major disk exec" confessing that "I expect in a short time to give *Billboard* a story of how the country bumpkins are putting things over on us."[49]

Yet alongside what had by now become well-worn topics of conversation whenever folk music was discussed were a few new twists that served as additional indicators of folk music's changing status. One of these involved the slippage of folk music as a music industry category with its folkloristic connotations. Although the confusion between folk as a commercial category and folkloristic uses of the folk had dogged the commercial category since its inception, the newfound acceptance of commercial folk produced fresh associations.[50]

An important discursive trope emerged around this time in the value given to rural authenticity. In earlier discussions about the slippage between corn novelty and hillbilly music, it was clear that, for music industry journalists, whether or not folk music was an act or the unvarnished expression of the folk was unimportant.

After all, Meyer Horowitz ("who ought to know") preferred Jewish and Italian hill-billies to "real" ones, and Edgar Grunwald could claim (without making an argument about the performative or citational aspect of identification) that the hillbilly was invented by the radio. The distinction between real and imitation hillbillies began to assume greater importance as rural authenticity was increasingly stressed as an important ingredient. Writing in *Billboard* in 1944, Nat Green put it this way: "A synthetic cowboy or hillbilly is anathema to the average listener. As audiences are made up largely of people living on farms and in small towns, or who have come from the rural districts, a phony is quickly spotted and is not likely to climb far."[51] Although a positive valence is imputed here to country music audiences, traces of the condescension that previously dominated music industry discourse still persisted. Elsewhere in the same issue of *Billboard,* these audiences were described as not caring about which hillbilly or cowboy they were listening to.[52]

Even as old negative tropes persisted, the new level of discrimination granted to fans undoubtedly stood in for the new level of discrimination possessed by the journalists themselves, now able to discern real hillbillies and cowboys from those who rehearsed in apartments in the Bronx (this formulation forecloses as a possibility that real hillbillies might be rehearsing in the Bronx). By 1946 the prestige granted ersatz hillbillies seemed to be long forgotten in the extolling of folk music as something "written from the heart" that "express[es] the feeling of the people more clearly than would even perfect poetry."[53]

Record reviews could refer to Ernest Tubb as "the soulful cowboy," or to the "sincerity" of Bob Atcher's "exposition of cowboy chants." George Frazier, a reviewer for *Variety,* even seized on this quality of folk music in the midst of a patronizing rant: "It is corny, overly sentimental, frequently illiterate, and on occasion dirty, but for all this it is more in touch with the times than any other form of music. . . . 'The Death of Floyd Collins' and similar things remain authentic Americana." The strongest assertion of folk music's authenticity came in a letter to *Billboard*'s column "American Folk Tunes." Appearing below a header titled "Folk Defense," the author asserts that "American folk music is the real strain of this country, and I find the simple and appealing so-called hillbilly ballads the music expression of the common man—the little people, and God made them in the majority."[54] These passionate attachments occurred more often with non-crossover artists such as Roy Acuff or Ernest Tubb than with purveyors of novelty corn such as the Hoosier Hot Shots.

Such defenses of rural authenticity would have significant reverberations, especially among the audience for non-crossover country music, as well as for future generations of roots music connoisseurs. For the moment, however, the rapprochement of folk tunes with the mainstream would be dominated by another trope, familiar to us from the previous chapter and the journey of "Open the Door, Richard": that of the novelty song and the echoes of minstrelsy.

WHERE THERE'S "SMOKE!" THERE'S FIRE

As we have already seen, the greatest commercial successes in the world of folk music in the years following "Pistol Packin' Mama" often bore sonic traces of that recording and/or a relationship to western swing (and/or were recorded by Al Dexter, Mr. "Pistol Packin' Mama" himself). Some of these recordings emerged from a thriving ballroom scene in Southern California. With audiences populated largely by transplants from the Southwest—and aided by the entrepreneurial skill of Foreman Phillips, who operated several ballrooms in Southern California—a style of western swing emerged that was derived from Bob Wills and Milton Brown but adapted toward its new milieu.

Phillips initially opened the long-dormant Venice Ballroom on the Venice Pier; it was a huge hall that could pack in more than six thousand dancers. Large crowds were common up and down the coast, and could stretch the bounds of legality; the fire department closed a ballroom in Oakland after it oversold a Bob Wills performance in 1944.[55] Phillips gradually built a network of ballrooms that expanded to include Compton, Baldwin Park, and Culver City. Other promoters latched onto the idea, and more halls featuring western swing–derived country sprouted in locations such as Riverside and Glendale.

Of the performers already mentioned with large hits in the period from 1944 to 1946, two participated directly in this scene: Spade Cooley and Merle Travis. Of their hits, Cooley's "Shame on You," with its multiple fiddles, jazzy electric guitar, and alternations between carefully arranged passages and improvisation, more closely approximated the Bob Wills model of western swing, while Travis's "Divorce Me C.O.D." derived more from "Pistol Packin' Mama" in its use of accordion, muted trumpet, and a novelty lyric. "Divorce Me C.O.D." has the added interest of being the first popular song to use the word "divorce" in the lyric, which Travis tempered with humorous novelty lyrics ("I ain't no college p'fessor / I ain't got no PhD / but if you want your freedom PDQ / divorce me C.O.D."). Despite the humor, the song was banned by two of the three major radio networks.

Cooley and Travis both played a major role in what would be the only major crossover country hit in the immediate postwar years, "Smoke! Smoke! Smoke! (That Cigarette)" by Tex Williams and His Western Caravan. Williams's professional career flourished during his time as the vocalist in Cooley's band, and he provided the distinctive baritone lead in "Shame on You." He split from Cooley due to what one writer termed Cooley's "megalomaniac tendencies," taking much of Cooley's band with him, and set up shop at the Palace Barn Dance in Glendale, California.[56] After signing with Capitol Records and releasing a single in October 1946, *Billboard* quoted Williams on the subject of recent trends in entertainment. According to Williams, fans are no longer satisfied to dance: "Now they want to be entertained. . . . Every musician in a Western band today has to be a showman. He must be able to either sing, clown or do solo work on his particular instrument."[57] Cooley's take on western swing, Travis's form of country novelty, and Williams's savvy notion of entertainment came together in "Smoke! Smoke! Smoke! (That Cigarette)," recorded in March 1947 and released in May of the same year.

Taken at a rapid tempo, the song relies on the conventions of popularized western swing. Featuring a boom-chuck rhythmic groove, improvised fills by accordion and electric guitar, orchestrated fills with accordion and fiddles acting like a horn section, an improvised trumpet solo reminiscent of New Orleans jazz, an improvised fiddle solo, and an arranged interlude for multiple fiddles, the recording's connections to previous hits of the immediately preceding period are clear, even if the arrangement presents a sonic variety exceeding its predecessors. The humorous lyrics also reiterate the type of humor found in Travis's "Divorce Me C.O.D.," a reference that is rather unsurprising in this case, as Travis wrote the song (Williams received a co-credit).

Several factors set "Smoke!" apart from its predecessors, however. Williams's relaxed Southern accent and baritone voice had been heard on Cooley's recordings, but in the verses of "Smoke!" Williams delivers the lyrics patter style, or in a rhythmic spoken declamatory manner. The resonance of his deep speaking voice is highlighted by the clear low frequencies of the recording, adding to the novelty (in both senses of the word) effect. The chorus is unusually catchy, and harmonized by two other male singers who join in with Williams. The orchestration, while featuring instruments already familiar to listeners through the conventions established by previous successful recordings, surpasses these in invention, featuring a kaleidoscopic swirl of different instruments, both in fills between lines of sung text, and as obbligato accompaniment.

Then there are the lyrics. If the sonic dimensions of the recording offered the usual repetition-with-a-difference that we've grown accustomed to expecting in these situations, then the words offered something new, with only "Divorce Me C.O.D." standing as a possible precedent. The lyrics detail the frustration that ensues when the song's persona must put on hold certain activities while the other party on which the activity depends has a smoke. The situation is established in the first verse, when Williams raps that "Nicotine slaves are all the same / at a pettin' party or a poker game / Everything gotta stop while they have a cigarette." Thus the song's persona ("Tex" from now on) has a great hand in poker but can't close the game because the only other player still in the game stops to light up. In the third verse, Tex finds himself deeply involved in a "smoochin' party," only to have it interrupted when his date indulges her inconvenient (for him) habit.

Unlike "Pistol Packin' Mama" or even "Open the Door, Richard," no explosion of discourse greeted "Smoke! Smoke! Smoke! (That Cigarette)." What was in retrospect almost every bit as extraordinary an event as the surprise success of "Pistol Packin' Mama" passed with nary a peep. The first notice to appear, in *Variety*, provides an inkling of the reception of the recording among the mainstream audience, declaring that "it should have almost universal appeal." *Billboard,* though initially somewhat more circumspect in its first review, eventually concurred with *Variety* in its second review a month later, describing "Smoke!" as "a dilly of a novelty disk that may well give Capitol . . . its first big hit." The review concludes with speculation about the potential audience: "Tho aimed at the cowboy crowds, side isn't restricted to Western locations."[58] This review made it plain that, whether the recording was western, cowboy, or novelty, it had what would later be recognized as crossover potential. An advertisement published at the same time also suggests a possible reason that Tex Williams and "Smoke!" might have seemed distinct from other folk recordings of the period. Williams is shown as a clean-cut, mature adult, facing the camera without a cowboy hat. By way of contrast, an ad for four folk artists signed to Columbia show all but one in a cowboy hat, and the fourth, Roy Acuff, looking decidedly rustic. These artists are advertised as "First String Favorites," punning on a sonic attribute by referring to the pickings and pluckings noted in earlier record reviews.[59]

The Minstrelsy-Novelty Connection

In some ways, the type of humor used in "Smoke!" can be traced back to that found in nineteenth-century songs such as "Arkansas Traveler," which in turn derived from minstrel shows but referenced a form of humor that appeared as always already associated with white, Southern identity. Such a chain of associations was recognized, albeit in a somewhat hazy manner, in the little journalistic commentary that "Smoke!" received.[60]

The chain of associations that emerges in the brief reviews of "Smoke!" helps explain the strange sense of familiarity that even non–folk fans might have felt upon first encountering the recording. One review stated that "Williams slings the wordage in typical Phil Harris fashion," while another referred to "the Phil Harris–type delivery by Tex Williams."[61] Granted that both blurbs were probably written by the same person given the many resemblances between them, still the question arises: Who was Phil Harris? What most sources identify as Harris's signature song, "That's What I Like About the South," provides some clues. The song, written by the African American songwriter Andy Razaf (well known as a collaborator with Fats Waller) and subtitled "The Groove Song," is an up-tempo patter number with a musical background similar to "I've Got Rhythm" minus the B-section. Harris recorded the song several times, first in 1937 for Vocalion, then early in 1946 for ARA, and again later in 1946 after signing with RCA Victor. *Billboard* reviewed the ARA release, noting that "Harris is best when singing of candy yams and butterbeans in 'That's What I Like About the South.' And the minstrel man is just as effective as he tells the fanciful story of the 'Brazen Little Raisin,' of the grape which shriveled up and became a raisin."[62] RCA Victor released Harris's latest remake about six months before "Smoke!" in December 1946. This time around, *Billboard*'s review praised "the effervescent Phil Harris singing in his inimitable minstrel style that spots the light on these sides."[63]

Other Harris recordings, such as "The Darktown Poker Club," released in 1946 but a mainstay of his repertoire for many years before then, also support the connection with minstrelsy. In addition to his musical repertoire, a clue to mainstream performance conventions across media is provided by considering Harris's other activities. During the period following the release of "That's What I Like About the South" and "The Darktown Poker Club," Harris became well known as a radio personality hosting "The Phil Harris–Alice Faye Show" in tandem with his wife, the actress Alice Faye. At least one of their broadcasts interpolated an extended citation of a minstrelsy performance, when Harris and the guitarist on the show get covered in soot during a skit and then slip into blackface dialect.[64] The establishment of a semiotic chain—Tex Williams = Phil Harris = minstrelsy—helps explain how hillbilly numbers that were marketed to the mainstream as novelties were also heard to have connections to minstrelsy.

We may also recall from the previous chapter that "Open the Door, Richard," although projecting somewhat less subtle associations with minstrelsy than "Smoke!," was also received within a general context of novelty that trafficked in stereotypical others of all denominations. The still pervasive, though no longer officially acceptable, tropes of minstrelsy could occasionally join with the generalized hilarity of othering found in the novelty song. For example, toward the end of the chart run of "Smoke!" a recording appeared that situated the other in central Africa. "Civilization (Bongo, Bongo, Bongo)," as recorded by Danny Kaye and (once again) the Andrews Sisters, entered the charts in November 1947 and told the tale of a native who mocks the uncivilized ways of those living in the very "civilization" that those "civilized" people were training him to desire. This might seem like a critique of imperialism and capitalism, but the song's persona uses skewered grammar ("Each morning, a missionary advertises neon sign") and portrays himself as a happy savage ("Bingo, bangle, bungle, I'm so happy in the jungle, I refuse to go") who uses humor to reinforce exotic images of the Congo dweller. As sung by Danny Kaye, the recording makes no attempts at ethnographic fidelity to the experience of life in central Africa.

In August 1947, at the height of the popularity of "Smoke!" a cartoon appeared in *Billboard* that resonated uncannily with the topoi that would be presented three months later in "Civilization (Bongo, Bongo, Bongo)."[65] The cartoon features a radio announcer for "WOR" who is reading an advertisement for "Boopy-Doopy Soapy Suds" that will provide "whiter washes." The next panel shows "natives," who resemble nothing other than blackface minstrel performers, "cooking" up a white person whom they presumably captured. Upon hearing the ad, they eject the person from their kettle and start using "Boopy-Doopy Soapy Suds" in their boiling water to wash their clothes. Advertising promotes civilizing effects upon unsuspecting minstrel performers, it would appear, even as the persona of Civilization would resist the clarion call of such promotions.

"Smoke!" on the Charts

The argument thus far is that the following contributed to the success of "Smoke!": 1) mainstream audiences' memories of the sound and spirit of "Pistol Packin' Mama"; 2) folk audiences' recent experiences with a variety of western swing–derived material that drew on the sound of "Pistol Packin' Mama"; and 3) the use of humor related to other minstrel-derived novelty numbers. Did these factors manage to help the recording evade the representational biases built into the construction of popularity charts at that time? By this point, the popularity-tracking apparatus had expanded greatly since the heyday of "Pistol Packin' Mama." The "Record Buying Guide" had transformed into the "Most Played Juke Box Records" chart, the "Best-Selling Retail Records" chart more or less remained in place, changing its name in a subtle yet telling way to "Best-Selling *Popular* Retail Records," and a new radio chart, "Records Most Played on the Air," had been added, which tracked which recordings (rather than songs) were played. The "Honor Roll of Hits," "The Chart of Charts," began in 1945, and combined the mainstream charts for recordings and publishing, while the "Most-Played Juke Box Folk Records" chart will be familiar from the discussion earlier in this chapter. In a move that possibly signified conceptual ambiguity, during the reign of "Smoke!" atop the "Most-Played Juke Box Folk Records" chart, the name of this chart changed to "Most-Played Juke Box *Hillbilly* Records" on September 6, then on November 8 the name changed back to "Most-Played Juke Box *Folk* Records."

Table 12 displays the remarkable success of "Smoke!" across the different charts responsible for tracking specific recordings. Its path established what would become a classic crossover pattern of success in a marginal chart followed by success, albeit lesser, on the various mainstream charts. "Smoke!" held the number one position for sixteen weeks on the "Most-Played Juke Box Folk/Hillbilly Records" chart, and the number one position on the "Records Most Played on the Air" chart (one week), the "Most Played Juke Box Records" chart (four weeks), and the "Best-Selling Popular Retail Records" chart (six weeks). One notices that "Smoke!" performed somewhat less well on the "Honor Roll of Hits," which incorporated data based on record sales, radio play, sheet music sales, and radio plugs. This chart, then, strove to balance the competing notions of the work concept and the sonic aesthetic, as well as the competing interests of music publishers and record companies.

A more detailed look at the rankings for "Smoke!" for the week of September 6, one of the three weeks in which it held the number one ranking in three different charts, helps shed light on its relatively poor performance on the "Honor Roll of Hits." In addition to the charts shown in table 12, all of which were based on the song as a recorded, sonic artifact, there were two other charts devoted to the song

TABLE 12 Comparative Chart Performance of "Smoke! Smoke! Smoke! (That Cigarette)," July 5, 1947–December 6, 1947

Week	MPJBF/HR	RMPOTA	MPJBR	BSPRR	HROH
July 5	#2	#15	—	—	—
July 12	#3	#15	—	—	—
July 19	#1	#3	#9	—	—
July 26	#1	#9	#7	#8	—
Aug. 2	#1	#8	#7	#6	—
Aug. 9	#1	#2	#5	#1	—
Aug. 16	#1	#1	#6	#1	—
Aug. 23	#1	#2	#2	#1	—
Aug. 30	#1	#6	#1	#1	#3
Sept. 6	#1	#3	#2	#1	#4
Sept. 13	#1	#2	#1	#1	#4
Sept. 20	#1	#2	#1	#2	#3
Sept. 27	#1	#2	#1	#2	#5
Oct. 4	#1	#2	#3	#2	#8
Oct. 11	#1	#4	#3	#4	#10
Oct. 18	#1	#6	#5	—	—
Oct. 25	#1	#10	#6	—	—
Nov. 1	#2	—	—	—	—
Nov. 8	#1	—	—	—	—
Nov. 15	#2	—	—	—	—
Nov. 22	#5	—	—	—	—
Nov. 29	#5	—	—	—	—
Dec. 6	#5	—	—	—	—

MPJBF/HR: Most Played Juke Box Folk/Hillbilly Records

RMPOTA: Records Most Played on the Air

MPJBR: Most Played Juke Box Records

BSPRR: Best-Selling Popular Retail Records

HROH: Honor Roll of Hits

as notated text: "Songs with Greatest Radio Audiences" and "Best-Selling Sheet Music." "Smoke!" did not appear at all on these two charts. Its absence there may explain how a recording ranked at number one or number two in the mainstream charts for best-selling records, radio play, and jukebox play could be ranked only at number four in the "Honor Roll of Hits," the master "Chart of Charts." Such a formulation illuminates the continued power of the publishing industry to affect the circulation of an idea about a given recording's popularity.[66]

• • •

The breakthrough success of "Smoke!" remained sui generis. Although the trade publications continued to speak of the success of folk music, the various forums in which notions of mainstream success circulated remained mute for the most part. Other tropes, well worn by this point, persisted. "Cornbilly" troupes would still "corn-quer" audiences by surprise in northeastern cities, the role of the migration of Southerners during the war in facilitating the spread of hillbilly music became further entrenched, and the importance of the sincerity and authenticity of country performers gained strength to the point where no one could question it any longer, especially for music that did not appear to pander to mainstream taste.[67] The idea that folk music consisted of two main genres, hillbilly and western (or cowboy), was increasingly clear, but at the same time, the confusion sowed by the continued usage of "folk" as a label for this type of music became harder to ignore, and eventually consensus emerged among music industry agents that, as a label for a category, "hillbilly" just would not do. Thus did "country and western" become the accepted name for the category at exactly the same moment (June 25, 1949) as the commercial breakthrough for Hank Williams, the performer who would become the icon for postwar country music.[68]

Crossovers from country and western remained largely a hit-or-miss affair. "Softshell" artists such as Eddy Arnold occasionally graced the lower reaches of the mainstream charts during the late 1940s and early 1950s, and Hank Williams's songs succeeded in mainstream cover versions while he managed a few minor hits himself during the same period. The sudden emergence of rockabilly in the mid-1950s reaped categorical confusion for several years as artists such as Elvis Presley, Jerry Lee Lewis, and Johnny Cash appeared in country and mainstream (and even occasionally rhythm and blues) charts. The countrypolitan moment of the late 1950s and early 1960s seemed to blur musical sensibilities between country and mainstream and resulted in pop success for Jim Reeves, Patsy Cline, and Skeeter Davis. The pattern of a cluster of crossover successes followed by years of almost complete separation between country and the mainstream continued, more or less, up to at least the early 1990s, when the method of calculating the sales of recordings changed, resulting in an immediate transformation in the representation of country's mainstream popularity, if not the greater inclusion of country music in contemporary hit radio.[69]

The resistance to such a blurring of categorical boundaries could be witnessed in a recording that was released toward the end of the countrypolitan period. Sung in a down-home manner recalling the heyday of honky-tonk, Carl Butler and Pearl's "Don't Let Me Cross Over" scored the largest hit in country and western music in late 1962 and early 1963, cresting at number one on the country chart for eleven weeks. The line that could not be crossed in this case did not constitute the boundary between musical categories but rather the line between marital fidelity and infidelity, a lyrical trope that also recalled classics from the late 1940s such as Floyd Tillman's shame-filled "Slippin' Around."[70] Carl Butler and Pearl (who were married themselves) may have sung about resisting the lure of crossing over, but that didn't prevent them from acknowledging the financial benefits delivered by their recording. They named their ranch near Franklin, Tennessee, Crossover Acres.

The reflexive quality of lyrics in country music has been often recognized, both then and now, and this extends to commentary on commercial processes as much as it does to puns that comment on the genre itself.[71] Because so much of this chapter has been taken up with the tracing of crossover processes between country music and the mainstream, it is worth remembering a claim from chapter 1, to wit, that instances of generic crossover often highlight those moments when identification with a category of music shifts from a homologous to an imaginary form. The case of country music in the 1940s does not offer a simple movement from a time when no recordings crossed over to the mainstream to one when many did, but rather a series of flirtations between country music and the mainstream, in which an opening might occur, only to close partially and then open again. In some cases, country artists adapted elements from mainstream popular music that seemed to facilitate their crossing over, a practice that happened in dialogue with cover versions of hillbilly songs by mainstream artists. Each movement of this sort disturbed notions of homological identification and required a new formulation, however slight, of both rural, white, Southern identity and urban, white, Northern identity.

Yet at the same time, the erratic and inconsistent nature of these crossovers reinforced the sense of difference between the two. The use of corn novelty retained the sense in which hillbilly identity was a convention that could be already known, cited, and a source of humor for those who identified as hillbillies as well as for those who didn't, and who thus were defined in opposition to an imagined, stable hillbilly identity.

Nevertheless, an awareness spread of the insufficiency of the categorical labels then in circulation for the music associated with rural, white Southerners. If these people remained legible for others as a source of humor and pathos, then "country and western" made sense as a non-pejorative label that could encapsulate the disparate musical threads that were already grouped together discursively. However, even country and western, which referenced this stylistic diversity, would eventually prove to be too cumbersome, and the unruly stylistic multiplicity of the 1940s would become a distant memory to most. On November 3, 1962, on the eve of the success of "Don't Let Me Cross Over," *Billboard* dropped the "western" and the category acquired the name it has held ever since: simply "country."

NOTES

1. I will alternate between the use of "country" (the dominant term since the early 1960s), "folk," and "hillbilly" (the terms used during the historical period in question) to refer to the music that forms the subject of the chapter.

2. This is not to say that hillbilly music was not internally differentiated in terms of musical style or subgenres, but only that a subset did not exist that was marked because of its mainstream success. Previous studies of country music in the 1940s include the following: Bill C. Malone, *Country Music U.S.A.* (Austin: University of Texas Press, 1985); Bill C. Malone, *Southern Music/American Music* (Lexington: University Press of Kentucky, 1979); Richard Peterson, *Creating Country Music: Fabricating Authenticity* (Chicago and London: University of Chicago Press, 1997); Jeffrey J. Lange, *Smile When You Call Me a Hillbilly: Country Music's Struggle for Respectability, 1939–1954* (Athens and London: University of Georgia Press, 2004); and Diane Pecknold, *The Selling Sound: The Rise of the Country Music Industry* (Durham, NC, and London: Duke University Press, 2007).

3. "The Case for Hillbillies: Biggar of WLW Says They Help Theaters, Vaudeville, Stations, Instrument Firms, You 'n' Me," *Billboard*, April 13, 1940, 12.

4. See H. M. Jones reporting from Stephenville, Texas, in "WTRADFM," *Billboard*, February 18, 1939, 69.

5. Ibid. For the comments from New York and Buffalo, see "WTRADFM," *Billboard*, November 11, 1939, 67; and "WTRADFM," *Billboard*, November 18, 1939, 65.

6. See for example comments from Willie L. (Bill) Eidt of Natchez, Mississippi, in "WTRADFM," *Billboard*, April 15, 1939, 15; Bob Lancaster of Ferriday, Louisiana, in "WTRADFM," *Billboard*, June 17, 1939, 78; Bill Paradise of Spokane, Washington, in "WTRADFM," *Billboard*, October 21, 1939, 63; and Frank Miles of Danville, Illinois, in "WTRADFM," *Billboard*, May 6, 1939, 77.

7. Western swing was itself a categorical label that arose after the fact, as is made plain by Jeffrey J. Lange in *Smile When You Call Me a Hillbilly*, 89. The same can be said for some of the other country subgenres discussed in this chapter, such as honky-tonk.

8. "WTRADFM," November 11, 1939, 67. See also the comment by Ted Mills of Buffalo, New York, published a week later in "WTRADFM": "'It Makes No Difference Now' is one of our best records and Dick Robertson deserves full credit" (November 18, 1939, 65).

9. The desirability of stocking hillbilly records in taverns comes from a detailed analysis of the impact of different types of locations on music machines. See Sam Lerner, "Picking the Right Records for the Right Spot," *Billboard*, September 28, 1940, 6, 58, 59. Lerner makes the following recommendation of "The ideal record selection . . . for the average tavern": two Viennese waltzes, two hillbilly numbers, five popular dance numbers, four novelty records, four songs of the Bing Crosby, Dick Todd, or Tony Martin type, two polkas or international numbers, and five records selected especially to fit the individual tastes of the patrons of the location.

10. "Talent and Tunes," *Billboard*, April 5, 1941, 72. See also "WTRADFM," *Billboard*, November 11, 1939, 67; "Hillbillies Like Broadcastin' Better 'n Stayin' on the Farm; One Feller Makin' 35G One Year," *Billboard*, December 21, 1940, 7.

11. Richard Peterson, *Creating Country Music*.

12. On the role of the barn dances such as the Grand Ole Opry in preparing non-Southern audiences for country music, see Jeffrey J. Lange, *Smile When You Call Me a Hillbilly*, 30.

13. As we saw in chapter 4, the idea of the hillbilly as someone who might have a particular allegiance to corny music and humor was already made possible by a discourse about Southerners and the South that was both romantic and patronizing. For the long history of

this discourse, see Anthony Harkins, *Hillbilly: A Cultural History of an American Icon* (New York and Oxford: Oxford University Press, 2005).

14. "West Virginia Hills Are in the Bronx, Says Barn Barnum," *Billboard*, March 4, 1939, 1, 8. The Hoosier Hot Shots were more likely to be recognized as a country band by other country musicians than Freddie "Schnicklefritz" Fisher owing to their regular inclusion in radio programs such as the WLS *National Barn Dance*.

15. Edgar A. Grunwald, "The Radio Hillbilly Still Wows 'Em," *Variety*, January 3, 1940, 89.

16. "Band Reviews: Fiddle Bow Bill's Dew Valley Acorns (8)" (Midway Gardens, Minneapolis), *Variety*, December 20, 1939, 32. Such reviews also speak to the centrality of the radio barn dance in promoting an image of country music articulated to popular notions of the hillbilly-as-rube. On this connection see Pamela Fox, *Natural Acts: Gender, Race, and Rusticity in Country Music* (Ann Arbor: University of Michigan Press, 2009), 17–62; and Richard Peterson, *Creating Country Music*, 97–117. Diane Pecknold, while not claiming that country music was an "invention of the radio," does describe it as "above all a creature of radio" in her discussion of the history barn dance broadcasts in *The Selling Sound*, 15–24.

17. Edgar A. Grunwald, "The Radio Hillbilly Still Wows 'Em." Other examples of this type of condescension abound, and arose in almost any account of the music appearing in mainstream journalism. See for example "Flowers That Bloom in Spring Return to Hillbillies in Philly," *Billboard*, May 25, 1940, 6.

18. The Grateful Dead also included "El Paso" in live performances, featuring it regularly beginning in 1969. Both this song and "Mexicali Blues" were sung by Bob Weir, leading one to wonder if borderland romance was a personal obsession of his.

19. Rich Kienzle, liner notes for Bob Wills and the Texas Playboys, *The Essential Bob Wills, 1935–1947* (Sony Music Entertainment / Columbia Legacy, 1992).

20. Ibid. and Charles R. Townsend, *San Antonio Rose: The Life and Music of Bob Wills* (Urbana and Chicago: University of Illinois Press, 1976). Diane Pecknold affirms the idea that metric irregularity was incompatible with popular music conventions of the time in her description of the crucial role played by Fred Rose in the transformation of country music: "Rose took country material and brought it into line with standard pop conventions. His ability to regularize meters, polish lyrics, and simplify melodies was employed over and over." Diane Pecknold, *The Selling Sound*, 62.

21. "Talent and Tunes," *Billboard*, November 30, 1940, 99. Release date courtesy http://www.secondhandsongs.com/performance/19914, accessed July 20, 2015.

22. "Record Buying Guide," *Billboard*, January 11, 1941, 64; "Record Buying Guide," *Billboard*, January 25, 1941, 75. My emphasis.

23. "Record Buying Guide," *Billboard*, February 22, 1941, 77; "Record Buying Guide," *Billboard*, March 8, 1941, 71.

24. For more on Crosby's recordings of cowboy songs, see Don Cusic, *The Cowboy in Country Music: An Historical Survey with Artist Profiles* (Jefferson, NC: McFarland, 2011), 112–13.

25. Review of Al Dexter and His Troupers, "Honky Tonk Chinese Dime" and "Sundown Polka," *Billboard*, March 14, 1942, 71; review of Ernest Tubb, "Time After Time" and "When the World Has Turned You Down," *Billboard*, March 14, 1942, 71.

26. *Billboard,* March 6, 1943, 1. Reviews of Elton Britt and the Hoosier Hot Shots, *Billboard,* July 4, 1942, 69. Reviews of Gene Autry and Spike Jones, August 1, 1942, 68. See also "Gold in Them Thar Hillbillies" (subtitled "B'Way Pubs Hungry for Corn as Rural Rhythms Skyrocket in Disk and Music Sales—ASCAP-BMI War Gave Push to Shoutin' Stuff"), *Billboard,* August 21, 1943, 12.

27. "Coast Orks Go 'Billy: Khaki and Overalled Oakies Make Metropolitian Maestri Feed 'Em Down Home Tunes," *Billboard,* May 29, 1943, 25. The popularity of hillbilly music was not limited to Southern California, as evidenced by the following: "Demand for mountain musikers was also pointed up when Tex Ritter and 'billy band was signed for a week at the Orpheum Theater, Oakland, but was only able to round up four men." "'Billies Reaping Harvest on Coast," *Billboard,* October 23, 1943, 13.

28. The video for "Cocktails for Two" (1944) may be seen at http://www.youtube.com /watch?v = lvt4b_qwC_Q, accessed May 10, 2014.

29. *Billboard,* October 16, 1943, back cover.

30. "Thar's Gold in Them Thar Hillbilly and Other American Folk Tunes," *Billboard,* September 26, 1942, 86. For the inclusion of folk music to combat the corn label, see "American Folk Tunes and Tunesters: 'Taint Corn, Says Bradley," *Billboard,* February 5, 1944, 63.

31. "On the Records," *Billboard,* April 17, 1943, 62.

32. "American Folk Records: Week's Releases," *Billboard,* December 12, 1942, 68.

33. "Record Buying Guide—Part 2," *Billboard,* December 4, 1943, 102.

34. "Record Buying Guide: Coming Up," *Billboard,* June 19, 1943, 65. This idea was echoed repeatedly; for example see *Billboard*'s "Record Buying Guide" from a month later, July 17, 1943, 65.

35. One can find numerous instances of these sorts of quotes. For examples see "American Folk Records," *Billboard,* August 1, 1942, 68; and "American Folk Records," *Billboard,* August 22, 1942, 69.

36. "Talent and Tunes on Music Machines," *Billboard,* July 3, 1943, 65.

37. "Hillbillies Owe Rise to Jukes: Lack of Other Recordings Forced Operators to Use Mountain Music," *Billboard,* August 28, 1943, 70, 75. See also "Record Buying Guide: Coming Up," *Billboard,* July 17, 1943, 65.

38. "Many Trends Combined to Give Folk Music a Wider Audience," *Billboard,* February 27, 1943, 93–94. For an earlier discussion of country crossover recordings and cover versions by mainstream artists, see "Thar's Gold in Them Thar Hillbilly and Other American Folk Tunes."

39. "Hillbilly Music Is Big Favorite with Baltimore Patrons," *Billboard,* July 3, 1943, 62. For more on the popularity of hillbilly music in Baltimore, see "Ex-Hillbillies Find Music They Like at Baltimore Spots," *Billboard,* August 28, 1943, 71; "Hillbillies Prefer Own Songs, Ops in Baltimore Find," *Billboard,* October 16, 1943, 64; and "American Folk Tunes and Tunesters," *Billboard,* October 30, 1943, 62. For a more general account of the effect of migration, see "Servicemen, Workers Bring 'Corn' to Cities," *Variety,* August 11, 1943, 1, 42.

40. This is the case for example with "Many Trends Combined to Give Folk Music a Wider Audience," *Billboard,* February 27, 1943, 93–94.

41. "Record Buying Guide," *Billboard,* January 9, 1943, 65.

42. "Record Buying Guide," *Billboard,* July 10, 1943, 65.

43. "Gold in Them Thar Hillbillies," 12, 14. This discussion has other ramifications in terms of the sonic aesthetic and work concept opposition. At one point the author reports that "Up to now no publisher has ever printed a hillbilly arrangement as mountain bands are generally recognized as ear musicians."

44. *Billboard*, November 13, 1943, 66.

45. I've tried not to use terminology in this description that is implicitly judgmental, such as "interrupting the flow," "dropping two beats," et cetera, as the flow probably did not feel interrupted to the musicians and primary audience for this tune, not did it probably feel as if beats had been dropped. I am aware, however, that even terms such as "irregularities" and "inconsistencies" carry with them more than a whiff of value judgment.

46. That is to say, race records as represented by the Most-Played Juke Box Race Records (MPJBRR) chart by 1944 seemed relatively coherent compared to folk records. Recall from chapter 5 that the "Harlem Hit Parade" was also extremely diverse in terms of the artists and genres it included, especially in its earliest incarnations. Diane Pecknold argues that the term "folk" was employed by country music insiders as a means to legitimate the music. Diane Pecknold, *The Selling Sound*, 60–61. The songwriter and publisher Fred Rose used the term in this manner, equating "hillbilly music" and "folklore" in his "open letter" published in *Billboard*, "American Folk Tunes: Cowboy and Hillbilly Tunes and Tunesters," August 3, 1946, 123.

47. "Folk Music Finds Its Way to the City: City Record Retailers Who Once Gave Folk Disks the Go-By, Now Find Sales Soaring . . . and the Upswing Has Only Begun," *The Billboard 1944 Music Year Book*, October 28, 1944, 353; "Folk Music Takes Hold in the Jukes," *The Billboard 1944 Music Year Book*, October 28, 1944, 343; "Folk Music Here to Stay in Jukes," *Billboard*, March 3, 1945, 92–93. An article from 1945 provides a more quantitative take on the popularity of folk disks. In this case, "25 per cent of advisory committee tab folk tunes" as the type of "platters" that lack sufficient supply, and folk tunes were followed closely by "Latin American, Hawaiian, novelty, quartets and foreign music," a list showing that certain groupings of genres had a long life. "More Folk Disks Say Ops: Juke Men Tell Industry Types of Platters Needed," *Billboard*, May 12, 1945, 65.

48. These two explanations are the topics of two articles in the "Folk Music" section of *The Billboard 1944 Music Year Book*, October 28, 1944: Nat Green, "Folk Airshows Hold and Build Audiences" (349–50), and Nat Green, "Fantastic Grosses Are Routine with Folk-shows" (344–45).

49. *Billboard*, January 18, 1947, 13, 31. An article with a similarly paranoid tone appeared a year earlier in *Billboard*: "Today's Platter Pilgrimages Show Folk Fellahs Plenty Hep," *Billboard*, February 16, 1946, 20.

50. One finds the folkloristic usage of "folk" more often in *Variety* than in *Billboard*, perhaps because *Variety* paid less attention to the nuances of the popular music field at this point than did *Billboard*. For a usage of "folk" that anticipates that of the late 1950s and early 1960s folk revival, see "Carnegie Becomes Keeper of the B's," *Variety*, April 24, 1946, 49. Another usage of the folkloristic conception of "folk" appeared in *Billboard* with the following startling claim: "For the first time . . . American folk music is being assembled, categorized and cataloged." "American Folk Tunes: Cowboy and Hillbilly Tunes and Tunesters," *Billboard*, May 25, 1946, 138.

51. Nat Green, "Folk Airshows Hold and Build Audiences," 349. For an in-depth study of the authenticity concept in country music, see Joli Jensen, *The Nashville Sound: Authenticity, Commercialization, and Country Music* (Nashville, TN: Country Music Foundation Press, 1998); and Richard Peterson, *Creating Country Music*.

52. "Folk Music Takes Hold in the Jukes."

53. "American Folk Tunes: People's Music," *Billboard*, August 17, 1946, 120. This article is also a good example of different usages of "folk music" (traditional and commercial) and the migration narrative.

54. "Record Reviews," *Billboard*, October 12, 1946, 102; "Record Reviews," *Billboard*, December 28, 1946, 88; George Frazier, "Jocks, Jukes and Disks," *Variety*, November 20, 1946, 56; "Folk Defense" in "American Folk Tunes: Cowboy and Hillbilly Tunes and Tunesters," *Billboard*, January 18, 1947, 98.

55. This anecdote and the general history of the California ballroom scene are indebted to the account in Jeffrey J. Lange, *Smile When You Call Me a Hillbilly*, 105–12. See also Peter La Chapelle, *Proud to Be an Okie: Cultural Politics, Country Music, and Migration to Southern California* (Berkeley: University of California Press, 2007), 76–110; and Gerald W. Haslam, *Workin' Man Blues: Country Music in California* (Berkeley: University of California Press, 1999), 87–128. Numerous stories about this scene also appeared in the "American Folk Tunes" feature in *Billboard* during the 1940s.

56. Jeffrey J. Lange, *Smile When You Call Me a Hillbilly*, 110.

57. "American Folk Tunes," *Billboard*, November 23, 1946, 106.

58. George Frazier, "Jocks, Jukes and Disks," *Variety*, June 4, 1947, 38; "Record Possibilities: "Smoke, Smoke, Smoke (That Cigarette)," *Billboard*, June 7, 1947, 30; "Record Reviews: Tex Williams, 'Smoke! Smoke! Smoke!' b/w 'Round Up,' *Billboard*, July 12, 1947, 124. A review of Williams's live act several months later repeated these assessments: "It should appeal to the hep as well as the novelty clan." "New Acts," *Variety*, October 15, 1947, 48.

59. Ad for Capitol Records, *Billboard*, July 12, 1947, 24; ad for Columbia Records, *Billboard*, July 26, 1947, 31.

60. For more on the figure of the hillbilly or rube and its connection to minstrelsy, see Pamela Fox, *Natural Acts*, especially 17–62. Other discussions of the relation between country music and minstrelsy may be found in Robert Cantwell, *Bluegrass Breakdown: The Making of the Old Southern Sound* (New York: Da Capo Press, 1992), 249–74; Nick Tosches, *Country: Living Legends and Dying Metaphors in America's Biggest Music* (New York: Charles Scribner's Sons, 1985), 162–217; and Charles K. Wolfe, *A Good-Natured Riot: The Birth of the Grand Ole Opry* (Nashville, TN: Country Music Foundation and Vanderbilt University Press, 1999).

61. "Record Possibilities," *Billboard*, July 12, 1947; "Record Possibilities," *Billboard*, June 7, 1947.

62. "Record Reviews: Phil Harris, 'That's What I Like About the South' b/w 'Brazen Little Raisin,'" *Billboard*, May 5, 1945, 66.

63. "Record Possibilities: Phil Harris, 'That's What I Like about the South,'" *Billboard*, December 28, 1946, 24. The song was also recorded by Bob Wills and His Texas Playboys (1938) and Cliff Bruner (1944, with a vocal by Moon Mullican).

64. For this episode, see http://podbay.fm/show/161481381/e/1403964000?autostart = 1, accessed July 14, 2014. The minstrel show segment begins about twenty-four minutes into the broadcast.

65. "Boopy-Doopy Soapy Suds," *Billboard,* August 30, 1947, 9.

66. An article on "Billboard's First Annual Chart Count" extols the objectivity of the "Honor Roll of Hits" and music popularity charts without calling attention to the differences between how the two are constructed. "1946 Music-Disk Toppers," *Billboard,* January 4, 1947, 3, 12. Comparisons with "Open the Door, Richard" are instructive in that the latter did not follow the prototypical crossover pattern, but experienced simultaneous success in the race and mainstream charts. "Open the Door, Richard" also evinced greater support in the charts related to the publishing industry.

67. The quote comes from "Hillbilly Bash in Carnegie Perks Stem Interest," *Billboard,* September 27, 1947, 3, 21. For other examples of mainstream discourse about country music in the late 1940s and early 1950s, see the following: "Hillbilly Boom Can Spread Like Plague," *Down Beat,* May 6, 1949; "Corn of Plenty," *Newsweek,* June 13, 1949; "Tin Pan Alley's Git-Tar Blues," *New York Times Magazine,* July 15, 1951; "Hillbilly Heaven," *American Magazine* (March 1952); Rufus Jarman, "Country Music Goes to Town," *Nation's Business,* 41, no. 2 (February 1953); James R. Denny, "Why the Upsurge in Country Music?," *Down Beat,* June 30, 1954, 66.

68. For a more extended discussion of Hank Williams's career at this moment of categorical redefinition, see David Brackett, *Interpreting Popular Music* (Berkeley and Los Angeles: University of California Press, 2000), 101–7.

69. The most extensive previous discussion of crossover processes involving country music during the late 1940s and early 1950s may be found in Philip P. Ennis, *The Seventh Stream: The Emergence of Rocknroll in American Popular Music* (Hanover, NH: University Press of New England, 1992), 161–228.

70. Carl Butler and Pearl might as well have been making their request to the popular music field itself: the recording did not cross over musical categories, reaching only number eighty-eight on *Billboard's* mainstream chart, the Hot 100. It is worth noting that the moment of Carl Butler and Pearl's success also witnessed the reemergence of the corn trope (although not identified as such) in another medium: the televisual situation comedy, as evidenced by *The Beverly Hillbillies* (1962–71), *Petticoat Junction* (1963–70), and *Green Acres* (1965–71). These shows relied on a form of corny humor long associated with white Southerners, such as (famously) Minnie Pearl, a veteran of the Grand Ole Opry. On the tail end of these shows' success, a variety show began, *Hee-Haw* (originally on CBS 1969–71, then syndicated 1971–92), which reprised the trope of corny humor more directly and with amazing endurance; one of its recurring skits featured cast members popping up from a cornfield to tell jokes. During this period, CBS was sometimes referred to as the "Country Broadcasting System." The cancellation of these shows in 1970–71 is known as CBS's "rural purge." Anthony Harkins, *Hillbilly,* 203.

71. The most in-depth study of reflexivity in country music may be found in Aaron Fox, *Real Country: Music and Language in Working-Class Culture* (Durham, NC: Duke University Press, 2004).

7

The Dictionary of Soul

Soul music arrived on October 23, 1965. At least, this was the claim made by an advertisement in *Billboard*. The two singers featured in the ad, Roscoe Shelton and Sam Baker, do not currently form part of the soul music canon, yet the sound of the songs featured in the advertisement, "I Know Your Heart Has Been Broken" and "Sometimes You Have to Cry," arguably participates in the category of soul music as we recognize it today.[1] "I Know Your Heart Has Been Broken" employs the 6/8 rhythms and gospel-rooted vocals familiar from the contemporaneous ballads of better-known singers such as Solomon Burke and Otis Redding, even if the distorted electric guitar and female backing chorus would be less likely to appear on one of those artists' recordings. "Sometimes You Have to Cry" mines these associations even more directly, with the singing of Sam Baker strongly reminiscent of other Southern soul artists such as Redding, Percy Sledge, or Wilson Pickett, and with the recording very much in the mode of a string of Redding's hits dating back to 1962 with "These Arms of Mine."[2] Existing as little more than a footnote in most histories of soul, the company that produced these recordings, Sound Stage 7, recorded at two of the genre's most famous sites, alternating between the Stax and Muscle Shoals studios.

Soul music may have arrived in October 1965, but the idea of soul as a category of popular music associated with African Americans had yet to be firmly installed across the discursive terrain of popular music, where "rhythm and blues" still reigned as the categorical label for African American popular music. Popular music historians have retroactively located the origins of soul music in the period from 1965 to 1967, with the efflorescence of Stax and Motown, the rise of the Muscle Shoals recording studios, the breakout proto-funk hits of James Brown, and

Aretha Franklin's first recordings for Atlantic among the historical milestones occurring during these years.[3] Following the procedures in earlier chapters, the aim is to analyze the stakes involved for the musicians, fans, journalists, and music industry personnel who came to associate the label "soul music" in a more or less consistent way with certain musical processes and gestures. The process of establishing the interests of the various parties involved will suggest reciprocity between the racial politics of the period, and the politics of musical popularity and popular music categories.

The history of black popular music during the 1960s presents an opportunity for more than simply revisiting a historiographical challenge. The label of "soul" itself provides a brilliant example of what Rick Altman observed as the propensity of genre labels to move from adjective to noun.[4] At the beginning of the 1960s, one finds the terms "soul-jazz" and "soulful" used to describe recordings and performances of R&B, while by 1969 "soul" has been widely adopted as a label for popular music associated with African Americans. This instability in the labeling of black popular music was nothing new in the 1960s. Returning to table 2 in chapter 1, it is striking how many changes this category underwent relative to the two other enduring categories, country and mainstream pop. Although the years between 1949 and 1969 appear as a period of stability in this table owing to the fact that the name "rhythm and blues" was used consistently to refer to this music in industry discourse, such a fact conceals the continuing uncertainty of the status of black popular music in relation to the mainstream U.S. music industry. Such remappings speak to a struggle over racial classification itself (and the shifting names for African Americans), with all the attendant implications of a political intervention into the "practices of exclusion, segregation and hoarding of opportunities which sort people out into ranked groups."[5]

The history of musical categories, however, can also be understood as possessing a certain degree of relative autonomy. The previous chapter detailed how country music after 1962, despite its instability before 1949, led a remarkably stable life. In contrast to country music's stability, the story of rhythm and blues was considerably more complicated—so complicated, in fact, that a moment came in the mid-1960s when *Billboard* appeared not to know what to do with the category any longer. One of the strangest events in the history of *Billboard*'s popularity charts occurred when the "Rhythm and Blues" chart disappeared in the November 30, 1963, issue. *Billboard* provided no explanation, and no questions seemed to have been raised by this curious turn of events. Given the important role of popularity charts in the symbolic communication about categories of popular music, and that popularity charts are one of the main ways in which the industry recognizes the commercial importance of a category of music, this turn might have amounted to a crisis of legitimation for black popular music. One particularly interesting feature of this event is the divergence between the level of discourse projected by *Billboard*'s popularity charts and the discourse around categories found in other forums of the time: critic-fan discussions, debates about radio formats, and even the popularity charts of other publications. After examining the particularly turbulent period from November 23, 1963 through January 30, 1965 (when the R&B chart reappeared) for signs indicating what the disappearance meant, along the way exploring ideas about crossover and public notions of African American identity, the chapter will return to the question of soul music. For in the latter half of the 1960s, as rhythm and blues turned into soul music, the position of black popular music within the popular music field underwent a radical shift as the field itself experienced a seismic transformation.

THE DISAPPEARANCE

Several different, albeit related, explanations are usually given for the disappearance of *Billboard*'s R&B chart. The popular music historian Charlie Gillett, in one of the first pieces of scholarship to address the issue, surmised that the large number of R&B tunes crossing over in 1963 obviated the need for a separate chart. The chart historian Joel Whitburn, in his compilation of *Billboard*'s R&B charts, stated, "It is our understanding that there was so much crossover of titles between the R&B and pop singles (Hot 100) charts that *Billboard* considered the charts to be too similar." Echoing these statements, an explanatory lacuna occurs in several *Billboard* articles from the late 1980s to the early 1990s that provided a history of the R&B charts: the first of these declared that the chart disappeared in 1963 because it was becoming "the mainstream for American pop music" and that it reappeared because (in what could be viewed as a contradiction) "many R&B records continued to record hits that did not show up on the pop chart." The second portrayed a similarly rosy picture for R&B artists, stating that "all black artists were charted in the pop category."[6]

Observation of the 1963 charts, however, doesn't support these rather positive assessments of the fate of *Billboard*'s R&B chart. The November 23, 1963, issue of *Billboard* (the last issue to include an R&B chart before its disappearance) reveals six songs by black artists in the top thirty slots of the Hot 100, and, oddly enough, the R&B chart includes eleven songs by white artists in its top thirty. The distinction between the charts was weakening, but not because of the number of songs by African American artists in the Hot 100. As witnessed in previous chapters, the racial identity of the performers, while important, was not the sole factor in how popular music categories were interpreted. If the number of recordings listed in the R&B charts crossing over to the mainstream was high, but not the number of recordings by African American artists, could it be that the association between African American identity and the R&B category, so carefully woven together through numerous musical and discursive performative acts and citations, had somehow been torn asunder?

Before attempting to answer this question directly, however, it is necessary to revisit the processes through which categories of music and humans become associated with one another. Given the repeated assertions in earlier chapters of the heterogeneity of both the taste of people within a given demographic group and the musical styles within a given musical category, it should be clear that the sound and social meaning of a category are continually sutured together through countless citations of musical styles articulated to identifications. At the same time, one of the guiding assumptions of this book has been that the formation of categories and their representations tells a story about widely shared perceptions of the popular music field, the connotations of categories, and their cultural value. That is, despite their complexity and constant transformation, musical categories project a circumscribed field of meaning that relates to widely shared social preoccupations. In other words, a given genre or identity formation may experience relative stability.

Analyzing the disappearance of a category from one of the most important forums for the exchange of information about popular music consumption, therefore, would seem to be of paramount importance. Lacking explicit insider information about how this decision was made, we must rely on the evidence provided by the constitution of the charts themselves, and other discursive clues found in trade publications. Such an analysis will also attempt to reconstruct the logic of the categories as they were deployed during this particular historical moment. At stake is not only the presence, or lack thereof, of a popularity chart, but the meaning and constitution of the rhythm and blues category at that moment, its relation to African American identity, and its position relative to other categories of popular music.

Retroactive Formation of R&B

Was *Billboard*'s treatment of its R&B chart (the BRB) anomalous? That is, even though the BRB disappeared, did this then mean that R&B as a marketing category, radio format, and critic-fan genre no longer existed? The short answer to this question is no. What then was the relationship between the BRB (before it disappeared), *Billboard*'s Hot 100 chart (the B100), and R&B as it circulated in other contexts? If *Billboard*'s R&B chart and *Billboard*'s Hot 100 chart were understood as being so similar that the BRB was no longer needed, and if the BRB is assumed to have a relationship to a category of music called R&B that continued to circulate in other forums, then this implies that there was something anomalous about *Billboard*'s conception of R&B. This anomaly, in turn, may be related to differing conceptions of the socio-musical conventions of R&B.

Retroactive histories of rhythm and blues and of popular music more generally, as well as the discursive traces published during the interregnum of *Billboard*'s R&B

chart, attest to the continuation of the R&B category during this period. These histories, as well as compilation recordings, documentaries, interviews with agents involved with popular music at the time who were and are explicitly identified with R&B, and other historical forums have created a notion of R&B during the mid-1960s that projects certain socio-musical regularities. As in chapter 5, we are confronted with a challenge: to analyze the components that were articulated together to render these recordings legible at that moment as R&B rather than something else. To reiterate a point made in chapter 1, these components do not exist in an organic totality, but rather in a relationship of exteriority in that they can appear in other genre formations, and that their meaning as elements of R&B comes about through their interaction with one another. Just as the elements that form part of a genre's assemblage may function as part of another genre, recordings may participate in more than one genre at any given moment. The relational quality of genre, also discussed in chapter 1, in which a genre is defined by what it is *not*, plays a role as well. R&B at the level of a marketing category is therefore established during this time because it is *not* mainstream popular music, country music, or middle-road/pop-standard music (due to the existence of popularity charts for these categories).

The socio-musical regularities adduced from retroactive formations of R&B include an unsurprising cluster of musical style tendencies—most prominently those derived from gospel music, such as a distinctive approach to vocal ornamentation and melisma, rhythmic playfulness with respect to pulse, use of blues-inflected tonality, and lyrics with a tendency to be directed toward a more adult audience than mainstream pop—along with one dominant social feature—the African American identity of the featured performers. Other factors were specific to the early 1960s, such as interjected sermons serving as a bridge, and recording quality, with non-mainstream R&B recordings occasionally featuring relatively crude recordings with distorted instruments and voices. As in the discussion of non-crossover black popular music of the 1940s, many R&B-associated recordings have an African American–identified vocal timbre.[7]

How does this description square with what would have been projected as R&B at the time by *Billboard*'s popularity charts? This is what *Billboard*'s "Hot R&B Singles" chart (the BRB) looked like in the November 23, 1963, issue:

1. Jimmy Gilmer and the Fireballs, "Sugar Shack"
2. Impressions, "It's All Right"
3. Garnet Mimms and the Enchanters, "Cry Baby"
4. Nina Tempo and April Stevens, "Deep Purple"
5. Rufus Thomas, "Walking the Dog"
6. Dale and Grace, "I'm Leaving It Up to You"
7. Sam Cooke, "Little Red Rooster"
8. Roy Orbison, "Mean Woman Blues"

9. Little Johnny Taylor, "Part Time Love"
10. Ray Charles, "Busted"
11. Mary Wells, "What's Easy for Two Is So Hard for One"
12. Major Lance, "Hey Little Girl"
13. Sunny and the Sunglows, "Talk to Me"
14. Solomon Burke, "You're Good for Me"
15. Marvin Gaye, "Can I Get a Witness"
16. Mary Wells, "You Lost the Sweetest Boy"
17. Dion DiMucci, "Donna the Prima Donna"
18. Ronettes, "Be My Baby"
19. Lloyd Price, "Misty"
20. Elvis Presley, "Bossa Nova Baby"
21. Betty Harris, "Cry to Me"
22. Village Stompers, "Washington Square"
23. Barry and the Tamerlanes, "I Wonder What She's Doing Tonight"
24. Ricky Nelson, "Fools Rush In"
25. Orlons, "Crossfire"
26. Robin Ward, "Wonderful Summer"
27. Lesley Gore, "She's a Fool"
28. Roy Orbison, "Blue Bayou"
29. Beach Boys, "Be True to Your School"
30. Martha and the Vandellas, "Heat Wave"

Many of the recordings in the BRB do not seem to fit the socio-musical regularities described in the preceding section, to say the least. These anomalies range from novelty-inflected, teen-idol rock 'n' roll ("Sugar Shack") to standards done in a folk-novelty style with a touch of a rock-a-cha-cha beat ("Deep Purple") to a country-ish male-female duet ("I'm Leaving It Up to You") to Elvis Presley's middle-of-the-road mutation of his early rock 'n' roll sound ("Bossa Nova Baby," but also Roy Orbison's "Mean Woman Blues" and Ricky Nelson's "Fools Rush In") to white girl group sounds ("Wonderful Summer," "She's a Fool") to the Beach Boys and the Village Stompers, the last of which became known for their folk-Dixie fusion style. This list of reverse crossovers (recordings that either began on the mainstream chart and crossed over to one of the specialized charts, or were ranked more highly on the mainstream chart) also captures some of the diverse subgenres then prominent in the mainstream: folk revival, surf music, teen novelty, and girl groups. On the other hand, the recordings by the Impressions, Garnet Mimms, Rufus Thomas, Sam Cooke, Little Johnny Taylor, Ray Charles, Mary Wells, and Major Lance (as well as many of the girl group recordings), while quite diverse, all fit comfortably into the retroactive formulation of the R&B category. If these conventions correspond in some sense to what R&B fans of the time liked, it is difficult to imagine from our current vantage point how people who identified strongly with this latter group of artists would prefer "Sugar Shack" (ranked number one) over the Impressions' "It's All Right" (ranked number two).

To some extent, the incoherence of *Billboard*'s R&B chart is symptomatic of the general sense of chaos pervading the popular music field, where Nino Tempo and April Stevens, the Singing Nun, Kyu Sakamoto, the Four Seasons, and the Village Stompers went cheek by jowl in the Hot 100. This state of affairs extended to the BRB, which featured the same diversity and chaos found in the Hot 100, even if it did remain slightly more "specialized" (*Billboard*'s term of choice for marginalized categories). In other words, by 1963, the BRB projected no consistent sense of R&B in terms of socio-musical regularities, a lack of consistency mirrored in the mainstream. Yet the very idea of a mainstream invokes the idea of a category that can assimilate difference in the pursuit of the broadest audience. What can it mean when one of the tributaries of the mainstream begins to assume a similar level of stylistic heterogeneity?

Historicist Formation of R&B

Before simply dismissing the constitution of the BRB at this moment as a deviant whim, we should entertain the possibility that the socio-musical regularities of rhythm and blues were understood very differently in 1963 than they have been after the fact. As a check to the retroactive formation of R&B, we can resort to an interpretation of R&B's historical horizon, which can be attempted via recourse to a variety of different discourses, one of them being other rhythm and blues charts published at the same time. *Cash Box* was one of *Billboard*'s competitors. Table 13 presents the *Cash Box* "Top 50 in R&B Locations" chart (the CRB) from November 23, 1963, the same date as the *Billboard* chart reproduced earlier.

Although the recordings in this chart are fairly diverse, they certainly correspond more closely to retroactive conceptions of rhythm and blues than do those in the *Billboard* chart, and it is possible to imagine even the outliers, such as the Kingsmen's "Louie, Louie," and the Angels' "I Adore Him," finding favor with listeners whose taste centered around the other artists on this chart. The number of deep cuts (in contemporary parlance) in the CRB that did not appear in either the *Cash Box* Hot 100 (the C100) or the *Billboard* Hot 100 (the B100), or appeared ranked very low, reveal that this chart seemed to be tracking the playlists of R&B radio stations, the sales figures of retail outlets specializing in R&B, and the preferences of listeners who had a separate identity (albeit an overlapping one) from the mainstream. These recordings, which crossed over very little, if at all, included Betty Everett's "You're No Good," Tommy Hunt's "I'm a Witness," and Doris Troy's "What'cha Gonna Do About It," among others. In contrast to this, *Billboard*'s "Hot R&B Singles" included only songs evidencing a strong crossover effect. With the benefit of hindsight, one can speculate about why some recordings crossed over

TABLE 13 *Cash Box* "Top 50 in R&B Locations" Chart, November 23, 1963

1. Impressions, "It's All Right"	26. Lou Johnson, "Reach Out for Me"
2. Sam Cooke, "Little Red Rooster"	27. Nat King Cole, "That Sunday, That Summer"
3. Rufus Thomas, "Walkin' the Dog"	28. Garnet Mimms, "Baby Don't You Weep"
4. Sunny and the Sunglows, "Talk to Me"	29. Fats Domino, "Red Sails in the Sunset"
5. Ray Charles, "Busted"	30. Drifters, "I'll Take You Home"
6. Marvin Gaye, "Can I Get a Witness"	31. Jerry Butler, "Need to Belong"
7. Major Lance, "Hey Little Girl"	32. Stevie Wonder, "Workout Stevie Workout"
8. Ruby and the Romantics, "Young Wings Can Fly"	33. Angels, "I Adore Him"
9. Chubby Checker, "Loddy Lo"	34. Ronettes, "Be My Baby"
10. Lloyd Price, "Misty"	35. Chiffons, "I Have a Boyfriend"
11. Garnet Mimms, "Cry Baby"	36. Chiffons, "A Love So Fine"
12. Mary Wells, "You've Lost the Sweetest Boy"	37. Martha and the Vandellas, "Quicksand"
13. Kingsmen, "Louie, Louie"	38. Essex, "Out of Sight, Out of Mind"
14. Patti Labelle and the Bluebells, "Down the Aisle"	39. Chuck Jackson, "Any Other Way"
15. Solomon Burke, "You're Good for Me"	40. Doris Troy, "What'cha Gonna Do About It"
16. Brook Benton, "Two Tickets to Paradise"	41. Lena Horne, "Now"
17. Betty Everett, "You're No Good"	42. Miracles, "I Gotta Dance to Keep from Crying"
18. Tommy Hunt, "I'm a Witness"	43. Johnny Mathis, "Come Back"
19. Charmettes, "Please Don't Kiss Me Again"	44. Brook Benton and Damita Jo, "Stop Foolin'"
20. Shirelles, "31 Flavors"	45. Wilson Pickett, "I'm Down to My Last Heartache"
21. Marvelettes, "As Long as I Know He's Mine"	46. Wilbert Harrison, "Near to You"
22. Miracles, "Mickey's Monkey"	47. Mary Wells, "What's Easy for Two's Hard for One"
23. Freddie Scott, "I Got a Woman"	48. Janettes, "Sally Go 'Round the Roses"
24. Garnet Mimms, "For Your Precious Love"	49. Orlons, "Crossfire"
25. Darlene Love, "A Fine, Fine Boy"	50. Four Seasons, "New Mexican Rose"

while others did not, although cause-and-effect analysis is more effective in this situation when based on a herdlike, statistical causality rather than on a one-to-one direct correspondence between cause and effect. The term "statistical causality" refers, in this case, to how large samples of individual musical texts create an overall pattern to which numerous exceptions may exist.[8]

The recordings in the CRB also provide sonic clues as to the elements of the R&B marketing category at this moment, conforming for the most part to the socio-musical regularities adduced in the retroactive analysis of R&B. Expanding the view of R&B beyond the week of November 23, 1963, to the end of 1964, and taking into consideration the CRB during this period and the end-of-the-year rankings from *Billboard* and *Cash Box*, the category of R&B can be broken down into numerous subgenres.[9] The purpose of this is to broaden the understanding of

R&B beyond the listing of traits to show how its internal diversity also relates it to the other marketing categories of the time (i.e., those with their own popularity chart in *Billboard*), which were mainstream pop, country, and middle of the road (MOR).

Based on retroactive grouping, the most popular R&B recordings for the period from November 1963 to November 1964 can be divided into the following subgenres: secular gospel, Motown pop, blues-retro throwbacks, 6/8 gospel-country ballads, uptown Brill Building pop-R&B, MOR-R&B, retro (mostly vocal groups), Curtis Mayfield–inspired, dance crazes, and girl groups. This group of subgenres could be expanded to many more, all of which balance citation of previous or contemporary genres such as gospel, 1950s vocal group arrangements, 1950s rock 'n' roll, 1950s blues and R&B, Latin rhythms, country music, and MOR pop. (Note that the three categories existing on the same level as R&B—mainstream pop, country, and MOR—feature prominently as components of the different R&B subgenres.) Most strikingly, in what might appear to confirm previous analyses of why *Billboard* discontinued its R&B chart, mainstream pop (featuring girl groups, dance crazes, teen-idol transformations of rock 'n' roll, and Brill Building pop as subgenres) overlaps considerably with R&B. These subgenres and their interconnections with the other large categories of popular music demonstrate how the components that make up R&B were already part of the other large categories of popular music. Note that several of these subgenres share many components (e.g., girl groups, Motown pop, and Brill Building pop-R&B) and that the subgenres could be further subdivided (within the girl group and dance crazes, for example, individual recordings fall along an R&B–pop spectrum). Figure 11 summarizes these observations, with the dotted lines showing that these subgenres participated less in the mainstream (both in terms of musical style and chart performance) than those with a solid line. The very light dotted line between country and 6/8 gospel-country ballads indicates a sharing of musical resources even though 6/8 gospel-country ballads (e.g., Garnet Mimms's "Cry Baby" or Solomon Burke's "Goodbye Baby") never appeared in the popularity chart for country music. The wealth of subgenres and possible combinations of the components of R&B attest to its internal heterogeneity. At the same time, the interconnections between R&B and the other marketing categories facilitated the participation of individual recordings in multiple categories at varying levels.

For an example of such multiple participation, Dionne Warwick's "Walk On By" from spring 1964 (CRB: 1; C100: 6; B100: 6; "Pop-Standard (MOR) Chart": 7) could be interpreted as participating in uptown Brill Building pop (overall sound, quality and location of production), MOR pop (complexity of harmony and melody reminiscent of Tin Pan Alley pop), or girl group (gender of vocalists, use of call and response, conversation-like dialogue between lead singer and backup singers).[10] Attesting to the independence of the different elements associated with

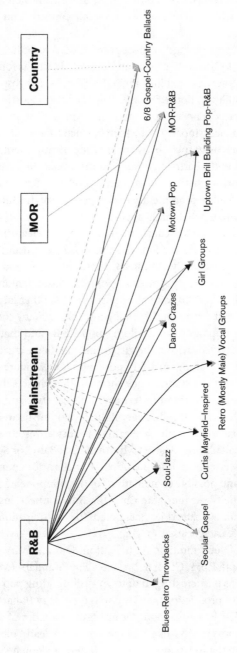

FIGURE 11. Relationships Between Marketing Categories and R&B Subgenres, ca. 1963–64.

the various subgenres are the song's Latin-derived rhythms and lyrics in which the song's persona is warned about an unfaithful man and/or a man with dubious personal characteristics, which are historically specific but cut across sub-generic divisions.[11]

Throughout the interregnum of the BRB, *Billboard* continued to publish articles about rhythm and blues, indicating that, even if tracking the popularity of rhythm and blues recordings no longer warranted attention, the category of rhythm and blues still concerned the music industry. A regular columnist for *Billboard*, Bill Gavin—author of the influential *Gavin Report*, a programming guide for Top 40 radio that he began producing in 1958—published an article in April 1964 that provides insight into how this topic was understood at the time. The article, titled "No Musical Color Line," expresses and analyzes many of the paradoxes of genre that have formed the central concerns of this book. Gavin begins by stating that while "rhythm and blues . . . is a term used to identify a particular kind of music . . . like other verbal-type tags, such as 'pop' or 'classical,' the term is at best loosely descriptive and is frequently misunderstood." He then emphasizes the role of social identity in the definition of the term, as "rhythm and blues refers to almost any music that is preferred by most Negroes." However, the contradictions of such a definition appear in his admission that a recording can be reclassified in what we would now recognize as a crossover process: "When a record that is a hit in the Negro market attains widespread acceptance with other record buyers, it then is called a 'pop' hit." He implies that his readership believes that classification is, or should be, a matter of musical style (and that it is also a matter of politics and power) when he admits to the unfairness of "such classification of music according to its audience." However, his emphasis on social identity underscores one of the main points of the article, which is to call attention to "the importance of the Negro in record sales, as well as in radio programming."[12]

Gavin anticipates what would now be called a critique of the essentialist implications of such a formulation (or of what could also be called a straightforward homology model for the social interpretation of genre) by recognizing that "Negroes buy and enjoy many different kinds of music, while many rhythm and blues records are well received by whites." Nevertheless, while a strict homology is untenable, this does not mean that general tendencies (i.e., statistical causality) do not exist: "About all that we can safely conclude is that recording artists, as well as certain musical sounds and subject matter find a readier acceptance among Negroes than elsewhere." Gavin also reports that competition for African American listeners was driving the programming of rhythm and blues by Top 40 stations. And if "non-Negro" listeners responded favorably to rhythm and blues, the reverse was not necessarily true. Despite his earlier point about the variety of taste among African Americans, Gavin asserts that "Negroes . . . consistently display a deep and lasting affection for the music that is most meaningful to them." This seems to indicate an aversion to "white" popular music, as "the recent teen-age obsession with the Beatles was almost entirely a non-Negro phenomenon."[13]

Gavin then takes a musicological turn, and the musical style factors that he discusses closely resemble the retroactive position that I presented earlier. That said, the main "musical" factor that he cites is not, strictly speaking, musical, but rather focuses on the orientation of R&B toward adults. Along with emotional maturity, he mentions an emphasis on improvisation related to the aesthetic practice of jazz, which is "completely foreign to the square and prescribed framework of the conventional 'rocker.'" As with the popular music most strongly associated with African Americans in the 1940s (discussed in chapter 5), improvisation in many different aspects of the music, including the approach to melody, accompaniment, and composition, would appear to connote both rhythm and blues–ness as well as African American–ness.

An article appearing in *Cash Box* at almost exactly the same time as Gavin's essay does not offer the same kind of precision as Gavin, but does provide a list of "artists who rely on the 'soul' approach," including "Ray Charles, Dionne Warwick, James Brown, Mary Wells, Ben E. King, Betty Everett, Timi Yuro, Aretha Franklin and Irma Thomas, to name a few."[14] All of these artists, with the exception of Yuro, were African American. Yuro, described as "a white, female artist with the emotional firepower of an African-American soul singer," was heavily influenced by Dinah Washington and experienced her first success with a version of Roy Hamilton's 1954 R&B hit "Hurt," produced by Clyde Otis, who was also Dinah Washington's producer.[15] Both the *Cash Box* editorial and Gavin agree, then, that the social identity of the artists associated with R&B is the most consistent factor in identifying texts that participate in the category, although the interaction of this social component with musical elements, and the citation of previous R&B artists and recordings, is also crucial. These articles also suggest that the previous classification of an artist plays a role as important, if not more so, in the categorization of texts as musical style.

Another stream of discourse existed in the black press of the period. Throughout the interregnum of the BRB, the *Chicago Defender* published a column titled "Platters," hosted by a series of high school–age music lovers. In addition to short commentaries on the social use of music among African American teenagers in Chicago, the column featured a list of "Top Ten" recordings. Initially based on the listening preferences of the columnist and her friends (the writer was usually female), the column eventually featured reports from area record stores. The contents of this list overlapped to some degree with the CRB (increasingly so after the reports became based on record store reports), but also featured a greater emphasis on soul-jazz recordings than what appeared in other forums for rhythm and blues. With the exception of "Louie, Louie," no recordings by non–African Americans appeared in these listings.

Although the rhythm and blues chart had disappeared from *Billboard,* the concept of R&B still figured into other taxonomies during this time, primarily at the level of radio formats. In a section titled "Programming Specials," *Billboard* listed the following: "Hot Pop," "Pop Standard," "Country Music," "Rhythm and Blues," and "Jazz." Tracks that would in some contexts be considered R&B, such as those by Barbara Lewis and Big Joe Turner, were listed under "Hot Pop," suggesting that "Rhythm and Blues" was reserved for those recordings deemed less likely to cross over. In another section devoted to radio, the programming for different regions was featured each week, listing stations by format. For example, for the week of May 2, 1964, the formats for Atlanta included "Popular Singles," "Popular LPs," "R.&B.," "Jazz," "Country Music," "Folk," "Comedy," and "Classical." This listing does not correspond in a one-to-one fashion to the popularity charts, due to the stratified nature of categories, but it provides another mapping of the popular music field, albeit one with finer distinctions than that provided by the charts. Figure 12 adds radio formats to figure 11, summarizing the relationship between marketing categories, radio formats, and the subgenres of R&B, with arrows indicating the relationship between the R&B subgenres and the various radio formats in which they might participate. The spatialization of relationships displayed in figure 12 makes no claim to exhaust the full range of possible connections; left out are elements such as the lateral influence between categories, components shared between formations on different levels, and the importance of the precise manner in which components interact with each other.

A concern with radio programming during this period also resulted in features on "Programming Specials," "D.J. Roundups," and "Market Analysis" focused on particular regions, all of which included discussions of R&B. Many of the recordings listed in these market analyses of R&B audiences never appeared at all on the B100; these included Bobby Bland's "After It's Too Late," Ben E. King's "What Can a Man Do," Kip Anderson's "That's When the Crying Begins," and Nathan McKinney's "Weep No More." Such accounts attest to an audience with preferences that had not been assimilated to mainstream tastes, but which were nevertheless not being tracked in the same fashion as mainstream, country, and MOR audiences, as evidenced by the lack of a popularity chart for R&B.

How Did Billboard's R&B Chart Get That Way?

The preceding discussion of the BRB's disappearance clarified that the chart had become disconnected from the preferences of those who identified as participants in the R&B category. A question then arises: Was this sense of disconnection something new? If not, how did the BRB get that way?

The music critic Chris Molanphy is one of the few writers to discuss this period of *Billboard* and analyze the conditions and effects of the disappearance of the R&B charts in a way that goes beyond merely repeating *Billboard's* own explanations.

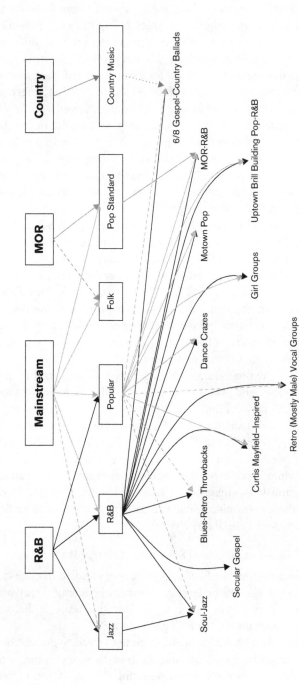

FIGURE 12. Relationships Between Marketing Categories, Radio Formats, and R&B Subgenres.

Molanphy unraveled the effect of changes in *Billboard*'s "R&B/Hip-Hop" chart in October 2012 in response to the incorporation of digital sales and streaming. In the course of pondering the shift created by changes in medium and technology, Molanphy argues that the period in late 1963 is analogous in that it provides an example of another time when "*Billboard* has run an R&B chart with so many white faces." He describes Jimmy Gilmer's "Sugar Shack" (the number one recording in the last BRB before it disappeared) as a "hokey song," that "whatever its merits . . . beggars belief" that it "was a major hit among black audiences." Molanphy ascribes the eclectic assortment of recordings in the BRB in November 1963 to "retailers and radio stations . . . reporting all manner of popular records with even a hint of a beat, by black or white artists, as R&B." This was at least partly due, according to Molanphy, because "one imagines the magazine was having a tough time finding record-shop managers and radio programmers able (or willing) to accurately reflect what African-Americans were listening to and buying." *Billboard* thus resorted to tracking a particular conception of R&B based on a single musical trait ("a hint of a beat") as reported in non-R&B-specific media rather than tracking the preferences of the R&B audience.[16]

Molanphy's conclusion is convincing and accords with the discussion earlier in this chapter that contrasted the CRB and *Billboard*'s own market analysis to the late-1963 iteration of the BRB. Clearly, the BRB in late 1963 was out of touch with R&B radio, judging from all the other evidence available, especially the comments of R&B DJs beginning in mid-1964 found in *Billboard* itself. But Molanphy's point still begs several questions: If *Cash Box* could track the audience for R&B more accurately, why couldn't *Billboard*? And was this extravagant eclecticism always characteristic of the BRB, or did it represent a new development?

The difference in approach to the R&B chart between *Cash Box* and *Billboard* at this time can partly be explained by the histories, status, and clienteles of the two publications. In contrast to *Billboard,* which was more established, more widely circulated, and more sought after by high-profile advertisers, *Cash Box* functioned as a young upstart that prided itself on its close connection to small independent record companies. Because of this, *Cash Box* put a priority on cultivating close relationships with smaller companies specializing in R&B and country that could not necessarily afford advertising in *Billboard*. This made it imperative that *Cash Box*'s R&B chart not become disconnected from R&B audiences in the way that *Billboard*'s apparently had.[17]

All of which leaves us with the ongoing strangeness of the composition of the BRB in the period immediately before its hiatus. The second question posed above— whether this extravagant eclecticism was always characteristic of the BRB, or if it represented a new development—forces consideration of the history of the BRB.

Prior to November 1963, the last major change to how *Billboard* represented the popularity of African American popular music occurred five years earlier. From

June 1956 to October 1958, tracking occurred along two axes: an "R&B Best Sellers in Stores" chart and a "Most Played R&B by Jockeys" chart. The descriptions for these charts make plain their connection to consumers affiliated with R&B. Another feature, "R&B Territorial Best Sellers," explicitly references a specialized R&B market, framed with a sense of great urgency, as it explains that "listings are based on late sales reports secured via Western Union messenger service from top rhythm and blues dealers and juke box operators." The new chart introduced on October 20, 1958, "Hot R&B Sides," took the place of the previous three charts, thereby (in *Billboard*'s words) "streamlining its record research operation."[18] While it is difficult to understand this as the improvement that *Billboard* claimed, it did, however, make the whole process of representing popularity less transparent.

Between 1958 and 1962, the recordings presented in the BRB retained a relationship to historicist-presentist conceptions of R&B similar to what had existed previously. Early in 1962, however, a shift occurred. Throughout 1962 the BRB transformed gradually from a chart that overlapped greatly with the CRB and was relatively consistent with R&B conventions to a grouping that was categorically incoherent. Most of the outliers crept in through the concept of novelty, which was extremely popular in the mainstream during this period, as it was during the late 1940s, another time when no one trend dominated the mainstream. The trend of including novelty tunes and middle-of-the-road recordings gained in strength until the end of 1963, when the BRB arrived at the brink of its own extinction.[19] Because of the divergence between the BRB and other discourses about R&B at the time, as well as from earlier instantiations of the BRB, the situation with the BRB in 1963 clearly differs from that of the "Harlem Hit Parade" in 1942 (discussed in chapter 5), in which preconceptions about race music as a commercial category did not seem to influence the makeup of the chart. Nor could these changes be attributed to the heterogeneity of African American audiences.

One possible factor in the increasing porousness of the boundary between the BRB and the B100 was the aforementioned diversity of the R&B category at this time. Middle-of-the road recordings were already a component of R&B via people such as Nat King Cole,[20] and R&B also included many dance craze numbers, girl group recordings, Brill Building pop-R&B, and Ray Charles country recordings. The CRB and the BRB prior to summer 1962 featured a music-stylistic eclecticism similar to that of the mainstream. In other words, if R&B included novelty tunes, girl groups, pop-soul, dance songs, and MOR material, and the mainstream included novelty tunes, girl groups, pop-soul, dance songs, and MOR material, then what *was* the difference? As noted by Gavin, the artists in the R&B category were almost all African American. But once a few white artists started to be included that overlapped sonically with black artists, particularly in the MOR and novelty categories, then the BRB's floodgates swung wide open. Assuming that *Billboard* had changed its consultation habits with R&B insiders sometime during the period between 1958 and 1962, the magazine had fewer sources to check a chainlike logic that could lead from an R&B category consisting of (among other things) MOR and girl group recordings by African American artists, and the occasional wildly popular white novelty song, to an R&B category consisting of MOR hits and girl group recordings by black *and* white artists, and more novelty recordings by white artists. What this chainlike logic lacked, however, was a sense of the importance of both the interaction of the individual components of R&B with each other and the citation of the social identities of R&B artists.

Moreover, simply using sales charts without feedback from agents working in the R&B field could lead to conflicting representations of popularity. The articles by both Gavin and *Cash Box* discussed earlier present other reasons for the under-representation of rhythm and blues recordings in sales charts. Recalling statements about the underreporting of the sales for country music in the 1940s, Gavin argued that "total sales of a r.&b. hit may not be reflected in a sales survey." This was because "r.&b. sales are frequently concentrated in a few specialty stores and will therefore not be reflected in the greater number of retail outlets whose reports are compared." Gavin counterbalances the reports used to construct popularity charts with "manufacturers' reports," which reveal that "chart listings of numerous r.&b. hits fail to show their true selling power." *Cash Box* took a slightly different angle, adding that R&B lacked "the immediate attention-getting approach of other types of rock-inspired sounds," and thus required "extensive airplay to gain chart-hitting sales."[21]

From the point of view of the citationality of genre, one could say that in the case of the BRB, the chain of citations of previous R&B conventions, or of subgenres associated with R&B, had collapsed to the point where *Billboard*'s conception of "R&B" was no longer legible (for whatever reasons) at the level of the popularity charts. In other words, R&B as produced by *Billboard*'s charts no longer referred to a sign that others could recognize as R&B. The question that arises is why didn't *Billboard* simply recalibrate the chart so that it was legible? While it is not possible to answer this question with certainty, we can refer to a discursive thread in the music industry press that pondered the relationship between R&B and the mainstream.

The discussions that appeared in *Billboard* offer a few hints. The idea that R&B was merging with popular music in general was voiced in prose as well as in the numeracy of the charts. Already early in April 1963, a survey of radio program directors referred to the blurring of boundaries in these terms: "A great many records produced today are basically of a rhythm and blues character. Yet they . . . have broken out of the narrow, regionalized bounds of a specific rhythm and blues market and have, in a sense, lost their separate identity." This statement is a little bit different from what we observed in *Billboard*'s R&B chart wherein the R&B category appears to be "losing its identity" because of many recordings that did *not*, from the point of view of participants in the genre, have a "rhythm and blues character." The article then refers to the temporal aspect of genre, observing that "many disks programmed broadly by pop stations today, might once have been called pure r&b. in content."[22] An article in the African American press took an even more extreme view, predicting that "Negro radio" was "destined to die out as the Negro and white cultures merge in America." Although the prognosticator, a general manager of a radio station directed toward the African American community, didn't expect this merger to occur for "maybe 20 years," it was foretold by "the sudden popularity of gospel music among white people," and because "for the past five years or so, white teenagers have fast been turning to rhythm and blues."[23]

To summarize, then, the BRB did not disappear, contra many previous descriptions of this event, because R&B was no longer distinct from the mainstream. Rather, the heterogeneity of both R&B and the mainstream had led, step by step, to a broadening of the BRB to include more white artists and recordings that did not cite the conventions of R&B. The makeup of the chart did not correspond to the R&B formation as described in other discourses about R&B at the time, and the BRB appears to have become disconnected from the audience most identified with R&B.

White DJs Need Help

For a type of music that had supposedly lost its separate identity, R&B continued to lead a very active existence. Discussions about the significance of rhythm and blues as a musical category and about the infiltration of mainstream pop by rhythm and blues recurred repeatedly over the next few years. During the interregnum of the BRB, one topic occurred more than the others: the difficulty of white DJs, radio programmers, and retailers in assessing the suitability of rhythm and blues recordings as crossover material. Anxiety surfaced in the acknowledgment that, despite its patent importance and popularity with "non-Negro" audiences (as they were often called at the time), white DJs at "contemporary pop" radio stations had difficulty picking rhythm and blues hits, and thus relied on African American disk jockeys at rhythm and blues radio stations for clues as to what to program. Discussions of the importance of the African American audience would appear several times in *Billboard* during the period in which the R&B chart had gone missing, almost as if to recognize the general utility of the information provided by this absent chart to music retailers and radio programmers. That the magazine had eliminated one of the resources that would help with the challenge in assessing rhythm and blues recordings remained a blind spot.[24]

Gavin, in the editorial discussed earlier, addressed the difficulties of white programmers with R&B, as did other features, including a profile of the R&B DJ Montague the Magnificent.[25] Gavin's article also anticipated another major thread that would run through several articles appearing in *Billboard* during 1964: that of the integration of the Top 40. A discourse arose that connected the relationship of rhythm and blues to pop with broader social struggles around civil rights. The growing popularity of rhythm and blues with white audiences could appear as a parallel to the weakening of social boundaries dividing African Americans and Euro-Americans.[26]

The civil rights struggle drew attention to how the musical integration of the Top 40 was not matched by these stations' hiring practices. The NAACP in Philadelphia and CORE in Los Angeles successfully pressured nonintegrated radio stations to hire African American DJs. Black DJs explicitly linked the hiring of African Americans to the musical practices already taking place, arguing that since Top 40 stations were programming so many recordings by black artists, they should hire a "competent Negro deejay as well."[27] If the integration of the Top 40 could lead to demands for integrating the staffs of Top 40 radio stations, a move that would presumably obviate the need to poach off the playlists of R&B stations, some recognized that the musical integration of the Top 40 might have a downside. At least one *Billboard* staff writer voiced concern, stating that the "the eventual integration of Negro and white could spell the end of Negro radio as we know it today."[28] At the same time, other commentators recognized that the social value of black radio extended beyond its playlist, in that radio served an important role as a community focal point for African Americans, and that the need for stations catering to African Americans would persist regardless of the degree of integration in the Top 40.[29]

In response to the integration of a few Top 40 stations, and demonstrating that charges of reverse racism are nothing new in the era of affirmative action, music industry and mainstream news publications labored to reassure their readers that R&B stations were integrating as well.[30] One of the issues arguing for the integration of R&B radio was the idea of soul as a musical element that some white artists might possess. As *Billboard* commented, "One of the key reasons for the extended playlist, of course, is to make room for white artists with soul feeling."[31] This illustrates what happens when one component is detached from a generic assemblage and then made to stand in for the whole of the category. In other words, and contrary to the arguments about integrating R&B radio, soul, while a component of R&B, could also participate in recordings in other categories as well without turning those recordings into R&B. By substituting a part for the whole, *Billboard* once again evinced a type of chainlike logic, detached from the feedback of participants in the field and the socio-musical conventions of R&B, a type of reasoning which had only recently led, step by step, to the situation encountered in 1963 when *Billboard*'s formulation of the R&B category had become incoherent.

After the burst of attention accorded R&B as a separate radio market in *Billboard* during the latter half of 1964, interest suddenly seemed to evaporate. Even the "D.J. Roundup," used to track the regional preferences of R&B radio, disappeared without notice in the December 19, 1964, issue. The "Market Analyses" and

"D.J. Roundups" may have answered the demand to provide more information and assistance to white music industry people, but the best answer to this demand was staring the magazine in the face: it needed to reinstate the R&B chart, which is exactly what happened in the January 30, 1965, issue.

THE REAPPEARANCE

The new and improved *Billboard* "Hot R&B Singles" chart did not pick up where the old BRB had left off. Gone were the teen idols, the folk novelties, Elvis Presley's mild-mannered rock 'n' roll from his movies, the surf tunes, and folk-Dixie. This is what it looked like:

BILLBOARD HOT R&B SINGLES CHART, JANUARY 30, 1965

1. Temptations, "My Girl"
2. Joe Tex, "Hold What You've Got"
3. Supremes, "Come See About Me"
4. Righteous Brothers, "You've Lost that Loving Feeling"
5. Marvin Gaye, "How Sweet It Is (To Be Loved by You)"
6. Sam Cooke, "Shake"
7. Shirley Ellis, "The Name Game"
8. Alvin Cash and the Crawlers, "Twine Time"
9. Larks, "The Jerk"
10. Sam Cooke, "A Change Is Going to Come"
11. Ben E. King, "Seven Letters"
12. Dobie Gray, "The 'In' Crowd"
13. Mary Wells, "Use Your Head"
14. Ray Charles, "Makin' Whoopee"
15. Marvelettes, "Too Many Fish in the Sea"
16. Radiants, "Voice Your Choice"
17. Impressions, "Amen"
18. Contours, "Can You Jerk Like Me"
19. Ad Libs, "The Boy from New York City"
20. Gene Chandler, "What Now"
21. Manhattan, "I Wanna Be (Your Everything)"
22. Little Anthony and the Imperials, "Goin' Out of My Head"
23. Lee Rogers, "I Want You to Have Everything"
24. Otis Redding, "That's How Strong My Love Is"
25. Kingsmen, "The Jolly Green Giant"
26. Barbara Lynn, "It's Better to Have It"
27. Velvelettes, "He Was Really Saying Something"
28. Ronettes, "Walking in the Rain"

29. Walter Jackson, "Suddenly I'm All Alone"
30. Lee Lamont, "Crying Man"
31. Barbara Mason, "Girls Have Feelings Too"
32. Major Lance, "Sometimes I Wonder"
33. Jan Bradley, "I'm Over You"
34. Joe Hinton, "I Want a Little Girl"
35. Impressions, "Long, Long Winter"
36. Effie Smith, "Dial That Telephone"
37. Contours, "That Day When She Needed Me"
38. Harold Melvin, "Get Out"
39. Mitty Collier, "No Faith, No Love"
40. Sam Cooke, "Cousin of Mine"

A newfound socio-musical stylistic consistency was evident. *Billboard* recognized this event with two statements, calling attention to its "expanded effort into the rhythm and blues field" via its tracking of emerging hits around the country in its "DJ Spotlight" (analogous to the earlier "D.J. Roundup") and "Territorial Break-outs" sections.[32] In a brief article at the bottom of the page, titled "Blues News," *Billboard* provided a clue to the adjustments that had been made since the last appearance of its R&B chart, thanking "all the disk jockeys, program directors and retail outlets for their splendid co-operation in helping to kick off the new r&b page." Molanphy comments on this passage, making the point that it reflects recognition on the part of *Billboard* that, rather than a core musical style, the industry would be better off tracking the core *audience* for R&B, and that the radio and retail outlets referenced in this passage are the means by which the industry would henceforth track that audience.[33] The blurb in "Blues News" does seem to admit a debt to music industry agents who are active participants in rhythm and blues, referencing a form of collaboration that may well have been absent before the disappearance of the R&B chart. Another way of putting this would be to say that the new *Billboard* chart aligned itself with the contemporary conventions of R&B as produced both discursively (including the *Cash Box* R&B chart) and via citationality, as well as with the relationship the BRB had had with R&B conventions prior to 1962.

By aligning the representation of R&B in the BRB with R&B's discursive and citational conventions, *Billboard* also reassessed the relationship between R&B and the mainstream, a relationship that a comparison of R&B and mainstream popularity charts can throw into relief. The recordings in the R&B charts reveal that a general shift had occurred in terms of the socio-musical conventions of R&B in the fourteen months since the BRB had last appeared. The influence from 1950s vocal groups had weakened considerably, and Motown had established a sound and dominance in both the R&B and pop charts. Some aspects of Motown's sound were shared across the R&B field, such as rhythmic grooves derived from bass riffs, vocal backgrounds derived from gospel (overlapping call and response) but with a strong focus on the lead singer, even eighth-note rhythmic subdivisions, and de-emphasis of MOR influences and of Latin rhythms in ballads. As befitting their motto, "The Sound of Young America," the songs, with their melodic hooks and teen-friendly lyrics, even lessened the "mature effect" of their music relative to other R&B and succeeded in attracting a large, interracial teen audience.[34] Subgenres such as the 6/8 ballad with interjected sermon largely disappeared, and when they did appear, as in Joe Tex's "Hold What You've Got," the elements of the song had been rearranged and reapportioned so that the sermon now occupied the majority of the recording, thus highlighting the sermon as a novelty effect.

Several recordings that evinced a weak crossover effect, such as Alvin Cash and the Crawlers' "Twine Time" (peak positions: CRB: 1; BRB: 4; C100: 9; B100: 14), Mitty Collier's "No Faith, No Love" (CRB: 4; BRB: 29; C100: 74; B100: 91), and other deep cuts lower down on the CRB and BRB, speak to distinctive listening practices among the constellated communities comprising the denizens of R&B radio and record stores, and provide strong clues as to the distinctiveness of R&B vis-à-vis the mainstream. These practices were surveyed tentatively during the latter part of 1964 through Billboard's "Market Analysis" and "D.J. Roundup," and with the CRB throughout the BRB's interregnum. One recording in particular stands out for its citation of a performative mode still resonant within the world of R&B, but which had lost its place within the ambit of mainstream taste by early 1965: Effie Smith's "Dial That Telephone (Parts One and Two)" (CRB: 26; BRB: 36). It reaches back to the humor of "Open the Door, Richard" and beyond in its novelty-parody depiction of the type of person who finds peculiar consolation in telephonic communication. First recorded in the 1950s, "Dial That Telephone" begins with a slow, blues-inflected groove and a sung refrain. "Part One" of the skit commences with a framing device, in which two male neighbors of "Ruby Lee" agree to listen in on her phone conversation with her friend "Mabel," whom Ruby Lee is sure to call because her partner "Henry" hasn't come home yet. The recording continues with a (one-sided) phone "conversation" in which listeners hear Ruby Lee describe the behavior of her no-good man. At the end of "Part One," Henry knocks on the door (a reference to "Open the Door," perhaps?) and comes in. "Part Two" revolves around an argument between the unhappy couple. Henry encourages Ruby Lee to listen to their party line, where he accurately predicts that she will hear Mabel criticizing her to a third person. This type of humor still clearly resonated within the African American community, even if it no longer found acceptance in mainstream circles.

Such non-crossover recordings were contrasted mightily by Motown's releases. Such was Motown's success that it moved the New York Times to gush to its readers about the "Detroit sound," and to provide a general explanation of R&B. Motown's "musical style stems from what is called rhythm-and-blues," explained the author,

Richard H. Lingeman, which "in the past, [was] a trade euphemism for a kind of music performed by Negroes and sold mainly to a Negro market." Thanks to the Supremes, "Motown's records have attained national, as opposed to racial, best-sellerdom." Later in the article, Lingeman uses the term "pop breakout" to describe R&B recordings that are "played by pop 'top 40' disc jockeys, and achieve ranking on the pop charts, which reflect sales in the broader mass market"—in other words, these recordings are crossover hits. Lingeman quotes an editor from *Record World* (a competitor of *Billboard* and *Cash Box*), who credits Motown with breaking "across racial barriers" and easing the way for other companies.[35]

In support of this last claim, well-established stars such as Sam Cooke and Ray Charles, or flamboyant takes on old genres such as Joe Tex's "Hold What You've Got," fared well on the mainstream charts, and other companies specializing in R&B, such as Atlantic and Stax, experienced consistent success. None could compete with Motown, however. When *Billboard*'s R&B chart returned, the number one song was a Motown recording, the Temptations' "My Girl," which was already rapidly ascending the *Billboard* Hot 100, jumping from number forty-one to number twelve that same week. Other Motown crossover sensations at this moment included the Supremes' "Come See About Me" (BRB: 3; B100: 8—eventually to reach number one) and Marvin Gaye's "How Sweet It Is" (BRB: 5; B100: 6).

Another new development was the recognition of the Memphis sound, which provided a tempting analogue to the Motown sound. Mostly consisting of recordings released by the Stax/Volt label or recorded at the Stax studios and released by other companies (e.g., Atlantic), artists such as Otis Redding, Booker T. & the MGs, and Rufus Thomas became identified with a sound traceable to the locale. Visitors from the North, such as Atlantic Records engineer Tom Dowd and producer and executive Jerry Wexler, were quick to notice the loose, spontaneous methods used to produce recordings, in which head arrangements were worked out by the musicians collectively rather than based on the notated work of an arranger.

Representatives from record companies located in Memphis agreed on aspects of the distinctive sound, describing it variously as "raunchy with a blues influence," or "a real danceable type beat with heavy bass and drum." Jim Stewart, the owner of Stax/Volt, weighed in, citing the importance of the "beat—a hard rhythm section" and "the combination of horns, [which] instead of a smooth sound, produces a rough growly, rasping sound, which carries into the melody." Stewart also noted the "addressivity" of their production process, observing that "all our artists are Negros. Naturally, our sound is directly oriented in that direction." The commentators, including Joe Cuogui, president of Hi Records and Sam Phillips of Sun Records (famed producer of Elvis Presley's early recordings and other 1950s rockabilly and R&B), as well as Stewart, all recognized the importance of identification in the Memphis sound, emphasizing the importance of place (the South) and race (African Americans).[36] These comments positioned the Memphis sound more firmly within the socio-musical conventions of R&B than Motown, a position that also aligned with the lesser crossover effect experienced by recordings emanating from Memphis.

The British Are A-Comin' and the Folk Are A-Rockin'

Few events roiled the popular music field like the British Invasion, the reverberations of which were felt in the category of R&B. In addition to the newfound dominance of Motown, during the fourteen months of the BRB's interregnum the arrival of the Beatles and other musicians from the United Kingdom resulted in a profound stylistic reorganization of the mainstream, which in some ways paralleled the changes already observed within R&B during this time. The influence of MOR, 1950s-style vocal groups, dance crazes, surf music, folk music, international tunes, and novelty numbers all declined in frequency.[37] It wasn't difficult to find the source of this displacement: the Top 40 of the B100 for January 30, 1965, featured not only the Beatles, but other British artists such as the Kinks, Gerry and the Pacemakers, Peter and Gordon, the Zombies, the Rolling Stones, Chad and Jeremy, the Searchers, and the Dave Clark Five.

Contributing to a shift not only in the disposition of the popular music field, but in the possibilities of socio-musical identification as well, was the emergence of a new genre. Folk-rock had become a mass media sensation by the summer of 1965 due in large part to the Byrds' recording of Bob Dylan's "Mr. Tambourine Man" followed by Dylan's own "Like a Rolling Stone." Usually explained as the marriage of folk lyrics and a rock beat, nothing attracted more interest to the new genre than the release and success of Barry McGuire's "Eve of Destruction" in August 1965. Many noticed that previous songs with protest lyrics had not fared as well with Top 40 radio; the difference in the case of "Eve of Destruction" was variously attributed to the fact that "many of radio's young disk jockeys have beliefs which coincide with those of Sloan's" (the songwriter of "Eve of Destruction") and the more "commercial" sound of the recording.[38] Not all reports confirmed the easy acceptance of the McGuire recording, however, citing the resistance of MOR stations to playing songs with controversial lyrics (commercial folk recordings often fared quite well in the MOR chart), even if such songs represented a new trend. In Oakland, California, radio stations felt pressure from "right-wing political groups who consider[ed] ['Eve of Destruction'] 'subversive' and want[ed] it banned," even as the recording's popularity on jukeboxes sent it ever higher in the charts.[39]

Billboard had difficulty differentiating recordings within the new genre, lumping together anyone who recorded a song decrying the treatment of long hair, or covered a Dylan song. All writers seemed to agree, however, that the difference between folk-rock and other rock and pop genres depended on a newfound seriousness of purpose, displayed most obviously in the lyrics. One analyzed the impact of Bob Dylan, whose economic capital had soared over the summer, as "48 different Dylan records have been cut within the past month." The author, Eliot Tiegel, was one of the first music industry writers to delve into the notion that Dylan might possess symbolic capital as well as economic capital, revealing that his "albums are loaded with message, protest and satire songs, very cerebral and complex, which have not yet been 'discovered' by the long-haired folk-rock performers and the awakening a&r men." Tiegel, in the course of discovering the appeal and secret of folk-rock, turned to one of the icons of the late-1950s urban folk revival, Harry Belafonte, who explained that "folk and rock have their roots in Negro music.... The intensity of Negro music is part and parcel of the music reflecting the world's changing society." Belafonte's reflections, in turn, led to Tiegel's consideration of the impact of "the current message trend," which "has all but eliminated Caucasian groups from singing 'let's go to the hop–type songs.'" The influence of folk-rock, however, had its limits: Dylan and folk-rock had not yet been "discovered" by rhythm and blues groups, who are "singing in their soulfully shouting style, with enough drums and 'yeah babies' to satisfy listeners."[40]

The discussion of race at the end of this article is telling, as is the earlier mention of the symbolic capital associated with Dylan, clearly indicated by the mention of his albums being "loaded with message, protest and satire songs, very cerebral and complex." The significance of folk-rock lies in its relationship to other genres. Unlike the earlier forms of rock 'n' roll and post–rock 'n' roll popular music that it was partially responsible for displacing—such as dance crazes, girl groups, and the early 1960s folk revival—folk-rock emerged as a music that was not only more serious (i.e., directed toward an older, better-educated audience) than other forms of post–rock 'n' roll popular music, but also one that distanced itself from black popular music. Drawing on the folk revival's aura of anti-commercialism, which was simultaneously projected within a fully commercial milieu, folk-rock fulfilled the need for a music that was distinctively both white and bohemian, achieved through alternative practices of accreditation, such as the approval of other artists, rather than from economic success. These factors helped differentiate folk-rock from less hip, white-associated genres such as teen pop, and pre-rock 'n' roll-styled pop. In other words, while the popular music field had previously included rock 'n' roll, girl groups, MOR, novelty tunes, and dance craze numbers recorded by both African Americans and Euro-Americans, the idea of an African American folk-rocker was difficult to imagine. Although other hip styles performed by white musicians coexisted at this time with folk-rock, these genres, such as blues-rock and hard rock, all maintained obvious ties to historical and contemporaneous genres that were strongly associated with African Americans.[41] The status and prestige of folk-rock and its descendants thus threatened to create greater distance between R&B and the mainstream at precisely the moment when the importance of R&B to the music industry as a whole had begun to receive greater recognition than it had for several years.

A Slice of the Charts, May–November 1965

The period following the reappearance of *Billboard*'s R&B chart illustrates how complex the relationship between the categories of R&B and the mainstream could be, especially when compared to the situation in the 1940s. The months between May and November 1965 provide a particularly excellent range of contrasting R&B styles and differential crossover effects that exemplify this complexity. While previous discussions in this chapter may have implied a direct correspondence between the degree of musical African American–ness (based on socio-musical conventions) and a lack of mainstream success, two factors in particular mitigate this. The first of these is what the anthropologist Alfred Gell dubbed protentions, meaning, the extent to which a work anticipates future artistic developments within an oeuvre or genre.[42] In this case it is possible to retroactively analyze how certain stylistic components would become more central to a category in the future than they were at the time of a recording's initial release. Thus, crossover engages in multiple levels of temporality, including both the cycle of a recording's rise and fall in popularity during the period of its public emergence, and the way in which its effects will be echoed by musical texts of the future. The second factor has already been mentioned: this is the degree to which an artist or recording cites previous crossover successes. The following examples demonstrate how numerous exceptions exist within patterns of general statistical causality that posit a relationship between musical style and crossover success, and how black popular music was now both more separate from certain genres of mainstream popular music (such as the hyphenated rock genres) and more tightly interwoven with them than ever.

At the end of 1965, "I Can't Help Myself" by the Four Tops was rated the number one R&B single and the number two pop single of 1965 by *Billboard*. By these standards of measurement, it earns the honorific of crossover song of the year. Table 14 shows the week-by-week rankings of "I Can't Help Myself" in *Billboard*'s R&B and pop charts. Although "I Can't Help Myself" started off much higher in the R&B chart, by the fourth week, it was in the same basic range in both charts, eventually reaching number one in both by the sixth week. Although it evidenced considerable longevity in both charts, it did fade more rapidly in the pop chart.

In the same end-of-year polls, Wilson Pickett's "In the Midnight Hour" was ranked the number two R&B song of the year, but not listed in the Top 100 pop singles of the year. In contrast to "I Can't Help Myself," then, "In the Midnight Hour" did not display a strong crossover effect. Table 14 reveals that "In the Midnight Hour" only gathered momentum in the pop chart after six weeks of popularity in the R&B chart. While it remained for twenty-three weeks on the R&B chart, its stay on the pop charts was limited to twelve weeks. Only for one week were the positions on the two charts within ten slots of each other (and when this occurred,

TABLE 14 Crossover Chart, May–December 1965

Title	"I Can't Help Myself"	"In the Midnight Hour"	"Papa's Got a Brand New Bag"	"Tracks of My Tears"	"Pretty Little Baby"
Artist	Four Tops	Wilson Pickett	James Brown	Miracles	Marvin Gaye
	R&B/Pop				
May 15	29/67				
May 22	6/32				
May 29	2/17				
June 5	1/7				
June 12	1/4				
June 19	1/1				
June 26	1/2	35/—			
July 3	1/1	19/135	action*/—	38/103	action/66
July 10	1/2	12/83	39/80	34/81	action/49
July 17	1/2	8/79	30/65	26/61	39/37
July 24	1/3	6/77	13/44	14/51	39/30
July 31	1/6	2/62	4/30	5/37	33/27
Aug. 7	2/9	1/52	1/20	3/30	23/25
Aug. 14	4/35	2/37	1/14	3/23	22/33
Aug. 21	7/—	5/27	1/10	3/19	22/—
Aug. 28	9/—	8/24	1/8	2/16	17/—
Sept. 4	13/—	12/21	1/8	3/20	16/—
Sept. 11	28/—	12/25	1/12	4/20	20/-
Sept. 18		11/39	1/28	5/31	29/-
Sept. 25		9/48	1/37	5/46	
Oct. 2		6/-	2/49	8/-	
Oct. 9		12/-	7/-	9/-	
Oct. 16		15/-	10/-	16/-	
Oct. 23		15/-	16/-	23/-	
Oct. 30		10/-	26/-	28/-	
Nov. 6		12/-			
Nov. 13		20/-			
Nov. 20		27/-			
Nov. 27		31/-			
Dec. 4		2/-			
year-end rankings	1/2		6/33	7/78	-/-

* "Action" R&B singles," according to *Billboard*, were "records registering solid sales in certain markets and appearing to be a week away from meriting a listing on the national Hot R&B chart above."

the recording was already declining in the R&B chart), and "In the Midnight Hour" never rose higher than number twenty-one on the pop chart although it reached number one on the R&B chart and made two resurgences after two initial declines. "In the Midnight Hour" presents the case of a song that was hugely popular in the R&B market but evidenced a fairly weak crossover effect.

Several other songs presented cases falling in between "I Can't Help Myself" and "In the Midnight Hour." James Brown's "Papa's Got a Brand New Bag" was every bit as big an R&B hit as "I Can't Help Myself," but its pop success fell somewhere between "I Can't Help Myself" and "In the Midnight Hour." Marvin Gaye's "Pretty Little Baby" traced yet another pattern: it started off much higher in the pop charts than in the R&B charts, peaked at number twenty-five, and then dropped off five weeks before it disappeared from the R&B chart. It is especially interesting to compare "Pretty Little Baby" to "Papa's Got a Brand New Bag" and the Miracles' "Tracks of My Tears," all of which entered the charts at the same time. While "Pretty Little Baby" didn't end up being anywhere near the hit of "Papa's Got a Brand New Bag" and "Tracks of My Tears," it initially had much more of the appearance of a hit in the pop charts, remaining ahead of the other two songs for five weeks, thus receiving more exposure on Top 40 radio.

What could account for the discrepancies in crossover effect between these songs? Both "Tracks of My Tears" and "Pretty Little Baby" were Motown releases, so company affiliation could not account for this difference. The difference may lie in the expectations that the industry had for the songs, or, as proposed earlier, in the differing degree to which the recordings cited previous crossover successes. Gaye's previous two songs ("How Sweet It Is to Be Loved by You," and "I'll Be Doggone") had been top-ten pop hits, whereas Pickett had only placed one song as high as number forty-nine, and that had occurred two years earlier; Brown had not released a single for a year since "Out of Sight," which had been a modest pop hit; and the highest spot for the Miracles' last four singles had been number sixteen. A similar set of expectations does not seem to have affected the performance of the songs on the R&B chart, where initial placement and movement in the chart corresponded to the peak popularity of the songs. These observations suggest that even if the BRB now more closely tracked the taste of the participants in R&B, the B100 continued to heavily weight expectations about an artist's commercial performance. Such examples also provide evidence for the "intuition" mentioned in chapter 1 as guiding the formulation of the charts.[43]

Three of the recordings discussed above ("Papa's Got a Brand New Bag," "In the Midnight Hour," and "I Can't Help Myself") will exemplify the aforementioned complexity between the degree of crossover effect and the socio-musical conventions of R&B. "I Can't Help Myself" as "crossover song of the year" reveals its relation to the conventions of R&B via its vocal timbre, call-and-response technique, overall rhythmic feel, and insistently repeating instrumental riffs, and the use of the baritone sax harks back to earlier R&B styles in instrumental timbre (as well as to previous Motown hits, thus providing a kind of sonic trademark for the label). The voice also makes spare use of melisma, paralinguistic effects, melodic variation, and pitch inflection. It does include more than a nod to pop style, as we might expect from a product emanating from Motown. These nods include a complex instrumental arrangement, fairly limited extemporization by the lead vocalist, the use of closed-periodic phrase structure and functional harmony, and the use of Western orchestral instruments. The eight-measure phrase structure repeats a great deal, yet this does not serve as a basis for constant variation by the lead singer, nor are the extemporizations of the singer the focus of the song. Rather, the focus falls on the overall sound of the song, and the hook, which emphasizes the words of the title in the consequent part of its antecedent-consequent phrase structure.

"In the Midnight Hour" as "non-crossover hit of the year" emphasizes musical conventions rather different from those found in "I Can't Help Myself." By comparison, "In the Midnight Hour" makes more explicit its connections to gospel and blues in almost every way. The vocal is harsher and makes more use of paralinguistic grunts and groans, the timbral variety is wider, and perhaps most importantly the phrasing is more open-ended, with the first eight measures being based on a riff-like pattern. This throws the focus on the singer's variations, which include a wide range of vocal techniques to convey a sense of emotional engagement. This is the result we would expect: the song that crosses over less has more audible links to "standards and aesthetics understood by the black community."[44] This is true of the lyrics as well. While "I Can't Help Myself" presents a typical (albeit clever) pop narrative of a jilted lover pleading with the object of his desire, the protagonist of "In the Midnight Hour" makes it clear that he can indeed "help himself," presenting a grown-up approach to physical love that suggests another possible factor in its failure to cross over. But the comparison of these two songs can only take us so far, for how can it explain the fact that James Brown's "Papa's Got a Brand New Bag" experienced greater crossover success than Wilson Pickett?

"Papa's Got a Brand New Bag," if anything, emphasizes the variative technique of the lead singer and the riff-like repetitions of the band even more than "In the Midnight Hour." The "Brand New Bag" here is musical as well as social: the spare instrumental parts combined with the extreme complexity of their interlocking accents made the song Brown's first studio recording to imply so strongly the style that would become known as funk. The song's title was heard by many at the time as a reference to the civil rights movement.[45] Musical example 22 shows the way in which voice, horns, and bass all occupy their own rhythmic space, creating a variety of call-and-response effects, most noticeably between voice and horns (the vocal "call" is marked "a," the instrumental response "b"). While the horns play a one-measure pattern and the bass plays a two-measure pattern, both coinciding with the bar lines, the vocal calls begin and end in the middle of measures. Both

MUSICAL EXAMPLE 22. "Papa's Got a Brand New Bag": Call and Response Between Voice and Horns

"Papa's Got a Brand New Bag" and "In the Midnight Hour" use phrases that contrast harmonically with the stable riff passages, but these contrasting phrases belong to patterns that derive from blues phrasing patterns, and as such are not based on the hierarchical patterns of Tin Pan Alley pop.[46]

In addition to this, musical examples 23, 24, and 25 demonstrate how both Brown and Pickett superimpose at key moments (usually over the bar lines) an implied meter based on an approximate triple subdivision of the pulse with complex internal accents, a device Levi Stubbs, the lead singer of the Four Tops, only hints at once (these passages are marked by brackets).[47] Both Brown and Pickett also use microtonal inflection, particularly of the third scale degree, much more than Stubbs. (It should be noted here that I arbitrarily selected the first three repetitions of the first four measures of the chorus of all three songs; these passages in no way represent the most complex rhythmic flights of the three vocalists.) The passages with triple subdivision are those that best illustrate the inadequacy of Western notation in representing the rhythmic play of these performers. This notation is at best an approximation that shows where the voice's pitches lie in relation to the underlying beat. In these passages, the effect is that of the voice disengaging from, or playing with, the beat. In most of the cases, this play results in eliding an accent on beat one, the normative downbeat and most strongly accented beat in most Western music.

In terms of subject matter, Brown's words do not convey a narrative, but rather, in their exhortations to the implied listeners to dance, invoke a participatory aesthetic in a way the other songs don't. In a sense these words conjure up an imaginary audience to respond to the song. Brown recounts that he knew he had a take when he looked around the studio during playback and saw everybody dancing.[48] Yet as we can see in table 14, the success of "Papa's Got a Brand New Bag" was more intense and immediate in the R&B charts than "In the Midnight Hour," and after it

MUSICAL EXAMPLE 23. "Papa's Got a Brand New Bag": Comparison of the First Four Measures of the Vocal Line, Verses 1–3

had been number one in the R&B charts for about five weeks it entered the top ten of the pop chart. What can account for this? One possibility is that while "In the Midnight Hour" had great longevity in the R&B chart, its performance in the charts suggested a steady sales pattern rather than a sudden explosion.[49] Thus it was less likely than "Papa's Got a Brand New Bag"—with its rapid ascent up the R&B chart— to attract attention as a possible crossover. James Brown had experienced a few minor pop hits before this time while Wilson Pickett had not, so expectations differed for the two artists as well. Figure 13 summarizes these observations, dividing the R&B category into "inconsistent crossover" and "consistent crossover," with "non-R&B mainstream" occupying the third term in this comparison.

Overall, there appears to have been a loose correlation between the style of a song and its ability to cross over, granted that it was successful initially on the R&B charts. The rapidity with which a song was promoted as pop had something to do

MUSICAL EXAMPLE 24: "In the Midnight Hour": Comparison of the First Four Measures of the Vocal Line, Verses, 1–3

MUSICAL EXAMPLE 25: "I Can't Help Myself": Comparison of the First Four Measures of the Vocal Line, Verses 1–3

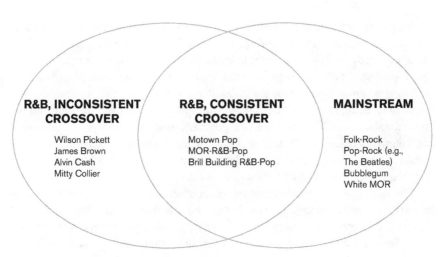

R&B, INCONSISTENT CROSSOVER

Wilson Pickett
James Brown
Alvin Cash
Mitty Collier

R&B, CONSISTENT CROSSOVER

Motown Pop
MOR-R&B-Pop
Brill Building R&B-Pop

MAINSTREAM

Folk-Rock
Pop-Rock (e.g.,
The Beatles)
Bubblegum
White MOR

FIGURE 13. The Circular Logic of R&B Crossovers, 1965.

with its closeness to pop conventions and its distance from the socio-musical conventions of R&B as well as with industry expectations based on previous chart performance by a particular artist. The impact of these expectations put a debut record by an R&B artist who had had no previous releases at a great disadvantage compared to white pop performers of the time such as Petula Clark or Gary Lewis, white contemporaries of Brown and Pickett whose recordings entered into an apparatus designed to promote them to a mainstream audience. If one assumes some sort of correlation between popularity charts and what people like, an enigma yet remains. For even statistical causality and the concept of relations of exteriority cannot adequately explain why or how one recording finds a larger audience (or audiences) than another. In retrospect, a retro recording could be viewed as succeeding because of its retentions, while a forward-looking song might succeed due to its protentions. But anyone who pays close attention to popular music history will know many recordings that were equally forward- or backward-looking and did not succeed or cross over. Nevertheless, by analyzing how the notions of popularity of particular artists and recordings in different categories are produced, it is possible to understand the role of racial connotations in the socio-musical conventions of large popular music categories.

FROM R&B TO SOUL

In the discussion of the R&B category between the years 1963 and 1965, the term "soul" has arisen repeatedly, usually as a component of R&B. At times, soul functioned as a synecdoche for R&B, so that when it was attributed to a particular artist, that artist was then interpreted as an R&B artist. Many of the uses of "soul" in journalistic discourse in 1965 and 1966 continued to highlight its relation to whiteness, especially in *Billboard*, where it appeared most often in the context of "blue-eyed soul" and in discussions of how many white artists were being played on R&B radio, apparently a matter of much greater concern than the number of R&B recordings being played on the Top 40. During this time, however, "soul" did not have the status of other labels used for popular music categories at that time, such as "country," "folk-rock," "Latin," or "easy listening," a status that "soul" clearly *did* attain by 1969. "R&B" remained the default term in the music industry in 1965 for popular music associated with African Americans.

The term "soul" had circulated in conjunction with certain forms of African American music since the late 1950s, but this was not music riding high on the R&B charts, for the most part, but rather soul jazz. An *Ebony* article from December 1961, "The Soul of Soul," clarifies the usage at this time. "Soul music," according to the author, Lerone Bennett Jr., is an "extraordinary movement in contemporary jazz" and an "outgrowth of a bitter musical war with muted racial undertones." "Soul music" or "soul jazz" is contrasted with "the rather anemic West Coast school" and described as "stress[ing] a hard-swinging, gospel flavored blues feeling."[50] Yet the author of the article finds it necessary to qualify further this label:

> Soul, to be sure, *is not even a music*. It is the feeling with which an artist invests his creation. And, above all, it is of the musical spirit rather than the letter. Guy Lombardo, for example, playing "See See Rider" is Guy Lombardo playing "See See Rider." One and one, in this case are two. But Jimmy Smith [soul jazz organist] playing "See See Rider" is another thing. One and one are three. The man adds something. The added increment? Soul—a certain way of feeling, a certain way of expressing oneself, a certain way of being. Similarly, Ray Charles or Mahalia Jackson singing "Twinkle, Twinkle, Little Star" is soul par excellence. Soul is the interpretation, not the song. (112, my italics)

Bennett clarifies that soul is not a category of music but rather a component of African American–associated genres, an affect, a performance practice. The article then closes with an observation that closely anticipates a connection between black popular music and the idea of "soul" that would become common by the late 1960s: "There is in the music a new note of racial pride, a celebration of ties to Africa and a defiant embrace of . . . all that middle-class America condemns" (116).

I cite this article at some length because its discussion of soul seems to typify the usage of the term for the next five years or so. It is associated with music, but it is "not even a music," even when it is conjoined to the word "music" to form "soul music" as in the Sound Stage 7 ad from 1965 that began the chapter.

A discussion of soul that illustrates its use as a component of R&B and its reliance on non-musical factors even cropped up in the profile of DJ Montague the Magnificent mentioned earlier with reference to the socio-musical integration of radio stations. In response to the realization by Top 40 stations that they would benefit from the expertise of African American DJs, Montague offered the following concise explanation of what the "Negro" DJ "has that cannot be captured by the white deejay": "It's SOUL, man, SOUL," opined Montague. In response to questions about the definition of soul, Montague answered in sociological terms: "It's the last to be hired, first to be fired, brown all year-round, sit-in-the-back-of-the-bus feeling. . . . You've got to live with us or you don't have it." This feeling is, in turn, an integral aspect of soul in music, a point that Montague emphasizes with a broadside launched at the British bands then dominating the Top 40: "The black brothers are the mainstay of our pop music today. Artists like John Lee Hooker, Otis Redding, and others are heavy on soul—one thing our English friends can't imitate."[51] Such a formulation of soul obviously flies in the face of other accounts in *Billboard* that would detach soul from social identity and view it as an abstract musical quality. Montague's statement also reinforces the new sense of a divide discussed earlier in this chapter between white rock and black popular music.

A few examples from 1965 and 1966 will clarify that "soul" had not yet acquired stability as a categorical term. Another article from *Ebony*, "Rock 'n' Roll Becomes Respectable" (this one from November 1965), refers to all current non-Tin Pan Alley-based popular music as "rock 'n' roll," but the article also adds that all "rock 'n' roll music" used to be called race music, thereby conflating rock 'n' roll with black popular music in general. The respectability of rock 'n' roll, according to this article, rests on the increasing number of television shows that feature it, and the author suggests that rock 'n' roll, in any form, should be celebrated as a triumph of African American music. This line of reasoning, although plausible in many respects and echoing the celebration of integration found in many other forums of the period, reaches a point of absurdity when the article begins to celebrate white artists, such as bubblegum star Bobby Sherman, as part of the success of black music.[52] What is striking in this article is not only the absence of the term "soul music" to talk about contemporary black popular music, but also the avoidance even of the label "rhythm and blues" in favor of the more race-neutral term "rock 'n' roll"—a label that was quickly becoming obsolete at the time of the article's publication.

An April 1966 article in *Jet* that contrasted Martha and the Vandellas with the Supremes indicates some of the tensions flowing around the genre terminology for black popular music at the time. Whereas "the Supremes have 'toned down' their driving sound and replaced it with material reminiscent of the Andrews Sisters and other white groups," "the most notable thing about Martha Reeves and her group is their stirring—strictly 'soul' sound. And their audiences are predominantly Negro." Soul, in this case as with soul jazz before it, was associated with musical approaches derived from gospel and with African American audiences, but rendered more as a quality that could be added to rhythm and blues, rather than a type of music unto itself.[53]

At the same time, the language for discussing African American identity underwent its own transformation. From the language of the early civil rights movement, with its emphasis on integration, acceptance, and assimilation, came a new rhetoric that grew in importance following the assassination of Malcolm X in 1965 and the landmark achievements of the civil rights movement, with the Civil Rights Acts of 1964 and 1965. The Black Panther party formed in Oakland, California, in 1966 (October 15); Stokely Carmichael first publicly used the term "black power" in 1966 (June 16); the Black Arts movement with its ideas of a distinctive black aesthetic took shape during the years between 1965 and 1968; and the ideas of "black power" and "black is beautiful" entered public discourse in the period between 1966 and 1968. Integration was no longer necessarily seen as the only goal of the civil rights movement; rather, pride in black cultural difference and the desire for recognition of the achievements signified by this cultural difference ascended in importance. The most commonly accepted designation for African Americans shifted from "negro" to "black" and the term "soul" circulated increasingly as a designation not only for a musico-spiritual quality, but as a sign of racial pride and activism as well.[54]

Thus, in the field of black popular music, "soul" went from being a component of R&B to the designation for a whole category of music. The titles of albums and songs bear witness to this transformation, as the term appears and changes function, moving from Otis Redding's *Dictionary of Soul* and Lou Rawls's *Soulin'* in 1966 to Arthur Conley's "Sweet Soul Music" and Sam and Dave's "Soul Man" in 1967.[55] Illustrating how quickly language can shift, by the latter part of 1966 the term "soul" was already appearing to nudge "R&B" aside as the categorical term of choice, albeit as a term still requiring quotation marks. The *New York Times* critic Robert Shelton, for example, in a review of a performance by Otis Redding, informs readers that Redding "has enjoyed a spiraling reputation in recent months as a 'soul' singer of uncommon power. . . . He even fell to his knees, overwhelmed with feeling, a device shared by gospel and 'soul' singers."[56]

The history of "Soul Man" is particularly instructive. Isaac Hayes, the composer of "Soul Man," says that he got the idea for the song while watching coverage of the Detroit riots in July 1967. Hayes noticed that African Americans who had written the word "soul" on their windows owned all the stores that had not been destroyed.[57] Although a sign of solidarity among African Americans, in the white-oriented press such usages could have ominous implications. Published a few months before Hayes's observations, the *New York Times* recalled that the "fraternal term, 'soul brother'" was used "in the Watts riots when Negro businessmen chalked it on their stores so the antiwhite rioters would pass them by." The same article does note (reassuringly?) that soul could "operate as a commercial thing, as when New York's WWRL calls itself 'soul brother radio,'" and that it "has entered the vocabulary as a loose description of the kind of music made by invariably Negro performers."[58]

However, despite its growing frequency, the usage of "soul" as a term designating a type of music was not consistent across a broad range of media in 1967. "Sweet Soul Music" and "Soul Man" may have been hits, *Jet* magazine may have begun its "Soul Brother Top 20" popularity chart in April 1967 in which readers wrote in with their favorite songs, Atlantic Records may have used the term profusely in its advertisements, and *Billboard* may have published a special edition titled "The World of Soul" in June 1967. Yet in that very same issue of *Billboard,* the only text that uses the term "soul" to refer to a type of music is found in the advertisements. All the articles in "The World of Soul" prefer the terms "rhythm and blues" or "blues," which are presented as genres within which individual artists might display a soulful quality. The usage of "soul" in 1966 and 1967 implies a disconnect between fan-musician usages and record company advertisements (especially Atlantic's), in which the use of "soul" was more common, and more official discourses, such as those found in *Ebony, Jet,* and *Billboard,* in which "rhythm and blues" remained the default genre term to which soul could be added. "Soul" still had the status of an adjective rather than a noun, even as its use proliferated across a broad range of media.

It was clear by the latter half of 1968 that "soul" was well on the way to becoming the de facto term for black popular music. This process was consecrated in August 1969 when *Billboard* changed the name of the chart used for representing the popularity of black popular music to "Soul." In the words of the anonymous *Billboard* editorialist:

> Beginning with this issue dated Aug. 23, Billboard uses the designation "soul" in place of "rhythm and blues." The editorial department, in making this change, is motivated by the fact that the term "soul" more properly embraces the broad range of song and instrumental material which derives from the musical genius of the black American. . . .
> Billboard's decision is in keeping with a policy formulated decades ago: that is, to give suitable designation to musical categories. Thus, many years ago Billboard dropped the term "race" in favor of rhythm and blues.[59]

Black popular music went from teetering on the brink of extinction to being the "most meaningful development in the broad mass music market within the last decade" in the pages of *Billboard* in a period of less than five years.[60] It is telling that during this transformation in the prestige and mainstream recognition of the music that the term "soul," once a component of R&B, and one with a strong charge of African American identity, became the default term for this music, installed across the different levels of genre.

. . .

In the early 1960s, a resonance occurred between a discourse of integration and civil rights on the one hand, and ideas about musical boundaries on the other. The political struggle over civil rights for African Americans fueled ideas about the dissolution of the border between R&B and the mainstream, as single musical components that were shared between categories were read as signs of musical merger. Indeed, forecasts of the fusing of musical categories were even at times echoed in optimistic remarks about the eventual loss of distinction between African Americans and Euro-Americans. The participation of individual elements of the African American socio-musical assemblage in mainstream society and music, however, led to the terminus of neither a distinct community identity nor the category of music associated with it.

The trajectory of this integrationist discourse, followed in the recordings released during this period and in the pages of the popular press, demonstrates the political function of the language used to discuss music and to name categories. When a disjunction occurs between categorical labels and social practice, it prompts recognition that categories are not based solely on music-stylistic characteristics, and that the classification of texts cannot be assumed based on what is already known about a category in advance. On the other hand, the reformulation of the rhythm and blues category after its reappearance in January 1965 could be read as emphasizing the value of ethnographic information, enabling the construction of a statistical aggregate about what people believed about categories.

One of the arguments of this chapter has been to emphasize the difficulty of separating two concepts, which could be summarized as the music-stylistic and the discursive (consisting of both historical and ethnographic threads). While the participation of agents who could act as representatives of the African American community acted as a crucial check and balance to the isolation of a formal feature in matching text to category, the intense identification of African Americans with rhythm and blues and soul meant that the re-citation of the category for black popular music could never be separated from what was already believed about that category. When detached from social identity and reduced to style traits, the category became illegible, as happened during the disappearance of *Billboard*'s rhythm and blues chart, and as has threatened to happen several times since.

What this chapter has sought to underscore, furthermore, through abundant examples of how people connected different categories of music with categories of people, is that such connections are anything but an academic concern. Such discourse functions as a riposte to strict anti-essentialists, who often make the same mistake as *Billboard* by equating a part with the whole. This type of chainlike logic argues (often through implication) that because a musical component appears in another assemblage, such an appearance contradicts the possibility that a musical category can have a homological relation with a category of people.[61] The evidence presented here for the importance of how people use these categories attests to the subtlety of the judgments made about which texts belong in which categories, and how crucial attestations of social identity are to these judgments.

At the same time, the story of the transition from rhythm and blues to soul illustrates how increases in cultural status are not without a countermovement of some kind. If, by the end of the 1960s, black popular music had acquired more prestige, it had become less integrated into the mainstream, a development with important consequences for the decades to follow. The chart for African American popular music remained the "Soul Music" chart until 1982, when, on the eve of Michael Jackson's *Thriller* and a fresh wave of black crossover successes, *Billboard* changed the chart's name to "Black Music." Between 1969 and 1982, crossover as a concept gained a higher profile, even as the commercial fortunes of black popular music suffered. The next chapter charts the countervailing fortunes of cultural prestige, economic success, and the politics of categorization during (and immediately after) the years of the transition from the marketing category of "soul" to that of "black music."

NOTES

1. Advertisement for Sound Stage 7 Records, *Billboard*, October 23, 1965, 29.

2. Both Brian Ward and Barney Hoskyns have pointed to "Sometimes You Have to Cry" as exemplifying a country-soul hybrid. See Brian Ward, *Just My Soul Responding: Rhythm and Blues, Black Consciousness, and Race Relations* (Berkeley: University of California Press, 1998), 221; and Barney Hoskyns, *Say It One Time for the Broken Hearted* (Glasgow: Fontana, 1987), 132.

3. See for example Peter Guralnick, *Sweet Soul Music: Rhythm and Blues and the Southern Dream of Freedom* (New York: Harper and Row, 1986); Gerri Hirshey, *Nowhere to Run: The Story of Soul Music* (New York: Penguin Books, 1984); Brian Ward, *Just My Soul Responding*; Robert Gordon, *Respect Yourself: Stax Records and the Soul Explosion* (New York: Bloomsbury, 2013).

4. Rick Altman, *Film/Genre* (London: British Film Institute, 1999), 50–53.

5. Manuel DeLanda, *A New Philosophy of Society: Assemblage Theory and Social Complexity* (London: Bloomsbury, 2006), 62.

6. Charlie Gillett, *The Sound of the City: The Rise of Rock and Roll*, revised and expanded edition (New York: Pantheon Books, 1983), 233; Joel Whitburn, *Top R&B Singles, 1942–1999* (Menomonee Falls, WI: Record Research, 2000), x; "Trade Debates Black Terminology," *Billboard*, February 25, 1989; "*Billboard* Adopts 'R&B' as New Name for 2 Charts," *Billboard*, October 27, 1990. Another article recounting the history of the black charts—"Saluting the Roots: Five Decades of R&B Hit-Makers," *Billboard*, June 12, 1993, special section, R3—omits any reference to the 1964 disappearance. See also Brian Ward, *Just My Soul Responding*, 174.

7. The ways in which these conventions are interpreted in terms of the category of R&B, and hence of black popular music, correspond in many respects to the descriptions of African American music found in the writings of (among others) Olly Wilson, "The Significance of the Relationship between Afro-American Music and West African Music," *The Black Perspective in Music* 2 (Spring 1974): 3–22; Pearl Williams-Jones, "Afro-American

Gospel Music: A Crystallization of the Black Aesthetic," *Ethnomusicology* 19, no. 3 (September 1975): 373–85; Portia Maultsby, "Soul Music: Its Sociological and Political Significance in American Popular Culture," *Journal of Popular Culture* 17, no. 2 (Fall 1983): 51–60; Portia Maultsby, "Africanisms in African-American Music," in *Africanisms in American Culture,* ed. Joseph E. Holloway (Bloomington: Indiana University Press, 1990), 185–210; Samuel A. Floyd "Ring Shout! Literary Studies, Historical Studies, and Black Music Inquiry," *Black Music Research Journal* 11, no. 2 (Fall 1991): 265–88; Samuel A. Floyd, *The Power of Black Music: Interpreting Its History from Africa to the United States* (New York: Oxford University Press, 1995).

8. This usage of "statistical causality" comes from Manuel DeLanda, *A New Philosophy of Society*, 21.

9. *Billboard* continued to publish an end-of-the-year chart for R&B for 1964 even though they had discontinued the weekly chart.

10. More subgenres and sub-generic connections are undoubtedly possible, and one could certainly quibble with my-as-yet-barely-stated criteria (which include musical style, performer identity and history, recording company, and record production values). Of these subgenres, girl groups have received the most scholarly attention. My description is indebted to the following: Barbara Bradby's notion of call and response, or conversation-like dialogue between lead singer and backup singers, in "Do-Talk and Don't-Talk: The Division of the Subject in Girl-Group Music," in *On Record: Rock, Pop and the Written Word,* ed. Simon Frith and Andrew Goodwin (New York: Pantheon, 1990), 341–68; Jacqueline Warwick, *Girl Groups, Girl Culture: Popular Music and Identity in the 1960s* (New York: Routledge, 2007); and Charlotte Greig, *Will You Still Love Me Tomorrow? Girl Groups from the '50s On* (London: Virago, 1989).

11. Of course, lyrics about unfaithful men are not specific to this period. I'm thinking here of lyrics in which a woman's friend or mother encourages her to be suspicious, which tend to reference the girl group genre. For example, in Maxine Brown's "Oh No, Not My Baby," the lyrics begin: "When my friends told me you had someone new / I didn't believe a single word was true." Other examples include Jan Bradley's "Mama Didn't Lie," the Sapphires' "Who Do You Love?," Mary Wells's "Two Lovers," and Skeeter Davis's "I Can't Stay Mad at You." Some songs preach acceptance of the no-good man, while others assert independence. Probably the most notorious example of this lyric type is the Crystals' "He Hit Me (and It Felt Like a Kiss), which, while sui generis in its over-the-top quality, can also be heard as a particularly extreme example of the type of female masochism presented in these other songs. For a more detailed analysis of this last recording, see Jacqueline Warwick, *Girl Groups, Girl Culture,* 66–70.

12. Bill Gavin, "No Musical Color Line," *Billboard,* April 25, 1964, 46. Some two years later, the *New York Times* offered this definition of R&B, once again displaying the centrality of race: "Rhythm-and-blues music [was] in the past, a trade euphemism for a kind of music performed by Negroes and sold mainly to a Negro market." This article notes that (as of 1966) "record-trade publications still maintain separate R&B charts, measuring air play by Negro-oriented radio stations and sales in predominantly Negro outlets." Richard H. Lingeman, "The Big, Happy, Beating Heart of the Detroit Sound," *New York Times Sunday Magazine,* November 27, 1966, 48, 162.

13. The comments on the Beatles in a column written by African American teenagers and published by the *Chicago Defender* at this time support Gavin's assertion. See "Platters," *Chicago Defender,* February 8, 1964, 16; "Platters," *Chicago Defender,* April 4, 1964, 17; "Platters," *Chicago Defender,* May 9, 1964, 16.

14. "'Soul' Disks Sell," *Cash Box,* May 16, 1964, 1.

15. Bob Dickinson, "Timi Yuro: Feisty White Singer with a Black Soul Voice," *The Guardian,* April 9, 2004, http://www.theguardian.com/news/2004/apr/10/guardianobituaries .artsobituaries1, accessed October 23, 2014.

16. Chris Molanphy, "I Know You Got Soul: The Trouble with *Billboard*'s R&B/Hip-Hop Chart," *Pitchfork,* April 14, 2014, http://pitchfork.com/features/articles/9378-i-know-you-got-soul-the-trouble-with-billboards-rbhip-hop-chart/, accessed October 26, 2014.

17. This history is recounted by several of *Cash Box*'s staff in John Broven, *Record Makers and Breakers: Voices of the Independent Rock 'n' Roll Pioneers* (Urbana and Chicago: University of Illinois Press, 2009), 187–207.

18. Sam Chase, "Charts Link New Clarity with Depth," *Billboard,* October 20, 1958, 3, 34.

19. The strangeness of this turn of events is highlighted by the admission by one of *Cash Box*'s editors of the time that "his editorial team used to eye *Billboard* charts to ensure there were no serious discrepancies with the *Cash Box* charts, and no doubt their rivals [i.e., *Billboard*'s editorial staff] did the same." John Broven, *Record Makers and Breakers,* 202.

20. For more on the relationship between African American popular music and MOR during this time, see Mark Burford, "Sam Cooke as Pop Album Artist—A Reinvention in Three Songs," *Journal of the American Musicological Society* 65, no. 1 (Spring 2012): 113–78; and Vincent Stephens, "Crooning on the Fault Lines: Theorizing Jazz and Pop Vocal Singing Discourses in Rock," *American Music* 26, no. 2 (Summer 2008): 156–95.

21. Bill Gavin, "No Musical Color Line"; "'Soul' Disks Sell."

22. "Billboard 1963 Radio Program Directors Survey," *Billboard,* April 6, 1963, 35.

23. Bob Hunter, "Radio Stations War for Negro Market," *Chicago Defender,* January 12, 1963, 6.

24. See Bill Gavin, "No Musical Color Line." In fact, an awareness of the importance of "negro radio" spread beyond that of its utility to Top 40 programmers to include that of advertising in general. An article in the *New York Times* published during this period stresses the importance of "Negro-oriented radio" in that these stations have "a personal relationship with local Negro communities that is unknown in general radio." William D. Smith, "Advertising: Drives Aim for Negro Market," *New York Times,* October 11, 1964, F14.

25. Bill Gavin, "No Musical Color Line"; "WWRL Example of Negro Radio's Vital Resurgence," *Billboard,* May 2, 1964, 12, 37; "Focus on the DJ Scene: The Magnificent Puts Soul Behind His Work," *Billboard,* May 23, 1964, 14, 39. This interest in the "negro market" did not necessarily find favor among African Americans. Only a year earlier the *Chicago Defender* had published Bob Hunter's article "Radio Stations War for Negro Market," arguing that the belief in the importance of radio for the African American community was a form of racism that implied illiteracy and the inability to resist advertising directed toward them.

26. Bill Gavin, "No Musical Color Line."

27. "WWRL Example of Negro Radio's Vital Resurgence." An article from almost a year later uses strikingly similar language to describe the argument for hiring African American DJs on Top 40 stations: "Negro deejays are actively seeking executive and on-the-air positions with other than Negro stations reasoning that many of the top-rated contemporary music stations are featuring a preponderance of r&b music and Negro recording artists. They should have a Negro deejay as well, they say." "Negro Radio an Ever-Increasing Influence," *Billboard*, March 27, 1965, 52, 54. On the NAACP's campaign in Philadelphia, see "NAACP Says: Hire Philly Air Negroes—Or Else," *Billboard*, November 30, 1963, 3.

28. "Negro Radio an Ever-Increasing Influence." As noted earlier, an article in the black press also predicted the eventual musical and social merger of African American and Euro-American "cultures." Bob Hunter, "Radio Stations War for Negro Market."

29. "WWRL Example of Negro Radio's Vital Resurgence."

30. "KGFJ Emphasizing Rhythm & Blues," *Billboard*, September 12, 1964, 14, 19; "WWRL Example of Negro Radio's Vital Resurgence." The discourse of a fear of reverse racism was not limited to *Billboard*; the *New York Times Sunday Magazine* published an article on Motown that, while noting that the company was "a predominantly Negro corporation," approvingly observed that "one sees a *healthy* sprinkling of white faces in every department." Richard H. Lingeman, "The Big, Happy, Beating Heart of the Detroit Sound," 162, my emphasis. Steve Chapple and Reebee Garofalo argue that "black stations were so squeezed for advertising dollars in the face of the predominance of white groups that they had no alternative but to add pop material to their playlists and in many cases hire white djs." Steve Chapple and Reebee Garofalo, *Rock 'n' Roll Is Here to Pay* (Chicago: Nelson-Hall, 1977), 249.

31. Claude Hall, "R&B Stations Open Airplay Gates to 'Blue-Eyed Soulists,'" *Billboard*, October 9, 1965, 1, 49.

32. "Billboard's R&B Section," *Billboard*, January 30, 1965, 14.

33. "Blues News," *Billboard*, January 30, 1965, 14; Chris Molanphy, "I Know You Got Soul."

34. Note that one of the major R&B hits of the year, "Shotgun," which was released on a Motown subsidiary called (not coincidentally) the Soul label, contained none of the above-mentioned concessions to pop. The Motown style itself was diverse, including the gospel-oriented records of Marvin Gaye, "Can I Get a Witness" and "Pride and Joy"; the intense crooning, rhythmic intricacy, and verbal wit of Smokey Robinson; and the updated doo-wop of the early Temptations, in addition to the recordings most resonant with the pop mainstream, such as the work of the Supremes and the Four Tops. For an early and thorough history of Motown, see Nelson George, *Where Did Our Love Go? The Rise and Fall of the Motown Sound* (New York: St. Martin's Press, 1985). For a detailed analysis of Motown songwriting and recording that debunks the myth of Motown's sameness and whitewashing, see Jon Fitzgerald, "Black or White: Stylistic Analysis of Early Motown Crossover Hits," *Popular Music* 14, no. 1 (January 1995): 1–11. For the most thorough scholarly musicological account of Motown, see Andrew Flory, *I Hear a Symphony: Listening to the Music of Motown* (Ann Arbor: University of Michigan Press, forthcoming). For a study of Motown in the context of the racial politics in Detroit during the 1960s, see Suzanne E. Smith, *Dancing in the Street: Motown and the Cultural Politics of Detroit* (Cambridge, MA: Harvard University Press, 1999).

35. Richard H. Lingeman, "The Big, Happy, Beating Heart of the Detroit Sound," 48, 162–71, 184. Not too surprisingly, the African American press had early on promoted Gordy and Motown as part of a general campaign of cultural uplift. See Bob Hunter, "Barry [sic] Gordy, Driving Force Behind Top Rock 'n' Roll Singers," *Chicago Defender*, May 14, 1963, 16. Gordy's own reflections can be found in Berry Gordy, *To Be Loved: The Music, the Magic, the Memories of Motown* (New York: Warner Books, 1994); and those by the Motown singer, songwriter, and bandleader Smokey Robinson in a 1968 interview: Michael Lydon, "Smokey Robinson," *Rolling Stone*, September 28, 1968, 21.

36. Elton Whisenhunt, "As 4 Musicmen See It: Memphis Sound: A Southern View," *Billboard*, June 12, 1965, 6. See also Peter Guralnick, *Sweet Soul Music*; Rob Bowman, *Soulsville U.S.A.: The Story of Stax Records* (New York: Schirmer Trade Books, 1997); Gerri Hirshey, *Nowhere to Run*; Jerry Wexler and David Ritz, *Rhythm and the Blues: A Life in American Music* (New York: St. Martin's Press, 1993), 169–78; Robert Gordon, *Respect Yourself.*

37. A *Cash Box* editorial, for example, declared 1963 the year of the international recording. This was the year of Kyu Sakamoto's "Sukiyaki" and the Singing Nun's (aka Soeur Sourire) "Dominique," both number one hits.

38. The quote comes from the producer Lou Adler in Eliot Tiegel, "Record of Absurd Gets Serious Play," *Billboard*, August 14, 1965, 1, 57. Such statements seem to overlook previous hits such as Peter, Paul, and Mary's recording of Bob Dylan's "Blowin' in the Wind," which soared to number two on the B100 in the summer of 1963. See also Elliot Tiegel, "Folkswinging Wave On—Courtesy of Rock Groups," *Billboard*, June 12, 1965, 1, 10.

39. Nick Biro, "'Eve of Destruction' Has Its Day," *Billboard*, August 21, 1965, 12; "Destruction Causes Furor," *Billboard*, September 4, 1965, 55.

40. Eliot Tiegel, "West Coast Clamors for Dylan Tunes," *Billboard*, September 4, 1965, 12, 47. The impact of folk-rock was such that it caused the *New York Times* to depart from its former, almost exclusively condescending approach to popular music in an August 11, 1965, article by Robert Shelton ("The Beatles Will Make the Scene Here Again"). Several months later, a pair of articles appeared in the *New York Times* that recognized Bob Dylan's special status, including another article by Shelton, who could now explain the difference between authentic and non-authentic folk-rock to his readers: see Robert Shelton, "On Records: The Folk-Rock Rage," January 30, 1966, X21–22; and Thomas Meehan, "Public Writer No. 1? Because of Dylan, Song Hits Now Are About War, Not Love," *New York Times Sunday Magazine*, December 12, 1965, 44–45, 130, 132–36. Further attesting to Dylan's specific capital at this moment, another feature article appeared in late 1965 in another New York daily: "A Night with Bob Dylan," *Sunday Herald Tribune Magazine*, December 12, 1965, 8–13.

41. For a more detailed examination of how certain characteristic musical gestures of folk-rock excised connotations of musical blackness, see David Brackett, "Elvis Costello, the Empire of the E Chord, and a Magic Moment or Two," *Popular Music* 24, no. 3 (October 2005): 357–67. For other discussions of folk-rock in terms of the redistribution of symbolic capital, see Bernard Gendron, *Between Montmartre and the Mudd Club: Popular Music and the Avant-Garde* (Chicago and London: University of Chicago Press, 2002), 180–87; and Keir Keightley, "Reconsidering Rock," in *The Cambridge Companion to Pop and Rock*, ed. Simon Frith, Will Straw, and John Street (Cambridge: Cambridge University Press, 2001), 109–42. Elijah Wald makes a similar argument in *How the Beatles Destroyed Rock 'n' Roll: An*

Alternative History of American Popular Music (New York: Oxford University Press, 2009), 230–47.

42. Alfred Gell, *Art and Agency* (Oxford: Oxford University Press, 1998). For the application of this concept to music, see Georgina Born, "On Musical Mediation: Ontology, Technology and Creativity," *twentieth-century music* 2, no. 1 (2005): 7–36.

43. John Broven, *Record Makers and Breakers*, 201.

44. Portia Maultsby, "Soul Music," 51.

45. "Think" from *Live at the Apollo* (1962) reveals that he was already using arrangements similar to this in live performance as early as 1962. "Out of Sight" from the TAMI show, recorded in 1964, is another clear, pre-1965 example.

46. See the discussion of "musematic repetition" in Richard Middleton, *Studying Popular Music* (Milton Keynes, England: Open University Press, 1990), 269–84.

47. The variation in verse 3 of "I Can't Help Myself" is necessitated by the lyrics and does not result from the kind of extemporaneous variation technique employed by Brown and Pickett.

48. James Brown (with Bruce Tucker), *The Godfather of Soul* (New York: MacMillan, 1986), 158.

49. See Bill Gavin's observations earlier about how popularity charts routinely underrepresented the sales of R&B recordings due to the greater prevalence of slow but steady sales patterns in R&B in "No Musical Color Line."

50. Lerone Bennett Jr., "The Soul of Soul," *Ebony* (December 1961): 112–16. Bennett observes that "qualities deemed soulful" could also be described as "funky" (112). Subsequent citations of this article will be noted by page numbers in parentheses.

51. "Focus on the DJ Scene: The Magnificent Puts Soul Behind His Work," *Billboard*, May 23, 1964, 14, 39.

52. "Rock 'n' Roll Becomes Respectable," *Ebony* (November 1965): 52. It is possible that *Ebony* is celebrating sequences such as what occurred on *Shindig*'s August 18, 1965, broadcast. Sherman was featured during the "Bo Diddley Medley" on the show, a performance that also included several other white performers—the Shindogs, Jay P. Mobey, Eddie Hodges, Glen Campbell—and Bo Diddley himself, see http://www.youtube.com/watch?v = dcBIop5VHhE, accessed October 30, 2012. Such a usage of "rock 'n' roll" was not unique to *Ebony*, however. Robert Shelton, in a portrait of the panorama of popular music in mid-1965, describes the "Detroit sound" (i.e., Motown) as "the strongest element of American rock 'n' roll" ("The Beatles Will Make the Scene Here Again"). Multiple articles from the *Chicago Defender* during this time provide further examples of the elision between the terms "rhythm and blues" and "rock 'n' roll." Among others, see Bob Hunter, "Barry [*sic*] Gordy, Driving Force Behind Top Rock 'n' Roll Singers."

53. "Martha and the Vandellas, No. 2," *Jet*, April 21, 1966, 60–63. See also "Spotlight Singles, Pop Spotlights, Top 60: Martha & the Vandellas—Never Leave Your Baby's Side," *Billboard*, January 15, 1966, 63; "Spotlight Singles, R&B Spotlights, Top 10: Sam and Dave—It Feels So Nice," *Billboard*, March 5, 1966, 12. Whether or not a release appeared in the pop or R&B section of "Spotlight Singles" seemed to depend on the crossover history of the artist.

54. Two collections that were instrumental in circulating the creative and theoretical work of the Black Arts movement were LeRoi Jones (Amiri Baraka) and Larry Neal, eds.,

Black Fire: An Anthology of Afro-American Writing (Baltimore: Black Classic Press, 2007) (originally published in 1968); and Addison Gayle, ed., *The Black Aesthetic* (New York: Doubleday, 1971). Baraka was one of the central figures (some would say *the* central figure) in the movement. His writings on music from the period were collected in *Black Music* (New York: William Morrow, 1968).

55. "Sweet Soul Music" name-checks the soul canon: Lou Rawls, Sam and Dave, Wilson Pickett, Otis Redding, James Brown.

56. Robert Shelton, "Otis Redding Stars in 2 Park Concerts," *New York Times,* August 18, 1966, 28.

57. Rob Bowman, *Soulsville U.S.A.,* 128.

58. Richard H. Lingeman, "The Big, Happy, Beating Heart of the Detroit Sound," 48.

59. "Editorial: R&B Now Soul," *Billboard,* August 23, 1969, 3.

60. Ibid.

61. Within popular music studies, one of the best-known (and oft-cited) examples of such anti-essentialist reasoning is Philip Tagg, "Open Letter: Black Music, Afro-American Music, and European Music," *Popular Music* 8, no. 3 (1989): 285–98.

8

Crossover Dreams

*From Urban Cowboy to
the King of Pop*

"We're living in a crossover era." So proclaimed Ricky Schultz, national promotion manager for the Warner Bros. jazz division in a 1981 *Billboard* article.[1] This casual usage of the term "crossover" referred to a shift in music industry discourse that had occurred during the previous decade. Despite my somewhat anachronistic usage of the term in earlier chapters to track musical and social boundaries in popular music categories, the term itself only really came into vogue in music industry discussions in the period immediately preceding Schultz's quote.

Since entering everyday discourse about popular music, the concept of crossover has steadily gained in cultural visibility. It has experienced an enormous spurt in popularity over the last twenty years, spanning a wide range of media: television (crossover events between connected television series, such as episodes of *Buffy the Vampire Slayer* and its spinoff, *Angel,* in the late 1990s and early 2000s), automotive advertising (car-based SUVs called "crossover vehicles"), and sports (the popular and difficult basketball maneuver, the crossover dribble).[2] In the context of popular music, however, a film released in 1985, *Crossover Dreams,* directs our attention to a historical moment in which the crossover concept had already achieved a high degree of cultural legibility.[3]

Crossover Dreams narrates a tale of a *salsero,* played by the real-life salsa musician Rubén Blades, and his efforts to cross over, which in this case means attempting to broaden his audience by courting mainstream success in the United States. In the course of the film, a dilemma emerges: Will Rudy Veloz (the character played by Blades) remain true to his musical roots, his audience of salsa fans, and his friends from the barrio, or "dilute" his music in an attempt to gain fans (and friends) who are not necessarily part of his core audience of salsa lovers?[4] The opposition between commercial opportunism and personal authenticity based on a truth to an inner self (which often implies a racial essence shared with the audience) is a familiar one in popular music scholarship and cultural studies. But how did we arrive at this point, where a film could take as its theme the crisis brought on by the decision to cross or not cross musical categories? Before analyzing the conditions of possibility for *Crossover Dreams* (as well as for the headline that opened this chapter), we will retrace the emergence of the crossover concept into the quotidian lexicon of music critics and music industry agents. The chapter will then explore how the crossover concept played out in both the country and the soul music categories at the beginning of the 1980s.

A BRIEF HISTORY OF CROSSOVER

The dilemma narrated in *Crossover Dreams* was anything but new. In fact, this particular debate around authenticity, which binds together questions about the artist's motivations and the ties between identity and genre, is virtually indissociable from the rise of the concept of crossover itself in the fifteen years preceding the film's release. Firmly establishing itself as a common term in music industry discourse in the years 1971 and 1972, discussion of the concept exploded in 1973 and 1974, during which time it attained something of the same everyday ubiquity it currently enjoys.

Before the term began to be used in this fashion, however, a number of barely perceptible moves had to be made that date back to the emergence of rock 'n' roll as a popular music genre during the years 1955 and 1956. Rock 'n' roll, in addition to upending many music industry verities, generated a new form of interest focused on the relationship between music and racial identity. Even in these somewhat distant and indistinct beginnings, rock 'n' roll encouraged media writers to think of the crossing of music-categorical boundaries as the transgression of social categories in a way that the boundary blurrings and crossings of earlier decades had not.[5] Usages of "crossover" to refer to the movement between musical categories were far and few between in the period from the late 1950s up to the early 1970s. Nevertheless, its continued and regular, albeit sparse, usage to describe movement from the rhythm and blues and country categories to mainstream pop suggests a broadly understood acceptance of the term.

A new era for crossover dawned at the beginning of 1971, instituting a far-ranging shift in the usage of the term, both with respect to its frequency and the discursive topoi with which it was associated. The initial boost responded to the mainstream popularity of country songs such as Lynn Anderson's "Rose Garden," Ray Price's "For the Good Times," and Sammi Smith's "Help Me Make It Through the Night." By 1972 the term was being used more frequently, not only to describe country to pop movement, but to refer to boundary crossing that included a wide range of categories such as soul, Latin, classical, jazz, and MOR (middle-of-the-road).

During this period debates arose about the effect of crossover. Formerly seen as an unalloyed benefit for the minority categories of rhythm and blues and country (with occasional mention of other genres, such as gospel), a more conflictual view began to emerge. The minority categories of country and soul music were recognized as expressing some essential quality of the identity of those assumed to be participating in those musics. At its most basic, the quest for popularity might thus be seen to compromise the ability of a category to act as the mouthpiece of a demographic group.[6] This debate—anticipating the movie *Crossover Dreams,* and relying on notions of the homological purity of certain genres—differed from the discussions about the R&B radio format during the period of 1963 to 1965 discussed in the last chapter, in which the argument for the continued survival of African American–oriented radio hinged on its utility for the African American community.

The uneasiness over crossover could also have an economic component. Once viewed as a positive commercial force, crossover was now occasionally viewed as dulling the force of separate, competing markets. In other articles from this period, crossover was criticized for having a homogenizing effect on radio stations; if a high percentage of recordings were to cross over from soul and country to Top 40, then "country and soul stations may lose some audience" and "a good portion of their uniqueness."[7] Another, similar objection was raised that concerned the motivations and target audiences of producers and musicians. Charges about motivations, which took the form of accusations about selling out, could be countered by reassurances (to R&B producers and consumers, at any rate) that when recordings "become large sized r&b hits they usually go pop."[8]

By 1973 soul music in particular had begun to receive a great deal of attention, as many record companies who had formerly ignored black popular music scrambled to create soul music divisions in response to the notorious Harvard Report.[9] The term "crossover" traveled into unforeseen territory, becoming the name of a record company founded by Ray Charles as well as the main topic of music industry conferences and large corporate meetings. The apparent increase in the number of crossover artists and recordings created a crisis in the music industry in which the process of crossover could be blamed for creating problems of classification. The screening committee for the 1974 Grammy awards had difficulty deciding into which category the recordings of artists such as Stevie Wonder and Barry White should be put, leading to the notion that the categories should be abolished.[10]

The question arises: Why 1973? Why would the concept of crossover, which had lain dormant, or at best been invoked sporadically for some fifteen years, suddenly take hold during the years from 1971 to 1974 (with 1973 representing a tipping point of sorts) and become ubiquitous? Why did the arguments about crossover, pro and con, consolidate into the terms that have dictated the debate ever since? In addition to soul music, the answers to these questions would have to address the role of country music, which, as we have seen, also figured prominently in discussions of crossover in the early 1970s. Might the interest in crossover have to do with the consolidation of the categories themselves, their synchronization? Examining these questions first at the level of popularity charts reveals that both the country and the soul charts expanded to one hundred positions in July 1973, responding to the growth of the industrial apparatus supporting these types of music and the resultant increase in the number of recordings circulating through the apparatus. Could this stability of the apparatus for the promotion and circulation of the different musics, which in some respects heightened and strengthened the sense of a boundary between categories, have been a factor in the perception that recordings were crossing over more?

The answer to this question is not very promising, for in terms of how many recordings from the soul or country chart appeared on the Hot 100, one cannot really observe any significant change from the mid-1960s up through the years in question. After all, as we already saw in the last chapter, the disappearance of the rhythm and blues chart for fourteen months from November 1963 to January 1965 was also retroactively explained by the claim that so many recordings were crossing over that a separate chart wasn't needed. So, why, then, 1973?

The heightened discourse of crossover responded in part to the increased range of tastes within the mainstream popular music audience, a symptom of what popular music histories have described as the splintering of that audience at the turn of the 1970s. This divide in the audience, which has often been read as generational, responded to the extension of popular music fandom past the teenage years, and to a corresponding growth in the audience, which became internally divided by age. Discussed in the previous chapter as the split of white rock (in the form of folk-rock and the British Invasion) from African American–associated genres, the continued involvement of fans with popular music well into adulthood corresponded to the cultural legitimation of certain popular music genres in the wake of the success of the Beatles and Bob Dylan, while other forms of popular music (particularly genres directed to younger audiences) failed to gain the same level of critical acclaim.

Another possibility is that the appearance of increased discourse around the idea of crossover responded to changes in how categories were understood and in how they were functioning, but that had not yet materialized in the appearance of actual popularity charts. In other words, the discourse of crossover may have been responding to the sense that the categories as they existed were insufficient to map the practices of musicians and consumers. Here it is instructive to examine relationships of scale, particularly that of radio formats to the marketing categories with which popularity charts were most closely related. The chaos that existed in

Top 40 radio in the early 1970s suggests a restructuring of the field at the level of radio format. Top 40 in the early 1970s was characterized by an extreme form of eclecticism. Don and Jeff Breithaupt, authors of *Precious and Few: Pop Music in the Early '70s,* offer the following pithy observation:

> These were the last days of radio's unformatted innocence; MOR, country, bubble-gum, hard rock, folk, soul, and sundry oddities could coexist on an urban playlist with no fear of listener backlash.[11]

"Unformatted innocence": described longingly here as the last glimpse of Top 40 paradise before the descent into hyperformatted radio hell, this quote captures the range of music that could still be contained in the "mainstream."

The reshuffling of radio formats, of which the eclecticism of the Top 40 was a symptom, responded to an increase in demographic research among advertisers interested in radio. This development in turn anticipated the expansion of popularity charts and factored into the new interest in crossover. If the actual number of types of formats did not increase during this period, the attempts to delimit the audience for these formats became more energetic, creating sharper format-audience boundaries as well as narrower and newer homological relations. Following from the aforementioned generational split among white audiences, the audience was further specified along the lines of gender, with MOR targeting adult women and underground or progressive radio targeting white males over the age of eighteen. Top 40, presumably, was left to cobble together the remainder, which resulted in the hodgepodge noted by Don and Jeff Breithaupt above, and a newfound openness to music appealing to young teens and preteens.[12] Country and soul radio also received interest for their ability to deliver demographic segments whose tastes could be measured and known with a new degree of precision.[13]

If this splintering and formatting of the audience did factor into a discourse of crossover and a new way of conceptualizing categories, this did not appear in actual labeling practice until the late 1970s. The division of the Top 40 radio format was signaled by the emergence as the decade proceeded of new formats (consecrated at the music industry level by popularity charts) such as "Rock Singles Best Sellers," "Rock LPs Best Sellers," "Album Radio Action Chart List," and "Disco Action Top 40." The discourse of crossover and discussions about the splintering of the audience earlier in the decade, and the increased attention to defining radio formats, thus appeared to anticipate the formation of new marketing categories. The racial politics of this splintering can be gleaned from observing that of the four new categories listed above, three explicitly referred to (white) rock, while one was dedicated to disco (the racial connotations of which were not primarily white). While disco recordings came to dominate the pop charts, and even required their own chart, other forms of African American–identified music began to be excluded, especially in radio programming, where all-disco formats and pressure on DJs in black radio to play more disco increased the homogeneity of the African American–associated music heard over the airwaves.

Another impact of the splintering was the fact that it became more difficult to find a mainstream or a center with which to contrast the margins. Mike Harrison, writing for *Billboard* in 1980, even attempted to redefine what crossover meant on this basis, describing how the process had changed because no one radio format was capable of representing the mainstream any longer:

> Now, on the fractionalized playing-board of the widening mainstream, in which the various standard formats of radio and music particularly want to be different from each other on the levels of lifestyle and image, all records start out as specialty items.
>
> Crossover simply takes place when the record gains acceptance in another (perhaps, neighboring) minority-genre.
>
> There is no longer a monolithic, unofficial national network of homogeneous, mass appeal, monster radio stations. There is, thus, no singular on-air step or path to mass-appeal acceptance.[14]

Although the radio format and popularity chart associated with the idea of the mainstream may have ceased to represent the mainstream on a statistical basis, sites such as the Hot 100 popularity chart and the Top 40 radio format (or contemporary hit radio, as it was coming to be called) continued to evoke the mainstream in a symbolic sense in order to convey mass acceptance. These symbolic sites of mass acceptance were reinforced during the early 1980s by the initial programming choices that were made for MTV, a topic that will be explored in greater detail later in this chapter. At any rate, the rhetoric of Harrison contrasts mightily with that of the Breithaupts, in which the mainstream acquired its meaning on account of its inner heterogeneity, and speaks to a shift in the organization of the popular music field (especially in the domain of radio formatting) that transpired during the 1970s.

Discussions of crossover figured prominently in music industry discourse about both country music and soul music in the early 1980s. The *Urban Cowboy* phenomenon, led by the movie of the same name and numerous Top 40 radio–friendly country tunes, created a boom in country music crossover to pop from 1980 to 1982. The value of these crossover recordings in terms of the identity of country music and the relations of crossover to country music's core audience were debated extensively. During that same period, the idea of a barrier that prevented recordings by African American musicians from having access to mainstream channels of distribution received increased attention. As this discussion has already demonstrated, the debate over the value of crossover has a history dating back to the late 1960s. In the 1980s, however, the debate took on a more urgent tone and assumed a higher public profile, with several writers at *Billboard,* including Nelson George most prominently, drawing attention to the racial politics of crossover.

URBAN COWBOY: CROSSOVER AND GENDER IN EARLY 1980S COUNTRY

Returning now to the period when this chapter began, we find that a generalized rhetoric of crossover filled the trade magazines at the dawn of the 1980s. Few discussions of radio formats were complete without mention of the term, which found its way into profiles of record companies, retailers, and distributors of soul, country, jazz, Latin, and disco recordings. In the midst of this heated rhetoric, a movie appeared in the summer of 1980 that fleshed out discussions of crossover with a narrative and, at the same time, appeared to add sociological depth. *Urban Cowboy's* plot derived from a profile of a "new phenomenon" published in 1978 by Aaron Latham, in which Latham described how "non-country cowboys" working in the petrochemical industry in the Houston area had begun to participate in a scene based around Gilley's nightclub, the self-proclaimed largest honky-tonk in the world.[15] Latham mentions the importance of music in passing, but devotes most of the article to detailing the war between the sexes among the participants in the scene, as well as the central importance of a peculiar ritual consisting of riding a mechanical bull. This activity, in Latham's account, becomes a symbol (and a near enactment) of castration. Men ride it even though "a honky-tonk cowboy has to risk his manhood in order to prove it" (22). As Latham describes in excruciating detail, the act of riding the bull results in pain due to repeated violent contact between the bull and the male participant's private parts. Women, due to their anatomical advantage, delight in outriding the men and taunting them with their superiority (25).

The conflict over mechanical bull riding is central to the movie, which is based on a script by Latham and James Bridges derived from the article. The film melds the acts described in the article with a Hollywood romantic narrative that achieves the closure left dangling by the article's description of its subjects' relationships. Certain elements at which the article barely hints are augmented in the movie, as characters are mapped onto social vectors such as class, attitudes toward gender roles, relationship to patriarchal authority, and fashion sense. These social positions are in turn related to genre positions within the field of country music.[16] Table 15 details these oppositions and correspondences among the primary characters in the film: the main couple, Bud and Sissy (Dew and Betty in the article), Wes (Steve), and Pam (Jan). This table provides a particularly clear example of how Pierre Bourdieu's notion of cultural capital (which theorizes the relationship between class, educational background, and taste in consumption and leisure) is related to long-held associations between mass culture and femininity, gender roles in general, and popular music genres.[17] The most important oppositions within the world of *Urban Cowboy* lie between crossover/modern/pop-country and two other genres: real/hard/traditional country and soft rock/adult contemporary. These oppositions are in turn articulated to the opposition in Latham's

TABLE 15   Socio-Musical Oppositions and Correspondences in *Urban Cowboy*

Character	Pam	Bud, Sissy	Wes
Music Genre	soft-rock / adult contemporary	all styles of country music ca. 1980, especially pop-country	hard country
Class	upscale, bourgeois	working-class, poor, but good-hearted (upwardly mobile?)	criminal, evil, a bad sport
Diet and Drink	drinks wine and eats beef stroganoff	drink Budweiser, eat lots of fried food and mayonnaise	similar food/drink pattern as Bud and Sissy, but eats worm out of mescal bottle
Makeup and Apparel	wears more makeup than Sissy, and wears a cowboy hat less often	cowboy hats and western apparel	cowboy hats and western apparel
Gender Aspects	feminine, "cunning, devious"	Sissy is a tomboy, wants to ride the mechanical bull; Bud likes to dance, is insecure about his masculinity	macho, confident in his masculinity

article between "non-country cowboys" (pop-country, adult contemporary) and "country cowboys" (hard country).

As mentioned earlier, *Urban Cowboy* was perceived at the time as sparking a wave of crossover country hits. The movie appeared to endorse the crossover process, as Bud and Sissy come to affirm the value of pop-country through Bud's rejection of Pam (soft rock / adult contemporary) and Sissy's rejection of Wes (traditional country), and through Bud and Sissy's subsequent reunification with each other. The soundtrack of the movie included numerous crossovers, including Johnny Lee's "Lookin' for Love," Mickey Gilley's (the namesake of Gilley's honky-tonk) cover of "Stand by Me," Charlie Daniels's "The Devil Went Down to Georgia" (already a crossover hit in 1979), and Kenny Rogers's "Love the World Away." On the level of cinematic genres, *Urban Cowboy* cited the best-known blockbuster film of the era featuring music and dance, *Saturday Night Fever*. *Urban Cowboy* achieved this referentiality through the casting of John Travolta, the actor who played the protagonist Bud in *Saturday Night Fever,* and the many scenes in *Urban Cowboy* centered around dancing in a nightclub. However much the movie may have called attention to the crossover phenomenon via citation, the soundtrack also produced its crossover effects by entering into a field of discourse in which music industry agents were already obsessed about the pros and cons of broadening the demographic of country's audience.

At the level of radio formats, programming directors were torn over whether seeking a younger demographic via pop-country would alienate their older listeners who valued traditional country. The music industry press discussed a spectrum of subgenres mainly in terms of the artists who were perceived to participate in them, with "modern" artists including Dolly Parton, Ronnie Milsap, Eddie Rabbitt, Kenny Rogers, the Oak Ridge Boys, Reba McEntire, and Dottie West, and "traditional" artists including Jeannie Pruett, John Anderson, Moe Bandy, Johnny Cash, Tammy Wynette, Merle Haggard, George Jones, and the duo of Porter Wagoner and Dolly Parton (again).[18] At the far end of the traditional side of the spectrum lay artists who might evoke a negative hillbilly image such as Ernest Tubb, Slim Whitman, and Kitty Wells, an image that some country radio stations were trying to expunge. While expansion of the audience was generally viewed in a positive light, doubts tended to surface around the identity of country music and the value of crossover-oriented country. After all, as one program director put it, "a lot of crossover isn't worth it. There are few Kenny Rogers [sic] around." In the even more pointed words of another program director, "What scares me is everybody jumping on the crossover bandwagon. I don't want to see country music lose its identity. When Porter Wagoner starts doing disco, you start to worry."[19]

The invocation of disco as the ultimate emblem of sellout crossover is telling, especially within the context of discussions of identity. For if anything did not correspond to the traditional, patriarchal, heteronormative, and white (by default) connotations of traditional country, it was disco. The style elements of country might overlap with and participate in album-oriented rock (AOR), 1950s-era rock 'n' roll, and adult contemporary, at times to such an extent that these interminglings went virtually unnoticed (except to acquire "crossover," "modern," and "pop" as prefixes in discourse around country music). But the great terra incognita, the mixtures that remained unthinkable, were those blendings that involved contemporary black-associated genres.[20] And although funk or soul could have served almost as well to express the writer's distaste for what Porter Wagoner's imaginary future held, disco filled the role particularly well due to its abject status in relation not only to country, but to almost every other genre currently participating in the popular music field. This was, after all, the era of "disco sucks" rhetoric, attributable as much to disco's domination of the field at the beginning of the 1980s as to the homophobia generated by its association with gay identity.[21]

Discussions about country music in music industry discourse revealed sensitivity to music-stylistic elements that did and did not participate in a country music assemblage. Instrumentation in particular seems to have been recognized as important to the genre. Indeed, for one seeking historical continuity with previous citations of country music dating back to the 1940s, one need look no further than to how the almost magical properties of the steel (or pedal steel) guitar and fiddle could confer country-ness on songs that otherwise would blend seamlessly into other categories. The issue of instrumentation arose within the context of discussions about crossover when the country producer Ron Chancey "debated for several days before adding the strong horn fills to the Oak Ridge Boys' 'Elvira.'" "Elvira" hit the top of the country charts in April 1981, and rose to number five on *Billboard*'s Hot 100 (the B100) evidently confirming the correctness of Chancey's decision. He admitted as much, recognizing that "the horns were one of the single's most potent crossover factors."[22] Elsewhere, the rhetoric of genre was used to indicate the stylistic elements that would create crossover country hits, as when Elektra-Asylum board chair Joe Smith emphasized that a "continuing influx of *pop* producers into Nashville, coupled with increasing use of *rock 'n' roll* techniques in studio sessions, [would] be the key to strengthening the city's visage as a full-scale recording center."[23]

Awareness of the participation of individual recordings in multiple categories, as well as the sharing of elements between categories, surfaced especially with regard to the relationship between country and adult contemporary. Adult contemporary (or AC), the descendent of easy listening and MOR, had greatly expanded its generic range during the 1970s, and had developed by the early 1980s a type of ballad that easily traversed not only the country and mainstream categories, but soul music as well.[24] The crossover hits from *Urban Cowboy* benefited from this easy fraternizing between country and AC, both of which shared an emphasis on an adult demographic.[25] For example, the popularity of Johnny Lee's "Lookin' for Love" (Country: 1; B100: 5; AC: 10)—a song that, in the course of playing repeatedly in the movie, became a kind of leitmotif for Bud and Sissy—"result[ed] from the fact that the song received much crossover airplay on both pop and adult contemporary stations." Indeed, the AC radio format was seen as central to the crossover process and as "the most successful radio format of the 1980s" because of its "broad flexibility for playing crossover hits" (not to mention its appeal to the coveted twenty-five to forty-nine, mostly female, demographic).[26] The music supervisor of *Urban Cowboy*, Becky Shargo, discussed how she "updated" Mickey Gilley and Johnny Lee by pairing them with pop producers to "get them in a crossover situation so they could have more appeal." Shargo also mentioned how the source music (i.e., underscoring) for the film was selected because the producers were "leaning toward a pop audience."[27]

Kenny Rogers vs. Merle Haggard

Kenny Rogers, another artist already mentioned as the archetypal country crossover case, scored a crossover hit on the *Urban Cowboy* soundtrack with his ballad "Love the World Away" (Country: 4; B100: 14; AC: 8), as did Mickey Gilley with his cover version of the Ben E. King number from 1961 "Stand by Me" (Country: 1; B100: 22; AC: 3). The appearance of these country songs in the Hot 100 was abetted by the close relationship between pop-country and adult contemporary. Of these artists, Rogers had mastered this particular marriage of style and audience earlier and more consistently than the others. Beginning with the song "The Gambler" in 1978, Rogers had AC hits even on songs that more strongly evoked a (non-pop) country musical style, such as "Coward of the County" (1979). Having appeared in *The Gambler* earlier in 1980—a successful made-for-TV movie based on the song with the same title that further expanded his audience—nothing could derail the crossover juggernaut that was Kenny Rogers. His momentum, with its voracious taste for gobbling up ever-larger audiences, reached its apotheosis on his release following "Love the World Away": a recording of "Lady," a song written by Lionel Richie.

"Lady," at the time of its release, drew from the lingua franca of AC ballads with its modal harmony, quasi-rubato rhythm, and prominent use of instruments and effects such as harp, piano, English horn, recurrent cymbal swells, and strings. Although the texts participating in adult contemporary and country overlapped significantly, certain stylistic elements of "Lady" were about as non-country as could be (see musical examples 26 and 27). One of the more striking of these elements (in addition to those just mentioned) was the key of E-flat minor. Given the prevalence of guitar-friendly sharp keys in country, such as G major, D major, A major, and E major, E-flat minor would require a technique not familiar to many country guitarists (or, at the very least, the use of a capo), as would the chord changes themselves, including such non-country-ish chords as major sus and minor sevenths. The rhythm of "Lady," too, would tend to occlude stereotypical country procedures, featuring as it does constant complex subdivisions of the beat, lack of accent on the beat, and a tendency toward rubato—all characteristics common to a pop ballad style. The instrumentation also fails to include the most obvious timbral signifiers of country music, including fiddle, pedal steel guitar, and trebly electric guitars (usually made by the Fender company).

It is true, however, that the history of ballads categorized as country without overt country stylistic elements has a long pedigree, and stretches back at least as far as countrypolitan songs of the late 1950s and early 1960s, which would include recordings by Jim Reeves, Patsy Cline, and Skeeter Davis, and such big crossover hits as Glen Campbell's 1967 recording "By the Time I Get to Phoenix."[28] And this list does not even include earlier country recordings with strong mainstream leanings such as those by Vernon Dalhart in the 1920s and Eddy Arnold in the 1940s. Nor does it acknowledge the foundational stylistic hybridity of the country music category in the 1920s, as discussed in chapter 4. As with many of these examples, the identity of "Lady" as a country song depends on the citation of the performer's identity as a country performer, and whatever vestiges of country vocal twang that were not eliminated in the production. It also results from the gradual transformation of the category of country itself as it interacted increasingly over time with the AC category, a transformation that can be traced back to the early 1970s.[29]

MUSICAL EXAMPLE 26. "Lady," First Section

MUSICAL EXAMPLE 27. "Lady," Second Section

The compositional pedigree of "Lady" does add a new twist, however, to this history of impurity. Written by Lionel Richie for Rogers, the song traded on both Rogers's history of crossover success and Richie's track record with the Commodores, who had scored success on the soul, Hot 100, and AC charts with "Three Times a Lady" (1978), "Sail On" (1979), and "Still" (1979). Richie's identification as an African American and his prior participation in the soul music category even brought associations of African American popular music into play (Rogers's "Lady" hit number forty-two on the soul chart). This instance of crossover thus goes beyond previous acts of citationality in that it cites multiple performer identities (Rogers and Richie) that created a hybrid text that was already mixing categories that were already perceived as hybrid on multiple levels.[30]

If Rogers's "Lady" represents the extreme soft rock and AC end of the country spectrum, another recording, ascending to number one on the country charts seven weeks after "Lady," just as surely represents the hard country end of it. Merle

MUSICAL EXAMPLE 28. "I'll Just Stay Here and Drink," First Verse

Haggard's "I Think I'll Just Stay Here and Drink" hearkens back to the honky-tonk subgenre of the late 1940s and early 1950s, with a sound and lyrics that reference recordings by Hank Williams and Lefty Frizzell. The topic cites many previous country recordings, bearing a strong resemblance to a song like Webb Pierce's "There Stands the Glass" from 1953. In addition to this, "I Think I'll Just Stay Here and Drink" cites the topic of a whole string of singles that Haggard had released immediately before, including "Bar Room Buddies" and "Misery and Gin." Other stylistic elements cite those often associated with non-crossover country, be it hard or traditional or honky-tonk; these include blues tonality in the accompaniment and a predominantly pentatonic melody, featuring lowered third and seventh scale degrees in the melody (measures 14–15) with corresponding use of a dominant seventh as the IV chord; a vocal timbre stressing Southern regionalism; instrumentation relying on electric guitars, probably Fenders; and extended improvised solos with frequent blues inflections (see musical example 28).

The non-crossover sound of "I Think I'll Just Stay Here and Drink" projected stylistic elements that lay outside the mainstream at this time and thus indicated a distinct country assemblage when "country" was conceptualized in relation to the rest of the popular music field. Elements of the country assemblage thereby would include pedal steel guitar, fiddle, trebly electric guitars made by the Fender company, voices with a Southern twang, a groove with even eighths, lyric themes about drinking, failed relationships, and regret, the reification of emotions into objects, and performers previously identified as country performers.[31] All previous caveats about the exteriority of relations between these components still apply—they could all participate in other assemblages, and recordings lacking some (or possibly all) of the components could participate in country. It is the distinctive interaction of some or all of these components that would differentiate a country recording from the rest of the popular music field at this moment.

FROM SOUL TO BLACK AND BEYOND

The crossover process played out somewhat differently for African American popular music during the early 1980s. Part of the significance of this period was created by what didn't happen during the five years immediately preceding it. Indeed, the mid- to late 1970s were notable for the rarity of crossovers between the soul chart and the B100; this lack of chart crossover was paralleled by the segregation of the radio formats most directly associated with these charts. Although songs moved regularly between the R&B-soul chart and the Hot 100 or mainstream pop chart from the mid-1960s through the mid-1970s, the developments that appeared to aid country music—such as the easy mixing between country, AC, and mainstream rock—worked against the inclusion of black popular music in other categories as the 1970s progressed. Some of the issues at play in the discourse around country music, such as a concern with radio formats, also figured prominently in the circulation of black popular music during this time. As with the relationship of R&B to the mainstream in the 1960s, arguments were made for and against the maintenance of boundaries, often under the guise of promoting a race-neutral mode of musical categorization that would rely only on the sound of a recording and not take public knowledge of the performer's racial identity into account.

Race-neutral terminology most decidedly did not factor into the latest shakeup in the popularity charts. After thirteen years as the "Soul" chart, Billboard's chart for African American popular music changed to "Black" in the June 26, 1982, issue. The explanations given provide evidence that institutional memory is not particularly prized by trade magazines, and that causal analysis can prove exceedingly difficult at close historical range. The magazine's own anonymous statement averred that the change "reflect[ed] the diverse nature of music which that field now encompasses" (3). In the same issue, the black music editor, Nelson George, echoed this view by emphasizing "the eclectic nature of black music today" (43). George expanded on the general notion of eclecticism by giving some specifics: "Any list that can accommodate the pop-rock of [Ray Parker's] 'The Other Woman,' the hard funk of [the Gap Band's] 'Early in the Morning,' the MOR-ish 'Making

Love' [by Roberta Flack] and the avant-garde rap of [Afrika Bambaataa and Soul Sonic Force's] 'Planet Rock' defies easy categorization" (43). These explanations clarify that "soul" had acquired fairly specific connotations at the level of a critic-fan genre (and one with an increasingly specific historical provenance) and could no longer function adequately as a market category. In George's words, "Blacks have been making and buying pop music of greater stylistic variety than the soul sound since the early 1970s" (10).[32] "Black music" could therefore act as an umbrella label under which soul could be included.

It can hardly fail, however, to attract notice how similar these statements are to those that heralded the consecration of soul as a marketing category label in August 1969 (see chapter 7). In changing from "Rhythm and Blues" to "Soul," we may recall that *Billboard* stated that "this change is motivated by the fact that the term 'soul' more properly embraces the broad range of song and instrumental material which derives from the musical genius of the black American."[33] These statements indicate how the status of the signifier "soul" had shifted over the ensuing years, from a categorical term that itself encompassed many diverse genres to a specific genre (with a specific musical style—the "soul sound," as George puts it) that required another term that could in turn encompass *it*. Nevertheless, the similarity of these statements separated by more than a decade illustrates how, when dealing with minority categories of popular music, the present moment tends to seem heterogeneous, as the previous term of choice in turn comes to designate a kind of stylistic homogeneity. It is fairly easy to recall that "soul," while perhaps referring to a specific sound when it became a marketing category, at the same time included such diverse genres as funk (James Brown, the Meters), pop-soul (Diana Ross and the Supremes, Smokey Robinson and the Miracles, the Delfonics), neo-doo-wop ballads (the Dells, the Originals), psychedelic rock-funk-soul (Sly and the Family Stone, the Temptations), and secular gospel (Aretha Franklin, Gladys Knight), to name only a few of the most obvious.[34]

Although the marketing category of "black music" would eventually lead to its own conceptual impasse, in the early 1980s strong arguments could be made for its use. As observed in the previous chapter, one of the factors in the illegibility of *Billboard*'s R&B chart in November 1963 was its failure to acknowledge the crucial role of social as well as musical conventions in the formation of the R&B marketing category. Despite all the apparent contradictions involved—the heterogeneity of taste within the African American audience, the popularity of black popular music with non–African Americans, the occasional participation of non–African Americans in the production of black popular music—an industry insider such as Bill Gavin could still assert that African Americans "consistently display[ed] a deep and lasting affection for the music that is most meaningful to them" while simultaneously showing an aversion to white popular music. The shift from "rhythm and blues" to "soul" affirmed the importance of the citation of an African

American identity to this category, an affirmation that the change to "black music" made even more explicit.

The very explicitness of the new label with respect to racial identity, however, highlighted the contradictions between, on the one hand, the music's social connotations and its more concentrated popularity with African Americans, and, on the other hand, the larger-scale heterogeneity of its production and consumption. If various attempts to confer soulfulness on white artists relied on a logic of bracketing the social and emphasizing musical components, the usage of "black" as the label for a marketing category would call attention to the occasional disjunctions between widely shared social connotations and the occasional participant in the music who might not be African American. The tensions in these usages flared with occurrences such as George Michael's receipt of the "Black Music Artist of the Year" at the American Music Awards in January 1989. As Greg Peck, VP of black promotion and A&R at Island Records said at the time, "I don't have a problem with George Michael's album being the album of the year . . . but I do have a problem with him being the black artist of the year. When you make him black artist of the year, you know . . . he's not *black*."[35]

From Black to Urban Contemporary

The role of racial identity in the categorization of music also figured prominently in one of the liveliest topics of early 1980s music industry discourse: the realignment and redefinition of radio formats. At issue here was a new format, urban contemporary (UC), that appeared to usurp the role of "black" stations (prior to its use as the title of a *Billboard* chart, "black" was already in use to designate African American popular music at the level of radio formats). By the middle of 1982, the pros and cons of "UC" versus "black" as a format designator were being vigorously debated. On the pro side, some argued that the UC format recognized by default the importance and success of black radio, gave more exposure to black artists, and provided a larger audience to black DJs. On the con side, the format was criticized for attempting to "fool" advertisers who were leery of the potential of African Americans as consumers about the social connotations of the format; that UC stations hired white DJs even though Top 40 stations were as reluctant as ever to hire black DJs; that UC used a less adventurous playlist than black radio; and that, by playing more white artists, the format provided less exposure for black artists than black radio.[36]

The idea of a format like UC had already been floated in the early 1970s by stations such as WLBS in New York. In a change spearheaded by DJ Frankie Crocker, WLBS moved away from a diet of soul and funk and toward what Crocker called the "total black experience in sound," which included the pop-jazz of Grover Washington, the jazz-funk fusion of Miles Davis, and the jazz-influenced soul produced by artists such as Donny Hathaway, Stevie Wonder, Roberta Flack, and

Marvin Gaye. Crocker directed his sound toward middle-class African Americans and others with similar amounts of cultural capital, displaying a keen awareness of how such music could cross over and bring together what were usually conceived of as multiple and distinct audiences. Crocker's emphasis on musical style over social identity—in his words, "those artists where the music just transcends the color of the skin"—attracted advertisers who would have avoided black radio in the past. In the process, Crocker and WLBS shifted black radio away from its role as a community focal point and toward a new role as the purveyor of a musical style that could function as a component of an upwardly mobile lifestyle. By the late 1970s, WLBS's "total black experience in sound" had become simply the "total experience in sound."[37]

As with earlier arguments about the virtues of reverse crossover (and in line with the transition of WLBS), some proponents of the UC moniker stressed the importance of sound over social identity in the constitution of categories, emphasizing the possibility and even the desirability of subtracting race from the black music assemblage. DJs working in the UC format "claim[ed] increasing willingness to add records on the basis of their sound, even when the act involved is not usually associated with the format. This trend . . . is exemplified by Hall and Oates' 'I Can't Go for That.'" Mike Roberts [program director of Atlanta's WIGO-AM] opined that "the success of the 'urban contemporary' format . . . lies not in its mix of pop & black records but its presentation of black music in a non-ethnic setting." This "non-ethnic" setting was created in part by surrounding the music "with news, public affairs, and announcers that have no ethnic identification like it was a straight general market station."[38] Other DJs expanded on this idea of a race-neutral sound by stressing that they did not play records by white artists in order to court a white audience. As Jeff Harrison of Oakland's KDIA-AM explained:

> It would be crazy for me to start playing white records for that reason (to draw in white listeners) because they can always go to the competition and get as much white music as they want. If I play a record, it's because its overall appeal is for the audience I have, which is predominantly black.[39]

Even on the subject of playing white music for black audiences, however, other black music insiders were less than sanguine about this change, recognizing the unreciprocated nature of this emphasis on a race-neutral sonic approach. If black DJs felt that "music has no color," then this feeling was not necessarily shared by their "counterparts on the other side of the fence" (i.e., album-oriented-rock programmers), who "don't seem to understand that the younger generation likes music whether it's white or black."[40] Longtime DJ Jack "the Rapper" Gibson criticized "urban radio" for watering down exposure for black music. Nile Rodgers, guitarist for the band Chic, added some specifics, noting how a track from an album he coproduced with David Bowie, "Let's Dance," entered rotation on black and rock formats soon after its release, something that "could never have happened if 'Let's Dance' was being treated as a black record, no matter how good the song is."[41]

UC vs. AOR

Similar to how the rise of adult contemporary fueled new conceptions about the boundaries of country music and the possibilities of crossover, so did the rise of the album-oriented rock (AOR) format in the mid- to late 1970s play a pivotal role in how the black music format was defined. Rather than the newly expansive sense of possibility around country provided by AC, however, AOR reinforced a sense of a borders around black music. In narratives about the segregated nature of the popular music field in the early 1980s, no bigger culprit appeared than AOR. AOR had appeared in the mid-1970s as a more tightly scripted version of rock radio stations known as free-form, underground, or progressive, that had presented themselves as platforms for the more or less spontaneous whims of the stations' DJs and programming directors. These stations would play longer album cuts by (mostly) white rock artists rather than respecting the restrictions of Top 40, soul, or country, which focused on singles and a maximum length of four minutes. According to a laudatory retrospective published in 1977, AOR emerged as a response to the unattractive, ponderous quality of progressive radio, presenting "a more entertaining vehicle for aware people rather than one designed to educate." Similar to the economic motivation of the emergence of UC and AC, another important factor was the increased involvement of "the people with the radio bucks," who "viewed AOR as a term much more acceptable than 'free-form acid rock' and other Sixties descriptions. So did advertisers."[42] Evidently education didn't sell like entertainment.

This last quotation reveals a peculiar consistency and parallelism between the shift from "progressive" to "AOR" and the transformation of "black" to "UC." In the pursuit of greater revenue, a non-musical component (such as racial identity, political connotations, or social idealism) is drained from descriptions of the radio format assemblage. In the process, that assemblage is reduced to its sonic components, or perhaps to an apolitical lifestyle built around consumption choices that render the format more attractive to advertisers. As a result of these format changes, certain demographic groups who are believed to lack potential as consumers, such as working-class African Americans, or young, politically and culturally progressive whites, find that they are no longer being addressed by radio stations that formerly spoke to their constellated communities.

In practice, the programming of individual AOR stations varied more than the somewhat monolithic description just given may indicate. Eric Weisbard offers a spirited defense of the format through a detailed account of one station, Cleveland's WMMS (aka "The Buzzard"). The recounting of the history of WMMS as it transitioned from an underground format to various incarnations of AOR is instructive, as the station periodically recalibrated its sense of its target audience and the generic makeup of its playlist. And although the audience for AOR overlapped significantly with underground radio, the cultural capital meter shifted from middle class and college educated to blue collar and working class. Such a shift partly explains the critical disparagement of AOR, as underground radio's approach aligned well with the aesthetics of rock criticism and the emerging rock canon. Such aesthetics did not figure as prominently in AOR, with its tighter, more populist playlists.[43] On the other hand, the idea that the transition from underground to AOR can be characterized as a move away from any sense of a countercultural political coalition is supported by how free-form stations provided generous airtime to the Black Panther Party as well as, in the words of Kim Simpson, "functioning as a non-stop antiwar rally."[44] Such political involvement does not negate the fact that underground radio also catered to a fairly limited white, male, eighteen to thirty-four demographic, even if, according to Susan J. Douglas, underground radio served as "an especially powerful site for the reimagination of masculinity,"[45] and that underground radio's idea of counterculture as lifestyle, encapsulated in a just-say-yes-to-drugs policy, carried over to AOR.

The idea that AOR was particularly implicated in the racial segregation of popular music categories already arose in the earlier discussion of the UC format, but commentators of the time made other types of connections as well. Many noted the paucity of recordings by African American artists in the upper reaches of the mainstream charts, and how this represented a historic shift away from the integrated mainstream charts of the 1960s and early 1970s, with one writer, Robert Palmer, comparing the situation to that of the mainstream prior to the advent of rock 'n' roll in the mid-1950s.[46] Disco also figured briefly as another example of this type of narrowcasting, as all-disco radio formats emerged during the heyday of the genre's popularity in the late 1970s on stations such as New York's WKTU (1978). The success of disco contributed to the internal homogeneity of radio formats, as it temporarily raised the bar of success for other African American–associated dance genres. As disco came to stand in for the whole of black popular music for rock fans, program directors at Top 40 stations increasingly played disco in lieu of funk and soul. Program directors for black radio came under corporate pressure to play disco, which in turn crowded out non-disco artists, and many recognized that all-disco stations severed the sense of "identification with the community [and] community service" traditionally performed by black radio.[47]

Even as AOR was blamed for the homogeneity and the racial segregation of radio formatting, its fortunes seemed to be fading. By 1982 the Arbitron ratings (which measured radio stations' audience share) were adjusted in a way that revealed that black radio stations had a larger listenership than previously believed, a development mirrored by the decline of AOR.[48] In search of greater programming consistency, the playlists of many AOR stations had shrunk to the point where blandness and predictability appeared to be alienating audiences, even though those strategies had been developed in order to guarantee greater commercial success. AOR was routinely portrayed as conservative and afraid to program new acts. The format was out of touch not only with non-rock genres, or so it would seem, but with new trends in rock music as well, eschewing punk and new wave acts in favor of groups that evoked the "classic rock group sound of the 1960s." Some of this had to do with regional markets: "The music out of the clubs on the East and West coasts wasn't the kind that middle America wanted to hear."[49] Against the trend toward ever-greater homogeneity in AOR, the move toward incorporating a greater range of genres made UC appear innovative. The discovery of the yuppie by radio advertisers also made the working-class audience of AOR less attractive.[50]

As discussed previously in this chapter, the increase in the number of formats and popularity charts during the latter half of the 1970s was anticipated by growing interest in crossover and demographics earlier in the decade, in which the increased categorical mobility of recordings and a more defined sense of the audience strengthened the sense of generic boundaries. The perception of a more finely segmented audience affected radio formats in two opposing ways. On the one hand, mainstream categories such as Top 40 and AOR became more homogeneous in terms of the genres and social identities that constituted their internal makeup and became more resistant to crossover to and from other categories. On the other, minority categories and formats such as country and UC became more internally diverse, facilitating greater crossover with other categories.

From AOR to MTV

The demographic homogeneity of AOR resembled that of the newest popular music medium of the early 1980s, the music video, which circulated most prominently in the United States on the new cable television network MTV. Criticisms of MTV for its segregated programming were legion. For their part, executives at MTV responded that their policies were not racist but merely responding to the tastes of their predominantly white, middle-American audience, who simply didn't like African American popular music. MTV's own executives constructed a popular music field in which their format fell "slightly left of center, between AOR (Def Leppard) and modern pop (Men at Work, Talking Heads). On the right are the verboten R&B and country music." Such race-neutral explanations collapsed upon further inspection of the musical style of many of the artists and songs in heavy rotation on the cable channel, which strongly resembled the music of African American artists whom the station refused to play.[51]

MTV, while relying to a large extent on AOR staples, did however draw on a larger range of critic-fan genres than the AOR radio format. In particular, the cable network featured genres described variously as new wave, the new music, synth-pop, and new romantic, produced largely in the United Kingdom. Insofar as these referenced new wave music, they evoked a British-based genealogy that can be traced to a complex of genres that emerged in the mid-1970s more or less simultaneously with punk. Punk in its British guise projected an anti-U.S. attitude that also included an explicit rejection of African American musics, partly because those musics were understood as being the root of the problem with the blues-based rock dinosaurs that punk sought to usurp. The two closest neighboring genres to punk, new wave and post-punk, are now recognized for consciously reintroducing black-associated musical components to music deriving its energy from punk, and for differing engagements with the mainstream (new wave being more pop friendly, post-punk more devoted to the pursuit of symbolic capital). Despite the reintroduction of black-associated musical components derived from disco, funk, and reggae, new wave and post-punk could not entirely escape racial connotations of whiteness. Thus, new wave was described by Robert Christgau in January 1979 as not just "White Music" but "WHITE Music."[52] Nevertheless, some five years later, Christgau observed how the "defanged funk" of the new wave tributary, synth-pop, was responsible to some extent for preparing white audiences for the music of artists such as Michael Jackson and Prince, who succeeded in crossing over during 1982 and 1983. As this British synth-pop also dominated the early years of MTV, some also viewed it as paving the way for black crossover artists in that medium as well.[53]

Juxtaposed with the debates about segregation in radio formats and cable television were other discussions about the recession gripping the U.S. economy in general, and the music industry in particular. While debates tended to cluster around the perils of home taping, overinflated record prices, and the foolhardiness of a blockbuster mentality (generated by *Saturday Night Fever, Frampton Comes Alive!*, and recordings by Fleetwood Mac and the Eagles, among others), the general trend of social conservatism and economic hard times framed the larger discursive context. John Rockwell, writing in the *New York Times* in March 1984, explained the greater segregation in popular music of the time relative to previous eras as a result of "the reactive shift to more conservative lifestyles and art forms in the country as a whole," evoking a parallel to the economic and social policies of Ronald Reagan and Margaret Thatcher.[54] The material consequences of these social and economic shifts for the circulation of African American popular music were addressed at the time in a series of articles by Nelson George, which described the deteriorating conditions for African Americans in the retail end of the business despite the healthy sales of black music relative to pop music.[55] Thus we have counterpoint during this period between, on the one hand, narratives that describe the increasing popularity of black popular music and a few extremely successful crossover acts (more about this in the next section), and on the other hand, narratives that describe the increasing difficulty of African Americans in benefiting from the success of black artists because of either failing retail businesses, a generalized social conservatism, or the tendency of black artists to hire white promoters for their concert tours. To this could be added the exclusion of black radio from advertising revenue due to the advent of UC, and the exclusion of black acts from MTV.[56]

ENTER MJ

The oppositions between differing marketing categories and radio formats, and the articulation of these with different genres, social identities, and a new medium (such as MTV), created a field of tensions into which Michael Jackson's *Thriller* was born. Following on the heels of his previous album, *Off the Wall,* and coming after more than a decade of spectacular success as a solo artist and with the Jacksons (the Jackson Five), the success of *Thriller* did not come as a surprise, even if the extent of its success did. Observers instantly saw *Thriller*—its music and its success—as a multimedia event that could transcend the dualities dividing the world of popular music. Because Jackson's appeal (based not only on his music but on his public persona as well) was already so wide, and because *Thriller* brought together what were commonly viewed as separate strands of popular music, his album early on held out promise that it could break into media that were off-limits for African American artists. Songs from *Thriller* were eventually to storm the barricades of both MTV and AOR, opening the door for a few other crossover-friendly black artists. By early 1984, long after the success of the album could be taken for granted, the increased public attention to Jackson also made it possible to see him as a quintessentially postmodern figure, transcending other, more basic dualisms, such as those based on race, gender, and sexuality.[57]

The watershed crossover success of *Thriller* figured in several discussions following its release in December 1982. As stated earlier, the album and its singles entered into a field of institutions, discourses, and values in which certain relationships between musical style, social identity, and genre were already assumed. Even at an early stage, writers recognized the genre-busting capabilities of the album, with the song "Beat It" generating particular interest. Allusions to these generic fusions often included glancing references to the challenges posed by such tracks to the social boundaries connoted by the citation of multiple genres. One front-page *Billboard* article, which focused on the generally favorable response to "Beat It" at AOR stations, nonetheless described listeners as having problems either upon discovering that Michael Jackson was responsible for the recording or with the idea that Eddie Van Halen was selling out by appearing on it. A further problem appeared to be indecision about whether to make "Beat It" the second single from *Thriller,* stemming from the reluctance of Jackson's record company "to hand black radio two pop-oriented singles in a row [when they] would prefer to follow 'The Girl Is Mine' with a more mainstream black track, probably 'Billie Jean.'"[58] It would appear from these statements that "Beat It" was doubly accursed: simultaneously given the cold shoulder by AOR listeners because of Jackson's image and Van Halen's sellout, and by black radio formatters as "too pop." Yet in the end the song provided a good example of how previously unexplored syntheses of genres can construct, or respond to, new (and very large) audiences. Eventually the third single released from *Thriller*, "Beat It" reached number one on the Hot 100 in April 1983 and remained there for three weeks.[59]

In terms of how the various components of marketing categories, radio formats, and critic-fan genres interacted with the representation of the popularity of individual songs on charts, the crossover process functioned much the same during this period as it had in the period analyzed in the previous chapter. Crossovers from the Black chart to the Hot 100 attracted a different sort of attention than had the R&B to Hot 100 crossovers of the mid-1960s, however, due to several factors. Foremost among these was the increased internal homogeneity of the Hot 100, attributable in large part to the exclusion of black popular music from the mid-1970s onward. The few crossovers preceding *Thriller* in the early 1980s, by artists such as Lionel Richie, Stevie Wonder, Diana Ross, Ray Parker Jr., and Kool and the Gang, bore a resemblance to examples from earlier chapters in that they generally responded to industry-wide expectations based on the artist's previous chart performance, initial strength of popularity in the R&B charts, and the musical style of the recording.

A closer look at two sets of two songs that were released and were popular at roughly the same time enables an exploration of the ideas of crossover and statistical causality broached in chapter 7 (see table 16). From this chart, we can see that "The Girl Is Mine" by Michael Jackson and Paul McCartney was earmarked for dual chart success from the beginning; its ascent and descent on both the Black and Hot 100 charts were roughly parallel. On the other hand, Chaka Khan's "Got to Be There" displayed a different type of crossover pattern. It fought its way onto the lower reaches of the Hot 100 after prolonged success on the Black chart. Similar to "The Girl Is Mine," Michael Jackson's "Billie Jean" appeared almost immediately on both charts. However, its ascent up the Black chart was much faster, landing it at number one a full three weeks before it hit number one on the Hot 100. In contrast to this, George Clinton's "Atomic Dog" followed a very different pattern, closer to that of "Got to Be There" but more extreme. Despite prolonged success on the Black chart, it didn't even crack the Hot 100, instead "bubbling under" (*Billboard*'s term) at number 101. In terms of the strength of their crossover effect, therefore, both "Got to Be There" and "Atomic Dog" were far weaker than even "Papa's Got a Brand New Bag" and "In the Midnight Hour," the two examples of relatively weak crossover from 1965. If one were looking for correspondences between musical style and marketing category, musical differences between "Got to Be There" and "Atomic Dog" on the one hand and "The Girl Is Mine" and "Billie Jean" on the other could indicate the distinctive components and modes of interaction between components of the black music category not shared with the mainstream.

TABLE 16 Comparison of Crossover Success for Four Songs, November 1982–July 1983

| Michael Jackson/ Paul McCartney, "The Girl Is Mine" | | Chaka Khan, "Got to Be There" | | Michael Jackson, "Billie Jean" | | George Clinton, "Atomic Dog" | |
Date	Black	Hot 100	Black	Hot 100	Black	Hot 100	Black	Hot 100
(1982)								
Nov. 6	—	#45	#69	—				
Nov. 13	#21	#36	#51	—				
Nov. 20	#10	#14	#38	—				
Nov. 27	#6	#9	#28	—				
Dec. 4	#3	#8	#20	—				
Dec. 11	#3	#5	#11	—				
Dec. 18	#3	#4	#8	—				
Dec. 25	#3	#3	#8	—				
(1983)								
Jan. 8	#3	#2	#8	#82				
Jan. 15	#1	#2	#8	#74				
Jan. 22	#1	#2	#5	#69	—	#47		
Jan. 29	#1	#5	#5	#67	#31	#37	#39	—
Feb. 5	#9	#16	#5	#92	#8	#27	#26	—
Feb. 12	#13	#34	#5	#98	#1	#23	#15	—
Feb. 19	#21	#82	#20	#98	#1	#6	#8	—
Feb. 26	#22	#91	#21	—	#1	#4	#6	—
Mar. 5	#25	#97	#22	—	#1	#1	#5	—
Mar. 12	#46	—	#23	—	#1	#1	#5	—
Mar. 19	#91	—	#33	—	#1	#1	#5	—
Mar. 26			#57	—	#1	#1	#3	—
Apr. 2			#91	—	#1	#1	#3	—
Apr. 9					#1	#1	#3	—
Apr. 16					#2	#1	#1	#101
Apr. 23					#2	#5	#1	—
Apr. 30					#3	#7	#1	—
May 7					#3	#14	#1	—
May 14					#11	#24	#4	—
May 21					#12	#29	#11	—
May 28					#23	#42	#16	—
June 4					#40	#58	#19	—
June 11					#66	#65	#27	—
June 18					#77	#70	#36	—
June 25					#84	#73	#42	—
July 2					#91	#98	#53	—
July 9							#70	—
July 16							#91	—
July 23							#98	—

"The Girl Is Mine" vs. "Got to Be There"

"The Girl Is Mine" is presented as a lighthearted song that might be found in a musical comedy, a quality that undercuts the passages with the most intense effects (such as Jackson's singing during the bridge). This affect contrasts mightily with the impassioned quality that characterizes Khan's performance throughout "Got to Be There." "The Girl Is Mine" also undoubtedly benefited from the fact that Jackson had such a long track record of crossover success that his releases were *expected* to cross over, even during periods when crossovers were rare. Sharing credit for the recording with Paul McCartney also didn't impede its progress on the Hot 100. Thus, even to say that "The Girl Is Mine" cited Jackson's previous crossover success would be a misnomer in that the whole production profited from an additional ingredient: the collaboration with a bona fide white rock star, fresh from a recent smash collaboration with Stevie Wonder (their summer of 1982 hit "Ebony and Ivory"), another African American musician with a spectacular history of bringing together disparate audiences.

By way of comparison, Khan had enjoyed a stretch of crossover success as a member of the band Rufus during 1974 and 1975, but this categorical mobility decreased after she went solo in 1978, with the exception of "I'm Every Woman" (B100: 21) in 1978. Khan's work with Rufus during the mid-1970s profited from a greater openness to African American artists in the mainstream, a situation contributing to the success of other funk units such as Kool and the Gang and the Ohio Players. These recordings continued to sound remarkably contemporary even in the world of early-1980s R&B, which was dominated by the skittering funk rhythms pioneered in the previous decade. Such stylistic components, protentions though they might have been for black music, were out of sync with mainstream taste by the early 1980s. For example, other solo recordings by Khan, such as her "What Cha' Gonna Do for Me" from 1981 (BRB: 1; B100: 53), produced a crossover effect as weak as "Got to Be There."

The comparison of these two recordings thus far implies that the difference in how "The Girl Is Mine" and "Got to Be There" were categorized rested largely on the previous history of the performers, and the expectations and "intuitions" of chart makers.[60] Michael Jackson and Chaka Khan were not merely public personalities who were placed into musical categories, but musicians who produced recordings that entered into a musical field arranged at least in part on the basis of sonic components. These two recordings bear interesting similarities in their basic harmonic language, tempo, and (to some extent) groove. "Got to Be There," the more harmonically sophisticated of the two, was first recorded, strangely enough, by Michael Jackson in 1971, and its harmonic language participates in a simplified form of the "modern ballad" developed by songwriters such as Burt Bacharach and Jimmy Webb—a post–Tin Pan Alley style that features chord extensions such as sevenths, ninths, and elevenths, and the frequent use of suspensions and polychords, in which a triad is superimposed over a bass pitch that is not part of the triad (as in F/G, interpreted as a F-major triad over G in the bass). This approach to harmony had already played a large role in the easy listening ballads of the 1960s, and it continued to be influential as easy listening turned to MOR and MOR turned to AC.

As with the songs of Bacharach, "Got to Be There" features notably irregular phrasing. I parse the first verse into six phrases, divided into 5 + 5 + 3 + 4 + 2 + 5 measures as shown below:

(A) Phrase 1 (5 measures): "Got to be there . . . when he says hello to the world"

(B) Phrase 2 (5 measures): "Got to be there, . . . and show him that I'm his girl"

(C) Phrase 3 (3 measures): "Oh, what a feeling there'll be"

(D) Phrase 4 (4 measures): "The moment . . ."

(E) Phrase 5 (2 measures): "'Cause when I look in his eyes . . ."

(F) Phrase 6 (5 measures): "I need him sharing the world . . . "

The discussion here of the irregularity of phrasing is not meant to suggest a correlation between asymmetrical phrasing and lack of mainstream popularity. After all, the song "Got to Be There," in the recording by Michael Jackson in 1971, did produce a strong crossover effect (BRB: 4; B100: 4). The impact of a single musical component on musical popularity cannot be divorced from how such a component interacts with other components within different assemblages operating on different levels within the musical field at a particular moment. To historicize this somewhat abstract statement, while irregular phrasing did not appear to have much impact on the representation of the popularity of "Got to Be There" as recorded by Jackson in 1971, it may have played a role in Khan's recording from 1982. At any rate, such irregularity certainly contrasts with the utter regularity of phrasing in "The Girl Is Mine," with its succession of four-measure phrases.

The groove of "The Girl Is Mine" is a bouncy, syncopated rhythm dominated by a repeated guitar riff of the type that was common in pop and black popular music of the period. The groove of "Got to Be There" alternates between two main underlying rhythms: a dotted-quarter eight-note Latin groove found often in pop ballads since the 1960s and a more syncopated groove (groove 2; first appearing briefly at 0:26 and then taking over at 0:40) typical of early-1980s R&B (a groove not found in Jackson's 1971 recording of the tune, but one not too distant from "The Girl Is Mine").

If the components of harmony and groove of the two songs are somewhat similar, then one stylistic component, vocal style, factored strongly in their differentiation. Vocal style here includes the basic timbre (or timbres) of the voice (or voices), timbral range and variety, frequency and complexity of ornamentation, relationship to the underlying beat, and the overall (pitch) range of the vocal. "Got to Be There" as a composed text already has a large range (an octave plus a fifth) that Khan extends and exploits. The contrasting timbres of even the first phrases of Khan's recording exceed what would be commonly found in the upper reaches of the Hot 100 at that time. For example, in the first twenty-eight seconds of the recording, which comprise an intro and the first phrase of the first verse, Khan produces at least six distinct timbres matched with pitch register and melodic direction, as detailed in the following (timings are given in parentheses, as are the lyrics on which the timbral changes occur):

INTRO

(0:00) Timbre 1—low/husky/breathy ("Got to be there")

(0:03) Timbre 2—ascend-middle-high/airy/breathy ("be there in the morning")

(0:12) Timbre 3—high/pure ("ooh")

VERSE 1

(0:14) Timbre 4—low/husky with body ("got to be there")

(0:17) Timbre 5—high/pure with light vibrato ("be there in the morning")

(0:26) Timbre 6—descend middle-low/body + extreme vibrato ("to the world")

In terms of ornamentation, melismatic runs such as those found in the extended coda of "Got to Be There" (musical example 29) would similarly be unlikely to be found in contemporary hit radio.[61]

The repetitions of the verse of "Got to Be There" feature considerable variation, a quality seemingly uniting the non-crossover qualities in the early 1980s with those of the mid-1960s (see, for example, musical examples 23, 24, and 25 from chapter 7). "The Girl Is Mine," although in a similar tempo and featuring some components of an R&B ballad of the time, shows considerably more restraint. Only a few ornamental flourishes and a grittier timbre in a higher register of the climax in the bridge by Jackson break out of the overall genteel quality of the vocals, in which variations between verses are minimal. These differences between the two recordings in timbre and melodic variation (or lack thereof) illustrate different aesthetic conceptions directed toward different audiences. At the same time, it is important to note that both recordings participate stylistically in multiple categories, principally R&B and black music, adult contemporary, and the mainstream, although admittedly to differing degrees. That is to say, even if both recordings participated in multiple categories in terms of musical style, only one of them, "The Girl Is Mine," managed to successfully transcend the institutional boundaries separating these.

MUSICAL EXAMPLE 29. Chaka Khan, Vocal Pyrotechnics, Coda, "Got to Be There" (3:34)

The previous discussion might give the erroneous impression that Jackson, whose voice has often been celebrated for its flexibility, was incapable of the type of timbral and melodic variation performed by Khan in "Got to Be There." Although not in evidence in his studio recording of "Got to Be There" from 1971, a live television performance of the song from the following year features melismatic embellishment of the melody that evokes conventions of African American gospel music similar to those referenced by Khan.[62] Even on *Thriller*, the two cuts that were not released as singles, "Baby Be Mine" and "The Lady in My Life," shared more with the musical conventions of non-crossover R&B than the rest of the album, with the variative vocal ornamentation and timbral variation of "The Lady in My Life" displaying close kinship with the technique of a singer such as Khan.

"Billie Jean" vs. "Atomic Dog"

The other two recordings featured in table 16, "Atomic Dog" and "Billie Jean," contrast even more than "The Girl Is Mine" and "Got to Be There." Basic differences in the two songs can be heard in their introductions: "Atomic Dog" presents a denser texture with more fragmented musical ideas overlapping one another than "Billie Jean." While the beat and groove are very clear in both examples, "Billie Jean," due to its sparser texture, presents a cleaner, lighter groove. The groove in "Atomic Dog," on the other hand, is heavier and feels more complex. In terms of timbre, or the sonic quality of particular instruments and voices, differences between the two songs are also striking: "Atomic Dog" features wildly varied, overtly synthesized sounds, synthesizer bass, and electronic handclaps. "Billie Jean" features synth keyboard along with drum and bass sounds that are non-synthesized (or sound non-synthesized). Michael Jackson's vocal quality in "Billie Jean," while recognizably African American, is also clearly singing (as opposed to speaking) in a somewhat cleaner timbre (including what were to become Jackson's trademark vocal hiccups) than that heard in the singing on "Atomic Dog," which mixes exaggerated gospel-derived mannerisms, sung by solo and group vocalists, with drawling spoken passages and even occasional barking dog–type effects.

In technical terms, the difference in rhythmic texture between the two songs can be described in terms of amount of syncopation or polyrhythm: very ("Atomic Dog") versus modest ("Billie Jean"). In "Billie Jean" the bass plays a steady eighth-note

MUSICAL EXAMPLE 30. "Billie Jean" (ca. 0:21–0:24)

+ = sounds one octave lower than written

pattern against the background of the drums, which provide an accent on the snare drum on the backbeat while also subdividing the beat into two on the hi-hat cymbal (a pattern that is reinforced by the maracas). The keyboard plays a pattern that produces some tension against the background beat, as every other chord arrives slightly ahead of the beat (see musical example 30). The even eight-note groove alludes to the new wave–ish synth-pop then dominating the mainstream as much or more than it does to the funk-post-disco prominent in the black music chart.[63]

In "Atomic Dog" (musical example 31) the drum part is sparser than in "Billie Jean," with the drums playing only on the beat, with other percussive sounds subdividing the beat during different passages of the song, including what sounds like a chorus of panting dogs. The drum sound is much heavier, however, with a backbeat thunderously reinforced by electronic handclaps. The bass, in contrast to "Billie Jean," plays a fragmented, syncopated pattern, and does not play continuously, leaving frequent gaps. Other synthesized instruments and chanting voices form a kind of collage effect of short, overlapping, syncopated musical ideas.

The harmony of "Billie Jean" relies on a modified form of tension and release, a process conveyed most vividly in the transition from pre-chorus to chorus that occurs around 1:25, resolving with the words "Billie Jean is not my girl," while its melody consists of clearly defined phrases that rise and fall, peaking in the chorus in a way that complements the aforementioned tension and release of the harmony. "Atomic Dog" features no such harmonically based sense of tension and release, relying instead on open-ended sections underpinned by either a single harmony or an alternation of two harmonies. Melodically, "Atomic Dog" relies on shorter, riff-like phrases, and the succession of phrases does not create the sense of melodic direction found in "Billie Jean." While sections of "Billie Jean" use func-

MUSICAL EXAMPLE 31. "Atomic Dog" (ca. 0:05–0:16)

tional harmony to generate musical interest, "Atomic Dog" relies more on changes of texture and the constantly shifting relationships created by different melodic fragments to create a kind of rhythmic tension and release.

Differences in the lyrics also play into distinctions of genre. "Billie Jean" employs a lyric depicting a domestic narrative focused on the drama of an individual, while "Atomic Dog" features playful, allusive lyrics lacking a clear narrative. The playful use of the signifier "dog," which describes its low-down qualities even as it revels in them, also references a mode of discourse widely understood in the United States as African American.[64]

Both "Billie Jean" and "Atomic Dog" had accompanying videos, which, in the case of "Billie Jean," played heavily into its reception. "Billie Jean" has assumed an prominent place in the lore of popular music as the video that broke MTV's color barrier after threats by CBS's president Walter Yetnikoff to withdraw all of the company's videos if it was not programmed.[65] MTV's decision to program "Billie Jean" undoubtedly aided in the transformation of *Thriller* from a fabulous success to an international phenomenon the likes of which the world had never seen before, yet CBS made a canny move in pushing for the inclusion of this particular video. "Billie Jean" (unlike other R&B videos) fit smoothly within the conventions of a certain type of video circulating on MTV in its use of a postmodern quasi-narrative, while at the same time surpassing previous videos in terms of its production values and the charismatic public persona of the video's main subject. These conventions include isolated jump cuts of images that rupture the narrative (the flipping coin, the glass that illuminates when the coin lands in it, the homeless person whose clothes transform into a tuxedo); the juxtaposition of film noir–ish images of the person (a detective?) in raincoat and fedora with Jackson walking down a similar street; Jackson's unexplained disappearances, which are shown in a polaroid photo; and the use of split screen and freeze frames for no apparent purpose. Disjointed narrative elements appear, such as a photo of two women, shots of someone in a bed in a sleazy motel, Jackson's entrance into the bed of the sleeping person, and a scene of entrapment with the "detective," who looks like he's going to take a photo, after which Jackson disappears and the detective is taken away by police. It is rarely clear, however, how these elements, which give the sense of being parts of a narrative, actually create one. Less information is provided than in all but avant-garde filmic or televisual narratives. The video images seem to be saying something about the images in the lyrics, but the relationship is allusive and elliptical, playing off public knowledge of Jackson and the assumption that the meaning of the lyrics is already known.[66] On the other hand, it is unlikely that the resolutely nonnarrative video for "Atomic Dog"—with its images of people partying (dressed up as a cats and dogs), intercut with animated images of dogs, cats, and dogcatchers—was ever played on MTV at all, confined instead to the few televised shows only beginning at the time to broadcast black music videos.

As in the contrast between "Got to Be There" and "The Girl Is Mine," this discussion of the sonic, lyric, and visual elements of "Atomic Dog" and "Billie Jean" clarifies how these recordings refer to conventions that overlap but also differ according to how they reference different categories. In addition to these textual factors, the reception history of George Clinton more closely resembles that of Chaka Khan than Michael Jackson. His work with the P-Funk aggregation prior to his solo career was notable for its low crossover differential—despite seventy recordings to appear on the rhythm and blues and soul charts, only two cracked the top twenty of the B100. As opposed to the critical reception of *Thriller*, which viewed it as the harbinger of greater crossovers yet to come, "Atomic Dog" was heard as one of the few popular recordings to evoke electro-funk rap and hip-hop—genres perceived at that time as part of the newly arisen underground of contemporary black music.[67]

Black Music, Crossover, and the Popular Music Field

The earlier discourse and chart analysis established how "The Girl Is Mine" and "Billie Jean" were crossover recordings that succeeded in both the black and mainstream popular categories, while "Got to Be There" and "Atomic Dog" experienced weak crossover effects. It would be difficult, however, to extrapolate from these examples to a general theory about the differences between black and mainstream popular music at this time without a broader awareness of larger populations of recordings that were categorized similarly and displayed similar ways of moving (or not moving) between categories. As with earlier chapters, the distinctive socio-musical conventions of black music would be established by a significant number of recordings that did not cross over. Several factors in the early 1980s complicate what is never an easy or simple task anyway.

The first complicating factor consists of the makeup of the Top 40 during 1982 and 1983, which was dominated by funk- and soul-influenced pop songs that featured liberal doses of newly developed digital synthesizers and older analog synths, which were in turn mixed with frequent dollops of heavy metal–influenced guitar. These were the days of Toto, REO Speedwagon, and Hall and Oates. New wave lingered on, adding new synthesized timbres and dance rhythms in bands such as Men at Work and the Cars. Aided by the strong and novel visual presence of MTV, many British techno-pop groups figured prominently, such as A Flock of Seagulls, Soft Cell, and Duran Duran. This trend overlapped significantly with the new romantic genre, which consisted of British-based groups who fused neo-soul singing with modified funk and disco rhythms, used plenty of synthesizers, and sported a fashion sense signifying a revolt against punk. While Culture Club was the most successful exponent of this trend in the United States, other bands such as the Fixx and Spandau Ballet achieved chart success during this period. And although heavy metal had not yet fully been accepted within the mainstream, several lite-metal bands such as Def Leppard and Quiet Riot had major hits, and, as mentioned above, many non-metal songs featured metal-influenced guitar solos. Figure 14 summarizes the relationships of the recordings and categories discussed thus far in this chapter in the now-familiar Venn diagram.

The most obvious sonic connection between "Got to Be There," "The Girl Is Mine," "Atomic Dog," "Billie Jean," and this mainstream lies in the general reliance on funk rhythms and synthesizers, which were widely recognized and disparaged by critics at the time for their domination of the instrumental texture of popular music. If synthesizers were shared across many generic borders, this did not mean that other instruments (or a lack of synthesizers) could not play a differentiating role. Like horns in country music, guitars in a black recording could signify a higher crossover differential, as witnessed already in "Beat It" (or a song such as Ray Parker Jr.'s "The Other Woman").[68]

The presence of aspects of funk style in the mainstream illustrates the difficulty (if not impossibility) of making airtight associations between musical style and race, as the mainstream was already saturated with musical style markers that bore strong associations with African Americans. Understanding the makeup of the

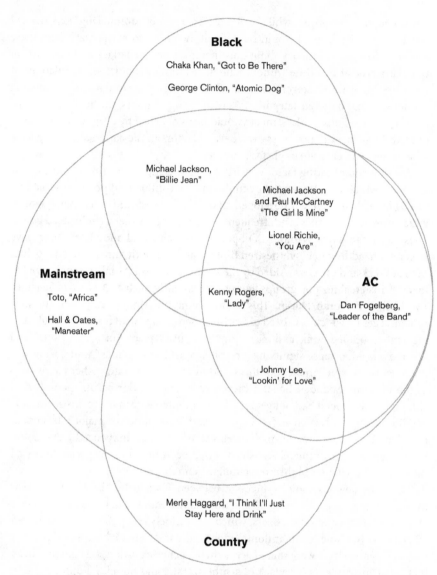

FIGURE 14. The Circular Logic of Radio Formats, 1980–83.

mainstream at this time, however, does highlight some important distinctions about which factors were involved in the ability of certain recordings to cross over. Songs that were too funky (such as "Atomic Dog" or the Gap Band's "You Dropped a Bomb on Me") or had too much gospel influence (anything by Chaka Khan or Maze featuring Frankie Beverly) had limited mainstream success—success that also correlated with the ability of the artist to cite (usually his or her own) previous crossover success. The role of race in the construction of the mainstream is revealed by the appearance of funky dance numbers by white artists, such as "Let's Dance" by David Bowie, in the Hot 100 immediately upon their release.[69] Once again, it is difficult to isolate musical style as a differentiating factor without recourse to knowledge about the social identity of the musicians. Artists and styles categorized as R&B or black existed along a spectrum of possibilities ranging from those artists and styles that were very likely to cross over, to those that were very unlikely to, with neither precluding the possibility that exceptions could occur within these general tendencies.

Another important axis of the mainstream during 1982 and 1983 revolved around lyric content and the use of a romantic ballad style. This realm of expression, however, was not open to R&B songs projecting a straightforward romantic message (such as "Got to Be There"), very few of which crossed over at this time. By way of contrast, soulful ballads were quite successful in the mainstream, but only when recorded by white singers such as Michael McDonald ("I Keep Forgettin' [Every Time You're Near]"), Joe Cocker and Jennifer Warnes ("Up Where We Belong"), and numerous new romantics (Lionel Richie stands as an exception to this rule). In a disturbing parallel to the situation that existed in 1920 prior to the success of Mamie Smith's "Crazy Blues" (or in the 1940s prior to the success of Nat King Cole), the inaccessibility of the widest public forum in popular music for the expression of serious emotions—given that crossover songs of the period were prone to be party and dance numbers—might tend to project an image of African Americans as frivolous, happy-go-lucky, and hedonistic, and therefore unready for the mature romantic commitments available to white pop artists. This partial access to the mainstream contributed to a double standard and higher bar for economic success for African Americans, a phenomenon that becomes more odious when we reflect back to earlier observations about how the economic rewards from black popular music were increasingly being diverted from African American entrepreneurs during this time.

. . .

The turbulence experienced by the black and country music categories in the 1980s arrived at the end of a period in which marketing categories and radio formats were subdivided and repositioned in the symbolic and monetary economies. Due in part to a belated recognition on the part of the mainstream industry of the economic value of these marginal musics, the whole idea of the mainstream underwent changes that led to a new way of conceptualizing the hierarchy of genres that might participate in it. One prominent casualty of this new conception was the dethroning of rock from its unquestioned position of supremacy within the mainstream.[70] Not that rock, particularly in the form of punk and post-punk, had lost symbolic capital with critics; it was rather that, unlike the period from the mid-1960s through the early 1970s, critically consecrated rock no longer could claim consistent popular approval as well. This critical vacuum at the heart of the mainstream led to a greater sense of a constellation of genres and formats that orbited around an absent center. In such a state of flux, different genres could claim popular and/or critical acclaim, resulting in the brief ascendance of country in the early 1980s and the sudden surge of interest in black crossover material in the wake of *Thriller*. These flirtations with the margins did not have the power to reorganize the mainstream, however. It took the arrival of new, automated methods of accounting for popularity in the early 1990s with SoundScan for the world to wake up to the fact that country music actually accounted for an *alternative* mainstream in the form of artists such as Garth Brooks and Billy Ray Cyrus (a shift experienced far more on the album charts than on the Hot 100). And it would take a steady stream of proponents of a new vocal lingua franca—in the form of a hyper-melismatic, neo-gospel approach—with artists such as Boyz II Men, Whitney Houston, and Mariah Carey, along with the absorption of hip-hop's rhythmic practices, to reintegrate African American popular music into the symbolic mainstream. By 1993, the *Billboard* end-of-the-year polls showed that thirteen of the top twenty recordings of the year were by African American and/or R&B artists.[71]

These developments in what was by then called R&B represented the culmination of a series of disparate trends. Fulfilling the recommendations of the Harvard Report of 1972, the major record companies had indeed finally woken up to the lucrative possibilities of African American popular music. These same companies underwent massive reorganization and consolidation during the 1970s, meaning that by the end of the 1980s, only six mega, multinational recording companies remained, with many indies existing as subsidiaries. Such institutional shifts certainly factored into what was broadly perceived as the growing homogenization of a variety of genres, categories, and formats throughout the 1970s and 1980s. With R&B, the loss of local entrepreneurs and community-based radio programming contributed to a situation in which the major companies, all of which now sported a black music division, would be less responsive to local trends. By the late 1970s a black music underground—in the form of rap and hip-hop music—arose as if in response to the growing corporate dominance of black popular music. At the same time, corporatization—the domination of the market by fewer and fewer multinationals—resulted in increased demographic research, the segmentation of the audience on this basis into ever-finer parcels, and the proliferation of categories, charts, and formats.

In addition to changes in the material conditions of the production of black popular music, a struggle over expressive resources had been taking place during the 1980s. Jesse Jackson exhorted the masses to enact consciously a shift in demographic nomenclature that was already under way, explaining the appropriateness of the term "African American" in his speech at the Democratic National Convention in 1988. "African American" would thus seek to put people of African descent on the same plane of signification as other demographic groups who used a hyphen with the suffix "American." The history of the naming of African Americans is much longer but every bit as turbulent as the history of the label for African American–associated popular music, expressing an awareness of the economic and legal significance of linguistic practice. Perhaps in acknowledgment of this longer (and more overtly political) history, when *Billboard* announced in 1990 the shift from "Black" to "R&B," the magazine evinced greater sensitivity to the significance of the change than it had in the past. After first acknowledging that their charts have "always attempted to reflect musical trends as well as *societal changes*," the editors noted how this change of name "is compatible with the desire in the black community *to redefine the terminology that society applies to the black cultural heritage*." Somewhat predictably, the music business executives who were interviewed for the article, all heads of promotion in their respective black music departments, stressed the importance of retaining an awareness of the music's racial background, even if admitting the utility of a race-neutral term for the music. In the words of one exec, "Black denotes the color of music. R&B talks about a style as opposed to a color."[72] As it just so happened, most believed that a race-neutral approach would prove more profitable than one focused on the race of the majority of those responsible for producing the music.

That the shift did seem to participate in greater access to economic and institutional resources can be gleaned from a quick comparison of the fortunes of a single artist. Luther Vandross had specialized in romantic ballads with a soulful edge throughout his career. Consistent crossover success on the singles charts eluded him, however, until the single "Here and Now" was released in 1989, after which almost everything he recorded for the next five years turned to mainstream gold.

The contrast between the 1980s and the 1990s could lead us to wonder what really was at stake in the obsession over crossover found in the fierce debates between critics such as Nelson George and Steve Perry in the early 1980s, and the attributions of pride or lack thereof in one's deepest sense of identification with other people based on musical style and genre that occurred so frequently during that time. The appearance of a "Crossover Chart" in 1987 tells us that certain forms of movement between categories had become conventionalized, and that crossover itself could become expanded to a market category or reduced to a musical style.[73] Crossover had become its own convention, and the stakes were lowered in terms of what the term meant for homologies between musical and social categories.

In the early to mid-1980s, however, the concept of crossover had a particular valence and expressive power. Little else could explain the appearance of a movie such as *Crossover Dreams* that thematized struggles over genre and identity. As we have seen, the crossover process was not necessarily viewed as an unalloyed benefit. For by the time of the release of *Crossover Dreams* it had become clear that what had been a dream for some had turned into a nightmare for others. Perhaps this is because the idea of crossover, as movement between musical categories that stand in for categories of people, is a dream, a phantasm, in that to dream of crossover is to imagine oneself as inhabiting a new identity, as appealing to those who identify differently, so that the artist must imagine an identification that is not felt as his or her own, but which may become second nature if assumed repeatedly.

NOTES

1. Sam Sutherland, "It's a Jazz Sales Spree at WEA-Marketed Labels," *Billboard,* August 29, 1981, 3, 50.

2. While the references to basketball and *Buffy the Vampire Slayer* are whimsical, important parallels exist between categories used for music and for automobiles. If one takes car type (rather than model) as the basis of comparison to genre, one can see how the idea of crossover serves an analogous function in the motor and music industries. Thus, instead of different copies of a given model, for example the Honda Civic, all of which are as identical as possible, one takes the sedan as the starting point, then a crossover between the sedan and the SUV would be designed to reach consumers attracted to both the sedan and the SUV, much as a crossover R&B recording is designed to attract both mainstream and R&B audiences. This is what, in fact, has happened with the most common form of crossover vehicles, which tend to combine aspects of a sedan or station wagon with an SUV.

3. An essay by Arlene Stein bearing the same title as the Rubén Blades movie and this chapter discusses crossing over in the context of obscuring one's lesbian identity in order to procure mainstream musical success. Arlene Stein, "Crossover Dreams: Lesbianism and Popular Music since the 1970s," in *Out in Culture: Gay, Lesbian, and Queer Essays on Popular Culture,* ed. Corey K. Creekmur and Alexander Doty (Durham, NC, and London: Duke University Press, 1995), 416–26.

4. For more on Rubén Blades and crossover in Latin popular music, see Don M. Randel, "Crossing Over with Rubén Blades," *Journal of the American Musicological Society* 44 (Summer 1991): 301–23.

5. For an example of an early usage of crossover as musical category boundary buster, see Bill Simon, "Jock Showcasing of New Talent Keeps Wax Fresh," *Billboard,* January 26, 1957, 45. An influential scholarly study of this moment of crossover, which occasionally occurred between all three major categories, is Charles Hamm, "The Fourth Audience," *Popular Music* 1 (January 1981): 123–41.

6. Hearkening back to some of the debates circa 1965, there was discussion at the time about whether or not soul radio should play white artists. For an example, see Claude Hall, "Soul Radio Gets Into the Roots of Its Community," *Billboard*, January 29, 1972, 38.

7. "Prog. Dirs. Forecast Radio's Continual Upgrading," *Billboard*, May 20, 1972, 24.

8. That this sentiment dates back to the late 1960s is clear from the provenance of this quote: Richard Robinson, "The Dilemma of the Soul Producer," *Billboard*, August 16, 1969, S-24. The "dilemma" of the article's title is twofold: how to create crossover success, and whether or not artists should try to create crossover success. Country music could also suffer anxiety about the effect of crossover. See Robert Sobel, "Northeast Country Music Men to Seek Piracy Bill," *Billboard*, May 4, 1974, 31.

9. Bob Kirsch, "Labels Formulate All-Out Soul Push," *Billboard*, March 17, 1973, 54. The Harvard Report recommended that the major recording companies invest in African American popular music. For more on the Harvard Report, see Nelson George, *The Death of Rhythm and Blues* (New York: Pantheon Books, 1988), 135–38; David Sanjek, "Tell Me Something I Don't Already Know: The Harvard Report on Soul Music Revisited," in *Rhythm and Business: The Political Economy of Black Music*, ed. Norman Kelley (New York: Akashic Books, 2005), 63–80; and Mark Anthony Neal, "Rhythm and Bullshit? The Slow Decline of R&B," *PopMatters* (2005), http://www.popmatters.com/feature/050603-randb/, accessed February 11, 2015. Mark Anthony Neal's book *What the Music Said: Black Popular Music and Black Public Culture* (New York and London: Routledge, 1999) addresses the social and political consequences of these structural changes in more detail.

10. Nat Freedland, "Crossovers Pose NARAS Problem," *Billboard*, December 7, 1974, 3, 4.

11. Don Breithaupt and Jeff Breithaupt, *Precious and Few: Pop Music in the Early '70s* (New York: St. Martin's Griffin, 1996), 3.

12. The title of a *Billboard* article from the early 1970s sums up the situation well: "Top 40 in Topsy Turvy Turmoil Is Consensus," May 13, 1972, 20, 24.

13. Kim Simpson presents a particularly clear version of this argument. See his *Early '70s Radio: The American Format Revolution* (New York: Continuum, 2011). For another study of the increased attention to radio formats in the 1970s, see Eric Weisbard, *Top 40 Democracy: The Rival Mainstreams of American Music* (Chicago and London: University of Chicago Press, 2014). And for a sustained study of the relationship of the radio and recording industries, see Will Straw, "Popular Music as Cultural Commodity: The American Recorded Music Industries 1976–1985" (PhD diss., McGill University, 1990).

14. Mike Harrison, "Crossover, Now and Then," *Billboard*, October 11, 1980, 31.

15. "The Ballad of the Urban Cowboy: America's Search for True Grit," *Esquire*, September 12, 1978, 21–30. All subsequent citations will be noted by page numbers in parentheses.

16. An analysis of character, plot, and genre relations of *Urban Cowboy* may be found in David Brackett, "Banjos, Biopics, and Compilation Scores: The Movies Go Country," *American Music* 19, no. 3 (Autumn 2001): 247–90, especially 259–62.

17. Pierre Bourdieu, *Distinction: A Social Critique of the Judgement of Taste* (Cambridge, MA: Harvard University Press, 1984); Andreas Huyssen, "Mass Culture as Woman: Modernism's Other," in *After the Great Divide: Modernism, Mass Culture, Postmodernism* (Bloomington: Indiana University Press, 1986), 44–64.

18. For a discussion of the breadth of Dolly Parton's appeal, see Eric Weisbard, *Top 40 Democracy*, 70–111. For a socio-musicological study of Parton's work during this period, see Mitchell Morris, "Crossing Over with Dolly Parton," in *The Persistence of Sentiment: Display and Feeling in Popular Music of the 1970s* (Berkeley and Los Angeles: University of California Press, 2013), 173–208.

19. Gerry Wood, "Old & New Conflict in South Central Radio," *Billboard*, July 19, 1980, 1, 27, 35. For a previous discussion about the importance of attracting "more upscale listeners" to country radio, see the special country issue of *Radio and Records*, October 1, 1976.

20. For an earlier statement that more overtly raises the fear of country's contamination by black popular music, see John Pugh, "Will Success Spoil Country Music?," *Music City News* (April 1971): 16, quoted in Kim Simpson, *Early '70s Radio*, 180.

21. The backlash against disco among rock fans led most infamously to a riot in Chicago's Comiskey Park during the intermission of a White Sox doubleheader. See Don McLeese, "Anatomy of an Anti-Disco Riot," *In These Times*, August 29–September 4, 1979, 23. For a discussion that details this backlash within the heightened visibility of gay subcultures occasioned by disco, see Andrew Kopkind, "The Dialectic of Disco: Gay Music Goes Straight," *Village Voice*, February 12, 1979, 1, 11–14, 16, 25, reprinted in David Brackett, *The Pop, Rock, and Soul Reader: Histories and Debates* (New York: Oxford University Press, 2014), 330–38.

22. Kip Kirby, "Country's Gold Grows," *Billboard*, August 29, 1981, 1, 54.

23. Kip Kirby, "Elektra Priority: Film Soundtracks," *Billboard*, August 30, 1980, 57. My emphasis. This is the context that spawned the Lonnie Mack song (released a few years later in 1988) quoted in chapter 1, "Too Rock for Country, Too Country for Rock and Roll." Other than in the refrain and title of the song, Mack also references marketing categories when he sings "Sometimes I think I'm standing in the *middle of the road*" (my emphasis).

24. Two music industry articles, published four years apart, illustrate this shift. The first, published in *Radio and Records* on May 30, 1975, asked "Where (What?) Is M.O.R.?," the two question marks in the title illustrating the amorphous quality of the format (29). The second, appearing in *Billboard*, noted MOR's incursions into the audiences for Top 40 and AOR, and its success in the highly coveted twenty-five to thirty-four demographic as it transitioned to A/C. Paul Grein, "MOR Artists Go to Funkier Sound," *Billboard*, May 5, 1979, 6.

25. For more on the AC format, see Ken Barnes, "Top 40: A Fragment of the Popular Imagination," in *Facing the Music,* ed. Simon Frith (New York: Pantheon, 1988), 8–50. See also the relevant passages in Kim Simpson, *Early '70s Radio,* 55–89; Eric Weisbard, *Top 40 Democracy,* 112–54; and Will Straw, "Popular Music as Cultural Commodity," 222–37.

26. Robyn Wells, "Programmers Tout Country as No. 1 '80s Format," *Billboard*, October 18, 1980, 20, 46; "Radio Needs Flexible AOR/Crossover Format," *Billboard*, August 16, 1980, 54; and Will Straw, "Popular Music as Cultural Commodity," 222. The AC ballad had the power to transcend other significant socio-musical boundaries as well. For a fascinating account of how such ballads transcended radio formats during the 1980s based on musical *and* linguistic categories, see Line Grenier, "Canadian Radio Formats," *Popular Music* 9, no. 2 (1990): 221–33.

27. Rick Forrest, "In Search of the Celluloid Singing Cowboy," *Billboard*, August 2, 1980, M-4, M-6, M-10, M-12.

28. David Brackett, "Questions of Genre in Black Popular Music," *Black Music Research Journal* 25, nos. 1–2 (Spring–Fall 2005): 73–92

29. Observations about the similarity between country and AC can be found in the comments of Jim Fogelson, president of MCA Nashville, in *Radio and Records,* January 18, 1980. See also "Country Music: Today's MOR," *Billboard,* September 26, 1981, 16.

30. Rogers's "Lady" was widely recognized by radio programmers as "the 'perfect' mass appeal song, capable of breaking in country, black, Top 40 and adult contemporary formats." Richard M. Nusser, "Radio's Flux Mixed Blessing," *Billboard,* December 27, 1980, 17.

31. And Merle Haggard's greater popularity with non-crossover country audiences can be gauged by his ranking (number nine) above Rogers (number thirty) in the end-of-the-year country singles chart for 1981 (*Billboard,* December 26, 1981). Aaron Fox has extensively probed the linguistic properties of country lyrics. See his *Real Country: Music and Language in Working-Class Culture* (Durham, NC, and London: Duke University Press, 2004).

32. Nelson George's retroactive refashioning of "soul" from a marketing category to a critic-fan genre became the default for *Billboard* in subsequent accounts. See for example "Billboard's Black Charts: Changing with the Times," *Billboard,* February 25, 1989, 82.

33. "Editorial: R&B Now Soul," *Billboard,* August 23, 1969, 3.

34. Another usage of "black music," and one no doubt familiar to music scholars, entered circulation at roughly the same time as the change to the name of *Billboard*'s chart. As enshrined in black music scholarship, this usage would include Western art music created by African Americans, a component not included in the usage of the term in music industry discourse of the early 1980s. For examples and discussions of the scholarly use of "black music," see, in addition to many other publications, the back issues of the *Black Music Research Journal,* founded in 1980 by Samuel Floyd Jr., as well as Floyd's monograph *The Power of Black Music* (New York: Oxford University Press, 1995).

35. "Trade Debates Black Terminology: Does 'African-American' Strike a Musical Note?," *Billboard,* February 25, 1989, 1, 82. Elsewhere in the same article, Vernon Reid, guitarist for Living Colour and founder of the Black Rock Coalition, added "If George Michael can be the 'best black artist,' then what does it mean to *be* a black artist?"

36. Donna L. Halper, "Urban Image Blends Audiences: Radio Downplays Blackness," *Billboard,* June 5, 1982, BM-6, BM-11, BM-14.

37. This profile of Frankie Crocker and WLBS, as well as the general line of argumentation, is derived from Nelson George, *The Death of Rhythm and Blues* (New York: Pantheon Books, 1988), 126–31. Crocker, in a later interview, connected these changes at WLBS to racial uplift: "Black audiences were proud that the people on the radio were intelligent and could speak to them and could speak to anybody." This was opposed to the "jive talk" heard on other black radio stations. "In the Black," *Radio & Records: 30 Year Anniversary,* CD-2 (November 2003), cited in Kim Simpson, *Early '70s Radio,* 151.

38. Nelson George and Paul Grein, "Black Formats Offer More New Act Airplay," *Billboard,* June 5, 1982, 1, 22.

39. Ibid.

40. Ibid.

41. Donna L. Halper, "Urban Image Blends Audiences," BM-14; and Nile Rodgers, "Commentary: The Black Side of Censorship," *Billboard,* April 9, 1983, 8. William Barlow

makes a particularly pointed critique of the crossover effect for black radio in "Commercial and Noncommercial Radio," in *Split Image: African Americans in the Mass Media,* ed. Jannette L. Dates and William Barlow (Washington, DC: Howard University Press, 1990), 232. For a defense of crossover and the race-neutral concept during this period written as a response to George, see Steve Perry, "Ain't No Mountain High Enough: The Politics of Crossover," in *Facing the Music,* ed. Simon Frith (New York: Pantheon, 1988), 51–87.

42. Stephen Peeples, "Mike Harrison," *Rock Around the World* (March 1977): 21.

43. Eric Weisbard, *Top 40 Democracy,* 194–237. For other examples of programming variety on AOR, see Mike Harrison, "The R&R Interview: Bob Gooding," *Radio and Records,* April 1, 1977, 28, 30; and Mike Harrison, "The R&R Interview: Max Floyd," *Radio and Records,* August 19, 1977, 28.

44. Kim Simpson, *Early '70s Radio,* 106. The reference to free-form stations' support of the Black Panther Party comes from Kim Simpson, *Early '70s Radio,* 133. For more on free-form radio, see Michael C. Keith, *Voices in the Purple Haze: Underground Radio and the Sixties* (London: Praeger Publishers, 1997); and Susan J. Douglas, "The FM Revolution," in *Listening In: Radio and the American Imagination* (Minneapolis: University of Minnesota Press, 1999), 256–83.

45. Susan J. Douglas, "The FM Revolution," 276.

46. Robert Palmer, "Brazil's Beat Alters Black Pop: Pop Changes," *New York Times,* February 27, 1983, H21–22; John Rockwell, "Michael Jackson's *Thriller:* Superb Pop," *New York Times,* December 19, 1982, 25, 28; John Rockwell, "In Pop Music, the Races Remain Far Apart," *New York Times,* March 18, 1984, H1, 22.

47. Bill Speed, "Black Radio," *Radio and Records,* December 8, 1978, 44. For commentary on the negative effect of disco on African American popular music, see Nelson George, *The Death of Rhythm and Blues,* 150–55, 181; and Rickey Vincent, *Funk: The Music, the People and the Rhythm of the One* (New York: St. Martin's Press, 1996), 214–15.

48. In the words of Larry Williams, general manager and program director of WBLX in Mobile, Alabama, "They're just finding out what people at the grass roots level have been listening to all along, which is black music." Nelson George, "Arbitron DST Use Aids WBLX Ratings," *Billboard,* August 21, 1982, 18. See also "New Methodology Is Key to Black, Urban Increases," *Billboard,* July 17, 1982, 66, 72.

49. Leo Sacks, "Format Consultants: AOR Boon or Bane?," *Billboard,* June 12, 1982, 1, 45.

50. Sam Sutherland, "WB Aims for Reverse Crossover: Rock, Pop Acts Finding Increasing Black Acceptance," *Billboard,* October 2, 1982, 52, 54. On the supplanting of blue-collar audiences by yuppies, see Eric Weisbard, *Top 40 Democracy,* 217–26. Will Straw traces the decline of both AOR and country/AC during this period due to their relatively slow "rates of change and innovation" (i.e., restricted playlists) at a time when "rapid rates of innovation and turnover within the recording industry" had returned. Will Straw, "Popular Music as Cultural Commodity," 236–38.

51. The quotation is from Steven Levy, "Ad Nauseam: How MTV Sells Out Rock & Roll," *Rolling Stone,* December 8, 1983, 30–37, 74–79. A year earlier, Laura Foti, in a scathing *Billboard* editorial on MTV and music video, stated that "MTV's programming executives have defended themselves by comparing MTV to typical AOR radio stations," implying (or outright stating) that the equivalence between MTV and AOR was in large part responsible for

MTV's racist programming. Laura Foti, "Taste & Fairness on Video," *Billboard*, December 11, 1982, 10. Black artists such as Rick James also criticized MTV's policies, citing the limits placed on the economic potential of their recordings due to their exclusion from MTV. Nelson George, "Slick Rick Says MTV Is Sick," *Billboard*, February 19, 1983, 53.

52. Robert Christgau, "New Wave Hegemony and the Bebop Question," *Village Voice*, January 22, 1979, http://www.robertchristgau.com/xg/pnj/pj78.php, accessed January 31, 2015. "New wave" could even be employed as a sign of otherness in funk/R&B, as in the lyrics of Rick James's 1981 hit "Super Freak." The namesake of the song is "the kind of girl you read about in new wave magazines"; the majority of the women in the video for "Super Freak" are white. Such a view of "new wave women" as sexually promiscuous was not limited to R&B musicians, nor were visions of new wave as some sort of ultimate generic other. See (and listen to), for example, Rodney Crowell's 1978 country recording "Baby, Better Start Turnin' 'Em Down."

53. Robert Christgau, "Rock 'n' Roller Coaster: The Music Biz on a Joyride," *Village Voice*, February 7, 1984, 37–45. For more on the "new music" and its connection to MTV, see Parke Puterbaugh, "Anglomania: America Surrenders to the Brits—But Who Really Wins?," *Rolling Stone*, November 10, 1983, 31–32. Many of these observations about punk, new wave, and post-punk are derived from the work of Mimi Haddon. See her "What Is Post-Punk? British and American Popular Music on the Edge of the 1980s" (PhD diss., McGill University, 2015), especially the chapter "Situating Post-Punk in the Broader Pop Field."

54. John Rockwell, "In Pop Music, the Races Remain Far Apart." An excellent summary of these debates may be found in Robert Christgau, "Rock 'n' Roller Coaster."

55. See Nelson George, "Little Credit for Hitbreakers: Black Retailers Fight Industry Double Standards," *Billboard*, June 5, 1982, BM-6, 12; "The Rhythm & the Blues: The View from 125th St., Part II," *Billboard*, October 9, 1982, 46; and "Times Even Tougher for Black Retailers," *Billboard*, November 13, 1982, 58.

56. See Nelson George, "The Rhythm and the Blues: The Concert Issue Won't Go Away," *Billboard*, December 4, 1982, 48, 51; "The Rhythm and the Blues: Dimples Promotes His Opinion," *Billboard*, December 25, 1982, 48, 50; "The Rhythm and the Blues: Griffey Seeks Promoter-Talent Ties," *Billboard*, January 8, 1983, 65, 66.

57. Jon Pareles, "Michael Jackson at 25: A Musical Phenomenon," *New York Times*, January 14, 1984, 11; John Rockwell, "Michael Jackson's *Thriller*: Superb Pop"; Stephen Holden, "Pop Music Surges Along New and Unexpected Paths," *New York Times*, November 20, 1983, 1, 18; Robert Palmer, "Energy and Creativity Added Up to Exciting Pop," *New York Times*, December 25, 1983, H19, H25. In the wake of Jackson's death in 2009, a wave of scholarship has explored Jackson as exemplifying a new sort of post-identity public persona. See the essays published in special issues of *Popular Music and Society* 35, no. 3 (2011) and the *Journal of Popular Music Studies* 23, no. 1 (2011). For writing by critics in the 1980s that early on recognized the relationships between Jackson's boundary crossings in the musical and social realms, see Greg Tate, "I'm White! What's Wrong with Michael Jackson," in *The Pop, Rock, and Soul Reader*; Kobena Mercer, "Monster Metaphors: Notes on Michael Jackson's 'Thriller,'" in *Sound and Vision: The Music Video Reader*, ed. Simon Frith, Andrew Goodwin, and Lawrence Grossberg (London and New York: Routledge, 1993), 93–108; Michele Wallace, "Michael Jackson, Black Modernisms, and 'The Ecstasy of Communication,'" in *Invisibility Blues: From Pop to Theory* (London and New York: Verso, 1990), 77–90.

58. Paul Grein, "Michael Jackson Cut Breaks AOR Barrier," *Billboard*, December 18, 1982, 1, 58.

59. Even "Beat It," however, was not sui generis. The particular stylistic fusion projected by the recording closely resembles that of "Let It Whip" by the Dazz Band from earlier in 1982 (even the titles resemble each other). "Let It Whip" evidenced a fairly strong crossover effect for a black/R&B number; thus, the stylistic hybridity of "Beat It" could be understood as not only citing the previous recording's stylistic hybridity, but citing its crossover effect as well.

60. Again, see former *Cash Box* editor Irv Lichtfield's comments in John Broven, *Record Makers and Breakers: Voices of the Independent Rock 'n' Roll Pioneers* (Urbana and Chicago: University of Illinois Press, 2009), 201.

61. I am fully aware of the absurd aspects of this transcription. On one level it is woefully inaccurate, squeezing the flexible nuances of Khan's phrasing into what appears to be the arithmetic precision of Western notation. On the other hand, the sheer complexity of this attempt might give the transcriber pause; a more "accurate" transcription would probably resemble nothing so much as the "new complexity" of a composer such as Brian Ferneyhough. What this music has that Ferneyhough's lacks, however, is that Khan's rhythmic complexity is performed against a groove, and that its effect depends on how the apparent rhythmic freedom of an improvised ornament actually reinforces the groove rather than vitiating it. For the most thoughtful exploration of the issues involved in transcribing rhythmically complex music, see Peter Winkler, "Writing Ghost Notes: The Poetics and Politics of Transcription," in *Keeping Score: Music, Disciplinarity, Culture*, ed. David Schwarz, Anahid Kassabian, and Lawrence Siegel (Charlottesville and London: University Press of Virginia, 1997), 169–203.

62. For Jackson's live performance of "Got to Be There," see https://www.youtube.com/watch?v = e1ODaEq9n3Y, accessed February 5, 2015.

63. Such distinctions were apparent in other recordings of the period. Nelson George noted how, in Shalamar's "Dead Giveaway," the "pushed beat and slightly sinister synthesizer" referred to new wave while the vocal referenced soul. Nelson George, "Shalamar Crosses the Color Line," *Billboard*, August 27, 1983, 42.

64. Musical phrases from "Atomic Dog" were later adapted by Snoop Doggy Dogg in his "What's My Name." Paul Gilroy has written insightfully on the trope of the dog in Afrodiasporic discourse in general and how this figures in Snoop's name and public persona: "[Snoop's] filling the mask of undifferentiated racialised otherness with quizzical canine features reveals something about the operation of white supremacy and the cultures of compensation that answer it. It is a political and, I believe a moral gesture." Paul Gilroy, "'After the Love Has Gone': Bio-Politics and Etho-Poetics in the Black Public Sphere," *Public Culture* 7, no. 1 (Fall 1994): 73. Ricky Vincent, somewhat more prosaically, notes the "hilariously accurate expressions of the doglike nature of horny men (and women)" in "Atomic Dog," and goes on to note the numerous recordings that have sampled or copied the recording's hook, leading to his designation of "Atomic Dog" as "the *jam* of the 1980s." Ricky Vincent, *Funk*, 250.

65. Accounts vary about what Yetnikoff did or did not do, though for reports of the *rumors* about happened, see "'Billie Jean' Gets Her MTV," *Billboard*, March 26, 1983, 1, 70; and Robert Christgau, "Rock 'n' Roller Coaster."

66. One of the first and most sustained interpretations of early music videos as a post-modern, avant-garde visual medium was presented by E. Ann Kaplan in *Rocking Around the Clock: Music Television, Postmodernism, and Consumer Culture* (New York: Methuen, 1987). Andrew Goodwin produced what was probably the most thorough counterargument, stressing the important role of musical rhythm in the rapid editing of music videos, and the relation of music videos to television advertisements, in *Dancing in the Distraction Factory: Music Television and Popular Culture* (Minneapolis: University of Minnesota Press, 1992).

67. Robert Palmer, for one, heard "Atomic Dog" as Clinton's response to "the challenge of electronic funk and rap." Robert Palmer, "Brazil's Beat Alters Black Pop: Pop Changes," *New York Times,* February 27, 1983, H21–22. However, rather than rap, it's also possible to hear the spoken introduction as a citation of Clinton's own habit of rapping in recordings such as "Maggot Brain" (1971) and "Chocolate City" (1975). Mark Anthony Neal views Clinton and P-Funk's alienation from the mainstream as part of a strategic rejection of the "corporate imperialism that mined a valuable landscape of black cultural expression" and a "trenchant critique of black middle-class isolation and mass-market-driven aesthetics." Mark Anthony Neal, *What the Music Said,* 112–13.

68. The dominance of the synthesizer was recognized by several critics. Robert Palmer noted how "the synthesizer, which conquered the British pop charts in 1982, made itself felt in almost every corner of American pop in 1983." Robert Palmer, "Energy and Creativity Added Up to Exciting Pop," *New York Times,* December 25, 1983, H19, H25. Robert Christgau observed the next month how both the black and pop charts were laden with "synthesizer-based neo-professionalism galore." Robert Christgau, "Rock 'n' Roller Coaster." See also Vernon Gibbs, "The Synthesizer: Instrument, Not the Player, Changes Music," *Billboard,* June 16, 1984, BM-6, BM-12. For a discussion of the guitar as signifying non-blackness, see the discussion of Run-DMC's "Rock Box" in "High Profile for Profile Label," *Billboard,* March 3, 1984, 50.

69. For more on the double standard applied to songs such as David Bowie's "Let's Dance," see Nile Rodgers, "Commentary," discussed earlier.

70. For contemporaneous accounts of the changed position of rock, see Robert Christgau, "Rock 'n' Roller Coaster"; and John Rockwell, "In Pop Music, the Races Remain Far Apart."

71. For an excellent overview of the impact of institutional shifts on expressive resources in African American popular music from the mid-1970s through the mid-1990s, see Mark Anthony Neal, "Rhythm and Bullshit."

72. "Billboard Adopts 'R&B' as New Name for 2 Charts," *Billboard,* October 27, 1990, 6, 35. My emphasis. The awareness of the importance of names in practices of inclusion, exclusion, and access to resources has a long history among African Americans. Out of many possible examples, one can read Dizzy Gillespie's reflections on the benefits (in addition to the expression of religious freedom) of adopting an Islamic name by jazz musicians of the 1940s in *To Be or Not . . . to Bop,* excerpt reprinted in Robert Walser, *Keeping Time: Readings in Jazz History* (New York: Oxford University Press, 1999), 150–51.

73. For *Billboard*'s announcement of this chart and the discussion about what necessitated its invention, see "Kim Freeman, "Hot 30 Crossover Chart Tracks New Breed of Radio," *Billboard,* February 28, 1987, 1, 83.

9

Notes Toward a Conclusion

Once upon a time, before the earlier chapters of the book grew much larger than I had anticipated, I entertained an idea for a chapter on music videos in the 1990s, given that the perception of popular music categories seemed to have been fundamentally transformed by the newfound importance of the televisual medium. Music videos provided a different view into the components of the categories, particularly those having to do with social connotations, and with other visual, kinetic associations and kinds of synesthetic experiences. Many music videos produced an image of the assumed audience for the recording within the video text, compactly materializing associations that formerly could only be established by a series of analytical moves. At the same time, by the mid-1990s, music television channels and shows had proliferated to the point where they adopted some of the same narrowcasted targeting of demographic groups as had radio formats earlier. Thus, the musical, visual, and social components of popular music categories could be highlighted, one presumes, by the way in which individual video texts moved or did not move between different music video channels and shows.[1]

If video transformed the generic landscape in the 1980s and 1990s, then this in retrospect seems like a modest intervention compared to what has happened in the wake of the wide availability of transportable digital sound files. Chris Molanphy's article discussed in chapter 7, in which he looked back at the R&B chart of the 1960s, was a response to the difficulties created by new modes of tracking popularity such as digital downloads and YouTube views.[2] Earlier market research firms and techniques such as Arbitron, Nielsen, and SoundScan had attempted to track listener-viewer-consumer taste in an increasingly scientific manner. With hindsight, however, these attempts were crude compared to how every Internet user's mouse click can now be tracked, cataloged, and eventually used for market research or national security purposes. Despite these technological advances, and a recalibration of the role of popularity charts and their relationship to marketing categories, practitioners and contemporary analysts of popular music genres encounter many of the same obstacles as did their predecessors. For example, those working with music information retrieval (MIR) who attempt to use data extracted from digital sound files to analyze genre still struggle with the tension between, on the one hand, the reification occasioned by a reliance on style traits and notions of linear causality, and on the other, the recognition of culturally determined interpretations of texts, the incorporation of non-music-stylistic components in the description of the relation of text to category, the multiple possible classifications of individual texts, the sharing of socio-musical components between genres, and processes of nonlinear causality. These difficulties often result from difficulties found in pre-MIR uses and analyses of genre in their confusion of scale or level, a failure to recognize the role of distributed creativity and the relational nature of genres, a tendency to blur synchronic and diachronic relations, and the reliance on wildly different criteria for categories that are presented as being on the same level of scale.[3]

Based on this description of the state of MIR analysis, it would appear that many of the challenges of genre analysis have not changed. Nevertheless, the resources for researching popular music categories have expanded enormously, as have the circulation of elaborate generic schema. Websites such as Ishkur's Guide to Electronic Music present detailed taxonomies that feature divisions according to scale, musical examples, diachronic charts, and brief, irreverent descriptions of the genres and subgenres.[4] Heavy metal is another genre that has spawned an abundance of taxonomies, diachronic graphs of generic dispersion, and debates about criteria and the veracity of categorical distinctions.[5] In industry-based practice, Glen McDonald's work with EchoNest and Spotify illustrates some of the difficulties already discussed in connection to MIR work in general in its tension between trait-based reification and discourse-based folk taxonomies that guide quotidian use of genre labels. McDonald has explained that EchoNest's response has been to rely on connections between artists rather than individual songs or albums as a way of organizing the similarity relations on which the company's taxonomies are based.[6] In addition to MIR analysis, the Internet now produces its own form of constelled communities, in the discussion groups, music websites, and reference sources such as Wikipedia that provide ceaselessly mutating attempts at genre reification. Internet users are themselves nodes within larger networks of genre users and producers, as their constant modifications and input creates a kind of consensus, which then produces effects upon Internet users—who may perform a range of social functions, such as musician, critic, fan, music industry worker—who then create further modifications both within the Internet and in other media.[7]

It cannot be denied that digital file sharing, downloading, web-based consumption, and services such as YouTube have altered many things, from how popularity can be recorded to the relationship of sales of individual recordings to the categories in which they are placed, all the way to representations of popularity itself.[8] Nevertheless, millenarian claims made on behalf of the Internet's effect on musical categories can, at their most extreme, portend a liberation of consumers from the death grip of the music industry's relentless classification schemes. Although the points through which categories circulate have multiplied, and the manner in which texts circulate has changed, the basic conditions and concepts used in *Categorizing Sound*, I would argue, have not disappeared from discourses on genre. We will still want to know what conditions enabled a particular category to emerge, how borders blur between the category and its neighbors, what social relations are performed by the category, and whether the emergence of the category effected a rearrangement of the popular music field.

A Question of Method?[9]

One day, before I returned to working on these "notes toward a conclusion," I made the mistake of looking at my email inbox. There I spied a notice from a certain Internet-based retailer informing me of a new product that, evidently, the skein of my mouse clicks had directed to me: the latest "best of" compilation by the Grateful Dead. While I had no interest in purchasing this "ultimate gateway to the Grateful Dead," as the web copy described the CD, some information at the bottom of the page did attract my eye: the sales of this recording were ranked 191 in "music" and 95 in "rock," but 9 in "classic rock."

This anecdote returns us to one of the issues stressed repeatedly throughout this book, most notably the matter of scale or level. The importance of differentiating the level at which an analysis is taking place produces one of the greatest challenges in genre analysis: the difficulty in avoiding reductionism and the reliance on essences that tend to occur in a trait-based approach. In genre analysis, reductionism can take the form of assuming an unvarying relationship between a micro level—often consisting of an individual text or a category on a lower level—and a macro level—represented here by the category or categories within which that text or lower-level category might be grouped. Such an approach posits that a certain grouping of stylistic components will equate with a category and that a change in the stylistic components of a text will result in its automatic reclassification.

The idea of level and scale does not resemble the relations found between those Russian dolls, in which each successive level contains and absorbs the previous one.[10] Such a clear nesting (another form of reductionism) is present in a certain Internet-based retailer's presentation of the popularity of *The Best of the Grateful Dead* described above: "classic rock" is absorbed by "rock," which in turn is absorbed by "music." One could take this example (and many more like it) as a clear refutation of millenarian claims that the Internet has obliterated all prior modalities of comprehending musical categories.

A more detailed consideration of individual components of a genre, however, and how these interact with categories operating at different levels yields a more complex picture than that depicted by my web-based solicitor. Rather, these components and their relation to categories occurring on different scales function more like a constellation, in which components from a category on one level have the ability to participate in categories on other levels. Take the example of instruments used in different popular music genres during the 1980s, to return to the discussion from chapter 8. In a manner similar to how individual recordings may participate in multiple categories, the same instrument could participate in different categories operating on different levels without signifying a change of category. While Dave Chapelle's skit discussed in chapter 1 revealed important truths about the relation between instruments, genres, affects, and social identities, the following example adds a bit of nuance to the model he proposed. On one hand, for an early-1980s radio format (that approached the level of a marketing category) such as AOR, the electric guitar was ubiquitous, particularly when played with a fairly standardized overdriven tone. On the other hand, one particular electric guitar, the Fender Stratocaster, when played in a bluesy, staccato fashion, had an iconic relationship to hard (non-crossover) country, arguably a subgenre of country existing on the level of a critic-fan genre. The very same Fender Stratocasters, however, played slightly out of phase with a clean tone, could be heard often in mainstream and dance tracks (many cuts on *Thriller* included), which could be understood as participating in the marketing category levels of black music or mainstream pop, in addition to multiple radio formats and critic-fan genres.

The mere use of an electric guitar in a track therefore did not necessarily signify its potential to participate in multiple genres. Rather, in addition to the presence of the electric guitar, the guitar's role in the song, its tone, the way in which it interacted with other instruments, and the way in which it was played indicate how it may or may not have generated, cited, or referred to crossover conventions and effects. Indeed, looking more closely at Chapelle's skit, even his examples demonstrate that different types of guitars may signify different genres. The electric guitar played one way with a certain type of tone signified jam band music, while it signified heavy metal when played in a different fashion with a different tone. Chords strummed on an acoustic, steel-string guitar signified country music.

The discussion of the guitar in popular music of the early 1980s should clarify that merely discussing the components of a musical category need not reify either the constitution of the category or the relationship of the components to one another. This analysis of components and their relationship to categories is an example of nonlinear causality, in that one and the same cause (the use of an instrument, for example) may lead to different effects and interpretations, and at the same time different causes may lead to the same effect (e.g., recordings with very different instrumentation may be classified in the same genre). Rather than relying on individual instances in order to establish a theory about relationships between musical texts, categories of music, and categories of people at a particular point in time—which creates the problematic of direct correspondences via cause and effect—such analyses are more convincing when they consider large populations of objects that are classified similarly, creating the effect of statistical causality. And although Chapelle does rely on single instances, large populations of similar songs could be found that would bear out his theory. For these reasons, the guitars in Michael Jackson's "Beat It" (heavy metal–ish guitar solo) and Ray Parker Jr.'s "The Other Woman" (hard rock riff), for example, played a role in the process of those songs' participation in multiple genres, radio formats, and marketing categories. In contrast to these recordings, the guitar (a Fender Stratocaster!) in "And the Beat Goes on" (1980) by the Whispers (complementary rhythmic riff in a funk-soul groove) interacted with other musical-lyrical components that primarily referred to conventions in the soul and funk genres.

Micro-macro relations are not the only ways in which citationality and nonlinear causality might impact the emergence and stabilization of popular music categories. Macro-micro relations also play an important role. Thus, once a category (at any level) has achieved relative stabilization, it then may influence the creation of individual texts. Artists may absorb a sense of style-audience association and therefore imagine a particular destination for their music, a process evoking the idea of addressivity discussed in chapter 1. Macro-to-micro relations also have an important material dimension, as economic and other institutional resources are often allocated to particular artists based on the perception of how they fit a particular category, thereby affecting which songs are produced, recorded, and performed, and what the musical-lyrical components of those songs might be.

But notions of the components of an assemblage as a mobile constellation can be applied to more than just musical style components: individual linguistic statements also made up the texts of preceding analyses. These too can be analyzed in greater detail. The meanings of these statements are not assumed to be self-evident but rather are established through their relation to other statements circulating at the same time, to the individuals who uttered them, and to the institutions (including the publications) with which the individuals were associated. In addition to access to expressive resources (linguistic, musical), material resources figure into the analyses as well. These include access to monetary resources, other types of institutional support, and the institutional histories of inclusion and exclusion according to the social categories with which the agents identify. In all of these musical and verbal categories and expressive and material modes, components come with social connotations, constitute a network of texts operating on different levels of scale, and are defined in relation to one another in differing degrees of temporal stability.

The discussion of the previous chapters also refers to different scales of historical temporality. The first of these is the emergence of a concept based on an analysis of a particular moment. A focus on emergence revolves around a series of questions: How did people make sense of a musico-stylistic formation before the categorical concept existed with which that formation is now associated? How did public perceptions of this complex change as a more stable relationship formed between musical sounds, social identities, and verbal descriptions of the formation? The second temporal scale consists of long-range historical trajectories constituted by successive presentist impressions of a category and later retroactive histories of the category.

The networks of musical and linguistic texts, and their relations to institutional resources, yield verbal-musical associations that would not likely appear in the consideration of a diachronic study of a single genre based on present-day, self-evident truths about that genre. For example, without an awareness of the discursive network in which it circulated, we might assume that the trope of "that certain something" used to explain the ineffable qualities of genres associated with minority populations from the 1920s through the 1940s to be merely a quaint expression that does not accord with what we now think are the salient historical features of either race music, old-time music, African American swing bands, or 1940s hillbilly ensembles. Other examples from a far-from-complete list of verbal-musical tropes that became apparent from a historical emphasis on a genre's moment of emergence include the Yiddish minor found in Jewish music from the early decades of the previous century; lyrics about Chinamen and hop that appeared in the vaudeville blues, which, rather than signifying an early expression of gangsta affect, instead reflected the popularity of lyrics about the dangers of Chinatown; the emergence of legit vocal style in conjunction with disaster ballads in the 1920s; tropes that tied together ideas about aesthetics, volume, intonation, race, and genre in the late 1930s; the notion of corn, uniting novelty ensembles with a rural image, urban notions about farmers, contemporary slang, and country music in the 1940s; the shift of "soul" from adjective to noun; and the emergence of the crossover concept into mainstream discourse about music. And then we have the frequency with which Fender Stratocasters appeared in the early 1980s, cutting across individual genres (not to mention that even-more-ubiquitous marker of the early 1980s, the sound of the first commercially available digital synthesizers from Yamaha).

The concepts of relationality, citationality, the exteriority of the relations between the part and the whole, the tension between presentist and retroactive historical conceptions, the necessity of analyzing differences in scale and level—these all run through *Categorizing Sound*. None of these concepts are ideal types or static concepts that need be applied in a formulaic fashion. Rather, the emphasis in the analysis is on the events that form the basis of the analysis as singularities. This emphasis on singularity or individuality applies to each level or scale of the analysis, meaning that assumptions cannot be made in advance about the relations between the parts of the category that they constitute, nor between the relations of the different levels that form a field of categories during a particular historical moment. Continuities may emerge between one moment and the next—this type of analysis does not exclude that possibility. But it also does not assume continuity between the present and the past, that what are now "self-evident" truths were always thus. The question becomes how the self-evidence of these truths comes into being. If we now believe that it is natural to have certain categories for popular music; that charts exist with certain labels; that these have a certain relationship with radio formats and with the terms that musicians, fans, and critics use to communicate about music; and that these categories of music are related to categories of people, then it is important to recognize that these categories did not always exist, that they will not always exist in their current form, and that it is possible to imagine other sorts of relations. The same holds true for how humans are divided into categories.

What does it mean, then, to analyze the practice of categorization as an event? One might ask, to begin with, when approaching the emergence of a category, what practices of genrefication already exist? Taking the emergence of race music as one instance of the practice of categorization, one could then determine preexisting practices of articulating a category of people to a category of music: the already existing practices of how popular music categories became established, and how ideas about these categories circulated and took hold. But these practices are themselves extremely broad and abstract. Further subdividing them, we could then analyze the practice of articulating a category of people to a category of music, including the practices and discourses about the significance of social categories and musical taste; already-established practices of communicating the popularity of recordings both to music industry agents and potential consumers; preexisting notions about minority social categories in general, and African Americans in particular; and the status of already existing categories associated with African Americans, such as jazz and blues. These can be broken down further into their musical components, public associations of the musicians associated with the categories, the types of performance venues most associated with the musical categories, and so on.

In light of my pronouncements on the perils of reification and reductionism, do I think I have successfully avoided them? Perhaps it's better to ask: Do I think it is ever possible to avoid them? The answer is, of course, no. Once this is acknowledged, the challenge is to increase one's own awareness of the limits of analyzing events as singularities. Overly schematic notions of scale are perhaps the most obvious point at which reductionism could occur, and one can never specify the point at which one level blurs with the next.

Despite what might appear like a methodological laundry list in the preceding paragraphs, this work is not a prescription for "how to do genre analysis"; the relationships comprising a category cannot be known in advance. That is why I cannot predict what might be necessary to analyze genre in the context of 1990s music videos, or in the context of how Internet-based communication has altered the field of popular music genres. I can only assume that, as in the somewhat more distant historical cases analyzed in this book, the various meanings, connections, and networks of relations will be discovered through a patient establishment of filiations via textual traces that open outward from a single instance of genrefication. We cannot assume that new technology has in and of itself altered the practice of how categories emerge and stabilize without studying the details of a given category's formation. There we may discover startling new and revolutionary processes at work next to the familiar and banal. We do not know before doing the research which of these may play a bigger role in the social life of a genre.

What I have tried to present is a history of the practice of categorizing, not a history of the categories themselves. That is, the examples presented in this book provide a provisional history of how a certain concept of a category becomes accepted at a particular time and place—how it becomes legible. Put differently, this book is not so much about the contents of the categories as about how the categories are produced: the networks of discourses, people, and institutions that produce the concept of a category that is accepted across a range of different sites, how these categories of music are articulated to categories of people, and the ways of thinking about music and people that make these articulations capable of being accepted, and of then functioning in the world so as to direct resources toward particular combinations of musical sound and the actors who produce them. If I occasionally do pause and note the contents of the categories, this is in order to observe the relative stabilization of particular techniques and practices, and how their repetition has enabled them to become associated with a particular category. The argument is that particular articulations of music and people are not natural or inevitable, and that music that is reported as popular has not achieved this status due to the will of the people. The categories respond to emerging concepts about sounds and social groups, and generate effects that enter into musical practice and the role of music in other types of social interactions, thus creating a feedback loop, a circular process that blurs the lines between the ideas of power imposed from above and the grassroots creation of musical meaning.

I turned to the history of popular music categories, with its sudden ruptures and its enduring continuities, because of the power these categories hold in the daily texture of contemporary musical life. *Categorizing Sound* is a history of how this pervasive power took root, and of the many sites through which it makes itself felt. Perhaps there is a hint here in these concluding gestures, however, not only of ideas about how to understand the categories of the present, but of a utopian gesture toward the future. For if popular music categories are made without the conscious imposition of an agent's will ("they never even knew"), then these categories may be unmade as well. And if this is true for categories of popular music, then what of the larger social categories in which the musical categories participate, with those larger categories' asymmetrical apportioning of resources and opportunities? Even if we cannot will a change to occur, we may live to recognize when we reflect back to earlier times that we do, in fact, know that we are living within a new, unforeseen arrangement of genre. Although we do not know what form this will take, we do know that a transformation of the arrangement of musical categories will be related to a reclassification of social categories. And that might not be so bad.

NOTES

1. A brief analysis of this sort may be found in David Brackett, "What a Difference a Name Makes: Two Instances of African-American Music," in *The Cultural Study of Music: A Critical Introduction,* ed. Martin Clayton, Trevor Herbert, and Richard Middleton (New York and London: Routledge, 2012), 127–39.

2. Chris Molanphy, "I Know You Got Soul: The Trouble with *Billboard's* R&B/Hip-Hop Chart," *Pitchfork,* April 14, 2014, http://pitchfork.com/features/articles/9378-i-know-you-got-soul-the-trouble-with-billboards-rbhip-hop-chart/, accessed October 26, 2014.

3. For a further examination of genre analysis and MIR, see John Frow, "Scale and Taxonomy in Musical Genres," presented at the "Genre and Music: New Directions" conference held at McGill University, Montreal, September 27–28, 2014; Eric Drott, "Genre in the Age of Algorithms," also presented at the "Genre and Music: New Directions" conference; and Paul Lamere, "Social Tagging and Music Information Retrieval," *Journal of New Music Research* 37, no. 2 (2008).

4. "Ishkur's Guide to Electronic Music, v. 2.5," http://techno.org/electronic-music-guide/, accessed March 20, 2015.

5. For a detailed analysis of these taxonomies see Eric Smialek, "Expression in Extreme Metal Music, ca. 1980–2012" (PhD diss., McGill University, 2015). For an online example of a map and timeline, replete with sound files, see Nick Grant and Patrick Gilbraith, "Map of Metal," http://mapofmetal.com/#/home, accessed March 20, 2015.

6. Comments on Glen McDonald and EchoNest are based on Glen McDonald, "The Genre Grinder's Song (What It's Like to Run a Machine for Sorting Music)," presented at the "Genre and Music: New Directions" conference. The term "folk taxonomy" comes from John Frow, "Scale and Taxonomy in Musical Genres."

7. On the making and remaking of genres on the Internet, see the discussion in Mimi Haddon, "What Is Post-Punk? British and American Popular Music on the Edge of the 1980s" (PhD diss., McGill University, 2015), 66–71.

8. Eric Drott has argued convincingly that music recommendation engines have

enacted a telling shift in their understanding of genre from one of *kind* to an emphasis on *similarity* relations ("Genre in the Age of Algorithms"). Drott also makes the point that the rise of the playlist emphasizes different grouping factors than did previous conceptions of genre. See also Nicolas Scaringella, Giorgio Zoia, and Daniel Mlynek, "Automatic Genre Classification of Music Content: A Survey," *IEEE Signal Processing Magazine* 23, no. 2 (2006): 133–41.

9. The subhead here recognizes the indebtedness of the following discussion to that found in Michel Foucault, "Questions of Method," in *Power: Essential Works of Foucault, 1954–1984*, ed. James D. Faubion (New York: The New Press, 2000), 223–38.

10. The image of Russian dolls, as well as the following discussion of assemblage theory, is indebted to Manuel DeLanda, *A New Philosophy of Society: Assemblage Theory and Social Complexity* (London: Bloomsbury, 2006), 33.

BIBLIOGRAPHY

Abbott, Lynn, and Doug Seroff. *Out of Sight: The Rise of African American Popular Music.* Jackson: University Press of Mississippi, 2002.

———. *Ragged but Right: Black Traveling Shows, "Coon Songs," and the Dark Pathway to Blues and Jazz.* Jackson: University Press of Mississippi, 2007.

———. "'They Cert'ly Sound Good to Me': Sheet Music, Southern Vaudeville, and the Commercial Ascendancy of the Blues." *American Music* 14, no. 4 (Winter 1996): 402–54.

Abrahams, Roger. *Deep Down in the Jungle: Negro Narrative Folklore from the Streets of Philadelphia.* Chicago: Aldine Publishing, 1970.

Adorno, Theodor. "The Curves of the Needle." In *Essays on Music*, 271–76. Edited by Richard Leppert. Translated by Thomas Y. Levin. Berkeley and Los Angeles: University of California Press, 2002. First published in 1927.

Adorno, Theodor, with the assistance of George Simpson. "On Popular Music." In *Studies in Philosophy and Social Science*, vol. 9, 17–48. New York: Institute of Social Research, 1941. Reprinted in Richard Leppert, ed. *Essays on Music*, 437–69. Berkeley and Los Angeles: University of California Press, 2002.

Ake, David. *Jazz Cultures.* Berkeley and Los Angeles: University of California Press, 2002.

Altman, Rick. *The American Film Musical.* Bloomington: Indiana University Press, 1987.

———. *Film/Genre.* London: British Film Institute, 1999.

———. "A Semantic/Syntactic Approach to Film Genre." *Cinema Journal* 23, no. 1 (Spring 1984): 6–18.

Anderson, Benedict. *Imagined Communities: Reflections on the Origin and Spread of Nationalism.* London and New York: Verso, 1991.

Anderson, Tim J. *Making Easy Listening: Material Culture and Postwar American Recording.* Minneapolis: University of Minnesota Press, 2006.

Attali, Jacques. *Noise: The Political Economy of Music.* Translated by Brian Massumi. Minneapolis: University of Minnesota Press, 1985.

Austin, J. L. *How to Do Things with Words*. Cambridge, MA: Harvard University Press, 1962.

Badger, F. Reid. *A Life in Ragtime: A Biography of James Reese Europe*. New York: Oxford University Press, 1995.

Baker, Sarah, Andy Bennett, and Jodie Taylor, eds. *Redefining Mainstream Popular Music*. New York and London: Routledge, 2013.

Bakhtin, Mikhail. *The Dialogic Imagination: Four Essays*. Edited by Michael Holquist. Translated by Caryl Emerson and Michael Holquist. Austin: University of Texas Press, 1981.

———. "Problems of Speech Genres." In *Speech Genres and Other Late Essays*, 60–102. Edited by Caryl Emerson and Michael Holquist. Austin: University of Texas Press, 1986.

———. "Response to a Question from the *Novy Mir* Editorial Staff." In *Speech Genres and Other Late Essays*, 1–9. Edited by Caryl Emerson and Michael Holquist. Austin: University of Texas Press, 1986.

Baraka, Amiri (aka Leroi Jones). *Black Music*. New York: William Morrow and Co., 1968.

———. *Blues People: The Negro Experience in White America and the Music That Developed from It*. New York: William Morrow and Company, 1963.

Baraka, Amiri, and Larry Neal, eds. *Black Fire: An Anthology of Afro-American Writing*. Baltimore: Black Classic Press, 2007. First published in 1968.

Barber, Karin. *The Anthropology of Texts, Persons and Publics*. Cambridge: Cambridge University Press, 2007.

Barg, Lisa. "Paul Robeson's *Ballad for Americans*: Race and the Cultural Politics of 'People's Music.'" *Journal of the Society for American Music* 2, no. 1 (2008): 27–70.

Barlow, William. "Commercial and Noncommercial Radio." In *Split Image: African Americans in the Mass Media*, 175–252. Edited by Jannette L. Dates and William Barlow. Washington, DC: Howard University Press, 1990.

Barnes, Ken. "Top 40: A Fragment of the Popular Imagination." In *Facing the Music*, 8–50. Edited by Simon Frith. New York: Pantheon, 1988.

Basie, Count (as told to Albert Murray). *Good Morning Blues: The Autobiography of Count Basie*. New York: Random House, 1985.

Bean, Annemarie, James V. Hatch, and Brooks McNamara, eds. *Inside the Minstrel Mask: Readings in Nineteenth-Century Blackface Minstrelsy*. Hanover, NH: Wesleyan University Press, 1996.

Becker, Howard. *Art Worlds*. Berkeley: University of California Press, 1982.

Beebee, Thomas O. *The Ideology of Genre: A Comparative Study of Generic Instability*. University Park: Pennsylvania State University Press, 1994.

Benjamin, Walter. *The Origin of German Tragic Drama*. London and New York: Verso, 1998.

———. "The Work of Art in the Age of Mechanical Reproduction." In *Illuminations*, 217–52. Edited by Hannah Arendt. Translated by Harry Zohn. New York: Schocken Books, 1969.

Bennett, Andy, and Richard A. Peterson, eds. *Music Scenes: Local, Translocal, and Virtual*. Nashville, TN: Vanderbilt University Press, 2009.

Bhabha, Homi K. *The Location of Culture*. London and New York: Routledge, 1994.

Born, Georgina. "Music and the Materialization of Identities." *Journal of Material Culture* (2011): 376–88.

———. "Music and the Representation/Articulation of Sociocultural Identities" and "Techniques of the Musical Imaginary." In *Western Music and Its Others: Difference, Represen-*

tation, and Appropriation in Music, 31–47. Edited by Georgina Born and David Hesmondhalgh. Berkeley and Los Angeles: University of California Press, 2000.

———. "On Musical Mediation: Ontology, Technology and Creativity." *twentieth-century music* 2, no. 1 (2005): 7–36.

———. "The Social and the Aesthetic: For a Post-Bourdieuian Theory of Cultural Production." *Cultural Sociology* 4, no. 2 (2010): 171–208.

Bourdieu, Pierre. *Distinction: A Social Critique of the Judgement of Taste*. Cambridge, MA: Harvard University Press, 1984.

———. "The Field of Cultural Production: or The Economic World Reversed." In *The Field of Cultural Production: Essays on Art and Literature*, 29–73. New York: Columbia University Press, 1993.

———. "Opinion Polls: A 'Science' Without a Scientist." In *In Other Words: Essays Towards a Reflexive Sociology*, 168–74. Translated by Matthew Adamson. Stanford, CA: Stanford University Press, 1990.

———. "Public Opinion Does Not Exist." In *Communication and Class Struggle*, 124–30. Edited by Armand Mattelart and Seth Siegelaub. New York: International General, 1979.

Bowman, Rob. *Soulsville U.S.A.: The Story of Stax Records*. New York: Schirmer Trade Books, 1997.

Brackett, David. "Banjos, Biopics, and Compilation Scores: The Movies Go Country." *American Music* 19, no. 3 (Autumn 2001): 247–90.

———. "Black or White? Michael Jackson and the Idea of Crossover." *Popular Music and Society* 35, no. 2 (2012): 169–85.

———. "Elvis Costello, the Empire of the E Chord, and a Magic Moment or Two." *Popular Music* 24, no. 3 (October 2005): 357–67.

———. *Interpreting Popular Music*. Berkeley and Los Angeles: University of California Press, 2000.

———. "Questions of Genre in Black Popular Music." *Black Music Research Journal* 25, nos. 1–2 (Spring–Fall 2005): 73–92.

———. "What a Difference a Name Makes: Two Instances of African-American Music." In *The Cultural Study of Music: A Critical Introduction*, 127–39. Edited by Martin Clayton, Trevor Herbert, and Richard Middleton. New York and London: Routledge, 2012.

Brackett, David, ed. *The Pop, Rock, and Soul Reader: Histories and Debates*. New York: Oxford University Press, 2014.

Bradby, Barbara. "Do-Talk and Don't-Talk: The Division of the Subject in Girl-Group Music." In *On Record: Rock, Pop and the Written Word*, 341–68. Edited by Simon Frith and Andrew Goodwin. New York: Pantheon, 1990.

Bradford, Perry. *Born with the Blues*. New York: Oak Publications, 1965.

Breithaupt, Don, and Jeff Breithaupt. *Precious and Few: Pop Music in the Early '70s*. New York: St. Martin's Griffin, 1996.

Brooks, Tim. *Lost Sounds: Blacks and the Birth of the Recording Industry, 1890–1919*. Urbana and Chicago: University of Illinois Press, 2004.

———. Liner notes for *Lost Sounds: Blacks and the Birth of the Recording Industry, 1891–1922*. Archeophone, 2005.

Broven, John. *Record Makers and Breakers: Voices of the Independent Rock 'n' Roll Pioneers*. Urbana and Chicago: University of Illinois Press, 2009.

Brown, Bill. "The Meaning of Baseball in 1992 (with Notes on the Post-American)." *Public Culture* 4, no. 1 (Fall 1991): 43–71.

Brown, James (with Bruce Tucker). *The Godfather of Soul*. New York: MacMillan, 1986.

Burford, Mark. "Sam Cooke as Pop Album Artist—A Reinvention in Three Songs." *Journal of the American Musicological Society* 65, no. 1 (Spring 2012): 113–78.

Butler, Judith. *Bodies That Matter: On the Discursive Limits of "Sex."* New York: Routledge, 1993.

———. *Gender Trouble: Feminism and the Subversion of Identity*. New York: Routledge, 1990.

Cantwell, Robert. *Bluegrass Breakdown: The Making of the Old Southern Sound*. New York: Da Capo Press, 1992.

Caponi, Gena. *Jump for Joy: Jazz, Basketball, and Black Culture in 1930s America*. Amherst: University of Massachusetts Press, 2008.

Carby, Hazel. "It Just Be's Dat Way Sometime: The Sexual Politics of Women's Blues." *Radical America* 20 (June–July 1986): 9–22.

Chanan, Michael. *Repeated Takes: A Short History of Recording and Its Effects on Music*. London and New York: Verso, 1995.

Chapple, Steve, and Reebee Garofalo. *Rock 'n' Roll Is Here to Pay*. Chicago: Nelson-Hall Inc., 1977.

Charters, Samuel B. *The Country Blues*. New York: Da Capo Press, 1975. First published in 1959.

Christgau, Robert. "Rock 'n' Roller Coaster: The Music Biz on a Joyride." *Village Voice*, February 7, 1984, 37–45. Reprinted in David Brackett, ed. *The Pop, Rock, and Soul Reader*, 386–96. New York: Oxford University Press, 2009.

Cockrell, Dale. *Demons of Disorder: Early Blackface Minstrels and Their World*. Cambridge and New York: Cambridge University Press, 1997.

Cohen, Anne, and Norm Cohen. "Folk and Hillbilly Music: Further Thoughts on Their Relation." *JEMF Quarterly* 13, no. 46 (Summer 1977): 50–57.

Cohen, Lizabeth. *Making a New Deal: Industrial Workers in Chicago, 1919–1939*. New York: Cambridge University Press, 1990.

Crichton, Kyle. "Thar's Gold in Them Hillbillies." *Collier's*, April 30, 1938, 26–27. Reprinted in David Brackett, ed. *The Pop, Rock, and Soul Reader: Histories and Debates*, 28–32. New York: Oxford University Press, 2014.

Cumming, Julie. *The Motet in the Age of Du Fay*. Cambridge: Cambridge University Press, 1999.

Cusic, Don. *The Cowboy in Country Music: An Historical Survey with Artist Profiles*. Jefferson, NC: McFarland, 2011.

Dahlhaus, Carl. "New Music and the Problems of Musical Genre." In *Schoenberg and the New Music*, 32–44. Translated by Derrick Puffett and Alfred Clayton. Cambridge: Cambridge University Press, 1990.

Dance, Stanley. *The World of Count Basie*. New York: C. Scribner's Sons, 1980.

Dannen, Fredric. *Hit Men: Power Brokers and Fast Money Inside the Music Business*. New York: Times Books, 1990.

Davis, Angela Y. *Blues Legacies and Black Feminism: Gertrude "Ma" Rainey, Bessie Smith, and Billie Holiday*. New York: Pantheon Books, 1998.

de Certeau, Michel. *The Practice of Everyday Life*. Berkeley: University of California Press, 1984.

DeLanda, Manuel. *A New Philosophy of Society: Assemblage Theory and Social Complexity.* London: Bloomsbury, 2006.

Deleuze, Gilles. *Foucault.* Minneapolis: University of Minnesota Press, 1988.

Deleuze, Gilles, and Félix Guattari. *A Thousand Plateaus: Capitalism and Schizophrenia.* Minneapolis: University of Minneapolis Press, 1987.

Denning, Michael. *The Cultural Front: The Laboring of American Culture in the Twentieth Century.* London and New York: Verso, 1997.

Dennison, Sam. *Scandalize My Name: Black Imagery in American Popular Music.* New York: Garland Publishing, 1982.

Derrida, Jacques. "The Law of Genre." In *On Narrative,* 51–77. Edited by W. J. T. Mitchell. Chicago and London: University of Chicago Press, 1981.

———. "Signature, Event, Context." In *Margins of Philosophy,* 307–30. Translated by Alan Bass. Chicago: University of Chicago Press, 1982.

DeVeaux, Scott. *The Birth of Bebop: A Social and Musical History.* Berkeley and Los Angeles: University of California Press, 1997.

———. "Constructing the Jazz Tradition: Jazz Historiography." *Black American Literature Forum* 25, no. 3 (Autumn 1991): 525–60.

———. "Core and Boundaries." *Jazz Research Journal* 2 (2005): 15–30.

Dixon, Robert M. W. *Blues and Gospel Records: 1890–1943.* Oxford: Oxford University Press, 1997.

Dixon, Robert M. W., and John Godrich. *Recording the Blues* (1970). Reprinted in *Yonder Come the Blues: The Evolution of a Genre,* 243–342. Cambridge: Cambridge University Press, 2001.

Dormon, James H. "Shaping the Popular Image of Post-Reconstruction American Blacks: The 'Coon Song' Phenomenon of the Gilded Age." *American Quarterly* 40 (December 1988): 450–71.

Douglas, Susan J. *Listening In: Radio and the American Imagination.* Minneapolis: University of Minnesota Press, 1999.

Dowd, Timothy J. "Concentration and Diversity Revisited: Production Logics and the U.S. Mainstream Recording Market, 1940 to 1990." *Social Forces* 82 (2004): 1411–55.

Dreyfus, Laurence. *Bach and the Patterns of Invention.* Cambridge, MA: Harvard University Press, 1996.

Drott, Eric. "The End(s) of Genre." *Journal of Music Theory* 57, no. 1 (Spring 2013): 1–45.

———. "Genre in the Age of Algorithms." Paper presented at the "Genre and Music: New Directions" conference, McGill University, Montreal, September 27–28, 2014.

DuBois, W. E. B. *The Souls of Black Folks.* New York: Bantam Books, 1989. First published in 1903.

Dubrow, Heather. *Genre.* London: Methuen, 1982.

Ecker, Susan, and Lloyd Ecker. Liner notes for *Sophie Tucker: Origins of the Red Hot Mama, 1910–1922.* Archeophone 5010.

Ennis, Philip. *The Seventh Stream: The Emergence of Rocknroll in American Popular Music.* Hanover, NH, and London: Wesleyan University Press, 1992.

Escott, Colin. "The Talking Machine: How Records Shaped Country Music." In *The Encyclopedia of Country Music,* 465–69. Edited by Paul Kingsbury. New York and Oxford: Oxford University Press, 1998.

Ethnic Recordings in America: A Neglected Heritage. Washington, DC: American Folklife Center, 1982.

Europe, James Reese (as told to Grenville Vernon). "A Negro Explains 'Jazz.'" In *Keeping Time: Readings in Jazz History*, 12–14. Edited by Robert Walser. New York: Oxford University Press, 1999. First published in 1919.

Everist, Mark. *French Motets in the Thirteenth Century: Music, Poetry, and Genre.* Cambridge: Cambridge University Press, 1994.

Fabbri, Franco. "How Genres Are Born, Change, Die: Conventions, Communities and Diachronic Processes." In *Critical Musicological Reflections: Essays in Honour of Derek B. Scott*, 179–91. Edited by Stan Hawkins. Farnham, England: Ashgate, 2012.

———. "A Theory of Musical Genres: Two Applications." In *Popular Music Perspectives*, 52–81. Edited by David Horn and Philip Tagg. Göteborg, Sweden, and London: IASPM, 1982.

———. "What Kind of Music?" *Popular Music* 2 (1982): 131–43.

Filene, Benjamin. *Romancing the Folk: Public Memory and American Roots Music.* Chapel Hill and London: University of North Carolina Press, 2000.

Fish, Stanley. *Is There a Text in This Class? The Authority of Interpretive Communities.* Cambridge, MA: Harvard University Press, 1980.

Fitzgerald, Jon. "Motown Crossover Hits 1963–1966 and the Creative Process." *Popular Music* 14, no. 1 (January 1995): 1–11.

Flory, Andrew. *I Hear a Symphony: Listening to the Music of Motown.* Ann Arbor: University of Michigan Press.

Floyd, Samuel A. *The Power of Black Music: Interpreting Its History from Africa to the United States.* New York: Oxford University Press, 1995.

———. "Ring Shout! Literary Studies, Historical Studies, and Black Music Inquiry." *Black Music Research Journal* 11, no. 2 (Fall 1991): 265–88.

Foucault, Michel. "The Confession of the Flesh." In *Power Knowledge: Selected Interviews and Other Writings 1972–1977*, 194–228. Edited by Colin Gordon. New York: Pantheon, 1980.

———. *Discipline and Punish: The Birth of the Prison.* New York: Vintage Books, 1979.

———. *The History of Sexuality, Volume 1: An Introduction.* New York: Pantheon, 1978.

———. "Nietzsche, Genealogy, History." In *Language, Counter-Memory, Practice: Selected Essays and Interviews*, 139–64. Edited by Donald F. Bouchard. Translated by Donald F. Bouchard and Sherry Simon. Ithaca, NY: Cornell University Press, 1977.

———. "Questions of Method." In *Power: Essential Works of Foucault, 1954–1984*, 223–38. Edited by James D. Faubion. New York: The New Press, 2000.

———. *Security, Territory, Population: Lectures at the Collège de France, 1977–78.* Houndmills, England: Palgrave MacMillan, 2007.

———. "Theatrum Philosophicum." In *Language, Counter-Memory, Practice: Selected Essays and Interviews*, 165–96. Edited by Donald F. Bouchard. Translated by Donald F. Bouchard and Sherry Simon. Ithaca, NY: Cornell University Press, 1977.

Fox, Aaron. *Real Country: Music and Language in Working-Class Culture.* Durham, NC: Duke University Press, 2004.

Fox, Pamela. *Natural Acts: Gender, Race, and Rusticity in Country Music.* Ann Arbor: University of Michigan Press, 2009.

Freud, Sigmund. *Civilization and Its Discontents*. London: Penguin, 2002. First published in 1930.

Friedwald, Will. "The First of the Red Hot Mamas." *Wall Street Journal,* October 15, 2009.

Frith, Simon. *Performing Rites: On the Value of Popular Music*. Cambridge, MA: Harvard University Press, 1996.

Frow, John. *Genre*. London and New York: Routledge, 2006.

———. "Scale and Taxonomy in Musical Genres." Paper presented at the "Genre and Music: New Directions" conference, McGill University, Montreal, September 27–28, 2014.

Gabbard, Krin. *Jammin' at the Margins: Jazz and the American Cinema*. Chicago and London: University of Chicago Press, 1996.

Gaisberg, Frederick W. *The Music Goes Round*. New York: MacMillan, 1942.

Garofalo, Reebee. "Black Popular Music: Crossing Over or Going Under?" In *Rock and Popular Music: Politics, Policies, Institutions*, 231–48. Edited by Tony Bennett, Simon Frith, Lawrence Grossberg, John Shepherd, and Graeme Turner. London and New York: Routledge, 1993.

———. "Crossing Over: 1939–1989." In *Split Image: African-Americans in the Mass Media*, 57–121. Edited by Jannette L. Dates and William Barlow. Washington, DC: Howard University Press, 1990.

Garrett, Charles Hiroshi. *Struggling to Define a Nation: American Music and the Twentieth Century*. Berkeley and Los Angeles: University of California Press, 2008.

Gayle, Addison, ed. *The Black Aesthetic*. New York: Doubleday, 1971.

Gelbart, Matthew. *The Invention of "Folk Music" and "Art Music": Emerging Categories from Ossian to Wagner*. Cambridge: Cambridge University Press, 2007.

Gelder, Ken, ed. *The Subcultures Reader*. London and New York: Routledge, 2005.

Gell, Alfred. *Art and Agency*. Oxford: Oxford University Press, 1998.

Gendron, Bernard. *Between Montmartre and the Mudd Club: Popular Music and the Avant-Garde*. Chicago and London: University of Chicago Press, 2002.

———. "Theodor Adorno Meets the Cadillacs." In *Studies in Entertainment: Critical Approaches to Mass Culture*, 18–36. Edited by Tania Modleski. Bloomington and Indianapolis: Indiana University Press, 1986.

Gennari, John. *Blowin' Hot and Cool: Jazz and Its Critics*. Chicago and London: University of Chicago Press, 2006.

George, Nelson. *The Death of Rhythm and Blues*. New York: Pantheon Books, 1988.

———. *Where Did Our Love Go? The Rise and Fall of the Motown Sound*. New York: St. Martin's Press, 1985.

Giddens, Gary. "Stride and Swing: The Enduring Appeal of Fats Waller and Glenn Miller." *The New Yorker*, May 31, 2004, 85–87.

Gillett, Charlie. *The Sound of the City: The Rise of Rock and Roll*. New York: Pantheon Books, 1983. First published in 1970.

Gilroy, Paul. "'After the Love Has Gone': Bio-Politics and Etho-Poetics in the Black Public Sphere." *Public Culture* 7, no. 1 (Fall 1994): 49–76.

———. *The Black Atlantic: Modernity and Double Consciousness*. Cambridge, MA: Harvard University Press, 1993.

Gitelman, Lisa. *Scripts, Grooves, and Writing Machines: Representing Technology in the Edison Era*. Stanford, CA: Stanford University Press, 1999.

Goehr, Lydia. *The Imaginary Museum of Musical Works: An Essay in the Philosophy of Music.* Oxford: Oxford University Press, 1992.

Goodwin, Andrew. *Dancing in the Distraction Factory: Music Television and Popular Culture.* Minneapolis: University of Minnesota Press, 1992.

Gordon, Robert. *Respect Yourself: Stax Records and the Soul Explosion.* New York: Bloomsbury, 2013.

Gordy, Berry. *To Be Loved: The Music, the Magic, the Memories of Motown.* New York: Warner Books, 1994.

Gracyk, Theodore. *Rhythm and Noise: An Aesthetics of Rock.* Durham, NC, and London: Duke University Press, 1996.

Grant, Barry Keith. *Film Genre Reader III.* Austin: University of Texas Press, 2003.

Green, Archie. "Hillbilly Music: Source and Symbol." *Journal of American Folklore* 78 (July–September 1965): 204–28.

Grenier, Line. "Canadian Radio Formats." *Popular Music* 9, no. 2 (1990): 221–33.

Grieg, Charlotte. *Will You Still Love Me Tomorrow? Girl Groups from the '50s On.* London: Virago, 1989.

Gronow, Pekka. "Ethnic Recordings: An Introduction." In *Ethnic Recordings in America: A Neglected Heritage,* 1–49. Washington, DC: American Folklife Center, 1982.

Guralnick, Peter. *Sweet Soul Music: Rhythm and Blues and the Southern Dream of Freedom.* New York: Harper and Row, 1986.

Gussow, Adam. "'Shoot Myself a Cop': Mamie Smith's 'Crazy Blues' as Social Text." *Callaloo* 25, no. 1 (2002): 8–44.

Hacking, Ian. "Biopower and the Avalanche of Printed Numbers." *Humanities in Society* 5, nos. 3–4 (1982): 279–95.

———. *The Taming of Chance.* Cambridge: Cambridge University Press, 1990.

Haddon, Mimi. "What Is Post-Punk? British and American Popular Music on the Edge of the 1980s." PhD diss., McGill University, 2015.

Hakanen, Ernest. "Counting Down to Number One: The Evolution of the Meaning of Popular Music Charts." *Popular Music* 17, no. 1 (January 1998): 95–112.

Hall, Stuart. "Introduction: Who Needs Identity?" In *Questions of Cultural Identity,* 1–17. Edited by Stuart Hall and Paul du Gay. London: SAGE Publications, 1996.

———. "On Postmodernism and Articulation: An Interview with Stuart Hall." *Journal of Communication Inquiry* (1986): 45–60.

Hall, Stuart, and Tony Jefferson, eds. *Resistance Through Rituals: Youth Subcultures in Post-War Britain.* New York: Routledge, 1993. First published in 1976.

Hamberlin, Larry. "Visions of Salome: The Femme Fatale in American Popular Songs Before 1920." *Journal of the American Musicological Society* 59, no. 3 (Fall 2006): 631–96.

Hamm, Charles. "The Fourth Audience." *Popular Music* 1 (January 1981): 123–41.

———. *Yesterdays: Popular Song in America.* New York and London: W. W. Norton and Company, 1979.

Handy, W. C. *Father of the Blues: An Autobiography* New York: Da Capo Books, 1969. First published in 1941.

Handy, W. C., ed. *Blues: An Anthology.* Bedford, MA: Applewood Books, 1926.

Harker, Brian. "Louis Armstrong, Eccentric Dance, and the Evolution of Jazz on the Eve of Swing." *Journal of the American Musicological Society* 61, no. 1 (Spring 2008): 67–121.

Harkins, Anthony. *Hillbilly: A Cultural History of an American Icon*. New York: Oxford University Press, 2004.

Harrison, Daphne Duval. *Black Pearls: Blues Queens of the 1920s*. New Brunswick, NJ: Rutgers University Press, 1988.

Haslam, Gerald W. *Workin' Man Blues: Country Music in California*. Berkeley: University of California Press, 1999.

Hatch, David, and Stephen Millward. *From Blues to Rock: An Analytical History of Pop Music*. Manchester, England: Manchester University Press, 1987.

Hebdige, Dick. *Subculture: The Meaning of Style*. London and New York: Routledge, 1979.

Hesmondhalgh, David. "Subcultures, Scenes or Tribes? None of the Above." *Journal of Youth Studies* 8, no. 1 (2005): 21–40.

Hirshey, Gerri. *Nowhere to Run: The Story of Soul Music*. New York: Penguin Books, 1984.

Holt, Fabian. *Genre in Popular Music*. Chicago: University of Chicago Press, 2007.

Horricks, Raymond. *Count Basie and His Orchestra: Its Music and Its Musicians*. London: Victor Gollancz Ltd., 1957.

Hoskyns, Barney. *Say It One Time for the Broken Hearted*. Glasgow: Fontana, 1987.

Huber, Alison. "What's in a Mainstream? Critical Possibilities." *Altitude* 8 (2007): 1–12.

Huyssen, Andreas. "Mass Culture as Woman: Modernism's Other." In *After the Great Divide: Modernism, Mass Culture, Postmodernism*, 44–64. Edited by Tania Modleski. Bloomington: Indiana University Press, 1986.

Ivy, Marilyn. *Discourses of the Vanishing: Modernity, Phantasm, Japan*. Chicago and London: University of Chicago Press, 1995.

Jacobson, Matthew Frye. *Whiteness of a Different Color: European Immigrants and the Alchemy of Race*. Cambridge, MA: Harvard University Press, 1998.

Jasen, David A., and Gene Jones. *Spreadin' Rhythm Around: Black Popular Songwriters, 1880–1930*. New York: Schirmer Books, 1998.

Jauss, Hans Robert. "Theory of Genres and Medieval Literature." In *Towards an Aesthetic of Reception*, 76–109. Translated by Timothy Bahti. Minneapolis: University of Minnesota Press, 1982.

Jensen, Joli. *The Nashville Sounds: Authenticity, Commercialization, and Country Music*. Nashville, TN: Country Music Foundation Press, 1998.

Johnson, James Weldon. "Preface to *The Book of American Negro Poetry*" (1922). In *Voices from the Harlem Renaissance*, 281–303. Edited by Nathan Irvin Huggins. New York: Oxford University Press, 1995.

Kallberg, Jeffrey. "The Rhetoric of Genre: Chopin's Nocturne in G Minor." In *Chopin at the Boundaries: Sex, History, and Musical Genre*, 3–29. Cambridge, MA: Harvard University Press, 1996.

Kaplan, E. Ann. *Rocking Around the Clock: Music Television, Postmodernism, and Consumer Culture*. New York: Methuen, 1987.

Kassabian, Anahid. *Ubiquitous Listening: Affect, Attention, and Distributed Subjectivity*. Berkeley and Los Angeles: University of California Press, 2013.

Katz, Mark. *Capturing Sound: How Technology Has Changed Music*. Berkeley and Los Angeles: University of California Press, 2004.

Keightley, Keir. "Reconsidering Rock." In *The Cambridge Companion to Pop and Rock*, 109–42. Edited by Simon Frith, Will Straw, and John Street. Cambridge: Cambridge University Press, 2001.

———. "Tin Pan Allegory." *Modernism/Modernity* 19, no. 4 (November 2012): 717–36.

Keil, Charles. "People's Music Comparatively: Style and Stereotype, Class and Hegemony." In *Music Grooves: Essays and Dialogues*, 197–217. Edited by Charles Keil and Steven Feld. Chicago and London: University of Chicago Press, 1994.

———. *Urban Blues*. Chicago: University of Chicago Press, 1966.

Keith, Michael C. *Voices in the Purple Haze: Underground Radio and the Sixties*. London: Praeger Publishers, 1997.

Kenney, William Howland. *Recorded Music in American Life: The Phonograph and Popular Memory, 1890–1945*. New York and Oxford: Oxford University Press, 1999.

Kienzle, Rich. Liner notes for Bob Wills and the Texas Playboys, *The Essential Bob Wills, 1935–1947*. Sony Music Entertainment / Columbia Legacy, 1992.

Kittler, Friedrich. *Gramophone, Film, Typewriter*. Stanford, CA: Stanford University Press, 1999.

Krims, Adam. *Rap Music and the Poetics of Identity*. Cambridge: Cambridge University Press, 2000.

Kronengold, Charles. "Exchange Theories in Disco, New Wave, and Album-Oriented Rock." *Criticism* 50, no. 1 (Winter 2008): 43–82.

Kun, Josh. *Audiotopia: Music, Race, and America*. Berkeley and Los Angeles: University of California Press, 2005.

La Chapelle, Peter. *Proud to Be an Okie: Cultural Politics, Country Music, and Migration to Southern California*. Berkeley: University of California Press, 2007.

Lamere, Paul. "Social Tagging and Music Information Retrieval." *Journal of New Music Research* 37, no. 2 (2008).

Lange, Jeffrey J. *Smile When You Call Me a Hillbilly: Country Music's Struggle for Respectability, 1939–1954*. Athens and London: University of Georgia Press, 2004.

Laplanche, Jean, and Jean-Bertrand Pontalis. "Fantasy and the Origins of Sexuality." In *Formations of Fantasy*, 1–34. Edited by Victor Burgin, James Donald, and Cora Kaplan. London: Methuen, 1986.

Latham, Aaron. "The Ballad of the Urban Cowboy: America's Search for True Grit." *Esquire*, September 12, 1978, 21–30.

Latour, Bruno. *Reassembling the Social: An Introduction to Actor-Network-Theory*. New York: Oxford University Press, 2005.

Lee, Robert G. *Orientals: Asian Americans in Popular Culture*. Philadelphia: Temple University Press, 1999.

Lena, Jennifer C. *Banding Together: How Communities Create Genres in Popular Music*. Princeton, NJ, and Oxford: Princeton University Press, 2012.

Lhamon, W. T. *Raising Cain: Blackface Performance from Jim Crow to Hip Hop*. Cambridge, MA: Harvard University Press, 1998.

Lomax, Alan. *Mister Jelly Roll: The Fortunes of Jelly Roll Morton, New Orleans Creole and "Inventor of Jazz."* New York: Pantheon, 1993. First published in 1949.

Lott, Eric. *Love and Theft: Blackface Minstrelsy and the American Working Class*. New York and Oxford: Oxford University Press, 1993.

Mahler, Alma. *Gustav Mahler: Memories and Letters*. London: Cardinal, 1990.

Malone, Bill C. *Country Music U.S.A.* Austin: University of Texas Press, 1985.

———. Liner notes for *The Smithsonian Collection of Classic Country Music*. Washington, DC: Smithsonian Collection of Recordings, 1981.

———. *Southern Music/American Music*. Lexington: University Press of Kentucky, 1979.

Malone, Bill C., and Judith McCulloh, eds. *Stars of Country Music: Uncle Dave Macon to Johnny Rodriguez*. Urbana: University of Illinois Press, 1975.

Marcus, Greil. *Mystery Train: Images of America in Rock 'n' Roll Music*. New York: Plume, 1990.

Maultsby, Portia. "Africanisms in African-American Music." In *Africanisms in American Culture*, 185–210. Edited by Joseph E. Holloway. Bloomington: Indiana University Press, 1990.

———. "Soul Music: Its Sociological and Political Significance in American Popular Culture." *Journal of Popular Culture* 17, no. 2 (Fall 1983): 51–60.

McClary, Susan. *Conventional Wisdom: The Content of Musical Form*. Berkeley and Los Angeles: University of California Press, 2000.

McDonald, Glen. "The Genre Grinder's Song (What It's Like to Run a Machine for Sorting Music)." Paper presented at the "Genre and Music: New Directions" conference, McGill University, Montreal, September 27–28, 2014.

Medvedev, P. N. *The Formal Method in Literary Scholarship: A Critical Introduction to Sociological Poetics*. Translated by Albert J. Wehrle. Cambridge, MA: Harvard University Press, 1985.

Mercer, Kobena. "Monster Metaphors: Notes on Michael Jackson's 'Thriller.'" In *Sound and Vision: The Music Video Reader*, 93–108. Edited by Simon Frith, Andrew Goodwin, and Lawrence Grossberg. London and New York: Routledge, 1993. First published in 1986.

Middleton, Richard. *Studying Popular Music*. Milton Keynes, England: Open University Press, 1990.

———. *Voicing the Popular: On the Subjects of Popular Music*. New York and London: Routledge, 2006.

Miller, Karl Hagstrom. *Segregating Sound: Inventing Folk and Pop Music in the Age of Jim Crow*. Durham, NC, and London: Duke University Press, 2010.

Molanphy, Chris. "I Know You Got Soul: The Trouble with *Billboard*'s R&B/Hip-Hop Chart." *Pitchfork*, April 14, 2014. http://pitchfork.com/features/articles/9378-i-know-you-got-soul-the-trouble-with-billboards-rbhip-hop-chart/.

Moon, Krystyn R. *Yellowface: Creating the Chinese in American Popular Music and Performance, 1850s–1920s*. New Brunswick, NJ: Rutgers University Press, 2004.

Morris, Mitchell. *The Persistence of Sentiment: Display and Feeling in Popular Music of the 1970s*. Berkeley and Los Angeles: University of California Press, 2013.

Morson, Gary Saul, and Caryl Emerson. *Mikhail Bakhtin: Creation of a Prosaics*. Stanford, CA: Stanford University Press, 1990.

Muir, Peter C. *Long Lost Blues: Popular Blues in America, 1850–1920*. Champaign: University of Illinois Press, 2010.

Nasaw, David. *Going Out: The Rise and Fall of Public Amusements*. New York: Basic Books, 1993.

Neal, Mark Anthony. "Rhythm and Bullshit?: The Slow Decline of R&B." *PopMatters* (2005). http://www.popmatters.com/feature/050603-randb/.

————. *What the Music Said: Black Popular Music and Black Public Culture*. New York and London: Routledge, 1999.

Neale, Stephen. *Genre*. London: British Film Institute, 1980.

————. *Genre and Hollywood*. London and New York: Routledge, 2000.

————. "Questions of Genre." *Screen* 31, no. 1 (Spring 1990): 45–66.

Negus, Keith. *Music Genres and Corporate Cultures*. London and New York: Routledge, 1999.

Odum, Howard W. "Folk-Song and Folk-Poetry as Found in the Secular Songs of the Southern Negroes." *Journal of American Folk-Lore* 24, no. 93 (July–September 1911): 255–94.

————. "Folk-Song and Folk-Poetry as Found in the Secular Songs of the Southern Negroes (Concluded)." *Journal of American Folk-Lore*, 24, no. 94 (October–December 1911): 351–96.

Ogren, Kathy. *The Jazz Revolution: Twenties America and the Meaning of Jazz*. New York: Oxford University Press, 1992.

Oliver, Paul. *Blues Fell This Morning: Meaning in the Blues*. Cambridge: Cambridge University Press, 1990. First published in 1960.

————. *Songsters and Saints: Vocal Traditions on Race Records*. Cambridge: Cambridge University Press, 1984.

Palmer, Jack. *Vernon Dalhart: First Star of Country Music*. Denver: Mainspring Press, 2005.

Parker, Martin. "Reading the Charts: Making Sense with the Hit Parade." *Popular Music* 10, no. 2 (1991): 205–19.

Pecknold, Diane. *The Selling Sound: The Rise of the Country Music Industry*. Durham, NC, and London: Duke University Press, 2007.

Peress, Maurice. *Dvořák to Duke Ellington*. New York: Oxford University Press, 2004.

Perry, Steve. "Ain't No Mountain High Enough: the Politics of Crossover." In *Facing the Music*, 51–87. Edited by Simon Frith. New York: Pantheon Books, 1988.

Peterson, Richard. *Creating Country Music: Fabricating Authenticity*. Chicago and London: University of Chicago Press, 1997.

Pond, Steven F. *Head Hunters: The Making of Jazz's First Platinum Album*. Ann Arbor: The University of Michigan Press, 2005.

Porter, Eric. *What Is This Thing Called Jazz? African American Musicians as Artists, Critics, and Activists*. Berkeley and Los Angeles: University of California Press, 2002.

Radano, Ronald. *Lying Up a Nation: Race and Black Music*. Chicago: University Press of Chicago, 2003.

Ramsey Jr., Guthrie. *Race Music: Black Cultures from Bebop to Hip-Hop*. Berkeley and Los Angeles: University of California Press, 2003.

Rancière, Jacques. *The Politics of Aesthetics: The Distribution of the Sensible*. Translated by Gabriel Rockhill. London: Continuum, 2004.

Randel, Don M. "Crossing Over with Rubén Blades." *Journal of the American Musicological Society* 44 (Summer 1991): 301–23.

Rasmussen, Chris. "'The People's Orchestra': Jukeboxes as the Measure of Popular Musical Taste in the 1930s and 1940s." In *Sound in the Age of Mechanical Reproduction*, 181–98. Edited by David Suisman and Susan Strasser. Philadelphia: University of Pennsylvania Press, 2010.

Riis, Thomas L. *Just Before Jazz: Black Musical Theater in New York, 1890–1915*. Washington, DC, and London: Smithsonian Institution Press, 1989.

Roediger, David R. *The Wages of Whiteness: Race and the Making of the American Working Class*. London and New York: Verso, 1991.

———. *Working Toward Whiteness: How America's Immigrants Became White*. New York: Basic Books, 2005.

Rogin, Michael. *Blackface, White Noise: Jewish Immigrants in the Hollywood Melting Pot*. Berkeley and Los Angeles: University of California Press, 1996.

Romeyn, Esther, and Jack Kugelmass. *Let There Be Laughter! Jewish Humor in America*. Chicago: Spertus Press, 1997.

Ross, Alex. *Listen to This*. New York: Farrar, Straus and Giroux, 2010.

Rossman, Gabriel. *Climbing the Charts: What Radio Airplay Tells Us About the Diffusion of Innovation*. Princeton, NJ: Princeton University Press, 2012.

Russell, Tony. *Country Music Records: A Discography, 1921–1942*. Oxford and New York: Oxford University Press, 2008.

Rustin, Nicole T., and Sherrie Tucker, eds. *Big Ears: Listening for Gender in Jazz Studies*. Durham, NC: Duke University Press, 2008.

Ryan, John. *The Production of Culture in the Music Industry: The ASCAP-BMI Controversy*. Lanham, MD: University Press of America, 1985.

Sanjek, David. "Tell Me Something I Don't Already Know: The Harvard Report on Soul Music Revisited." In *Rhythm and Business: The Political Economy of Black Music*, 63–80. Edited by Norman Kelley. New York: Akashic Books, 2005.

Sanjek, Russell, and David Sanjek. *American Popular Music Business in the 20th Century*. New York and Oxford: Oxford University Press, 1991.

Scaringella, Nicolas, Giorgio Zoia, and Daniel Mlynek. "Automatic Genre Classification of Music Content: A Survey." *IEEE Signal Processing Magazine* 23, no. 2 (2006): 133–41.

Schaefer, R. Murray. *The Tuning of the World*. New York: Alfred A. Knopf, 1977.

Schuller, Gunther. *The Swing Era: The Development of Jazz, 1930–1945*. New York and Oxford: Oxford University Press, 1989.

Scott, Michelle R. *Blues Empress in Black Chattanooga: Bessie Smith and the Emerging Urban South*. Urbana and Chicago: University of Illinois Press, 2008.

Shank, Barry. *Dissonant Identities: The Rock 'n' Roll Scene in Austin, Texas*. Hanover, NH, and London: Wesleyan University Press, 1994.

Sharpe, Cecil. "Introduction." In *English Folk Songs from the Southern Appalachians*, vol. 1, xxi–xxxvii. Edited by Maud Karpeles. London and New York: Oxford University Press, 2012. First published in 1917.

Shelemay, Kay Kaufman. "Musical Communities: Rethinking the Collective in Music." *Journal of the American Musicological Society* 64, no. 2 (Summer 2011): 349–90.

Simpson, Kim. *Early '70s Radio: The American Format Revolution*. New York: Continuum, 2011.

Slobin, Mark. *Tenement Songs: The Popular Music of the Jewish Immigrants*. Champaign-Urbana: University of Illinois Press, 1996.

Smialek, Eric. "Expression in Extreme Metal Music, ca. 1980–2012." PhD diss., McGill University, 2015.

Smith, RJ. "Richard Speaks! Chasing a Tune from the Chitlin Circuit to the Mormon Tabernacle." In *This Is Pop: In Search of the Elusive at Experience Music Project*, 75–89. Edited by Eric Weisbard. Cambridge, MA: Harvard University Press, 2004.

Smith, Suzanne E. *Dancing in the Street: Motown and the Cultural Politics of Detroit*. Cambridge, MA: Harvard University Press, 1999.

Spalding, Henry D. "Dialect Stories." In *A Treasure Trove of American Jewish Humor*, 63–72. Edited by Henry D. Spalding. Middle Village, NY: Jonathan David Publishers, 1976.

Spottswood, Richard K. "Commercial Ethnic Recordings in the United States." In *Ethnic Recordings in America: A Neglected Heritage*, 51–66. Washington, DC: American Folklife Center, 1982.

Stein, Arlene. "Crossover Dreams: Lesbianism and Popular Music Since the 1970s." In *Out in Culture: Gay, Lesbian, and Queer Essays on Popular Culture*, 416–26. Edited by Corey K. Creekmur and Alexander Doty. Durham, NC, and London: Duke University Press, 1995.

Stephens, Vincent. "Crooning on the Fault Lines: Theorizing Jazz and Pop Vocal Singing Discourses in Rock." *American Music* 26, no. 2 (Summer 2008): 156–95.

Sterne, Jonathan. *The Audible Past: Cultural Origins of Sound Reproduction*. Durham, NC, and London: Duke University Press, 2003.

Straw, Will. "Popular Music as Cultural Commodity: The American Recorded Music Industries 1976–1985." PhD diss., McGill University, 1990.

———. "Scenes and Sensibilities." *Public* 22–23 (2002): 245–57.

———. "Systems of Articulation, Logics of Change: Communities and Scenes in Popular Music." *Cultural Studies* 5, no. 3 (1991): 368–88.

Suisman, David. *Selling Sounds: The Commercial Revolution in American Music*. Cambridge, MA: Harvard University Press, 2009.

Tagg, Philip. "Open Letter: Black Music, Afro-American Music, and European Music." *Popular Music* 8, no. 3 (1989): 285–98.

Tate, Greg. "I'm White! What's Wrong with Michael Jackson." In *The Pop, Rock, and Soul Reader: Histories and Debates*, 365–67. Edited by David Brackett. New York: Oxford University Press, 2014.

Taussig, Michael. *Mimesis and Alterity: A Particular History of the Senses*. New York and London: Routledge, 1993.

Taylor, Jeffrey. "The Early Origins of Jazz." In *The Oxford Companion to Jazz*, 39–52. Edited by Bill Kirchner. New York: Oxford University Press, 2000.

———. "With Lovie and Lil: Rediscovering Two Chicago Pianists of the 1920s." In *Big Ears: Listening for Gender in Jazz Studies*, 48–63. Edited by Nicole T. Rustin and Sherrie Tucker. Durham, NC: Duke University Press, 2008.

Taylor, Timothy D., Mark Katz, and Tony Grajeda, eds. *Music, Sound, and Technology in America: A Documentary History of Early Phonograph, Cinema, and Radio*. Durham, NC: Duke University Press, 2012.

Thompson, Emily. "Machines, Music, and the Quest for Fidelity: Marketing the Edison Phonograph in American, 1877–1925." *Musical Quarterly* 79 (Spring 1995): 131–71.

———. *The Soundscape of Modernity: Architectural Acoustics and the Culture of Listening in America, 1900–1933*. Cambridge, MA: MIT Press, 2004.

Thornton, Sarah. *Club Cultures: Music, Media and Subcultural Capital*. Hanover, NH, and London: Wesleyan University Press, 1996.

Toll, Robert. *Blacking Up: The Minstrel Show in Nineteenth-Century America*. New York and Oxford: Oxford University Press, 1974.

Tosches, Nick. *Country: Living Legends and Dying Metaphors in America's Biggest Music.* New York: Charles Scribner's Sons, 1985.

———. *The Unsung Heroes of Rock 'n' Roll: The Birth of Rock in the Wild Years Before Elvis.* New York: Harmony Books, 1984.

Townsend, Charles R. *San Antonio Rose: The Life and Music of Bob Wills.* Urbana and Chicago: University of Illinois Press, 1976.

Toynbee, Jason. "Mainstreaming: Hegemony, Market and the Aesthetics of the Centre in Popular Music." In *Popular Music Studies: International Perspectives*, 149–63. Edited by David Hesmondhalgh and Keith Negus. London: Arnold, and New York: Oxford University Press, 2002.

———. *Making Popular Music: Musicians, Creativity and Institutions.* London: Arnold, 2000.

Tsou, Judy. "Gendering Race: Stereotypes of Chinese Americans in Popular Sheet Music." *repercussions* 6, no. 2 (1997): 25–62.

Tucker, Sherry. "Big Ears: Listening for Gender in Jazz Studies." *Current Musicology* 71–73 (Spring 2001–2002): 375–408.

———. "Deconstructing the Jazz Tradition: The 'Subjectless' Subject of New Jazz Studies." *Jazz Research Journal* 2 (2005): 31–46.

———. *Swing Shift: "All-Girl" Bands of the 1940s.* Durham, NC, and London: Duke University Press, 2000.

Tynyanov, Yury. "On Literary Evolution." In *Readings in Russian Poetics: Formalist and Structuralist Views*, 66–78. Edited by L. Matejka and K. Pomorska. Cambridge, MA: MIT Press, 1971.

Vincent, Rickey. *Funk: The Music, the People and the Rhythm of the One.* New York: St. Martin's Press, 1996.

Waksman, Steve. *This Ain't the Summer of Love: Conflict and Crossover in Heavy Metal and Punk.* Berkeley: University of California Press, 2009.

Wald, Elijah. *Escaping the Delta: Robert Johnson and the Invention of the Blues.* New York: Amistad, 2004.

———. *How the Beatles Destroyed Rock 'n' Roll: An Alternative History of American Popular Music.* New York: Oxford University Press, 2009.

Walden, Joshua S. "The 'Yidishe Paganini': Sholem Aleichem's *Stempenyu*, the Music of Yiddish Theatre and the Character of the *Shtetl* Fiddler." *Journal of the Royal Musical Association* 139, no. 1 (2014): 89–136.

Wallace, Michele. "Michael Jackson, Black Modernisms, and 'The Ecstasy of Communication.'" In *Invisibility Blues: From Pop to Theory*, 77–90. London and New York: Verso, 1990.

Walser, Robert. *Keeping Time: Readings in Jazz History.* New York: Oxford University Press, 1999.

———. *Running with the Devil: Power, Gender and Madness in Heavy Metal Music.* Hanover, NH, and London: Wesleyan University Press, 1993.

Ward, Brian. *Just My Soul Responding: Rhythm and Blues, Black Consciousness, and Race Relations.* Berkeley: University of California Press, 1998.

Warwick, Jacqueline. *Girl Groups, Girl Culture: Popular Music and Identity in the 1960s.* New York: Routledge, 2007.

Waterman, Richard Alan. "African Influence on the Music of the Americas." In *Mother Wit from the Laughing Barrel: Readings in the Interpretation of Afro-American Folklore*, 81–94. Edited by Alan Dundes. Jackson: University Press of Mississippi, 1990. First published in 1952.

———. "'Hot' Rhythm in Negro Music." *Journal of the American Musicological Society* 1 (1948): 24–37.

Waters, Ethel (with Charles Samuels). *His Eye Is on the Sparrow*. New York: Da Capo Press, 1992. First published in 1951.

Weisbard, Eric. *Top 40 Democracy: The Rival Mainstreams of American Music*. Chicago: University of Chicago Press, 2014.

Wexler, Jerry, and David Ritz. *The Rhythm and the Blues: A Life in American Music*. New York: St. Martin's Press, 1993.

Whitburn, Joel. *Pop Memories, 1890–1954*. Menomonee Falls, WI: Record Research Inc., 1986.

Wilgus, D. K. *Anglo-American Folksong Scholarship Since 1898*. New Brunswick, NJ: Rutgers University Press, 1959.

Williams-Jones, Pearl. "Afro-American Gospel Music: a Crystallization of the Black Aesthetic." *Ethnomusicology* 19, no. 3 (September 1975): 373–85.

Willis, Paul. *Profane Culture*. London: Routledge and Kegan Paul, 1978.

Wilson, Olly. "The Significance of the Relationship Between Afro-American Music and West African Music." *The Black Perspective in Music* 2 (Spring 1974): 3–22.

Winkler, Peter. "Writing Ghost Notes: The Poetics and Politics of Transcription." In *Keeping Score: Music, Disciplinarity, Culture*, 169–203. Edited by David Schwarz, Anahid Kassabian, and Lawrence Siegel. Charlottesville and London: University Press of Virginia, 1997.

Wolfe, Charles. "Columbia Records and Old-Time Music." *JEMF Quarterly* (Autumn 1978): 118–25, 144.

———. *A Good-Natured Riot: The Birth of the Grand Ole Opry*. Nashville, TN: Country Music Foundation and Vanderbilt University Press, 1999.

Zak, Albin. *I Don't Sound Like Nobody: Remaking Music in 1950s America*. Ann Arbor: University of Michigan Press, 2010.

———. *The Poetics of Rock: Cutting Tracks, Making Records*. Berkeley: University of California Press, 2001.

INDEX

Locators with "fig" signify figures; locators with "tab" signify tables; locators with "mus" signify musical examples.

CPSIA information can be obtained
at www.ICGtesting.com
Printed in the USA
LVHW091909221120
672387LV00005B/869